Week

1	1, 2
2	3, 13
3	7, 18
4	4, 7
7	10
9	11, 12
10	13, 14
13	19

COMMUNICATION IN BUSINESS AND INDUSTRY

COM

MUNICATION IN BUSINESS AND INDUSTRY

WILLIAM M. SCHUTTE
LAWRENCE UNIVERSITY

ERWIN R. STEINBERG
CARNEGIE-MELLON UNIVERSITY

HOLT, RINEHART AND WINSTON

New York   Chicago   San Francisco   Philadelphia   Montreal   Toronto
London   Sydney   Tokyo   Mexico City   Rio de Janeiro   Madrid

Library of Congress Cataloging in Publication Data

Schutte, William M.
  Communication in business and industry.

  Includes index.
  1. Communication in management.   I. Steinberg,
Erwin Ray.   II. Title.
HF5718.S33 1983   658.4′5   82–21238

ISBN 0-03-056118-3

Portions of the material in this book first appeared
in a volume with the same title, copyright © 1960
by Holt, Rinehart and Winston.

CBS COLLEGE PUBLISHING
Holt, Rinehart and Winston
The Dryden Press
Saunders College Publishing

For Anne and Bev

PREFACE

In this book we have focused on the real needs of two audiences as we have come to know them: college or university students who have had a basic course in writing and want to learn how to communicate successfully in business, industry, or government; and those already employed who want to improve their communication skills. The text moves from a brief consideration of basic principles, derived largely from communication theory, rhetoric, and psychology, to demonstration of how these principles apply to writing and speaking on the job. Throughout it provides ample illustration from the business world and opportunities for the reader to gain experience in solving the type of communication problems most frequently found there.

The balance of theory and actual business practice in this book reflects our thirty years of experience in university teaching and in consulting and teaching in business. On campus, we have taught freshman composition and courses in business, professional, and technical writing. As communications consultants, we have worked with and taught accountants, engineers, lawyers, managers, marketing and public relations specialists, scientists, and many other professionals; and we have been asked for and have given advice on such widely different kinds of communications as letters, memos, proposals, specifications, manuals, surgical consent forms, company newspapers, reports, contracts, minutes of meetings, and speeches. Most of our examples from business and industry come from those consulting experiences with companies large and small, with local firms and multinational corporations.

Our purpose is to help individuals, both in the colleges and universities and in the business world itself, to develop the ability to communicate in ways that will enable them to move as rapidly as possible to ever more interesting and responsible positions in their companies. We have made no attempt, therefore, to provide instruction in minimum skills for students who are about to enter the business world or to discuss in detail such matters as specific forms or form letters used in business and industry. On the job new employees discover very quickly the nature and uses of those prescribed by their company; students, we believe, profit little from learning about forms that are inevitably quite different from those used at any company they may join. Thus, though we do not by any means neglect the routine aspects of business communication, we emphasize the more significant general principles every writer, in business or in any other field, must master if he or she is to succeed.

The materials in this book are grouped in six major sections, each of which concerns a significant aspect of communication on the job. The first, *Context and Principles,* is the foundation for the others. In it we present the essential elements in the communication process as we see it operating in the world of business and industry. We begin by providing an overview of that world with special emphasis on how its communication system operates. Chapter 2 concerns the relationship between writers and speakers and their audience as it has been defined by those who have studied how effective communication is achieved when messages are transmitted. And since one of the conclusions of researchers is that the function of almost every communication involves, in one way or another, both informing and persuading, Chapter 3 is devoted to a discussion of how these may best be accomplished.

The remaining materials are divided into five parts:

II. Writing Letters and Memos
III. Major Writing Assignments: The Report
IV. Economy, Clarity, and Unity
V. Reading, Listening, and Speaking
VI. Applying for a Job

Each of these sections builds on the base provided in Part I. We have placed them in an order that seems sensible and is likely to satisfy most readers, discussion leaders, and teachers; nevertheless, there is no reason an instructor who feels that his group needs to work on its prose should not assign Part V before turning to Parts II through IV. Similarly, a department head in a company who is primarily concerned about reporting may go directly from Part I to Part III and perhaps follow that with Chapter 20, "Communicating in Group Discussion."

Most users of this volume, nevertheless, will probably wish to move through it in the usual order. Part II provides a method for planning and writing memos and looks at some of the more common types of letters produced in a business establishment. Part III concerns the major report; how best to plan, organize, and write it. In this section we have also included a chapter on a subject of increasing importance to report writers: the use of layout and design—including such devices as tables, decision trees, flowcharts, graphs, and packaging—to increase effectiveness.

Part IV focuses on what we have found to be the three stylistic qualities most important to effective communication—economy, clarity, and unity—and suggests ways of increasing the impact of one's prose. The next section, Part V, applies the principles explored in Part I not only to speaking but also to reading, listening, and communicating in group discussions. Finally, we include a section on a subject of intensely practical concern to upper-class college students and those temporarily unemployed or seeking employment. This chapter, "Communications and the Job Hunt," incorporates the results of much recent research on how one may find and get the right position in the business world.

Throughout *Communication in Business and Industry* we have provided a great many problems and materials for revision, which readers may use to put into practice the principles discussed in the chapters. Additional materials of a similar nature may be devised by individual teachers or discussion leaders to meet the needs of their own group. We have also provided Illustrative Materials, supplementary materials related to subjects discussed in the chapter which precedes them. They are deliberately varied in form and content. Most are serious; others, like John Davenport's delightful "Slurvian Self-Taught" and the conversation between Tom and Bob at the end of Chapter 11, are not. But in some way all reinforce communication principles. Most of the illustrative materials are drawn from the contemporary business world, although we have been less concerned with where they came from than with how well they make their points. We have included among them an Old English sentence to illustrate the importance of word order in the sentence, newspaper headlines that show how lack of punctuation confuses, and a passage from Shakespeare to demonstrate how rhetoric can be used to sway an audience. The basic principles of communication operate, after all, in every area in which people communicate; and it is often easier for us to spot them and to see how they work in materials other than those with which we deal every day.

In short, we believe that the chapters in this text, together with the illustrative materials, the problems and exercises, and the materials for revision included in those chapters where they are appropriate, will enable the reader to develop a real understanding of the basic principles and skills needed to communicate successfully in the business world.

Over the years many people in business and industry and on the campus have contributed indirectly to this volume—so many that we cannot possibly mention them individually. But we do wish to express our appreciation to those of our colleagues who have worked with us in business, to the companies that have invited us to serve as consultants, and to the hundreds of their employees from whom we have learned so much and who, we trust, learned a few useful things from us.

We also acknowledge with thanks the reactions and suggestions of these teachers who read the book in manuscript: Rosemary Ascherl, Hartford State Technical College; Lois J. Bachman, Community College of Philadelphia; Dwight Bullard, Middle Tennessee State University; William G. Clark, University of Iowa; Andrea Corbett, University of Lowell; Virginia J. Cyrus, Rider College; L. W. Denton; George H. Douglas, University of Illinois; Phillip V. Lewis, Oklahoma State University; C. Glenn Pearce, Virginia Commonwealth University; William E. Rivers, Auburn University; William Speers, Oregon Institute of Technology; and Thomas L. Warren, Oklahoma State University.

More immediately we should like to thank our editors at Holt, Rinehart and Winston, Anne Boynton-Trigg and H. L. Kirk, for their good advice and patience; Ruth Lesselyong, Mildred Wallace, Lila Johnson, Karen Haney, Carol Janik, Paul Kravits, Joyce Swaney, and Karen Watts for typing the manuscript in its various stages; and our wives for support and counsel on yet one more collaboration.

W. M. S.

E. R. S.   ix

CONTENTS

CONTENTS

3
WRITING TO INFORM AND PERSUADE 48

The Importance of Proper Planning   49

1. Determine Real Purpose or Function   50
2. Select Materials   50
3. Order Materials   51
4. Check Against Purpose   51
5. Write   52
6. Recheck Against Purpose   52

The Psychology of Persuasion   53
Who: The Source   54

The Writer's Image   54
The Credibility of the Source   55

Says What: The Message   55

Organization   55
Explicit Conclusions   57
Humor   57

To Whom: The Receiver   58

Basic Needs   58
The Audience's Self-Image   59
Reader Cultural Patterns   59
Involving the Audience Actively   60
Really Understanding   61

In What Channel   61
What Every Writer Should Know   62

ILLUSTRATIVE MATERIALS   63
PROBLEMS   65

II
WRITING
LETTERS AND MEMOS

4
PLANNING   69

Case Study: A Confirming Memo   69
Steps in Planning a Communication   71

1. Determine Real Purpose or Function   71
   Routine Responses   72
2. Select Materials   74
3. Order Materials   74
   Why Order Is Essential   78

xii

CONTENTS

CONTENTS

IV
ECONOMY, CLARITY, AND UNITY

CONTENTS

16
COHERENCE   *294*

17
PUNCTUATION   *308*

V
READING,
LISTENING, AND SPEAKING

18
READING AND LISTENING   *325*

CONTENTS

19
SPEAKING   *339*

20
COMMUNICATING IN GROUP DISCUSSION   *360*

CONTENTS

VI
APPLYING
FOR A JOB

21
COMMUNICATION AND THE JOB HUNT   *379*

1

CONTEXT AND PRINCIPLES

The Climate
of Business

The growth of American business and the advances of American technology during the recent past are so remarkable that they would have astonished our ancestors. And though familiarity has made us less likely to marvel at the wonders of our time, now and then some particularly spectacular accomplishment of science or industry still shocks us out of our blasé acceptance of miracles. This is the age, too, of achievement in communication. A newsman interviews a tribal chief in the heart of Africa; a few hours later millions of families not only hear his words but see him speak as they watch the evening news. When a presidential candidate is nominated, the public sometimes knows about it before most of the convention delegates who did the nominating.

This is also an age of increasing paperwork. From every business establishment pours a steady stream of letters, memoranda, reports, news releases, advertising material. Each year the pile of mail and internal communications in every office mounts. Each year executives must make more decisions on the basis of the written matter on their desks, fewer on what they find out in face-to-face conference with employees, suppliers, and competitors. As the piles grow, there is less and less time to spend on each individual communication.

THE GROWING COMPLEXITY OF COMMUNICATION

We should not be surprised, therefore, that a major focus of executive and management-training programs today is communications: public speaking, group conference techniques, letter writing, report writing; public relations, employee relations, customer relations. The common denominator is the effective use of language. This increasing concern with communication reflects the increasing complexity of business and industry. At the turn of the century, when many of today's businesses were founded, they were one-man organizations. A Henry Ford or E. T. Weir could keep within his view all of the various aspects of his business. It was only a few steps from the front office to the plant. Today, however, the "front office" is likely to be in New York, Pittsburgh, Detroit, Chicago, or Los Angeles; the plants in Biloxi, Jersey City, New Orleans, or Cedar Rapids. Suppliers may be even more widely dispersed, for even a modest business frequently needs raw materials from all over the world. Customers may also be widely dispersed. Distance, however, is not the only problem.

Even when the home office and the plant are physically close, engineers developing a new process may well be as "far" from top management, who must decide whether to invest in the process, as if they were a thousand miles away. The engineers must put their findings in writing so that all interested individuals and departments can examine them, discuss them, and make the required decisions. Even if personal explanation to everyone involved were possible, the engineers would still have to write reports that their associates could turn to if they forgot the details, that technical writers could use in writing a manual, that development or marketing experts could use when determining costs, and that would enable an almost endless number of people to perform the daily miracle of turning words on paper into pharmaceuticals, or steel, or computers, or cloth, or airplanes.

THE IMPORTANCE OF WRITTEN COMMUNICATION

In business and industry, therefore, letters, memos, and reports are important for a number of reasons. They inform and record in a way that the spoken word cannot. Industry would be as helpless without them as without machinery or fuel. These days, as we all know, a company cannot afford to put up with inadequate equipment or costly power. Industry invests millions of dollars every year to improve machines and fuels. For the same reasons, industry and government have been attempting to improve their communications. Records show that their efforts have paid off. The complexity of business, vigorous competition, the continuing demand for increased production and a better product, customer insistence on speed and service, the importance of good

4

internal and public relations—all of these factors and many more have increased the need for *efficient* communication.

A board of directors or an operating committee, with many important decisions to make, has no time to decipher or untangle complicated, wordy reports. It must have information that is usable as well as useful. Similarly, specifications for production line orders must be concise and readable; if they are not, production lags in direct proportion to the time it takes to interpret them. Sales orders and reports must be complete and precise. Inadequate reporting leads to overflowing warehouses, orders returned to the factory, freight cars stacked up on sidings, extra correspondence, and mounting bills for long-distance phone calls. Installation and maintenance manuals must be simple and understandable. If they are too technical or not detailed enough, equipment may be installed improperly, with predictable results—breakdowns or inefficient operation. Reports on research must be written so that the general manager, who probably is not an engineer but an accountant (or a lawyer, or an advertising executive), can understand them. If they are full of unclear phrases and terms, the manager will not be able to recommend appropriate action to the board of directors or operating committee. Consumer inquiries, complaints, and suggestions pour into business establishments; each requires a tactful reply which will satisfy the customer. And direct-mail sales letters must be vigorous and effective if they are to do their job.

An inefficient letter or report costs money in a dozen different ways. It takes too long to write or dictate. It takes too long to transcribe and type. It takes too long to read and unravel. But even efficient business letters are far more costly than we like to think. More than twenty-five years ago, the National Archives and Record Service of the General Services Administration estimated that in salaries alone a typical half-page letter dictated to a stenographer cost between $0.70 and $2.45; machine dictation reduced the cost only slightly, to $0.60 and $2.25. The total cost of letter writing at that time was probably close to $5 billion a year. Today the work force has increased and the overall cost of a business letter is over $6.00. As a result, the total annual cost is now said to be well over $100 billion.

These figures, of course, cover only the cost of the letters up to the time they are put in the mail. If we add the cost of *inefficient* letters—letters which require further letters of clarification or which lose a sale or a customer because they are tedious or rude—the total will be multiplied manyfold. If to that figure we add the cost of producing reports and the further, but hidden, cost of inefficient reports, the total will rival that of the gross national product of many of the world's developed countries.

ORAL COMMUNICATION

The ability to communicate orally is equally important. Today managers, scientists, and engineers frequently find themselves before an audience or participating in a conference. The impression that they make when they speak

5

has an important bearing on their future. If they are well prepared, poised, and sensible, they will be remembered favorably. If they fumble for ideas, seem ill at ease, and speak erratically, they will leave a poor impression. Ineffective speakers do a disservice not only to themselves but also to the companies of which they are visible representatives.

INCREASED INTEREST IN BETTER COMMUNICATION

Today, management at all levels is becoming increasingly sensitive both to the waste involved in inefficient communication and to the importance of communication skills. Hence it looks very carefully at these skills in evaluating the potential of its employees.

Paradoxically, people who themselves tend to feel that writing is a secondary part of their job are frequently judged by their superiors largely on the basis of what they do write. In a technical report manual one major corporation has this to say:

> Experienced engineers recognize the value of a well-organized report. It is often their only tangible product. It represents their investigation, their testing and experimentation. If their efforts are to count in the judgment of their supervisors, they must describe clearly what they have done. They must show the significance of their work. And often the engineers' written reports are their only contact with management. This factor takes on added importance as the size and complexity of the organization increase.

COMMUNICATION SKILL AND THE INDIVIDUAL'S CAREER

Letter, memo, and report writers often fail to recognize the significance of the point made in the last two sentences of this statement. For many of them, promotion and the opportunity to grow in professional capacity depend ultimately on an executive whom they seldom or never see. To the executive, an individual under consideration for promotion or a raise is often little more than a name at the bottom of reports that periodically cross his or her desk. If these reports are clear, efficient, and usable, the executive, consciously or not, will form a good impression of the writer. But if they are poorly organized, wordy, clogged with unnecessary details or with technical terms and concepts that are difficult to understand, he or she will form, perhaps quite unconsciously, a poor impression of the writer. Many a capable engineer, for example, has been denied a promotion or a raise—or both—without either the person making the decision or the engineer knowing quite why. Too often, inadequate reports have been the cause.

It is just as important, of course, for memo and report writers to write well to supervisors whom they see regularly. A supervisor has reason to appreciate people whose reporting is clear and usefully organized and reason to be irritated by people who write memos and reports that have to be pushed off to the corner of the desk because they cannot be read but must be deciphered, frequently at home in the evening or over a weekend. As one business executive put it, "Every memo, letter, or report is a request for a promotion or a demotion." Certainly good personal relations are important in business, but they are no substitute for good professional communication.

Since management is becoming more and more aware of the importance of good letter and report writing and of good speaking, the individual's need to write and speak well is even greater. If a person is being considered for a position of increased responsibility, management can seldom allow time for improvement. If the candidate cannot write and speak well when the position opens, it will probably be filled by someone else. As communication consultants, we too often hear stories about the "very capable" engineer whose work was never recognized because he could not communicate his results and make clear the importance of what he had done; the salesperson who was not promoted to sales manager because as soon as he was removed from direct contact with his customers and had to write to them, he ceased to be an asset and became a liability; the young department head who became general manager of a profitable division, only to watch her excellent plans come to naught because she could not communicate adequately with her most capable subordinates and so was denied their coordinated strength and wisdom. These stories come to us from management. Increasingly, top management is insisting on the ability to communicate, not only from those who aspire to its ranks, but from employees at all levels.

What, for example, will a supervisor think about the writer of the following paragraph, taken from a progress report?

> This unit is being purchased on an R & D capital accounting basis. Consequently, avoid budget and tax complications, we request that all efforts be expended to ship and complete the financial transactions during the present calendar year. In addition, there are major practical reasons for my evaluating and approving this design prior to purchasing future production-scale units for a facility we are designing at the present time. Hence, please expedite the fabrication of this unit as much as is practical.

Any reader will stumble over the second sentence and will have to reread to discover that the word "to" has been left out before "avoid." And then, how does one "ship . . . financial transactions"? What, precisely, does the phrase "as much as is practical" mean in the last sentence? A discerning reader would also notice the pomposity of some of the language. How should one interpret the statement "we request that all efforts be expended to ship . . ."? Does it mean "we would appreciate your trying hard to ship . . ."? Or "please try hard to ship . . ."? Or "please ship . . ."? And why write "a facility we are designing at the present time" when "a facility we are designing now" is more efficient and more effective?

What will one's supervisor—and the reader of the letter—think about a letter which begins:

Dear Mr. Johnson:

The December 4 suggested date for the Priority Committee meeting has been postponed until early next year due to various schedule conflicts with the majority of the members because of prior plans such as startup of new facilities and the normal rush of the holiday season.

How does one postpone a date? And how useful is the last two-thirds of the sentence? Compare the impression such an opening sentence makes with that made by an opening like this:

Dear Mr. Johnson:

We have postponed the suggested December 4 meeting of the Priority Committee until early next year because most of the committee members have already made commitments for that date.

In the revision, the writer has properly announced the postponement of the meeting rather than of the date and has given his information clearly and efficiently (29 words as opposed to the original 46).

What kind of impression does a person make who writes, "The delivery of the four (4) string filters and the two (2) flotation cells which were scheduled to be on site by January 1 and December 19 respectfully, have not yet arrived"?

"The delivery . . . have not yet arrived"? "Respectfully"?

At the very least, a reader will suspect that the writers of these sentences were careless or that their minds were elsewhere when they were writing (or dictating). It is dangerous enough to leave the impression that one is careless or not paying attention to what one is doing; it is even more dangerous if the reader concludes that one is inept, pompous, or illiterate. What supervisor wants a subordinate who is likely to write this way to a customer? Letters and memos which include such passages are requests not for promotion, but for demotion.

Here is a letter that *did* go to a customer:

Dear Mr. Farmer:

I have just received your letter of March 25, and I fully understand your company's position about ordering material before you have a written purchase order. My requisition to our Purchasing Department was dated November 7; and, as you have probably surmised, I have no control after they receive the requisition. We are rescheduling the distillation test for early June based on the revised delivery date you indicated in your letter.

Yours truly,

The writer may have felt he was protecting his own reputation with the cus-
8 tomer. But was the letter effective? It did not solve the customer's problem or

even assure the customer that the problem would not arise again. Furthermore, it suggests buck-passing and disloyalty. This writer, too, has requested a demotion.

BURIED UNDER REPORTS

One afternoon several years ago we met with a division manager in one of America's large industrial firms who wanted our help in dealing with the writing problems of the department heads in his division. We asked our usual question: "What makes you think that these people have a writing problem?" The muscles around his jaw tightened. He opened his mouth. Then he snapped it shut and reached down behind him. Pulling up a pile of reports almost twelve inches high, he slammed it down on the desk in front of us and with a face and voice that expressed both satisfaction and exasperation announced, "This is what I'm going to be doing this whole weekend—reading these reports."

Clearly he had a problem. When we examined the reports that his department heads had written to him, we decided that they were indeed badly designed for his needs. Many were too wordy; others were poorly organized; none told him immediately and economically what he needed to know.

We mention the incident here because it is typical of the problems faced by managers at all levels, from the first-line supervisor to company president and chairman of the board. Typically, at each level a manager must digest a flood of information; too often it is not only inefficiently organized but written in wordy, cliché-ridden prose. Too many memos, letters, and reports cannot simply be read and acted upon. To understand them requires lengthy study, sorting out of materials, and requests for clarification. As a result, managers claim that they must spend far too much time reading and thus have too little left to plan and manage. "When we are able to pull our heads out of the piles of correspondence and reports on our desks," they say, "we seldom have enough time to do more than put out fires."

In the last few years the reporting problem has been made even more complicated by the steady increase in the use of computers, word-processing equipment, and photocopying machines. Sometimes it seems that every possible analysis of a given situation is made and that everyone who might conceivably want to know the results receives not merely a notice of their availability, but a printout as well. Managers sometimes feel that they spend all their days unfolding computer printouts and turning pages as they try to track down the vital bits of information that they need in order to do their job.

COMPANY AND CUSTOMER

Companies have also begun to recognize that all letters to customers are sales letters. It makes no sense for a company to spend thousands of dollars on advertising if the salesperson who is actually in communication with a customer concludes a letter with a routine "If we can be of further service, please do not hesitate to call." On the other hand, a well-written letter from a 9 field service engineer which solves a customer's problem can often be a better sales mechanism than an expensive advertisement in a national magazine. So can the reply to an unsolicited inquiry about a product line. Routine responses to such inquiries are opportunities wasted.

The relatively new consumer movement has also led companies to reconsider communications with their customers. In 1977, the New York State legislature passed the country's first "Plain English" law, which requires the use of understandable English in a broad range of consumer contracts. All residential leases and all contracts involving money, property, or service primarily for personal, family, or household purposes must be (1) written in nontechnical language and in a clear and coherent manner, using words with common, everyday meanings, and (2) appropriately divided and captioned. Similar legislation has been passed or is being considered throughout the country.

Pressure is also coming from the courts. A hospital, for example, failed to recover from the husband of a woman patient any costs other than those allowed by his insurance policy, even though he had signed a form agreeing to such payment. The judge felt that the husband had been misled:

Defendant's failure to read the document or to give it more than the most cursory attention [while his wife lay critically ill in a hospital emergency room] is understandable. It thus becomes vital that a document like the form involved here be clearly labeled and organized so that the signer is made aware of what it entails.

The form that the husband had been presented with—and had signed—was headed "Assignment of Insurance Benefits." The judge concluded:

Here the paragraph signed by defendant bore a heading totally unrelated to the sentence on which the plaintiff [i.e., the hospital] now relies to argue defendant's financial liability. Defendant would have been entirely justified in concluding from the heading that he was agreeing only to have his union insurance pay for his wife's hospital bills. This is a far cry from agreeing to assume personal liability. (*St. John's Hospital* v. *McAdoo*, 94 Misc. 2d 967—Civ. Ct. Kings Cty. 1978)

In recent years a growing number of similar decisions have rejected claims for payment because contracts have been misleading or unreadable.

Most companies have begun to make a virtue of necessity by advertising that their warranties or insurance policies are written in "Plain English" so that the consumer knows what he or she is buying. The cover of a policy recently issued by the Hartford Insurance Group, for example, is emblazoned with "Your Easier-to-Understand HOMEOWNERS POLICY." In its "Definitions" section near the top of page 1, Hartford begins to make good on its promise:

Throughout this policy, "you" and "your" refer to the "named insured" shown in the Declarations and the spouse if a resident of the same household, and "we," "us" and "our" refer to the Company providing this insurance.

The rest of the policy contains such statements as "If you and we fail to agree on the amount of loss, either one can demand that the amount of loss be set by appraisal," certainly more readable than the overblown statements of earlier policies.

With the help of Siegel & Gale, Citibank in New York has made some startling changes. Consider, for example, these "before" and "after" statements on default taken from its consumer loan form. In small print the old form said:

> In the event of default in the payment of this or any other Obligation or the performance or observance of any term or covenant contained herein or in any note or other contract or agreement evidencing or relating to any Obligation or any Collateral on the Borrower's part to be performed or observed; or the undersigned become insolvent or make an assignment for the benefit of creditors; or a petition shall be filed by or against any of the undersigned under any provision of the Bankruptcy Act; or any money, securities or property of the undersigned now or hereafter on deposit with or in the possession or under the control of the Bank shall be attached or become subject to distraint proceedings or any order or process of any court; or the Bank shall deem itself to be insecure, then and in any such event, the Bank shall have the right (at its option), without demand or notice of any kind, to declare all or any part of the Obligation to be immediately due and payable, whereupon such Obligations shall become and be immediately due and payable, and the Bank shall have the right to exercise all the rights and remedies available to a secured party upon default under the Uniform Commercial Code (the "Code") in effect in New York at the time, and such other rights and remedies as may otherwise be provided by law.

The new form is in larger print, and the comparable section reads:

> I'll be in default:
> 1. If I don't pay an installment on time; or
> 2. If any other creditor tries by legal process to take any money of mine in your possession.
>
> You can demand immediate payment of the balance of this note, minus the part of the *finance charge* which hasn't been earned, calculated as stated in the Prepayment paragraph. You will also have other legal rights, for instance, the right to repossess, sell and apply security to the payments under this note and any other debts I may then owe you.

Companies are also under pressure to make their warranty statements more precise and more understandable. Thus, although the concept of *caveat emptor*—"Let the buyer beware"—may not have disappeared completely from the marketplace, it is being radically modified, with important implications for business.

FEDERAL GOVERNMENT REGULATIONS

The Federal government has also begun to simplify its communications. For example, the *Federal Register* for July 20, 1977 (v. 42, no. 139) carried an announcement by the Federal Communications Commission of a proposed set of simplified regulations for Citizens Band radio service. Here, for example, are the existing and proposed sections on signing CB applications:

CONTEXT AND PRINCIPLES

EXISTING

95.421 Who may sign applications.

(a) Except as provided in paragraph (b) of this section, applications, amendments thereto, and related statements of fact required by the Commission shall be personally signed by the applicant, if the applicant is an individual; by one of the partners, if the applicant is a partnership; by an officer, if the applicant is a corporation; or by a member who is an officer, if the applicant is an unincorporated association. Applications, amendments, and related statements of fact filed on behalf of eligible government entities, such as states and territories of the United States and political subdivisions thereof, the District of Columbia, and units of local government, including incorporated municipalities, shall be signed by such duly elected or appointed officials as may be competent to do so under the laws of the applicable jurisdiction.

(b) Applications, amendments thereto, and related statements of fact required by the Commission may be signed by the applicant's attorney in case of the applicant's physical disability or of his absence from the United States. The attorney shall in that event separately set forth the reason why the application is not signed by the applicant. In addition, if any matter is stated on the basis of the attorney's belief only (rather than his knowledge), he shall separately set forth his reasons for believing that such statements are true.

(c) Only the original of applications, amendments, or related statements of fact need be signed; copies may be conformed.

(d) Applications, amendments, and related statements of fact need not be signed under oath. Willful false statements made therein, however, are punishable by fine and imprisonment, U.S. Code, Title 18, section 1001, and by appropriate administrative sanctions, including revocation of station license pursuant to section 312(a)(1) of the Communications Act of 1934, as amended.

PROPOSED

95.425 How do I sign my CB license application?

(a) If you are an individual, you must sign your own application personally.

(b) If the applicant is not an individual, the signature on an application must be made as follows:

Type of applicant	Signature of applicant
Partnership -----------	One of the partners.
Corporation -----------	Officer.
Association -----------	Member who is an officer.
Governmental Unit ------	Appropriate elected or appointed official.

(c) If the FCC requires you to submit additional information, you must sign it in the same way you signed your application.

(d) If you willfully make a false statement on your application, you may be punished by fine, imprisonment and revocation of your station license.

The FCC then offered this explanation:

> *Editorial changes.* This section has been redrafted in greatly simplified language to ensure that an applicant for a CB license knows how to sign his or her application. Paragraph (b) of existing 95.421 has been deleted as duplicative of 1.913(b) of the Commission's Rules. Paragraph (c) of existing 95.421 has been deleted as unnecessary.

With all of this interest, one may well wonder why our communication problems are not quickly solved. Is the problem of inefficient language any different from that of inefficient design of automobile engines? Why shouldn't industry work at it as seriously as it works at its other problems? There are many reasons.

BARRIERS TO IMPROVING COMMUNICATION

Probably the most important barrier to communication is that we are touchy about our ability to use our own language. We resent any suggestion that our writing is inadequate. Psychologists say that language is very personal, that it is "a projection of one's self." People never like to have an editorial pencil taken to their writing or to be told that their grammar is wrong, that a particular comma should be a semicolon, or that they should not use slang. The extent to which many people are embarrassed by these difficulties is suggested by the way they react when introduced to an English teacher: "Oh, you teach English, do you? I'd better watch my language." This half-guilty, half-resentful attitude toward language and language specialists is a major hurdle for anyone who attempts to improve the quality of communication in business.

Both the guilt and the resentment may be well founded. Having heard about rules for the "proper" use of the English language and suspecting that they probably violate them, people feel that they are somehow at fault. On the other hand, because the standards are so often presented as inflexible rules unrelated to practice, few people are well enough motivated to learn them and comply with them.

Those who think of instruction in "grammar" and in writing as instilling outdated, unrealistic rules for the proper use of conjunctions and prepositions naturally tend to resist any attempt to improve their work. After all, they have used language for twenty or thirty or even fifty years and have "gotten along"; they have argued with their parents over the family car (and generally gotten it), they have graduated from high school and perhaps college, they have proposed marriage and been accepted. They have applied for a job, bought their clothes, asked or given information about how to get to Broadway and Twenty-third Street. And they have almost always managed to get results. As far as they can see, their conjunctions and their prepositions seldom, if ever, have kept them from being understood.

A second reason that business and industrial writing is difficult to improve   13 is the way young employees are introduced to their jobs. There is nothing sacred, they soon learn, about current methods of production or merchandising. If they can develop better ones, they know they will be rewarded. Their suggestions are sought, and they are offered bonuses for workable improvements. But when it comes to writing, an entirely different attitude prevails.

Today, young people in industry may learn their jobs under a person of fifty-five or sixty who trained in the 1940s under someone who started out right after the first World War. This sequence suggests why the language of young people in industry today sometimes reminds us of the high, starched collar. In effect, only one business generation separates them from that period, and we still find occasionally in their letters such quaint phrasing as "Yours of the fourteenth instant received" and "I beg to remain, Yours sincerely." For the same reason, too many people still write "Enclosed herewith please find" when all they mean is "Enclosed are" and refer to "this writer" or "the undersigned" because they think that using "I" is immodest.

Though they are given a thorough introduction to production methods, new employees today are seldom given instruction in how to write. The only thing they can do, therefore, is to go to the files for copies of the boss's letters and to try to imitate them. After all, a letter in the style favored by the boss can hardly get them in trouble. If it does sound a bit pompous—well, nobody is likely to notice. Thus a lack of positive instruction and a temptation to follow bad models combine to discourage young writers from developing an effective style of their own.

Some companies do include an hour or two on communication in the training programs they run for new employees. The average person, however, will get little help from these sessions—even if he or she wants help. People do not learn to write by listening to a lecture or two. To break an old habit pattern, they must continue to work over a period of time to build a new one. Reading articles on business writing and attending brief writing clinics may convince them that they have a lot to learn; but it is no substitute for sustained effort, for taking part with co-workers in group discussion of writing problems, for discovering themselves what is wrong with certain kinds of writing, and for arriving at the solutions to various problems—all, of course, under proper guidance.

A final stumbling block is that sometimes an employee or a company which recognizes the problem and makes a real attempt to solve it expects results too quickly. A person of forty has been building and reinforcing writing habits for fifteen or twenty years. In a few months, only the unusual individual can break long-standing habits and substitute new ones. How many people resisted automatic transmission in automobiles when it was first introduced solely because they were suspicious of a device which, though it was much easier to operate, required a frustrating change of habit? Why should we not expect much greater uneasiness about changing habit patterns in using language, and still greater difficulty in actually making the adjustment?

We are always confused, frustrated, and irritated at any attempt to make us think through a habit pattern that has become automatic for us: explaining and demonstrating how to tie a bow tie, for example; or singing only the third line of "The Star-Spangled Banner." We share this quality with the well-known arthropod:

> The centipede was happy quite,
>   Until a frog in fun
> Said, "Pray, which foot comes after which?"
> That worked her mind to such a pitch
> She lay distracted in a ditch
>   Considering how to run.

Even more frustrating is attempting to *change* what we have been doing for years: correcting a fault in our driving technique or in the way we serve a tennis ball. Most men and women are similarly frustrated by any question that forces them to be self-conscious about and eventually to change their writing habits. Many in business complain when we come to the second or third of a series of weekly group conferences: "These sessions are killing me. This week while I was dictating, I got to worrying so much about how I was going to say things that I made a mess of every letter I wrote." Such a reaction is perfectly normal. It is a symptom of progress. And invariably we find that after a few *more* sessions new habit patterns have developed and the frustration is relieved. Individuals who have difficulty in adjusting must be guided and supported through their frustrated period until they are secure in new and more efficient patterns.

As these paragraphs have suggested, to write and speak well requires sustained effort. The proverbial sayings "Anything worth doing is worth doing well" and "You can't get something for nothing" both apply to improving communication skills. Catch phrases and magic formulas may inspire a brief flurry of enthusiasm for "doing something" about one's writing and speaking. But unless an individual is willing to follow up good intentions with solid work, the results will be negligible. The person who works conscientiously over the materials we have provided and thoughtfully studies our discussion of communication problems should be well on the way to becoming capable not merely of solving the specific problems covered in this book, but of bringing to the solution of any writing or speaking problem a flexible instrument which will serve well throughout his or her career.

ILLUSTRATIVE MATERIALS

1.

In recent years all businesses have concerned themselves much more than they once did with how women and members of other minorities are addressed and referred to. The guidelines below, developed by the College Department of Holt, Rinehart and Winston, consider ways to avoid both stereotyping and the use of language that suggests prejudice.

15

The Treatment of Sex Roles and Minorities

Authors and editors of college textbooks communicate to students, colleagues, and friends much more than is apparent in the broad subject matter of remarks or writings. Sometimes we are aware of this hidden content, but more frequently it is below the conscious level.

This subliminal communication takes many forms, but it is probably most frequently influenced by the attitudes we have, the tendencies we have to respond, favorably or unfavorably, to types of people, things, and ideas. If we believe that a young, American, male, middle-class WASP is the best kind of person to be—whether this belief is conscious or not—those who read or listen to us are quite likely, sooner or later, to get the message, particularly if they do not fit into one or more of these categories. And this will not do much for our powers of persuasion or exposition. Unconscious negative stereotypes are dangerous, although sometimes a positive attitude does inadvertent damage because of its negative corollaries: for example, if intellectuals are wonderful, nonintellectuals are not.

We live in a period of changing attitudes, of the rejection of discrimination, overt or covert, against any group, whether it be defined by race, sex, ethnic or national origin, age, religion, or physical condition. Because of the widespread effort to reject discrimination, the attitudes that remain are likely to be only dimly visible to everyone concerned, including the discriminator. As a result, this has also been a period of "consciousness raising"—of exploration of the meanings and implications of terms and habits of language, so that what appears as discriminatory to the listener or reader who is aware will be equally apparent to—and avoided by—the speaker or writer.

This learning process is not easy for at least two reasons. First, it is difficult to obtain consensus, in our changing social scene, on what is or is not discriminatory. Second, our habits of speech are deeply ingrained, and the elimination of terms now offensive to one or the other group may leave us with no substitute that does not—for the first few instances of its adoption—appear foolishly artificial.

It is consequently impossible to lay down a series of simple and unambiguous rules for the avoidance of linguistic bigotry. All we can do is suggest some general guidelines and give examples of their applications. We should realize that consensus cannot be expected and that, even with the best of intentions, errors of omission and commission may occur.

GENERAL CONTEXT

Authors and editors should keep in mind the following guidelines:

1. Avoid stereotypes of all kinds—race, sex, ethnic or national origin, age, religion, physical condition, or those relating to any "different" group.

A simple example is the picturing of women as harried homemakers and mothers unable to cope with mechanical problems in the home. Another example is the out-of-work black male.

2. Avoid unnecessary negative associations, such as the mention of ethnic or racial identity linked to negative situations or personality traits.

3. Include the positive contributions of minorities, women, and others to the development of the society. Prejudice can be expressed through emphasis on any one group, through lack of recognition of achievement or leading role of a group, by omission of certain persons as role models, and by assignment of certain roles to specific individuals.

4. Portray the history of various peoples with accuracy so that the lack of advantage for minority groups and women, for example, is explained in a historical context. Use currently acceptable ethnic descriptions (Chinese or Chinese-American, *not* Chinaman; American Indian or the tribal name, *not* red man; and so on).

5. Recognize that the United States is not the only country where English is spoken. If the material pertains to the United States, do not use America as a synonym. It may be that no geographic reference is needed; for example, the chapter title "Urban Life in America" might be appropriately retitled "Urban Life."

6. Represent many kinds of life-styles—urban as well as suburban and rural—and various socioeconomic classes; and do so within a realistic framework.

7. Be straightforward about the differences between people or groups and the relationships that have occurred between them in both the past and the present.

8. Do not allow titles or job descriptions to be stereotypes (for example, chairperson or chair, *not* chairman; postal worker, *not* postman; flight attendant, *not* steward or stewardess).

9. Show integrated groups in both text and illustrations where possible.

10. Balance artwork (both drawings and photographs) so as to include representatives of several groups. Picture individiuals in nonstereotypic roles.

11. In citing research from the literature, take care that the reader is made aware of any intentional or unintentional biases in the samples. For example, underprivileged children are not always black; nurses and elementary school teachers are not always women; aboriginal societies are not "primitive."

SPECIFIC EXAMPLES

In the following examples we will list common constructions and possible alternatives. While some of them may appear obvious, the purpose of including them is to alert you to the problems that do exist. A number of these examples were taken from recent manuscripts.

CONTEXT AND PRINCIPLES

1. *He* is the commonly accepted general singular pronoun. There are, however, many cases in which the use of *he* and *she* can be equitably arranged so as not to exclude or stereotype either sex. Similarly, *man* and *mankind* have traditionally been used to encompass both sexes, thus needlessly implying exclusion.

EXAMPLES

A. Studying the techniques by which a celebrated writer achieved his success can stimulate any writer faced with similar problems.

B. Inherited capabilities in man are transmitted through genes; at conception, his physical traits are partially determined.

POSSIBLE ALTERNATIVES

A. Studying the techniques by which celebrated writers achieved their successes can stimulate any writer faced with similar problems.

B. Human inherited capabilities are transmitted through genes; at conception, physical traits are partially determined.

2. Refrain from using characterizations that reinforce negative models or are unnecessary in the context (for example, the dumb blonde, lazy black, senile elderly person, helpless handicapped person, retarded spastic). Other more positive images can be found (for example, the successful businesswoman, black storekeeper, elderly person helping others, handicapped worker). Such images can and should be incorporated into the text without patronizing implications.

EXAMPLES

A. William Jones, the black foreman at General Motors, is active in Detroit politics.

B. A lady Bible School director wanted to determine the average daily contribution to the school. She computed it to be thirty-five cents.

C. The male kindergarten teacher took his students on a trip of the zoo.

D. Maggie Kuhn, the little old lady who is head of the Gray Panthers, gave a speech.

POSSIBLE ALTERNATIVES

A. William Jones, the foreman at General Motors, is active in Detroit politics.

B. A Bible School director wanted to determine the average daily contribution to the school. She computed it to be thirty-five cents.

C. The kindergarten teacher took his students on a trip to the zoo.

D. Maggie Kuhn, the leader of the Gray Panthers, gave a speech.

3. Persons mentioned together should be named in parallel style.

EXAMPLES	POSSIBLE ALTERNATIVES
A. Louis Pasteur, a doctor, and Madame Curie, a chemist, were pioneers in their respective fields.	A. Louis Pasteur, a doctor, and Marie Curie, a chemist, were pioneers in their respective fields.
B. President Kennedy and Martin Luther King, Jr., were two leaders assassinated during the sixties.	B. John F. Kennedy and Martin Luther King, Jr., were two leaders assassinated during the sixties.
	or
	President John F. Kennedy and Reverend Martin Luther King, Jr., were two leaders assassinated during the sixties.
C. The celebrated team of L. S. B. Leakey and his wife is known for its work at Olduvai Gorge.	C. The celebrated team of L. S. B. Leakey and Mary Leakey is known for its work at Olduvai Gorge.
	or
	The celebrated husband and wife team. . . .

2.

Pitman's Commercial Correspondence and Commercial English, published in London by Sir Isaac Pitman & Sons, probably in the early years of the century, instructed its readers on the proper way to write a business letter. In part it reads:

The Salutation is the complimentary term used to commence the letter. Custom has prescribed certain forms which are in general use; as *Sir, Dear Sir,* or *My Dear Sir,* when writing a business letter to a man, and *Sirs, Gentlemen, Dear Sirs,* or *My Dear Sirs,* when addressing a firm. The vulgar term *Gents.* should never be used. The salutation in a business letter should be followed by a *comma.*

The Body of the Letter is the part which contains the message or the information to be communicated; and, it is, of course, the part of first importance. In this, as in the other parts of a letter, good form is desirable. . . .

The body of a letter should be punctuated like ordinary printed or written matter. Well written letters do not require much punctuation, but such as is necessary should not be omitted. *Commas, full-stops,* and *notes of inter-* 19 *rogation* are the only stops usually required, as long sentences, requiring much punctuation, should not be used in business correspondence.

The Complimentary Close follows the body of the letter on the next line below, and consists of the words of respect or regard used to express the feelings of the writer toward his correspondent. The terms used are quite conventional, and are employed by many without the slightest thought as to their meaning, but the good correspondent will use the words most appropriate to the occasion.

The complimentary close should always be consistent with the salutation, and its words should never be abbreviated. The pairs of salutations and complimentary closings suitable for use together are arranged in the table below.

Salutations.	Suitable Complimentary Closings.
Sir or *Gentlemen; Madam,* or *Mesdames*	*Your obedient servant.*
Dear Sir, Dear Madam, or *Dear Sirs*	*Yours faithfully,* or *Yours truly.*
My Dear Sir, My Dear Madam, or *My Dear Sirs*	*Yours very truly.*

When the complimentary close is connected with the last sentence in the body of the letter, as *Hoping you will give this your immediate attention, We remain, Yours faithfully,* such sentence should always begin a new paragraph; *we remain,* or whatever words are used in this connection, should be placed on a separate line preceded and followed by a comma, and the initial letter of the first word should be a capital; then the complimentary close is placed on a line by itself. In official letters the formal style is observed; as

I have the honour to remain, Yours, etc.

The complimentary close may occupy two or even three lines according to the terms used, and its position is governed, to some extent, by its length. The closing terms should be arranged diagonally with the signature.

When the complimentary close consists of several parts they should be separated by *commas,* and a comma should also be placed after the last part.

The Signature is the name of the *writer* or of the *firm* or *company* he represents, placed after the complimentary close.

1. *Which of the Pitman instructions are not applicable today?*
2. *Which ones are?*
3. *What are some likely reasons for the continued acceptance of some and the rejection of others?*

3.

Pitman also included sample letters in his book. How would each be written today?

THE CLIMATE OF BUSINESS

London, 18th May, 19 . .

Messrs. Johann Werner & Co.,
Bremen.

Dear Sirs,

The goods invoiced by you on the 10th inst. have now safely arrived, and are satisfactory. In settlement of the amount of your invoice, less 5 per cent. discount, I enclose sight draft on Berlin, value Mks. 300—. Please acknowledge receipt in course of post.

Yours faithfully,
Henry Lomax

Bremen, 20th May, 19 . .

Mr. Henry Lomax,
London.

Dear Sir,

We beg to acknowledge receipt of your favour of the 18th inst., enclosing sight draft, value Mks. 300—, which amount, with 5 per cent. discount, will be duly passed to your credit, with thanks.

We hope to be favoured with your further orders, and meanwhile remain,

Yours faithfully,
Johann Werner & Co.

London, 10th June, 19 . .

Messrs. James Gray & Son,
Calcutta.

Gentlemen,

Your favour of the 18th ult., with draft at sight on Lloyd's, value £156 10s., duly to hand, with thanks, and the same will be placed to your credit.

We thank you for the interest you are taking in the matter of the Mohairs, and hoping soon to hear favourably from you,
We remain, Gentlemen,

Yours very truly,
W. Anderson & Co.

4.

The article below appeared in The Washington Post *for October 18, 1980. It was written by Gregory M. Jones, an attorney and former employee of the Federal Communications Commission, who with his wife prepared the revised CB radio rules which are discussed in this chapter. It is an interesting and thoughtful commentary by a one-time writer of government prose.*

Confessions of a Reg Writer

> A station in repeater operation, operating in conjunction with one or more stations in auxiliary operation relaying radio signals received at other locations to stations in repeater operation, may use input frequencies not available for repeater operation, provided the input frequencies to the stations in auxiliary operation are in frequency bands authorized for repeater operation.
> —*Federal Register,* Vol. 42, page 2091 (1977).

I wrote that regulation. I am not proud that I wrote it. Even now, 3½ years after the regulation was published in the *Federal Register,* it still embarrasses me that I permitted such a regulation to go out with my name on it. And it embarrasses me that the regulation's shortcomings were discussed, apparently in some detail, at a closed meeting of the Federal Communications Commission, my former employer. But most of all, it embarrasses me that the editors of *The Washington Star* selected "my" regulation (as I have come to think of it) for publication in *The Star*'s "Gobbledygook" column, which each day highlights egregious examples of the product for which Washington is so well, and so justifiably, known.

Contrary to what you may have been led to believe, federal employees do not consider it an honor to have their handiwork publicly ridiculed. I know that I didn't; and when, three weeks later, President Carter promised, in one of his first major addresses to the nation, that federal regulations would be "written in plain English for a change," my humiliation knew no bounds. For all I knew, Carter's speech writers (or Carter himself!) had spotted my regulation and decided that something had to be done—immediately. Hence, the President's plain-English exhortation.

Time and experience have allowed me to take a more detached view of federal gobbledygook, in general, and my contribution to it, in particular. The regulation I wrote in 1977 is really little worse than much of the flapdoodle that spews forth each day from agencies all over town. Those who read the *Federal Register* as part of their work see dozens of equally (well, almost equally) bad examples every week. My regulation was merely the latest in a continuing series.

Fortunately for me, my personal experiment in gobbledygook effectively ended with that one horrendous regulation. After a period of extensive reeducation at the hands of several gifted and ruthless fanatics, I emerged a new man, a maverick bureaucrat with a hatred of gobbledygook, committed to plain English in government at all cost. Incredibly, I soon found myself doing the impossible: writing regulations so that all but the functionally illiterate could understand them. With my wife, I rewrote the rules for CB radio operators into language most any good buddy could get a handle on; and in so doing, I concluded that it is possible, thought not terribly easy, for a federal agency to speak plainly.

Others have made the same discovery. Several federal agencies have made serious, and successful, efforts to write regulations so that non-bureaucrats without Washington connections can understand and comply with them. Former HEW secretary Joseph Califano, for example, launched "Operation Common Sense" to review all of his department's regulations, to get rid of the obsolete rules and to rewrite the remainder. The FCC recently released new radio regulations for America's 400,000 recreational boaters, revised for readers with 8th grade educations. President Carter even issued an executive order in 1978 requiring agencies of the executive branch to issue regulations only upon a finding that the regulations are comprehensible.

Considering the mind-boggling dimensions of the problem (there were 87,681 pages of federal regulations in existence at the end of 1979), progress toward making plain English the language of the federal government has been reasonably good, but it has been uneven. This is so, I am convinced, not because of a lack of commitment on the part of the administration; nor is it because Washington bureaucrats are uncaring, insensitive or inept: Carter has consistently advocated simpler federal regulations, and most government employees are, in fact, reasonably competent and dedicated guardians of the public trust. Rather, much of the gobbledygook can be traced directly to the average bureaucrat's understandable desire to make life as easy as possible by using language with which he or she is comfortable and familiar.

Those of us who live and work in Washington have our own patois, our own sort of bureaucratic cant. It is easy to use, and we use it every day. Some of us even love it. This is fine, I guess, as long as the only people with whom we attempt to communicate speak governmentese as fluently as do we. Bureaucrats, however, tend quickly to forget that 99 percent of the people don't speak governmentese, and that the average American could probably not distinguish between an ANPRM, an EIS and an RFP if his or her life depended upon it.

And that, I think, is the core of the problem: bureaucrats writing for bureaucrats and not for the 220 million other Americans who support the government with their taxes. Bureaucrats fail to recognize the bulk of their audience is composed not of GS15 program managers, but of common folk who want to be told simply and accurately what their government expects of them.

The federal government, unlike the private sector, has a special responsibility to communicate in a manner the public can understand, and it is a responsibility the government is, with some notable exceptions, not fulfilling.

And what of my infamous regulation? It is still on the books, albeit in a slightly more palatable form (*Code of Federal Regulations,* Volume 47, Section 97.86[b]). Maybe one of these days I'll figure out what it means.

Is Jones' analysis in the last five paragraphs of the reasons for the proliferation of gobbledygook in Washington relevant to the writing of the American business community? If so, in what ways and to what extent?

EXERCISE

Earlier books and articles about communication in business and industry reflected a world largely devoid of women, certainly of women in positions other than clerk or secretary. We now live in a changed business community, in which more and more women write and receive letters, memos, and reports. The presence of women managers in the structures of commerce and government forces us to deal with the problems that face the present-day writer who has to refer to both sexes. To illustrate the problem and the challenge, we have included two passages from an article we wrote more than a dozen years ago.

Revising these passages will be a valuable experience in removing what is frequently referred to as a "sexist" viewpoint. We recommend the exercise for several reasons:

1. It makes clear how pervasive is the masculine bias in writing.
2. It demonstrates how difficult it is to avoid reinforcing that bias.
3. It provides practice in a useful skill.

To the busy supervisor, any report—whether in set form, in a letter, or in a memo—is likely to seem an unnecessary nuisance, interfering with the "real work" he should be attending to. As he sees it, he must, more or less painfully, set down information on what for him is usually a dead issue for the benefit of someone who may do little more than file and forget it.

But the supervisor is mistaken if he believes that what he writes is filed unread or that it is of no importance. . . .

A supervisor's effectiveness may be judged to a greater degree than he realizes by his memos and reports. In many instances the men who make the final decisions about his future seldom see him; their impression of him and of his work must, therefore, depend very largely on the quality of what he writes.

Since his reports really are important, the supervisor owes it to himself and to his company to make them as good as he can. . . .

Isn't all this planning and checking going to take more of [the supervisor's] time than it's worth? Even if it did take more time, the increased value of his report to management and its effect on his own future would make it worthwhile. Actually, though, we have found that once a person begins to plan his writing he is able to turn out reports much faster than when he was trying to do everything at once—when he wasted time chewing his pencil and revising what he had written. If a supervisor thinks through a writing problem, he will not only do a better job but will also save time.[1]

[1]"Thinking Through a Writing Problem," *Supervisory Management* 6 (1961), pp. 8–9, 15.

An alternative exercise: Recast the extract from George De Mare's *Communicating at the Top* on pp. 336–337—in which the author seems to assume that all top executives, and even junior ones on the way up, are male—so as to remove the sexist language.

PROBLEMS

1. Inspect two years of the issues of a business journal (for example, *Business Week, Dunn's Review, Fortune,* or *The Harvard Business Review*). Read any articles you find on communication (reading, writing, listening, and speaking) and write a 750-word summary of the problems those articles discuss.

2. Ask an acquaintance who has a job in your field to make for one week an informal tally at the end of each day of roughly how much time he or she has spent that day reading, writing, listening, and speaking as part of that job.

   Ask a second acquaintance at another level or in another subspecialty of that field to do the same. (For example, the first might be a salesperson, the second a sales manager; the first might be an electrical engineer in production, the second an electrical engineer in research and development; or the first might be in marketing, the second in purchasing.)

   Write a paper summarizing and analyzing the results and explaining the reasons for similarities and differences.

3. Obtain loan forms from three different banks or savings and loan associations. Compare the layouts and the language used in the forms to determine which is most readable and understandable to a person who must complete such forms. (Many banks are now trying to provide forms which the borrower can fill out without help from a bank employee.) Write an analysis of the three forms that would be useful to a person responsible for improving the readability and design of such loan forms.

4. Write to your state legislator to ask whether your state has passed or is considering a "Plain English" law, and, if so, whether you may have a copy of the law or proposed law. When the legislator responds, write a 750-word story for a local newspaper on "The Plain English Movement," drawing on the legislator's response and the section of this chapter entitled "Company and Customer."

5. Obtain a copy of a local ordinance (often published in the local newspaper) or a state law. Write a report evaluating it for readability, using specific examples to support your conclusions.

Communication Theory: Considering the Audience

COMMUNICATION THEORY:
THE SHANNON-WEAVER MODEL

In any area effective training must be based on an understanding of the elements of the process involved: what causes an engine to run; what creates the sound when a guitar string is plucked. So here we should ask: What is communication, and how does it occur?

In its simplest form human communication is the transmission of messages, which may or may not be verbal, from one individual to another. If I say to you, "I like peas," and, as a result, you understand that I like peas, communication has occurred. We might diagram the interchange:

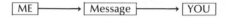

This diagram is very simple. It is the one in the mind of the person who says: "Well, if you want to get the message across, just tell it exactly like it is!" But communication is seldom that simple.

In seeking to understand and explain the communication process, communication theorists continue to develop more and more complicated equations and models. Most of the models, however, are based on a relatively simple one devised some years ago by Claude Shannon and Warren Weaver:

COMMUNICATION THEORY: CONSIDERING THE AUDIENCE

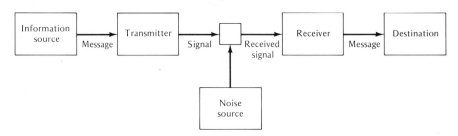

Figure 2.1. Schematic Diagram of a General Communication System. From Claude E. Shannon and Warren Weaver, *The Mathematical Theory of Communication* (Urbana: University of Illinois Press, 1949), p. 5.

In working with business people and students, we have found this model, which is not much different from the simpler one we offered first, to be very helpful in discussing both written and oral communication. Let's see how it works.

When a person speaks, the brain is the information source, the voice box the transmitter; the audience's ear is the receiver, the audience's brain the destination; and a jackhammer or radio operating nearby—quite literally making *noise*—may interfere with or distort the message. In a telephone conversation there are two transmitters, the speaker's larynx and the transmitter in the phone; there are also two receivers, the receiver in the phone at the listener's end and the listener's ear; and there may be a buzzing or a crackling on the line—again, literally noise.

In most everyday speaking situations, of course, the message does not flow only one way. There is conversation: dialogue or group discussion. Communication theorists, therefore, have introduced a variety of "feedback loops" into their models to show how speaker and listener interact and adjust their messages as speaker becomes listener, listener becomes speaker, and they continue to interchange roles. We will consider here, however, only the simple model. If one understands that, the more complex models with their interactive features do not offer serious problems. The person who understands the principle of adjusting a message to the needs of an audience will understand how to adjust successive messages to take account of audience response.

The same simple model is useful in considering written communication. Take, for example, a business letter or report. The brain of the writer is the information source, the typist and typewriter the transmitter; the eye of the reader is the receiver, the brain of the reader the destination. The term "noise" here is used metaphorically to mean anything that interferes with the message or distorts it as it travels from transmitter to receiver: a faulty sorting machine in the post office which punches a hole in a letter or sends it to Las Vegas, Nevada, instead of Milan, Italy; or a torn mail bag which allows the letter to get wet and blur.

Some communication theorists have expanded the metaphor to include almost anything that would interfere with or distort a message or distract an audience, including aspects of the message itself. Thus, for example, wordiness 27 may be considered noise if it distorts the kernel of information that a message is intended to carry, or if it distracts or otherwise prevents the reader from understanding the message. As we shall see later, in this sense any poorly chosen grammatical structure which interferes with the proper transmission of an idea may be "noise": instead of reflecting an idea and reinforcing it, an inappropriate grammatical structure sets up a dissonance, and works against it. Similarly, an inappropriate layout on the page or even a poorly chosen typeface can create dissonance and thus function as "noise."

Other communication theorists speak not of noise but of problems which interfere with the proper *encoding* (i.e., wording) of the message before it is transmitted. An endless variety of such problems, of course, can impair communication: lack of professional skill, a queasy stomach, a limited or ill-used vocabulary, preconceptions and prejudices, self-centeredness, and a host of individual psychological quirks in a speaker or writer. But if, as we believe, the function of written communication in business, industry, and the professions is to influence the thinking and hence the actions of the audience, these obstacles must be overcome.

Warren Weaver, co-author of *The Mathematical Theory of Communication*, put the matter very succinctly in discussing the implications of that theory for communication:

> The problems of influence or effectiveness are concerned with the success with which the meaning conveyed to the receiver leads to the desired conduct on his part. It may seem at first glance undesirably narrow to imply that the purpose of all communication is to influence the conduct of the receiver. But with any reasonably broad definition of conduct, it is clear that communication either affects conduct or is without any discernable and provable effect at all.[1]

COMMUNICATION THEORY:
THE LASSWELL MODEL

Another model which we have found useful in helping speakers and writers think about communication is one developed by a sociologist, Harold Lasswell:

> A convenient way to describe an act of communication is to answer the following questions:
>
> Who
>
> Says What
>
> In Which Channel
>
> To Whom
>
> With What Effect
>
> The scientific study of the process of communication tends to concentrate upon one or another of these questions.[2]

[1] Warren Weaver, "The Mathematics of Information," *Automatic Control,* by the Editors of *Scientific American* (New York: Simon & Schuster, 1955), p. 98.

[2] Harold D. Lasswell, "The Structure and Function of Communication in Society," *The Communication of Ideas,* ed. Lyman Bryson (New York: Harper & Brothers, 1948), p. 3.

COMMUNICATION THEORY: CONSIDERING THE AUDIENCE

In this model, the last line, "With What Effect," echoes Warren Weaver's statement. Lasswell's "Who" is the Shannon and Weaver "Information Source," his "Whom" is their "Destination," his "Says What" is their "Message" and "Signal," his "Channel" is their lines with arrows carrying the "Message" and "Signal." Each model, therefore, is based on the same principle: *the only way to evaluate the effectiveness of a message is to determine its impact on the audience,* that is, on the listener or the reader. A speaker or writer, therefore, must always seek to convey a message that will cause the audience to understand or consider or do what he or she wants that audience to understand or consider or do. No other criterion can be valid. A message may be so "beautifully" written that by some abstract standard it may be thought worthy to be carved in marble; but if it fails to influence the reader as the writer intended, it is ineffective, and thus an unsatisfactory piece of writing.

CASE STUDY I:
AN INSENSITIVE LETTER

Not long ago a secretary in a large steel company opened an envelope addressed to the company president. It contained this letter (names altered):

Dear Sir:

I am presently entering my senior year as a student at the Pitcairn University Institute of Business Administration, and I am now in the process of planning my graduation thesis: an analysis of the steel industry in the United States.

I have about six months to complete this thesis, but I have already started some basic research on it.

I would appreciate any and all information and assistance you would be able to give me in reference to all the facets of the industry, barring none.

When considering this request, please remember that this is a college thesis, and not a high school Science Fair project, and that the caliber of the source material should be commensurate with what the finished product should be.

I would also appreciate any information in relation to whom I should contact at the various company levels for more specific information.

If this letter is not being processed by the official whose job it is to process this kind of request, please forward it to the proper authorities.

Sincerely yours,

John H. Larkin

No doubt Mr. Larkin was well pleased with his letter. If it did its job—and he must have felt sure it would—he would have at his disposal virtually all of the materials he would need to write his thesis.

29

He did, in fact, receive some material from the company. These days companies go out of their way to be helpful in such situations; they have no interest in antagonizing potential customers. But he did not get what he seems to have hoped for. The Public Relations Department, to which his request was finally referred, sent him some pamphlets and recommended a few sources on the history of the steel industry. In the end the young man was forced to go to his university's library and dig for his facts.

Larkin's letter, however, was posted on the company's Public Relations bulletin board. Why? Because it had both amused and irritated the members of the department who had seen it. It amused them because it was so hopelessly naive; it irritated them because it was so insufferably arrogant.

"Who is this little pipsqueak," they must have said to each other, "who writes direct to the president of the company (Has he taken a course in aggressiveness training?) and demands that he be furnished with *all* information and given *all* assistance concerning *all* the facets of the steel industry—*barring none?* Does he think that supervisors *at the various company levels* are going to drop everything they are doing to answer all of the poorly thought-through questions he may dream up? And how nice of him to inform us that this is not a high school project but a college thesis. Now *that* is really impressive!" In short, the people who read his letter were astonished by his impudence and brashness.

But they were also amused. They were aware that they were dealing with a person who obviously knew nothing about the world of business, who was so thoughtless as to feel that the company would drop everything to satisfy his extravagant requests—which he phrased as demands—and who would address the president as "Dear Sir." Ultimately they put it all down to his inexperience. But they would not forget his name, and his letter would surface in their consciousness whenever the words "Pitcairn University Institute of Business Administration" came before them. What kind of a business school must it be, they would think, whose seniors are so abysmally ignorant of the world for which they are specifically being prepared?

One may well wonder how a presumably intelligent young man could write such a letter. That question can't be answered with any degree of accuracy. But it is clear that Larkin did not keep in mind the most important consideration for any writer, whether novelist, journalist, essayist, lover, or business person: he did not consider his audience. He did not ask himself: Who will be reading my letter? What will be that person's attitude toward my request? What do I want the person to do for me? What can he or she be *expected* to do for me? How much should I ask for? How can I phrase my request so that the recipient will be motivated to help me? If Larkin had asked these questions, and others like them, he would not have written a letter of such arrogance that it must have damaged the reputation of the Pitcairn business school not only among those executives who read it, but also among those whom they told about it.

Because it was addressed to a large corporation with which he probably— but not necessarily—would never have further dealings, it may have done

Larkin himself no great harm. If, however, he were to write similar letters for the company which employed him after his graduation, such insensitivity in approaching his business correspondents would be very damaging both to himself and to his company.

CASE STUDY II: A ROUTINE LETTER

Too often people in business are unaware that procedures and phrases that to them are routine may confuse a customer. Consider, for example, the following letter recently sent by a savings and loan association:

Dear Mr. Anderson:

We are returning herewith your personal check No. 272 in the amount of $385.00, dated the first of this month, remitted as the total monthly payment due on your mortgage, including principal, interest, and required escrow.

Mansfield Bank refused to honor the check due to lack of signature and returned it to us.

The sum of $385.00 has been added to the principal of your mortgage.

Yours truly,

John J. Opal, Jr.
Courtesy Savings & Loan Assoc.

When Mr. Anderson received the letter, he was concerned. Was the additional $385.00 a penalty to be added to his mortgage? Because he was going to be out of town for a week and couldn't call to inquire, he wrote the following letter:

Dear Mr. Opal:

I have two comments in reply to your letter returning my unsigned check:

a. Instead of adding the $385.00 to the principal of our mortgage, whatever that means, why didn't someone just call me up and tell me that the check had been returned for lack of signature? I would have come in immediately with another check.

b. Adding $385.00 "to the principal" sounds ominous. What does it mean? Will it cost me any more money?

You spend thousands of dollars advertising how friendly, courteous, and helpful you are and the pains you take to personalize your service; but none of your people thought to pick up the phone and short-circuit this whole problem. Incredible!

Yours truly,

Oscar J. Anderson

When Mr. Anderson returned home, he found the following reply waiting for him:

Dear Mr. Anderson:

I am in receipt of your letter questioning our policy on the handling of your unsigned check No. 272 in the amount of $385.00, remitted as the monthly payment on your mortgage.

We dealt with the matter according to our regular procedures for taking care of such discrepancies.

Please be assured that there are no penalties involved. As soon as you send us a substitute payment, we will subtract the amount added to the principal of your mortgage.

Yours truly,

John J. Opal, Jr.
Courtesy Savings & Loan Assoc.

Anderson was still not sure that he was not going to be penalized, and he felt that John Opal had not understood the last paragraph of his letter, so he called Opal to ask again about the details of the procedure and why someone in Opal's office hadn't simply called to explain the problem. The Andersons, after all, had been doing business with the Courtesy Savings & Loan Association for seventeen years and, as their address indicated, were only a mile away. When Anderson put the question to Opal on the phone, there was a long pause, and then Opal replied, "Well, we always do it by mail"—and presumably they would continue to do so. Opal couldn't understand the connection between the Association's advertising and Anderson's suggestion that a phone call is sometimes more appropriate than a letter. He seemed to feel that what the people in the Association's advertising department did was their business and didn't have anything to do with how he ran the mortgage department. Nor could he understand why Anderson had been concerned upon reading the last paragraph of his first letter. When he wrote the first letter it meant to him exactly what he explained at greater length in his second; and he couldn't see why Anderson needed that fuller explanation.

CASE STUDY III: A COSTLY LETTER

The Genung Manufacturing Company specializes in the production of custom-built laboratory equipment. Though small, it has built up a thriving business by providing special service at reasonable rates. Recently, Genung received an order for a specially designed cooling system to be installed in the laboratory of the Short Beach Chemical Company. The laboratory, then under construction, was to be in operation by July 1. Genung was able to fill the order by June 25 and shipped it on that date to the Short Beach Chemical Company. It arrived on June 30 and was eventually paid for. At that point Genung considered the transaction completed.

However, in March of the following year, Fred Peters of the order service department at Genung received a letter from Thomas W. Crosby of Short Beach Chemical Company saying that a prolonged strike had prevented their completing the laboratory by the expected date and that as a result the equipment designed by Genung had not been uncrated until three weeks before. After it had been installed, the thermostat assembly was found not to be in working condition. Crosby stated that although they should have inspected the equipment when it arrived at the construction site, they had not done so. Under the circumstances the only logical course seemed to be to return the thermostat assembly for reconditioning. Would Genung examine it, he asked, and quote a price for the repairs? Since Genung had not built the thermostat but had obtained it from the Thompson Industrial Equipment Company, Fred Peters referred the matter to Thompson. Thompson reported that the assembly was so severely damaged that repair would be impractical.

This was the situation when Fred Peters, having received his reply from Thompson, dictated this letter:

Mr. Thomas W. Crosby
Short Beach Chemical Company
376 Fosdick Avenue
New York, New York 10094

Dear Mr. Crosby:

With reference to your letter of March 1 in which you inquired as to the approximate cost for reconditioning the thermostat assembly supplied with your order No. A-626 for a specially designed cooling system for the Short Beach Chemical Company Laboratory, we have contacted the factory from which we obtained the assembly and they advise that they do not wish to have anything to do with repairing it, due to the fact that it is not practical and the expense would be exceedingly high. Therefore, since it was not our thermostat assembly and is not repairable, we also do not wish to have anything more to do with it. It is being returned to you this date.

Thank you.

Very truly yours,

Fred Peters
Genung Manufacturing Company

There was no reply to Peters' letter, and the correspondence went to the files. Over a year later, Tom Parsons, a salesman for Genung, made a routine call at the Short Beach Chemical Company Laboratory in New York. Here is his call report:

I unsuspectingly walked into this place and mentioned Genung and was almost forcibly ejected. Paul Mason, who is director of the Short Beach Lab, has hanging on his wall a thermostat assembly which Short Beach apparently obtained with a special cooling system from us. The assembly is there to remind them never to place another order with Genung.

Parsons then reviewed the sequence of events through Short Beach's discovery that the thermostat was inoperative and continued:

Up to this point everything is fine. The customer realizes he was in error in not inspecting the equipment sooner, and is prepared to pay the penalty. His only hope is to salvage what he can, and he requests a definite price for the repair. He then receives a letter from Peters telling them to take their thermostat and go to hell, not quite in those words but essentially to that effect. That did it as far as they were concerned. It was no longer a question of the thermostat but the fact that we refused even to discuss it that gave them the slow burn.

I suppose at this point you're asking yourself why Tom Parsons is bothering to exhume a corpse that's been buried for over a year on an account that probably doesn't give us the price of the thermostat assembly in profit in a year's time. This is the situation. The Short Beach Chemical Lab is only one, and the smallest, of several labs which are affiliated with the Marvin Chemical Corporation. Our total potential sales for the group probably run around eighty thousand dollars a year. This incident has jeopardized the entire account. It goes even beyond that. We have other substantial accounts in this area which are in constant contact with each other, and the word spreads fast. The Marvin Chemical Corporation plans to build two additional laboratories and both will be under the supervision of Paul Mason. Mason has this incident firmly impressed upon his mind, as the thermostat assembly hanging in his office would suggest, and under the circumstances I doubt whether we would receive any consideration for an order. On the other hand, this would appear to be an opportune time psychologically to apologize for Fred Peters' letter and offer some sort of adjustment. Even if the thermostat were a total loss, which I doubt, it would probably be worth the cost just to get it out of Mason's office, where it is collecting dust and is a constant reminder. On the other hand, we might obtain a substantial part of Marvin Chemical's business in our field, which would probably more than compensate for any loss we would suffer.

Fred Peters—who incidentally had left Genung by the time the salesman's report came in—jeopardized a significant portion of the Genung Manufacturing Company's business by writing one letter. Fred was a pleasant fellow and a loyal employee. He would have been shocked had he known the effect his letter had produced.

How did Fred happen to stir up this hornet's nest? The problem of the thermostat assembly probably struck him as routine. Short Beach Chemical had asked him a question, he had found the answer, and he gave it to them ("Well, if you want to get the message across, just tell it exactly like it is"). But the result was just as devastating as if he had *intended* to sabotage his company.

Perhaps Fred Peters was in a bad mood when he wrote the letter. Perhaps he had had an argument with his wife over the discipline of his children. Or perhaps one of his neighbors had dented a fender of his car the night before.

34

Fred may even have been feeling good when he began to dictate. Perhaps he was in a mood to say, "To heck with everything. Let's get this job done and go on to something interesting." Whatever his situation, one thing he clearly did not do: he did not ask himself, "How do the people at Short Beach, who made a costly error in not checking out the thermostat when it came, feel about this whole transaction?" He did not put himself in Mr. Crosby's place and ask himself: "How can I give him the bad news in such a way as to convey our sympathy for their plight and promote good relations between our companies?"

Instead Peters treated the whole matter as routine. He started off with the most impersonal of standard business openings: "With reference to your letter of. . . ." When the time came to give Crosby the bad news, he grabbed the first phrasing that occurred to him; he said that the Thompson Company did "not wish to have anything to do with" repairing the thermostat. It never occurred to him that he had chosen a phrase normally used to refer to something distasteful from which we wish to disassociate ourselves: cheating, deception, questionable behavior of all kinds. It was bad enough that Thompson didn't want to have anything to do with the thermostat. When Peters proceeded to announce that "we also do not wish to have anything more to do with it," the result was a sharp slap in the face for Mr. Crosby and his associates. Finally Peters signed off with a curt: "[The thermostat] is being returned to you this date." No expression of regret or sympathy. No expression of gratitude for previous orders. And, over a year later, Tom Parsons found the thermostat hanging on the wall. Thus a few careless phrases in one letter had cost Genung significant orders and might have produced even more damage had not Peters' superiors been able eventually to restore amicable relations through careful negotiation.

A few careless words. That's all it takes; for words, as every thoughtful person learns, are tricky. What works well in one situation may not be appropriate in another. In a letter to an unsavory character who has been attempting to persuade a company to adopt an unethical and possibly illegal course, the phrasing "we do not wish to have anything to do with it" might be exactly right. But for Mr. Crosby it was all wrong. The context—the dynamics of a particular situation—makes the difference.

CONSIDERING THE READER

Actually few of us are completely unaware of the reader. Up to a point we all realize that our communications will be read by someone, that they are not sent off into in a vacuum. Many a person in business, however, has failed to think through the implications of the reader-writer relationship; few, though, have trained themselves to take that relationship into account intelligently and unfailingly in every communication they produce.

Not a few seem to accept in some degree the view that if you want to give your correspondent information, or make a recommendation, or say that you cannot fill an order, "just put it down in black and white, and if he's got any brains he'll know what you're talking about." In theory, this approach is fine; 35 in practice, as the Genung story so clearly demonstrates, it can cause havoc. The company that sends its customers a letter saying "Effective July 1, this company will service its installations without charge only during the first ninety days after their purchase" will be getting its message across. But if its customers have been accustomed for years to free servicing for the first twelve months, they are going to be very unhappy about a curt note which tells them in effect: "This is what we're doing. If you don't like it, you know what you can do." To be sure, few executives would let a note of this type be sent to all of a company's customers. But we have seen many equally curt and offensive notes sent to an individual company by a sales representative or even by a sales manager.

Perhaps the most important cause of poor communication in business is the failure to remember that a human being will receive each communication—and to write accordingly. People get letters from "companies," but no "company" opens and reads a letter. Each letter is read by an individual, or perhaps a group of individuals. They do not like being slapped in the face. If they are slapped, they react in a very human way: in a case like the one just cited, they retaliate by placing future orders with a company that has the decency both to explain why it must change its service policy and to suggest that it wishes the change did not have to be made. The person who writes letters as if the reader were a robot should not expect them to be received cordially. On the other hand, a touch of warmth or good humor will sometimes do wonders.

COMMUNICATING UP AND DOWN THE LADDER

As our models and our examples suggest, consideration of the audience may involve a number of factors and the need to assess the importance of each as one composes a letter, memo, or report—or as one plans what is likely to be an uncomfortable half-hour on the phone or in a conference room. One such factor is the relative status of the writer and the reader (or speaker and listener).

The college student, like the first-grader, is well aware of the need to consider the reader when preparing written assignments. Indeed, one preoccupation, especially with marginal students, is "what old Smithers wants." Is it different from what Professor Watson wanted last term? Each year in each class the student adjusts subject matter (and perhaps style) to his or her perception of what each teacher wants. This is because the student and the teacher have different status. The teacher gives grades; the student strives to please.

In the business world, life is more complicated, relationships more complex. One's status, both within and without one's own organization, varies from individual to individual and even from day to day. Today's fellow worker may be tomorrow's counterpart in a competing division. Thus the effective communicator in business must adjust tone and language to take account of variations in his or her status in relation to that of others.

The most obvious distinctions to be made are determined by the well-known ladder which every employee must climb, the one up whose rungs one moves from new wage-earner to company president and board chairman. We are all aware of such distinctions, of course, and aware of our own place in the hierarchy. But if we are not careful, we may inadvertently damage ourselves by not being precise enough in what we say. Even what seems a simple writing situation may provide opportunity for disaster.

CASE STUDY IV: A LETTER OF CONGRATULATION

Take the letter of congratulation, for example. Here is a sentence from such a letter: "Your promotion is well deserved, and I know that you will provide the kind of leadership the company needs in the Marketing Division." Is this a "good" sentence? It would be appropriate in a letter from the executive vice-president of a company to a newly appointed division manger. As it happened, we found it in a letter written by a junior executive, a man in his middle twenties, to the new manager of his company's marketing division. The manager felt, understandably, that the junior executive's presumption was almost insulting. "Who does Foster think he is," the older man must have growled, "to tell me that *he* knows I'll provide good leadership?" Being an understanding and intelligent man, he quickly realized that young Foster was really trying to be complimentary, to express his admiration for his superior; nevertheless, the manager told us, it was a long time before he could look at Foster with complete objectivity and a still longer time before he came to feel that he could rely on Foster's judgment.

Once again we have a failure by a writer to put himself in the place of his reader. After he had drafted his letter, Foster should have said to himself, "Suppose I am Mr. Smith. This letter has reached my desk from a very junior executive in the marketing division. What does it sound like to me as manager?" Had he asked this question, Foster would have realized his mistake and phrased his sentence to remove the presumptuous implications.

Writing reports for the people "upstairs," for the boss, the boss's boss, the general manager, and the president, is not an easy job. It deserves careful consideration, and we will come back to it. However, it may be well here to indicate briefly how difference in status affects such communication. For one thing, people who prepare reports generally know more about the subject of their reports than anyone who will receive them. No one else will need *or want* to know as much as they do. Indeed, they dare not put into a written report all they know about their subject. No one at a higher level wants "all the details." Very busy, besieged on every side by reading matter demanding immediate attention, the executive complains bitterly about reports that fail to provide necessary information in brief form. Writing for the top requires that every word be carefully chosen, that every extra phrase, sentence, or paragraph be eliminated. We recall one president who was buried under reports and wanted to get out from under. After making a preliminary survey of the reporting procedures in his company, we came back to him with some proposals. 37

As we talked, we mentioned that one of his junior executives had recognized that his reports should be more concise. "But," this young man had told us, "it would take a lot of time to do that. And time costs the company money." We thought the president would explode. "Does he know how much *my* time is worth to the company?" he roared. To executives these days, time is a most important commodity. They do not appreciate having their subordinates waste it for them.

If one can make such errors in judgment when writing up the ladder in one's own company, one can also make them when writing down the ladder or to someone in another company. We know a personnel manager who heard that an old college friend had just been promoted to *assistant* manager of a firm about the size of his own. "I'm glad to see that at long last you have been given a much-deserved promotion," he wrote—and could not understand why his old friend was something less than cordial the next time they met.

Sometimes difference in status may also be aggravated by difference in background. An engineer communicating with a mechanic can make the same error in judgment that the Bureau of Standards did when a plumber wrote that he had discovered that hydrochloric acid was fine for cleaning out clogged drainpipes. The Bureau replied: "The efficacy of hydrochloric acid is indusputable, but the corrosive residue is incompatible with metallic permanence." The plumber thanked the Bureau for the information and was happy that the Bureau approved of his measures. The Bureau wrote back: "We cannot assume responsibility for the production of toxic and noxious residue with hydrochloric acid and suggest you use an alternative procedure." Again, the plumber said he was glad to know that the Bureau approved of his procedure. Desperate, the Bureau took the unprecedented step of using the plumber's own language: "Don't use hydrochloric acid. It eats hell out of the pipes."

This illustration may seem somewhat exaggerated, but similar misunderstandings are commonplace in industry. A survey of maintenance foremen in one company recently elicited such complaints about maintenance directives as "Call a spade a spade and not some engineering term" or "To the engineer at a desk the job can be done on paper and look fine; to the foreman on the job it may not be practical" or "Either use terms that are well understood, or else define them." Writing for subordinates, especially those not in management positions, is very difficult to do well. In this situation, the reader lacks status and is likely, therefore, to be insecure and tend to resent instructions from above, especially if they come from someone not very far above. It requires great tact and diplomacy to keep such a reader on the writer's side. Most of all, it requires careful thought about *the reader's* situation and probable reaction to what the writer has to say.

THE NEED FOR GOOD HABITS

Without effective communication, internal, external, and at every level, no business organization can adequately fulfill its mission. The new employee who sends out "routine" responses to letters of complaint, the chief executive officer of the company, and all of the employees whose functions lie between share the responsibility of representing their company in dealing with the general public, the government, and other companies. Within a company each member of a department or a divison represents that unit to management. Some communication is oral; but because much of what people in business do must be on record, they will spend a major portion of their working hours preparing memoranda, letters, and reports. A new employee who writes to a customer about a purchase with which she is dissatisfied *is* the company as far as she is concerned, and how he responds to her complaint may determine whether she continues to be a customer. A department head who is asked by her division manager to prepare for top management a report on why the department's production has fallen below expectations *is* for the moment the department, and how she responds may affect not only the department's future, but also her own.

Few individuals have risen to senior executive positions who do not have the habit of considering the audience, for it is one of the keys to effective management. Every report, we said earlier, is an application for either promotion or demotion. As we have pointed out, it is largely through reports that a junior executive is known to the "top brass" of the company. An outstanding report, one that meets the needs—not the prejudices—of the person for whom it is written, inevitably finds its way to the top. Its writer has made an impression that will not be forgotten and will not go unrewarded. On the other hand, an ineffective report—bulky, repetitious, containing extraneous material, impossible to find one's way around in—will probably go no further (fortunately) than the person for whom it was written. It, too, will be remembered—but not with favor.

Consideration of the reader, however, is not toadying to the reader's prejudices. A person may be considerate without losing integrity and self-respect. Blunt statements of fact or intention are necessary for some individuals who will not or cannot understand any but blunt language.

It takes more than intelligence to write good letters and reports. It takes also a mind trained and habituated to consider *all* of the factors involved, most especially the effect of a communication on the person or persons who will receive it. Some people have a special instinct for measuring this effect. But most of us have to train ourselves until consideration of the reader becomes habitual whenever we sit down to write a memo or a letter or a report.

ILLUSTRATIVE MATERIALS

1.

The damage which can occur when a person fails to think carefully about the effect that a communication will have on readers or listeners is graphically illustrated in this excerpt from an article by Edward A. Locke, Jr.[3]

CONTEXT AND PRINCIPLES

Lately I have come to think that the sector of our society that suffers most seriously from verbal incompetence is business. The misleading use of words is a major source of inefficiency and waste motion in business. . . .

I have seen more than one business shaken by a single letter or memorandum in which words were used loosely or wildly. A story was recently told to me by the head of an important company. Call him Mr. Brown. He was at the time trying to establish friendly relations with an executive of another company, a Mr. Slade, who was an important potential customer for Mr. Brown, and Brown had given a good deal of thought to the best way of cultivating him.

One day, a letter from Slade arrived at Brown's office. Slade said that he was reviewing his requirements for the year ahead, and that if Brown would like to talk with him, he would make himself available.

Now it happened that Brown just then was away on a trip. In his absence, Slade's letter went to one of his young assistants for reply—call him Harvey. This is what Harvey wrote to Slade. "Dear Mr. Slade: In Mr. Brown's absence, I am writing to say that your request for an appointment will be brought to his attention immediately on his return."

When Brown got back a few days later, he telephoned Slade at once. Slade shocked him by saying that he was no longer interested in pursuing the matter. He said that he judged companies by the tone of their correspondence, and after receiving Harvey's note he had got in touch with another company, a competitor of Brown's, and had concluded a deal with them. He added that he had been surprised to find that his letter to Brown was regarded as a request for an appointment.

When Brown hung up the phone, he sent for Harvey. Now the point that interested me most is that Harvey could not see that there was anything wrong with the letter he had written. He said, "But Mr. Brown, that letter from Mr. Slade *did* ask for an appointment."

Brown said, "You don't seem to understand. Slade wrote that if I wanted to see him, he would make himself available. He wasn't requesting an appointment. He was giving *me* a chance to request one."

And then young Harvey said, "But after all, it's practically the same thing, isn't it?". . .

Another costly aspect of verbal incompetence in business is what might be called the careless cliché. . . .

I know about a letter written by the sales manager of a well-known company to a customer. The letter explained why a certain salesman had left the company. The sales manager was angry at the salesman for quitting, and in his letter he said, "It's just a case of a rat leaving the ship."

He failed to remember that it is the *sinking* ship that rats desert. But this thought came to his customer, and he mentioned it to others. Soon people were gossiping that the company was in trouble. It took an investigation to unearth the source of the rumor, and a good deal of effort to undo the damage that had been done. The head of that company told me that he figured the cost of that one little misused cliché at about $10,000. . . .

2.

Read the following letter at least twice. Then answer the questions at the end.

Gentlemen:

In filling our order of June 16 (your Order No. 2693), you sent 200 round Wentworth electric wall clocks, No. 102-A, set in a cork base.

My order and your invoice call for 200 round Wentworth electric wall clocks, No. 102-AB, set in a mahogany base. Please send us promptly the ones called for (No. 102-AB, mahogany base). We will return the others for credit.

On this same order we requested immediate shipment of two dozen Went-worth "Charm Alarm" clocks which did not come, did not appear on invoice or packing slip, and had no "will follow" notice. Please send them also without fail, or notify me that you will not supply them.

I have dealt with your firm for years largely because of your promptness and accuracy in filling orders. We can easily procure annoyance and carelessness locally, and will do so if your service is deteriorating to the nuisance level. I will appreciate an acknowledgment of this letter as well as the merchandise ordered.

Yours very truly,

T. J. Barstow

a. *What do the first three paragraphs tell you about the writer of this letter?*
b. *What does paragraph 4 tell you?*
c. *Analyze carefully the effect which this letter is likely to have on the company to which it is sent. All of the facts presented by Mr. Barstow are accurate.*

Gentlemen:

In the past, our company has contracted your firm for numerous design and detailing jobs. It is about two of these jobs in particular I wish to write, namely the Pullin Screw Turner and Adler Belt Tightener. Generally, the work was correct. Admittedly we all make mistakes, though a number of them occurring in these jobs we feel were unnecessary. They resulted in considerable amounts of time and money expended by us.

We wish merely to point out these facts in the hope that those men involved might become aware of their occurrence.

Very truly yours,

C. W. Palmer

Compare this letter with Barstow's. Is there anything missing from the Palmer letter? What effect will it have on its audience? Which letter is likely to be received more kindly? Which is likely to get the better results?

3.

Here is a memo from "the main office" telling a man in one of the branches that a suggestion he made is not practical.

TO: Fritz Jackson—Detroit
FROM: John Gordon
SUBJECT: Lamp List, Green Co. vs. Linton Supply

Thanks for your suggestion that we have branches buy their lamps individually from Linton. Such a procedure would eliminate double handling but would cause several other difficulties. We checked past purchases by the branches from the shop and discovered that the duplication involved in having branches do individual buying would more than offset the saving. The change of procedure would require much more paper work to keep the branches informed of the specification changes on the various lamps.

I know that you are thinking primarily of customer service on small items like lamps. Central Control has been considering this problem for several weeks. I can tell you that we are opening a Small Parts Department, which we hope will provide better delivery on small items. Just as soon as the stocks have been moved from the Chicago shop to Central Purchasing, a general announcement will be made.

Thanks again for the suggestion. Keep them coming. We appreciate them.

a. *If you had received this memo, would you feel that your suggestion had been given careful consideration?*
b. *Does John Gordon sound like a "know-it-all" from the home office who likes to lord it over the men in the branches or like someone who appreciates the problems of the men in the field?*
c. *On what specific things in the memo do you base your opinion of Gordon?*
d. *What were John Gordon's problems in writing the memo?*
e. *How did he attempt to solve them?*

4.

This "Notice of Planned Action" was received by a 70-year-old man with a *second-grade education. Can you understand it?*

SUPPLEMENTAL SECURITY INCOME
NOTICE OF PLANNED ACTION 537

FROM: DEPARTMENT OF HEALTH,
         EDUCATION, & WELFARE
         SOCIAL SECURITY ADMINISTRA-
         TION   DATE: 8-22-80
TO: JAMES WEAVER
         OMRO, WISCONSIN 55623   FILE NO. *72-621-930-Q*

        YOUR PAYMENTS—OR THOSE OF THE INDIVIDUAL NAMED ABOVE—WILL BE CHANGED AS FOLLOWS.

THE AMOUNT OF YOUR CHECK BEGINNING OCTOBER 1980 WILL BE $94.10. THIS AMOUNT INCLUDES $66.20 FROM THE STATE OF WISCONSIN.

YOUR SUPPLEMENTAL SECURITY INCOME PAYMENT IS BEING REDUCED BECAUSE OF YOUR INCOME. THE AMOUNT OF YOUR PAYMENT DEPENDS IN PART ON THE AMOUNT OF OTHER INCOME AVAILABLE TO YOU.

ALTHOUGH SUPPLEMENTAL SECURITY INCOME PAYMENTS ARE MADE MONTHLY, WE AVERAGE YOUR INCOME OVER A CALENDAR QUARTER IN FIGURING THE AMOUNT OF YOUR PAYMENT. WE FIND THAT FOR THE CALENDAR QUARTER OCTOBER 1980 THROUGH DECEMBER 1980 YOUR AVERAGE MONTHLY INCOME IS $159.90.

YOUR AVERAGE MONTHLY INCOME IS BASED ON YOUR INCOME FOR THE CALENDAR QUARTER AS FOLLOWS.

YOUR SOCIAL SECURITY BENEFIT, BEFORE ANY DEDUCTION FOR MEDICARE MEDICAL INSURANCE PREMIUMS, OF $479.70.

SINCE YOUR AVERAGE MONTHLY INCOME INCREASED, YOUR SUPPLEMENTAL SECURITY INCOME SHOULD BE REDUCED EFFECTIVE OCTOBER 1980.

ALTHOUGH WE PLAN TO TAKE THE ACTION SHOWN ABOVE, YOU MAY HAVE YOUR PRIOR PAYMENT CONTINUED OR REINSTATED IF YOU REQUEST AN APPEAL WITHIN 10 DAYS OF RECEIVING THIS NOTICE.

Even if you cannot understand all of the details in the notice, can you suggest improvements in the way the material is presented here?

5.

The United States Army is a performance-oriented organization. It must train individuals to do specific jobs well, often in emergencies. Thus it has developed   43

what it calls "performance-oriented writing." Here is an excerpt from its Guidebook for the Development of Army Training Literature, *which gives two descriptions of what is done when a "local alarm" occurs. The first is topic
oriented: it treats the topic as a "body of knowledge" or the subject of an
expository essay. The second is performance oriented: it "organizes the information as a unit commander would have if he were to use it to guide the
development or check the completeness" of his unit's preparation for a local
alarm. Study the way in which the second version organizes and presents the
material in the first, and list the devices which will make the material easy for
the commander to use. (SOP means "standard operating procedure.")*

CBR: The Local Alarm

The local alarm (warning) is given by any person recognizing or suspecting the presence of a CBR hazard. Unit SOP's must provide for the rapid
transmission of the warning to all elements of the unit and to adjacent units.
Brevity codes should be used where feasible. Suspicion of the presence of
a chemical hazard is reported to the unit commander for confirmation. It is
important to avoid false alarms and to prevent unnecessary transmission of
alarms to unaffected areas. Consistent with the mission and circumstances
of the unit, the alarm will be given by use of any device that produces an
audible sound that cannot be easily confused with other sounds encountered
in combat. Examples of suitable devices for local alarms are empty shell
cases, bells, metal triangles, vehicle horns, and iron pipes or rails. The unit
SOP should specify the devices to be used, locations of the devices in the
unit area, and procedures to be followed. As a supplement to the audible
(sound) alarms or to replace them when the tactical situation does not permit
their use, certain visual signals are used to give emergency warning of a
CBR hazard or attack. These visual signals consist of donning the protective
mask and protective equipment, followed by an agitated action to call attention to this fact. In the event of a chemical agent attack, there is a danger
of breathing in the agent if the vocal warning is given before masking. The
individual suspecting or recognizing this attack will mask first and then give
the alarm. The vocal alarm for chemical agent attack will be "SPRAY" for
a spray attack, and "GAS" for an attack delivered by other means. The vocal
warning is intended for those individuals in the immediate vicinity of the
person recognizing the attack. The vocal alarm does not take the place of
the sound alarm or the visual signal to alert a unit of a chemical attack.

CBR: The Local Alarm

The local alarm or warning is given by any person who knows, or thinks,
that a CBR hazard is present.

Unit Commanders' Responsibility for the Local Alarm Procedure

The Unit Commander will prepare a Unit SOP describing the procedures to be followed in giving the local alarm. These procedures must provide for:

a. A vocal alarm to warn people who are near to the person who gives the alarm;

b. A sound alarm to warn people in the Unit's area—

   (1) This alarm should produce a sound that will not be confused with other sounds of combat. Examples of objects that might be used are empty shell cases, bells, metal triangles, vehicle horns, and iron pipes or rails.

   (2) The Unit SOP should identify the object to be used, where it is located, and how it is to be used to give the alarm;

c. A visual signal to be used in addition to the sound alarm, or, in place of the sound alarm when silence is necessary;

d. A way for members of the Unit to quickly report a suspected CBR hazard to the Commander for confirmation;

e. Rapid communication of the warning to other nearby units, making use of brevity codes if at all possible.

How to Give the Local Alarm

In case of Chemical attack, use these steps to give the local alarm:

a. Put your mask on first;

b. Give a vocal alarm—
   If spray attack, say 'SPRAY,''
   For all other kinds, say "GAS";

c. Give the sound alarm, visual signal, or both, as directed in your Unit SOP;

d. Pass the warning to the Unit Commander as directed in your Unit SOP.

6.

This audience analysis checklist has been developed by Siegel & Gale, a design and language simplification firm, for their own use in developing and preparing documents for their clients.

1. Who is the primary reader?
2. Who are the secondary readers?
3. How will the reader(s) use the document?
   as a reference guide to explain their obligations and rights.
   as a legal contract to be picked apart by courts and lawyers.
4. How often will the reader use the document?
   occasionally, when an incident occurs.

constantly, as a reference in explaining provisions to others.
rarely, and then only to check very specific provisions.
5. What are the document provisions?
are they new to the reader?
are they modifications of existing provisions?
6. What is the *technical background* of the audience?
are they *all* professionals in the same field?
are they professionals in different fields?
are they professionals and laymen?
are they business people?
what is their educational background or socio-economic status?
have they been exposed to comparable documents before?
what terms of art do they know from personal or home policies?

NOTE: The more diverse the audience, the more general (or self-explan-
atory) the language must be.
If uncertain of the audience's technical level, assume lowest possible level in writing.

7. What is the *attitude* of the audience?
is the reader hostile to the document?
does the reader see the document as beneficial, helpful?
does the document ask for personal information?
does the reader have any preconceived notions about the document that
you must surmount?
8. What *behavior* do you want as a result?
what reaction do you expect from the audience?

a. Which aspect of the Lasswell model does this checklist stress?
b. At which stage(s) in the writing process should particular questions on the
checklist be asked?
c. Analyze a writing assignment that you have already completed by asking
the questions on the checklist. Has the checklist helped you to see something about how to do the assignment that you didn't see before?
d. Which section(s) of the checklist do you find particularly helpful?

PROBLEMS

1. Many books on communication in business and industry begin with a consideration
of communication theory or communication models. Find such a book in your
company, college, or public library and read that section. Then write a 500-word
analysis for your instructor or for a fellow employee comparing the treatment of
communication theory in this book with the treatment in the other book you examined.

2. You are the personnel director of the steel company to which John Larkin sent his
letter (*Case Study I: An Insensitive Letter*) and see the letter on your company's

Public Relations Department bulletin board. Since you have gotten to know the Dean of Pitcairn University's Institute of Business Administration reasonably well on your recruiting trips there, you want to alert him to the fact that naive letters like Larkin's can harm his school's reputation; but you don't want to get Larkin in trouble. Write an appropriate letter.

3. You are the public relations consultant for the Courtesy Savings & Loan Association (*Case Study II: A Routine Letter*). John Opal of the Association's mortgage department shows you Oscar Anderson's letter and asks in some puzzlement what policy his department should adopt on calling customers rather than writing to them. He adds that similar problems have arisen in other departments. Write a policy statement on the use of the telephone by Association employees to communicate with Association customers. The statement will first be considered by the Association's lawyers and then by its Board of Directors.

4. You are the Sales Manager for the Genung Manufacturing Company (*Case Study III: A Costly Letter*). When you receive the call report that Tom Parsons wrote after his stop at the Short Beach Chemical Company Laboratory, you decide to write to Paul Mason, director of that laboratory, to see if you can repair the damage that Fred Peters caused with his thoughtless letter and win back the account. Write the letter.

5. Using the audience analysis checklist developed by Siegel & Gale (Illustrative Material 6), write an analysis to help someone preparing to be a technical writer understand why the second version of "CBR: The Local Alarm" is more effective than the first (Illustrative Material 5).

6. The next time you hear a talk delivered to a group, note what the speaker does to take into account the particular interests of the group. Then write a summary report of your findings.

3

Writing to Inform and Persuade

The fact that "to inform" and "to persuade" are two different verbs may suggest that informing and persuading are two quite distinct—and distinguishable—processes. Many communication theorists insist, however, that these are not as separate as they may seem, that in practice distinctions between them may become blurred.

In the last chapter we quoted Warren Weaver's statement that "communication either affects conduct or is without discernible effect at all." Thus if a letter, memo, or report does not have the desired effect on the person who reads it, it is not a successful communication. Even technical reports affect conduct. A report, for example, which concludes, "Thus the new procedures tested will offer at least a 30% cost savings over current processes without loss of quality or time" can be expected to affect conduct, to lead the reader to take certain actions. One might argue that the report *caused* or *induced* certain actions—rather than *persuaded* the reader to take them—on the grounds that *causing* or *inducing* implies an appeal to reason, whereas *persuading* implies an appeal to the emotions; but the distinction between *cause* or *induce* and *persuade* is even less clear than the distinction between

inform and *persuade.*

One might also argue that whatever the effect on the reader, the writer didn't intend to influence the reader's actions. Indeed, some might say, it would be improper for a report writer to attempt to influence a manager. Deciding which technical process to use in production is, after all, not only a managerial prerogative but a managerial responsibility. It should not, therefore, be assumed at the technical level. Theoretically, perhaps, the distinction is reasonable. Practically, it is not. In the first place, the reason a company hires people to do research is so that its managers will be able to make informed production decisions. Thus the basic function of research reports in business is to influence such decisions. Secondly, the engineer who writes a report on procedures that "will offer at least a 30% cost savings" can hardly avoid influencing management, and may be understandably annoyed if management ignores what seem to be obvious improvements.

THE IMPORTANCE OF PROPER PLANNING

Whether a message is intended to inform or persuade, it must be understood. To be understood it must be coherent, organized. It must persuade the reader that the writer has the subject under control. Its ideas must be developed in an orderly, meaningful fashion. Like an experiment, a sales campaign, or the construction of a building, a communication must be planned. Consider, for example, Mr. G. T. Stevens, who is faced with a difficult writing problem. He must refuse an invitation but maintain pleasant relations with the person and the group which invited him.

On October 21 Stevens received a call from Mary A. Rinton, Executive Secretary of The National Association of Hardware Wholesalers. Stevens understood from the conversation that Ms. Rinton was simply inviting him to attend the association's annual meeting on November 18, 19, and 20 and especially to attend a panel discussion on lawn-mowing equipment, a field which his company was planning to enter. Since several projects in which he was interested were likely to be in a critical stage in mid-November, Stevens was cordial but noncommittal about the invitation.

Ten days later a letter from Ms. Rinton reached Stevens' desk which clearly indicated that she thought she had invited Stevens to be a *member* of the panel. The letter renewed the invitation and asked for a prompt reply. Stevens, who was in South America on a special assignment, did not return to his desk until November 6. On November 7, we find him at his desk. He has finally been able to get around to his most important mail, which includes Ms. Rinton's letter. A telephone call discloses that she is on a business trip and will not return for two days. Stevens decides to write. An intelligent and thoughtful man, he uses an orderly procedure.   49

1. Determine Real Purpose or Function

The meeting is less than two weeks away. Stevens cannot afford to alienate either Ms. Rinton or The National Association of Hardware Wholesalers. He may want to display his products at future meetings of the association, advertise products in its trade journal, and sell to its members. On the other hand, he knows little about the panel topic and does not wish to get his company's venture off on the wrong foot. Furthermore, he has a very important meeting in Chicago on November 17 and may have to remain there until the late afternoon of the next day. Hence he must refuse—late as it is. But he must refuse in such a way that neither Ms. Rinton nor the association will be offended. In fact, he should, if possible, increase their good will toward his company. This is the real purpose of his letter.

2. Select Materials

Stevens' first step is to recheck his calendar. As he thought, he is firmly committed to a conference on November 17 with representatives of the Dill Company, and they may insist on his staying over for an extra day. Even if he were prepared to speak on the panel's subject, he couldn't be sure of making the conference on November 18. So he jots down on his scratch pad "Chicago, Nov. 17," and then adds "H. C. Dill Company—overnight?" Underneath that, he writes "not enough exp. with mowers yet." Then he adds "can't cancel Chi.—too many people involved." Thinking about the Dill Company, he puts down also "imp. customer." Those are the facts. What else does he want to say? He must be gracious about the invitation, so he writes "flattered." He must also apologize for replying late, so he adds "apology—out of town— phone call, too."

Now he looks at his list:

> Chicago, Nov. 17
> H. C. Dill Co.—overnight?
> not enough exp. with mowers yet
> can't cancel Chi.—too many people involved
> imp. customer
> flattered
> apology—out of town—phone call, too

There are some things he should not say. Calling the Dill Company "an important customer" might suggest that he considers the hardware wholesalers to be of lesser importance. Nor would there be much point in naming the Dill Company or in mentioning the number of people involved. Should he mention the Chicago trip at all? Probably so. That leaves:

> Chicago, Nov. 17
> ~~H. C. Dill Co.~~ overnight?
> not enough exp. with mowers yet
> can't cancel Chi. ~~too many people involved~~
> ~~imp. customer~~
> flattered
> apology—out of town—phone call, too

3. Order Materials

How should he begin the letter? Probably by expressing his pleasure at being asked. So next to "flattered" he puts a *1*. What should come next? After a few moments' thought, he decides that in this instance apology should precede excuses. Therefore he makes that *2*. Now the excuses. He decides to start with his inexperience and *then* mention his appointment in Chicago. He labels inexperience *3*, then connects the first two and the fourth items on the list and makes them *4*.

> **4.** Chicago, Nov. 17
> ~~H. C. Dill Co.~~ overnight?
> **3.** not enough exp. with mowers yet
> can't cancel Chi. ~~too many people involved~~
> ~~imp. customer~~
> **1.** flattered
> **2.** apology—out of town—phone call, too

4. Check Against Purpose

The approach he has worked out looks good. Is there anything else? He not only wants to stay in Ms. Rinton's good graces, but also wants to keep the door open for future invitations, so he adds a final item, which he numbers *5*:

5. perhaps next year

5. Write

Now he is ready to dictate. He calls in his secretary, and looking at his outline he dictates the following letter:

Dear Ms. Rinton:

I was flattered to learn from your letter of October 29 that you were inviting me not only to attend the coming meeting of the Association of Hardware Wholesalers, but also to participate in a panel discussion. And I owe you an apology both for misunderstanding you over the phone and for taking so long to answer your letter. I returned Monday from two weeks in South America. This morning I tried to call you, only to learn that you, too, have been away from your desk.

You may not know that we have only recently begun to consider manufacturing lawn mowers, so we don't have any practical experience with them yet. I'm afraid that my personal experience is confined to my weekly wrestling with an old Quick-Cut 720. Therefore, it would be presumptuous of me to accept an invitation to speak on that subject before your group, most of whom probably know much more about mowers than I do. As I told you over the telephone, I want very much to attend the meetings, but my interest is in learning from those of your members who have had long experience with mowing equipment.

As it turns out, I may even be cheated out of that. I have a longstanding appointment in Chicago for the seventeenth which I can't cancel. I may have to stay overnight. If so, I won't be able to attend the panel, though I'll certainly be there for the later sessions.

By the time of your next meeting I might possibly have some contribution to make. We hope by then to have experience with trial models and the results of some experiments we began recently. One of our engineers is working on a new type of motor that we hope will greatly reduce the weight of the standard mower.

I am sorry that I could not send this reply last week, for I know what a headache it is to set up panels. However, I am looking forward with great interest to the meetings at Stafford Springs and to the opportunity to meet you and other members of the association.

Sincerely,

6. Recheck Against Purpose

When his secretary brings in the typed letter, Stevens reads it carefully. Is the second apology in the last paragraph a little too much? Under the circumstances, probably not. After signing, he tells his secretary to send the letter special delivery, so that Rinton will have as much time as possible to get someone to take his place.

This procedure may at first seem involved and time-consuming. In practice it is not, especially after it becomes habitual. For a letter like the one we have been discussing, the first four steps (determining the real purpose, selecting the materials, ordering them, and checking against purpose) should take a minute or two—three at the most. On the other hand, Stevens does not waste dictating time, because he knows exactly where he is going. He does not, like so many letter-writers, have to keep his secretary waiting while he decides what to say next. Nor does he discover as he looks over the typed letter that it has to be rewritten because he has omitted an important item or because the emphasis—or even the clarity—of the message is obscured by ineffective order. Even if a poorly planned letter is not confusing, it is likely to be a third again as long as it need be. Thus in the long run careful planning saves both writer and correspondents a great deal of time.

By proceeding in an orderly fashion, therefore, Mr. Stevens has *informed* Ms. Rinton that he will be unable to accept her invitation to participate in the panel discussion. But, if she is a reasonable person, Stevens has also *persuaded* her that although he cannot accept this particular invitation, he is a responsible, clear-headed, articulate person whom she would do well to consider as a panel member or speaker for the next meeting. If Stevens had not thought his letter through as carefully as he did, he might have written simply that he could not accept the invitation. Ms. Rinton would probably have considered his reply unsatisfactory, would have been annoyed at having to find a last-minute replacement, and would have wanted to stay clear of him in the future. Fortunately, however, Stevens understood the function of his communication well enough to know that what was ostensibly only a letter informing Ms. Rinton that he was not available should also be persuasive.

THE PSYCHOLOGY OF PERSUASION

A recent bibliography of research on the communication process had seven thousand entries. One would think that such a bibliography would enable us to find the answers to any questions about persuasion that we might wish to ask. Unfortunately, we still have few answers. There is a good bit of information about individual components of the Lasswell model discussed in Chapter 2, but very little about their interaction. Furthermore, because many of the studies have been done on university campuses in situations unrelated to the business world, it is not clear how useful they are for business or technical writers.

If, for example, a study of one audience shows that information (Lasswell's "What") alone almost never changes attitudes, should one assume that the same generalization applies to all audiences (Lasswell's "To Whom")? Does it apply to technical communications? Mightn't it apply differently at different levels of a business organization? When one technical person writes to another of comparable training and understanding and at the same level of authority, the content of the communication may be largely informational (although dif- 53 ferent organizations of the material may be more or less persuasive). The same message aimed at a management audience might have a larger amount of analysis; adapted for a customer, its thrust might be more heavily persuasive.

On the other hand, suppose an engineer writes for a particular manager who is known to be suspicious of attempts at manipulation and to prefer antiseptic reports, or for a purchasing agent who takes pride in his or her engineering training and experience and resents being "talked down to." In such a case it would be best to stick to information and provide a minimum of analysis or persuasion. How the components interact is therefore very important. But because of the complexity of their interaction, no study of their relative impact is available or likely to become available. Writers and speakers must of necessity work them out individually for each communication.

The challenge, then, is always to determine what effect one wants to achieve (Lasswell's fifth component) and then to determine how to use the other four variables to achieve that effect:

Who is writing and to whom? How should the source present himself or herself to the particular audience: as an expert, as a fellow specialist, as a friend, as a subordinate, as a superior, as one who shares a certain set of opinions or assumptions, as a competitor or even an antagonist, as someone with inside information . . .?

How should the message be encoded and organized? Should the style be breezy or formal, the sentences and paragraphs long or short; should the sections be numbered or unnumbered, introduced by headings and subheadings; should the bad news or the good news be given first; should the message be humorous, friendly, sincere, or impersonal . . .?

What channel should be used—a hand-delivered handwritten note, a letter, a cablegram, a phone call, a printed document, a message sent from one person to another over the word-processing system . . .?

As we have indicated, no decision about any component can be made independently. Only by thinking through how it interacts with others will the writer or speaker achieve a desired effect with a particular audience.

Despite the complexities of their interaction, however, recent research has some useful things to say about at least three of the five variables in the Lasswell model: WHO—SAYS WHAT—TO WHOM. For most of us these are the significant variables; few writers or speakers have a choice of channel, and the fifth variable, impact on the audience, will be produced by our manipulation of the other four.

WHO: THE SOURCE

The Writer's Image

Many of the things that research on persuasion tells us we already know from experience. We know that the members of an audience will more likely be persuaded by a writer or speaker they think is like themselves than by someone they think of as different. Thus a letter to a potential customer in South America might better begin "As business people, you and I share a common aim . . ." than "We here in the United States think. . . ." Similarly, all other things being equal, a company selling to a customer whose chief engineer will have the final say on the purchase of equipment for a new process will do well to have as its major spokesman an engineer with practical experience, even though the research scientist who developed the process concerned may well know more about it. In such negotiations, the scientist might profitably play the role of "consultant."

The Credibility of the Source

Another common-sense principle supported by research studies is that an audience is most likely to be persuaded by a writer or speaker of high credibility, particularly for the short term. Thus a salesperson probably should reply to a customer, "Our Engineering Department [note the capitals, which make the statement more impressive than "our engineers"] tells me that if you use a lighter weight oil in your number 3 unit . . ." rather than "Your problem can best be solved by using a lighter weight oil in your number 3 unit."

Furthermore, a writer or speaker whose background or position seems likely to provide low credibility should make the case first and then display such credentials as he or she may have. Thus a proposal from an established industrial firm might profitably begin, "In our twenty-two years of building steel plants on three continents, we have developed a flexible planning procedure ideal for developing and building your Maroon Bay steel mill." A firm that is new to the field, however, would do better to begin by emphasizing its special competence to build the proposed steel mill and refer later, if at all, to what the audience will clearly perceive is its limited experience.

. . . SAYS WHAT: THE MESSAGE

Organization

The effectiveness of a message is increased if it begins with views shared by its audience. Thus a proposal for purchase of new equipment or use of new technology might better begin with a statement about how its cost effectiveness will increase profits than with analysis of its radical features.

Studies also show that if one has both desirable and undesirable information to transmit, presenting the desirable information first increases the possibility that the audience will pay attention to and understand it. Offering the undesirable information first decreases that possibility. The writer of the following letter made a serious mistake:

CONTEXT AND PRINCIPLES

Dear Mr. Carson:

The plastic baby bottles that you sent with the other items for our inspection are not up to your usual standard of quality. The eight-ounce size has an extremely thin bottom which developed a hole in the center when we tested it. The four-ounce size is not uniform in color and failed our pressure test. Therefore, we are returning them by parcel post today.

If we can have a modified exclusive on the bottle brushes, we will order 500 dozen. We would like to advertise them as a "SIMPSON FIRST." Could you hold off making them available to other dealers until we have had a chance to advertise them?

The Pyrex feeding dishes are fine. We'll let you know by the end of the week how many we will want.

Yours truly,

Simpson Baby Products

G. A. Farenol
PURCHASING AGENT

The opening paragraph of Mr. Farenol's letter certainly is not designed to put Mr. Carson in a pleasant frame of mind. If Carson has any alternative, Farenol is unlikely to get a "SIMPSON FIRST" on his bottle brushes. Nor is Carson's unhappiness likely to be alleviated by the final paragraph, which does not contain a firm order for the Pyrex feeding dishes. As a whole the letter is likely to damage rather than improve relations between the two companies.

Research suggests, too, that the reader who is first made to feel a need for a product will absorb more of the information presented. A proper approach in a sales message about a cleaner, then, might be:

Does your present upholstery shampoo soak your furniture clear through, leaving it uncomfortably damp for hours—even days? If it doesn't, you are probably using an inflammable cleaner which is dangerous to have around the house. To use it safely, you should drag your furniture outside. Either way, it's a mess.

Well, Soluol has changed all that. It's a completely safe, nonflammable cleaner that can be used on all colorfast fabrics. A foam, it rides on the surface and will not overwet the material.

Furthermore, you don't need to fuss with a separate applicator. Soluol comes in a handy plastic tube which doubles as a handle. All you do is screw the tube into the applicator head, squeeze gently, and out comes the foam. When the Soluol tube is empty, you simply unscrew it and screw in a new one. The refill costs no more than the can or bottle of the messy or dangerous cleaner you are using now.

Incidentally, Soluol also cleans car seats quickly and easily, whether they are fabric, vinyl, or leather. You'll probably want to buy two, one for the house and one for the car.

You can get Soluol in department, drug, hardware, variety, and grocery stores, as well as at your supermarket.

Presenting the information in paragraphs two and three first and then trying to convince the reader of the need for Soluol would be much less effective.

If an audience can be expected to be unfriendly to the view presented in a message or will hear opposing arguments from another source, the speaker or writer should present both sides of the case. If an audience is likely to be friendly, however, or if the other side of the case will not be presented by someone else, only the one side need be presented.

If a message carries both sides of an argument, it is not clear which side should be presented first. Presumably the nature of the audience will govern here. If an audience holds an opinion based on very narrow ground, which can be quickly, simply, and effectively countered, it may be appropriate to do that immediately. On the other hand, if there is strong emotional commitment to a point of view, it may be more effective to explore that view sympathetically before presenting an opposing view. It *is* clear, however, that arguments presented either at the beginning or at the end of a message are remembered better and are therefore more effective than those presented in the middle.

Explicit Conclusions

Recent investigations also show that whereas new information can strengthen a position that an audience already holds, information alone is unlikely to change attitudes. Similarly, a message with an explicit conclusion will produce more opinion change, particularly among less intelligent people, than one which simply provides information and lets the audience draw its own conclusions. Like all generalizations, however, this one must be used cautiously and with due attention to the other variables. We have already suggested that particular audiences may be left to draw their own conclusions. Indeed, such audiences may resent obvious attempts to influence them.

Humor

The person who attempts to use humor in a persuasive message is usually asking for trouble. Humor frequently is not understood and may well backfire. Editors of professional journals and of magazines designed for educated readers know that every satire, no matter how obvious, will draw irate letters to the editor from readers who do not recognize the satire for what it is. Writers or speakers, therefore, should rely on humor to carry the burden of their message only when they are absolutely sure how a particular audience will respond. Similar care should be taken with emotional appeals. They can be effective, but they, too, are likely to be misunderstood or resented.

. . . TO WHOM: THE RECEIVER

We have all heard much in recent years about how we differ from each other: our nervous systems differ, for example, as do our IQs; the sex drive varies from person to person, as does the need for approval. But for all our individual differences, we can still accept some general propositions about people and the way they act and react. Every individual, for example, has certain needs, has a self-concept, and reacts in typical ways to the world. Anything that frustrates those needs, violates that self-image, or throws the person into too sharp a conflict with the culture pattern will inevitably cause pain. Since causing pain is generally not an effective method of persuasion, the writer of a persuasive letter must be very careful to avoid doing so.

Basic Needs

Anyone attempting to persuade should be aware of basic needs and how they affect people. First, of course, comes the need to satisfy certain biological drives. Of these, we are probably most aware of hunger, thirst, and sex. But there are also excretory and maternal drives and the need for oxygen. These drives appear in many different patterns and proportions. What may be persuasive with one person may irritate another and leave a third cold.

Another important need is security. People want to feel that they belong. Hence the frequent management appeal for employees to contribute to a "team" effort. Belonging makes a person feel secure. So does status. Hence the strong drive toward a position carrying an impressive title, a handsomely appointed office—and a secretary. "Getting ahead" enables one to display status symbols which suggest that one has "made it."

People satisfy their needs and their drives in various ways, depending upon the strength of each and the method approved by their culture pattern. In certain parts of the world people satisfy hunger primarily by eating fish, in others by eating rice, in still others by eating meat. There are differences within subcultures, too. In the culture pattern which we know as "Western European civilization," the French still tend to satisfy their thirst more often with wine than do the English, the Germans more often with beer than do the Italians. Even within a single country there are marked differences. In some areas of the United States, hominy grits is a staple in the diet. In other areas it is virtually unknown.

To communicate effectively, any executive must be aware of these individual and cultural differences. An American agricultural expert working in Asia, for example, found it extremely difficult to persuade the people of a village to forsake their old-fashioned methods of cultivating for more productive ones. Even his promise to supply them with rice should his methods result in crop failure did not persuade them. In desperation he finally filled a warehouse with a year's supply of rice for every person in the village. Only then did the villagers try the methods he espoused. To the American their stubborn refusal seemed at first to be utter stupidity. But he soon realized that for the villagers hunger was a terrible reality, not something they had merely read about, as it was for him and most Americans. And their need to stay alive was a much stronger influence than the promises of an American stranger.

The Audience's Self-Image

As we have seen, a writer or speaker must be careful to keep clearly in mind the self-image of the individual or group being addressed. The skillful persuader will not make the same appeal to engineers as to millworkers. Engineers think of themselves as professionals. Thus an organization patterned on a professional association like the American Medical Association or the American Bar Association is likely to appeal to them more than one patterned on a labor union like the International Ladies Garment Workers Union or the International Union of Electrical Workers. The first two organizations are more compatible with an engineer's self-image; the others may violate it.

A brief examination of magazine advertisements will suggest that advertisers are very much aware of reader self-image. In homemaking magazines, for example, usually sold in supermarkets, the central figure is a woman who is still lovely (but needs the right soap and makeup to maintain her loveliness), still romantically appealing to her husband (but needs the right toothpaste and skin creme to maintain that appeal). A good hostess, she is not pretentious (she frequently uses silver plate or stainless steel rather than sterling); an efficient cook and baker, she uses packaged cake mixes (with which, however, she bakes "homemade" cakes). In her life there is always the right balance between domestic duty and domestic felicity, always the light brush of comfort to soften the bright and perhaps harsh lines of efficiency. To some this portrait may seem a distorting stereotype. But its persistence in advertisements suggests that it reflects the self-image of many women accurately enough to sell products. It must, therefore, be taken into account by anyone who wishes to write a successful sales letter to women.

Reader Cultural Patterns

Knowledge of the pressures and laws (written and unwritten) established by a particular culture pattern and of the ways people respond to them is also essential to effective persuasion. Americans pride themselves on their social mobility: from office boy to bank president, from farm boy or haberdasher to President of the United States. Our culture pattern encourages us to think in these terms. In many parts of the world, however, culture patterns—though seldom laws—support class consciousness and provide sanctions against upstarts who try to work their way above the positions into which they were 59 born. Anyone dealing with foreign customers should understand these and other cultural differences. A young businessman, for example, who was sent by his company to South America, found that his biggest problem was adjusting to what he felt was the relatively slow rhythm of business there. Only a moderately aggressive person here, he found himself much too brash by South American standards. He discovered very quickly that his new business companions were not impressed by "Yankee ingenuity" and "efficiency." Only when he adjusted to their tempo could he work effectively with them.

Subgroups within a particular culture pattern also have different standards and patterns of response. A study of dieting, for example, showed that the higher the class (as measured by education and occupation), the stricter the standard of weight control and the lower the percentage of overweight people. Clothing styles and preferences in art, music, and literature similarly reflect class. Western driving habits are often different from Eastern ones. Farmers do not go to sleep or wake up at the same hours as city dwellers. The owner of a business or an executive in a large company can generally be expected to take a dimmer view of government regulation than a member of a labor union. On the other hand, in some industries such as trucking, in which government regulation decreases competition, management may well favor at least certain kinds of regulation.

Similarly, among some groups of workers, voicing support for joint labor-management committees to improve plant efficiency may not be appropriate. Workers who aspire to management positions, however, may argue for such committees even in the face of disapproval or accusations of disloyalty by their peers. The effectiveness of peer-group pressure is strongly influenced by individual personality. The insecure employee is less likely than the secure one to express views contrary to those of the group. Similarly, it is harder to change the opinion of an individual who has taken a public stand than of one who, though holding a similar opinion, has not made it known.

Involving the Audience Actively

One conclusion confirmed by recent studies of group behavior is that active participation helps to overcome resistance to a point of view or a policy and also leads to effective opinion change over time. A manager seeking to establish standard procedures and specific formats for reporting would do well, therefore, to have those procedures and formats emerge from a series of group meetings with report writers, rather than imposing them by executive fiat. Even though discussion at such meetings may sometimes be heated, members are likely to accept a group decision. In the long run, therefore, managers will be wise to seek consensus, even though the process is time consuming and perhaps even occasionally aggravating. In the same way, the seller who involves a prospective customer in shaping a proposal can do a great deal to insure its
60   acceptance.

ally Understanding

ot all attempts to persuade are successful. Nor is it always possible to ver the real sources of an individual's opinions, for they are often buried in the subconscious and unknown even to the self. Therefore, when they are held with great tenacity or don't really explain the actions they are supposed to, they may appear to the observer to be irrational, even childish. A woman may refuse to place money in a savings bank because her father or grandfather lost everything through bank failure in the Great Depression. But she may give her children thirty other reasons for not doing so. A man may be overaggressive because as a child he saw his good-natured father trampled on by employers and associates. But he will talk about "the importance of drive" in business.

Although we can tell in general how people will react to various stimuli, we cannot predict accurately for any one individual or even for any one group. Still, we must understand the nature of prejudice and attempt to circumvent its effects as we can.

. . . IN WHICH CHANNEL

In business, industry, and government, people communicate most frequently by writing (letters, memos, and reports) and by speaking (face to face, in group discussion, or by phone). Sometimes, of course, a single message will go through two channels, as when a person follows a phone call with a confirming letter or memo or with a written order.

Given the nature of our business world and its need for precision, accuracy, and record-keeping, writing will continue to serve an important function. The pundits who predicted a few years ago that all business would soon proceed by tape cassettes and phone calls were simply wrong.

There is something to be said, however, for shifting occasionally from the relatively formal written channel to a less formal one, particularly when correspondence seems to be getting nowhere. A problem bogged down in an interminable exchange of mail can sometimes be solved by a phone call or a face-to-face conversation, or, as the following example shows, by a sudden change in tactics.

One of our clients told of sitting at his desk late one Friday afternoon looking despondently at a correspondence file an inch or more thick about a minor problem that seemed no nearer solution than when the first letter was written six months before. He doubted that another exchange of letters would be helpful. What to do? Since it was five o'clock, he just ducked the problem by going home.

Monday morning, however, it was there on his desk when he arrived. He sagged into his chair, staring at the correspondence. Then he had an idea. After tying some string around the file, he wrote on a blank sheet of paper: "Ralph Oberman: Isn't this getting silly? John Williams, 554-3382." Tucking the hand- 61 written message under the string, he had the package delivered by messenger to Oberman, whose office was in another part of the same city. In an hour, he received a phone call from Oberman, who agreed that, yes, it was getting silly and suggested that they meet and resolve the difficulties. They met the next day and found a solution.

The note-writer was convinced that the unexpected change in medium and channel had jolted the problem out of the rut into which it had fallen and had thus led to a solution. We do not propose that such a procedure become standard, but we do recommend a change of channel when the usual one seems unlikely to produce results.

WHAT EVERY WRITER SHOULD KNOW

As a writer one should understand that all of the needs and the tensions we have been describing exist in the sender of the message as well as in the receiver and that one must be constantly aware of them. An angry incoming letter may threaten our security and tempt us to reply angrily. If we recognize this reaction and its origins, we will be better able to resist that temptation. Understanding needs and tensions and how they are satisfied and understanding the concept of the self-image and the relation of the individual to society's various culture patterns should help us understand better not only our audience but also ourselves. And by thinking clearly about both ends of the communication channel, we will be able to communicate more effectively.

All of this may sound as if a person who wants to be a successful writer (or speaker) should plunge immediately into a study of psychology, sociology, and anthropology. Some knowledge of these areas is useful, of course. Business and professional people should not only be familiar with the elementary concepts presented in this chapter but also do what they can to expand their knowledge of how people interrelate. Certainly a salesman, purchasing agent, accounting, personnel or traffic manager, training director, or engineer does not have time to become an expert social scientist. By learning to "consider the audience," however, such a person will come to ask the right questions, and to create communications that will seldom alienate their readers.

None of us, for example, needs to have heard of "self-image" to know that we should not criticize a subordinate in public. It is only necessary to ask how we would feel under similar circumstances. Nor should it require a sociological analysis of the attitudes of his audience to convince an insurance salesman that in writing to professional men he should not stress the importance of insurance in protecting wife and children from hunger but rather its importance in providing an income that will allow a widow to keep the family residence and send the children to college.

What is needed, no matter what the position of the communicator or the nature of the communication, is careful, thoughtful, and consistent attention to the five variables in the communications theory model: Who? Says What? To Whom? In What Channel? With What Effect?

ILLUSTRATIVE MATERIALS

Since at least the fourth century B.C., *the art of rhetoric has been seen as being essentially the art of persuasion. Here are several definitions of rhetoric which explore some of the connections between the two.*

Aristotle, *Rhetoric* (c. 365. B.C.):

Rhetoric may be defined as the faculty [power] of discovering in any given case the available means of persuasion.

Isocrates, *Antidosis* (353 B.C.):

Because there has been implanted in us the power to persuade each other and to make clear to each other whatever we desire, not only have we escaped the life of wild beasts but we have come together and founded cities and made laws and invented arts; and, generally speaking, there is no institution devised by man which the power of speech has not helped us to establish.

Francis Bacon, *The Advancement of Learning* (1605):

The word eloquence, in its greatest latitude, denotes that art or talent by which the discourse is adapted to its end. All the ends of speaking are reducible to four; every speech being intended to enlighten the understanding, to please the imagination, to move the passions, or to influence the will.

A. S. Hill, *Principles of Rhetoric and Their Applications* (New York: Harper & Brothers, 1878), p. iii:

Rhetoric may be defined as the art of efficient communication by language. It is not one of several arts out of which a choice may be made; it is *the art* to the principles of which, consciously or unconsciously, a good writer or speaker must conform. . . . It is an art, not a science: for it neither observes, nor discovers, nor classifies; but it shows how to convey from one mind to another the results of observation, discovery, or classification; it uses knowledge, not as knowledge, but as power.

I. A. Richards, *The Philosophy of Rhetoric* (New York and London: Oxford University Press, 1936), p. 3:

Rhetoric . . . should be a study of misunderstanding and its remedies. We struggle all our days with misunderstandings, and no apology is required for any study which can prevent or remove them.

Cleanth Brooks and Robert Penn Warren, *Modern Rhetoric,* 2d Edition (New York: Harcourt Brace & Company, 1958), p. 280:

The basic distinction between grammar and rhetoric might be illustrated from the game of football. The "grammar" of the game would be the rules and conventions that determine the conduct of the game, including the system of scoring. The "rhetoric" of the game would be the knowledge of strategy and maneuver that leads to effective play and a winning game. To play the game correctly would not *necessarily* be to play it effectively,   63 though effective play would certainly have to conform to the rules of the game.

Most of the positive observations to be be made about the dispositions and arrangement of the various elements of a sentence properly fall under the heading, not of grammar, but of rhetoric; that is, they have to do with making the sentence effective rather than correct.

Francis Connolly, *A Rhetoric Case Book,* 2d ed. (New York: Harcourt Brace Jovanovich, 1959), pp. xx–xxi:

Rhetoric, then, has clear connections with grammar, logic, literature, psychology, and ethics; let us add, with all the arts and sciences. . . . Nevertheless, rhetoric, despite its multiple connections with all the arts and sciences, has its own special province. Its immediate aim is not knowledge or information, although it presumes both, but skill in the total processes that result in effective expression of a given topic to a given audience. Knowledge or information may serve to produce the correct grammarian, the expert logician, the literary scholar, the informed psychologist, the learned ethicist. But knowledge or information alone does not produce men who can effectively communicate their knowledge. . . . Knowing how to express effectively one's subject (and oneself) depends upon a faculty not merely of discernment but of creating, that is, the power to embody knowledge, information or thought in a meaningful structure of language. . . . Rhetoric, then, does have its own special province—it aims to discover the principles or rules that underlie effective expression and to apply those rules to any kind of prose discourse.

R. E. Hughes and P. A. Duhamel, *Rhetoric: Principles and Usage* (Englewood Cliffs, NJ: Prentice-Hall, Inc., 1962), p. 4:

Aristotle's definition of rhetoric in his treatise on the subject, *The Art of Rhetoric* (1355 b), can be translated as "The art of discovering all the possible means of persuasion on any subject whatsoever." . . . Its right to recognition lies neither in its source nor its age. It should be accepted for the same reason that any good definition should be accepted: it is the clearest statement of the nature of what it purports to define, and it applies to its subject and only to its subject. The significant words of the definition are: (1) art, (2) of discovering, (3) the means of persuasion.

a. *Do any of these definitions of rhetoric distinguish between informing and persuading?*
b. *Does the emphasis in these definitions vary? If so, how?*
c. *Would you prefer to read a book entitled* Principles of Rhetoric *or one entitled* Principles of Communication? *Why?*
d. *To what extent do the various definitions above agree or disagree with the principles inherent in the Shannon and Weaver and the Lasswell models?*
e. *Connolly's definition of rhetoric is the fullest of the group. What does it include that the others do not?*
f. *Could this book be considered a rhetoric? Explain the reasoning behind your answer.*

WRITING TO INFORM AND PERSUADE

PROBLEMS

1. From the section on "The Psychology of Persuasion" in this chapter, choose two concepts that you feel would be most useful to your fellow students or to your colleagues on the job. Write a five-minute talk (approximately 700 words) to give in class or at your weekly department meeting, explaining those concepts and why you think they are important. Provide examples appropriate to your audience.

2. Examine carefully the advertisements in a magazine, preferably one you read regularly. Then assume that you are an advertising salesman for that magazine. Keeping in mind the concepts discussed in this chapter, write a letter in which, by analyzing the advertising, you not only try to convince a potential advertiser that your magazine is a good medium for that company's ads, but also suggest the approach they might take. (Choose an appropriate company with an appropriate product.)

3. Write a model letter to be sent to individuals who might be interested in joining a business or professional organization in your field. Each letter will be individually typed and signed by the president of the organization. The letter should be aimed at a person who is a member of the natural constituency of the organization you choose. If the organization is a local group of training directors, you should write to training directors who are not members, not to sales managers or purchasing agents. If the organization is a local group of technical writers, you may want to write a letter appropriate to send to an engineer who writes many technical reports, but not to one who works mostly in the field and reports largely by telephone or by marking up blueprints.

4. Examine a college catalog or an annual report sent to its stockholders by a manufacturing or service company. For the president of the college or of the company, who is concerned about the effectiveness of the publication, write a report analyzing the publication's strengths and weaknesses and how it might be improved.

5. If you see regularly the letters sent out by one of the groups which seek support and contributions for a cause—the environmentalists, the oil companies, the pro- or anti-abortionists, the solar energy advocates, the groups supporting medical research or trying to feed and clothe the hungry, and others—select one group, analyze its letters (including enclosures), and write a report on how it attempts to persuade the recipients to support its efforts.

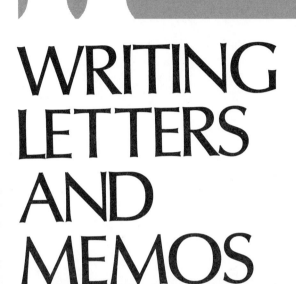

WRITING
LETTERS
AND
MEMOS

4.

Planning

CASE STUDY: A CONFIRMING MEMO

Recently a small tanker owned by a chemical company was damaged in a collision in the Gulf of Mexico. After a quick inspection, the captain radioed that the ship was still seaworthy, but that a considerable amount of water had contaminated the cargo. He was ordered to take the tanker to the nearest large port with appropriate docking facilities, and the company flew a young executive, Tom Morton, down to the port to make the necessary arrangements.

He and the captain inspected the ship carefully, and then Tom called his boss, J. C. Smith, at the home office. As they talked, Smith made notes on a pad that he always kept near his telephone. Although they would have seemed cryptic to anyone else, they recorded adequately the discussion that he and Tom Morton had had over the phone:

"RS" cargo ⟶ Anderson

Disch—WHJ

Est—H H Branscome

In port—T Pratt

Insurance estimate (Brans)

P W Iron—Emerg repairs (Send figs.)

Exp disch cargo (WHJ)

Siphon first using T P

Analyses—T Chem and cargo test reports

Tank-car shipment

Send unloading report (trip)

Also Brainard dope

Test reports $\begin{cases} \text{Krug} \\ \text{JCS} \end{cases}$

Auth to be sent

Anything else—send along

While the details were still fresh in his mind, Smith called in his secretary and, using his notes as a guide, dictated the following confirming memo to Tom:

This memorandum confirms the decisions which we made over the telephone today for handling the *Robert Slack* when she makes port this afternoon. We shall let you know as soon as arrangements have been completed for temporary storage and reclamation of the cargo at Anderson City.

W. H. Johnson and Company is the outfit to handle the discharge of the cargo, and you will contact Mr. H. H. Branscome of the Norbert Company for an estimate of the total damage. Tom Pratt will arrange for temporary care of the ship when it arrives, and you are authorized to hire a watchman if necessary.

We need to have Mr. Branscome's estimate for insurance purposes. Also you should get a bid from the Port Wells Iron Works on the emergency repairs. Please send figures on both promptly.

We also need a statement of expenses for salvaging the cargo. Arrange for this with W. H. Johnson and Company after you have siphoned off as much free water as possible using Tom Pratt's crew, and send a statement of all salvage expenses to this office.

Please have a water-content analysis run on the sample sent to you by the Thomas Chemical Company. Also, after the free water has been removed, each compartment should be agitated and samples taken for water content analysis.

The cargo is to be shipped by tank car to Anderson City. We shall need your barge unloading report in triplicate and a copy of the documents to be turned over to you by Mr. E. T. Brainard. Results of the test should be sent to P. J. Krug in Chicago with a copy to this office.

As soon as we have checked with the insurance people, we will give you authority to proceed with emergency repairs.

If you run across any other pertinent information, be sure to send it along too.

All of us up here appreciate your prompt and efficient handling of this emergency.

J. C. Smith

cc: Alvin Atherton

A quick reading shows that the memo is not a model of clarity. All the necessary details are included, but the sentences bounce from one idea to the next, reflecting the telephone conversation, which in turn is reflected in Smith's notes.

STEPS IN PLANNING A COMMUNICATION

With this example in mind, let us consider in more detail the useful procedure introduced in Chapter 3 for preparing any communication:

1. Determine real purpose or function
2. Select materials
3. Order materials
4. Check against purpose
5. Write
6. Recheck against purpose

For some writers, all of the steps may not be necessary, but only in planning the simplest messages can one safely omit more than one or two of them.

1. Determine Real Purpose or Function

Determining the real purpose of a communication is not always as simple as it seems. If someone had asked Smith after he had dictated his memo, "What was your purpose in writing that memo?," he would probably have answered, "To confirm our arrangements, of course." People in business frequently send confirming letters or memos—to make sure that both parties to a conversation understand or remember it the same way, to give written authorization to take certain actions, to provide the paperwork necessary to place an order, to record for all concerned the understandings reached in a conference.

Smith's memo would serve several of these functions. Tom, of course, began the necessary salvage and repair operations as soon as he finished talking to Smith on the phone, so the memo did not serve primarily as a set of instructions. But when it arrived, it did provide the necessary formal authorization for what he was doing, a fact which made him considerably more comfortable about approving the necessary expenditures. It also served to ensure that he and Smith had understood each other when they talked over the phone.

Tom was fully conversant with the problem and had taken his own notes on the phone conversation, against which he would check off the items in Smith's memo. But what of others who would read it? What would Alvin 71

Atherton, Smith's immediate superior, make of it? Or the insurance adjuster, who might use it as one of several documents presented in settling the claim?

If it had been more carefully written, furthermore, the memo could usefully serve another important function for both Tom and J. C. Smith—as a checklist of jobs completed and documents sent and received. For that purpose, Smith's memo is almost useless. As Tom sends off the various documents that Smith requested, how easy will it be for him to find the appropriate item in Smith's memo and check it off? As Smith receives those documents, how easy will it be for him to find the appropriate item and check it off? And if each uses Smith's memo as a checklist, how easy will it be for Tom to glance at it periodically to see what he still has to do or for Smith to see how much of the required information is still to come? By all these criteria, the memo is clearly inadequate.

Routine Responses

We see this failure to consider the possible functions of a letter most frequently in routine responses to routine inquiries. Many companies regularly receive requests for information about their products or services. Such simple inquiries seem to invite perfunctory replies.

The head of a university chemistry department, for example, writes to a chemical supply house to inquire about certain equipment:

Gentlemen:

Please send me information about the new electrophotometer you advertised in our local Chemical Society bulletin.

Thank you.

The typical response is:

Dear Dr. Spewock:

With reference to your inquiry of 7 October, enclosed is the brochure on the new Adler Electrophotometer about which you inquired.

Should you have any further questions, please do not hesitate to write or call.

Yours truly,

Frank O. Smather
Sales Order Department

One would think that, since Smather is in the *Sales* Order Department, he would recognize in Dr. Spewock's inquiry an opportunity to do some selling, perhaps like this:

PLANNING

Dear Dr. Spewock:

Everyone who has ordered the new Adler Electrophotometer reports excellent results from it:

1. It is simpler and faster to use than any other electrophotometer on the market.
2. It uses much less electricity.
3. It provides alternative methods of presenting results that allow for multiple uses.

I'm enclosing a brochure with basic information that should be helpful. If you will send me a sentence or two about the research in which you might use the electrophotometer or a photocopy of the catalog description of the courses in which you might use it, I'd be happy to give you the names of people who are using it successfully for similar purposes.

I'm sending a copy of this letter to Bill Johnson, our salesman in your area, so that he will be sure to see you on his next swing through Ruston.

Yours truly,

In a similar vein, compare the following two letters:

Dear Mr. Manley:

In regard to your letter of 15 May, enclosed is a report about coal cleaning equipment from one of our customers.

Thank you for your inquiry, and if you have any questions, do not hesitate to call.

Yours truly,

A better reply would be a sales letter:

Dear Mr. Manley:

The enclosed report from one of our customers will give you the basic information that you requested in your letter of 15 May. It not only describes our latest coal cleaning equipment, but reports on how effectively it operates. Our thirty-seven years of designing and building such equipment makes us a leader in the field.

If you will send us some information about the kinds of coal you mine, the tonnage, and other relevant details, we'll be happy to suggest what specific equipment might be most useful to you, based on similar installations we have made. With our wide experience, we are certain to have met and solved problems like the ones you are currently dealing with.

Yours truly,

Not every such reply will bring an order. But personalized responses will produce better results than routine ones.

73

2. Select Materials

J. C. Smith "selected" his materials, of course, when he took notes during his talk on the phone with Tom Morton. Frequently one "selects" materials in a similar way by underlining parts of an incoming letter and making marginal notations, as Randolph Aiken did when he received the one on the opposite page.

When Aiken received Calhoun's letter, he first scanned it and then read it carefully. He then read it again with pen in hand, making marginal and inter-linear notes as he went. Finally he went through those notes assigning numbers to each to indicate the order in which he would take them up in his reply to Calhoun. In effect, he used Calhoun's letter not only to select but also to order his materials. (He also made himself a note to select materials from his Country Dairy files and his Silo Stores files to send to Calhoun with his reply.) From his notes one can get a reasonably good idea of what his letter will be like, and a very clear idea—from the sketch in the lower right-hand corner—of what his last paragraph will say. If Aiken had wanted to, he could have prepared for writing or dictating his reply by sketching a complete outline on a separate sheet of paper. Many people, however, find themselves comfortable working directly from their notes on the incoming letter.

Frequently writing a letter or memo will require gathering diverse infor-mation and materials and selecting just the right ones: choosing an appropriate set of data from a report, calling someone in the Engineering Department for advice on treating rust in a particular climate, looking up statistics on popu-lation growth in a remote area, or finding information on competitive word-processing equipment. Sometimes such information gathering will go through two stages: a general gathering and then a more careful selection of just the right materials to solve the particular communication problem at hand.

3. Order Materials

As we saw, after Aiken selected materials for his reply to Calhoun, he went back and indicated how he would order them in his letter. That is what J. C. Smith failed to do before dictating his reply to Tom Morton. Here, again, are Smith's notes:

"RS" cargo $\longrightarrow$ Anderson

Disch—WHJ

Est—H H Branscome

In port—T Pratt

Insurance estimate (Brans)

P W Iron—Emerg repairs (Send figs.)

PLANNING

```
Mr. Randolph P. Aiken,
      President
Aiken Associates
Design Consultants
728 Lafayette Avenue
Chicago, IL 60680
```

Dear Mr. Aiken: *Volume?*

We are a <u>small</u> supermarket chain in Iowa with

fifteen stores. <u>Because of the recent failure of one</u> *IV Why?*

<u>of our competitors</u>, we see an opportunity to grow if

we can move quickly. *II Only if Iowa? elsewhere?* } *x, below*

(A) need photos of several store fronts showing name

We are concerned, however, about our looks. As a *V Corporate identity program (how deep?): a↓b below.* rural chain, our name, Rural Pride, and our (ads) with

young men and women in <u>country dance patterns</u> have

worked well for us. We are worried, however, that *III X--Which?* *(B) need 5 exs.*

they might work less well in <u>metropolitan areas.</u>

II Country Dairy (South Ill.) Silo stores (Ala.) ↑ senders

Have you ever worked on a <u>similar problem</u>? Do

you think that you can <u>help us</u>? What would that help

cost us? Could you work on our problem soon?

a. Give 3 levels, depends on extensiveness of work
b. start in 3 weeks, finish.

```
                          Yours truly,


                          Ernest S. Calhoun,
                          President
```

VI A-Colhoun send us: photos, exs. of ads, volume, proposed location
B. 10 days for us to analyse
C. Then we will call, visit (consulting fee), write 3 level proposal.

Exp disch cargo (WHJ)

Siphon first using T P

Analyses—T Chem and cargo test reports

Tank-car shipment

Send unloading report (trip)

Also Brainard dope

Test reports { Krug
               JCS

Auth to be sent

Anything else—send along

Instead of the J. C. Smith whom we saw at the beginning of the chapter, let us imagine a J. C. Smith who prepared as carefully to write or dictate as Randolph Aiken did. When he finished talking with Tom, he thought, "Who's going to read this? Tom, Alvin, an insurance adjuster, someone else, maybe, when I'm out of town. And me—as a checklist. For Tom, too." And in his mind he saw not a memo with blocks of paragraphs but one done in outline form. Glancing over his notes, he looked to see in what ways the ideas could be grouped. In a minute he had jotted down the following at the bottom of his pad:

Tom to handle

1. Salvage of cargo

2. Repair of ship

3. Send here for ins.

JCS to handle

4. Send notifications

Then he went through the list of notes he had jotted down. Before each item which had to do with salvage of the cargo, he wrote the figure *1*. Before each item having to do with repair of the ship, he wrote a *2*. Before each item having to do with the insurance information he himself needed he put a *3*.

Under *4*, the notifications which Smith had agreed to provide, there were only two items. He made a mental note that they probably need not be formally listed, especially as Tom did not have to take any action on them.

Smith's next step was to glance at the items before which he had placed a *1*. Since they fell naturally into a rough chronological order which was not the order in which he had them on his pad, he put (a), (b), and (c), after the three *1's*. After ordering the items under the other headings in the same way, he was ready to dictate:

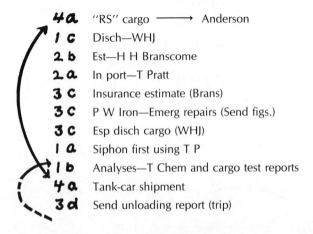

4a	"RS" cargo ⟶ Anderson
1c	Disch—WHJ
2b	Est—H H Branscome
2a	In port—T Pratt
3c	Insurance estimate (Brans)
3c	P W Iron—Emerg repairs (Send figs.)
3c	Esp disch cargo (WHJ)
1a	Siphon first using T P
1b	Analyses—T Chem and cargo test reports
4a	Tank-car shipment
3d	Send unloading report (trip)

PLANNING

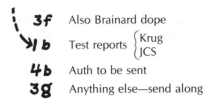

3f Also Brainard dope

1b Test reports {Krug JCS

4b Auth to be sent

3g Anything else—send along

This scheme may look complicated, but it took only a few minutes to prepare, was easy to dictate from, and helped Smith to write a clear and effective memorandum.

This memorandum confirms the arrangements that we made over the telephone today for handling the *Robert Slack* when she makes port sometime this afternoon. You agreed to do the following:

1. Arrange for the salvage of the cargo:
   (a) Siphon out as much free water as possible, using Tom Pratt's crew.
   (b) Run a water-content analysis on the sample sent to you by the Thomas Chemical Company and, after removing the free water and agitating each compartment, on samples of cargo.
   (c) Arrange for discharge of the cargo by W. H. Johnson and Company and shipment as soon as possible by tank car to Anderson City.
2. Prepare for repairs to the ship:
   (a) Arrange with Tom Pratt for temporary care, including a watchman if necessary.
   (b) Contact Mr. H. H. Branscome of the Norbert Company and ask for an estimate of the total damage.
   (c) Have the Port Wells Iron Works submit a bid for the necessary repairs.
3. Prepare information for this office:
   (a) A copy of the test results on the cargo.
   (b) The bid for the repair of the ship.
   (c) Branscome's estimate of the total damage.
   (d) Your barge unloading report (in triplicate).
   (e) A statement of expenses for salvaging the cargo.
   (f) A copy of each of the documents to be turned over to you by Mr. E. T. Brainard.
   (g) Any other pertinent information.

We shall let you know as soon as we have made arrangements for storage and reclamation of the cargo at Anderson City and will give you authority to proceed with the emergency repairs as soon as we have checked with the insurance people.

All of us up here appreciate your prompt and efficient handling of this emergency.

J. C. Smith

If there had been many more items, Smith would probably have entirely rewritten his original notes, a more time-consuming process. He would have

written down the first of the four types of information he was transmitting—
"Salvage of cargo"—and listed below the various items pertaining to it:

> Salvage of cargo
> Disch—WHJ
> Siphon using TP
> Analyses—T Chem and cargo—Krug

He would have crossed off these items on his telephone notes and then begun
to work on the second, third, and fourth categories. After numbering the items
on each list in an appropriate order, he would have been ready to dictate. For
a writer dealing with a complex communication, the added clarity is well worth
the investment of a few minutes.

Why Order Is Essential

The memorandum which we have been discussing is complex. Seldom is
a business person called upon to sort out so much specific information for a
short communication. Seldom, in fact, does the information come in such a
confused form. But to be effective, even a short letter or memo must be organized so that the writer gets the message across—which in the long run
always means that the reader or readers both understand and act upon the
message. Because the efficient Smith had done his job well, both he and Tom
could use the memorandum as a checklist, and both could easily monitor the
progress of the operation. Had Smith not done so, both men would have had
great difficulty in finding the items to check off, and some important action
might have been overlooked.

Finally, Smith provided a readily understandable memo for Alvin Atherton
or an insurance adjuster or anyone else looking into the file who was not
familiar with the situation.

We might note here that ordering notes for writing or dictation takes very
little time—sometimes a few seconds, seldom more than a minute or two.
Aiken's notes on Calhoun's letter shouldn't have required more than two minutes of writing time, his thinking about an appropriate order and his adding
the numbers perhaps an additional thirty seconds. Altogether J. C. Smith spent
a great deal of time on the *Robert Slack* accident. Reading and thinking about
the captain's message, conferring with associates about how to handle the
situation and whom to send down, briefing Tom, talking to him on the phone,
dictating memos, arranging for storage and reclamation of the cargo, as it came
in—these activities took many hours. The few minutes it took Smith to order
his notes before dictating were an insignificant part of the total—insignificant
in time, but very significant in effect.

Like selection of materials, appropriate order depends on the writer's purpose and on the readers'. An executive writing a recommendation for pro-

motion for a person in his or her department will almost always begin with the person's faults and end with the person's virtues. A recommendation not to promote will probably begin with the person's virtues and end with the faults. Why? Because the executive knows that readers will tend to be most influenced by what they read last. Similarly, in explaining why a machine has been modified, an engineer may choose one set of facts and a particular approach in presenting the story to the department head and perhaps a shorter list of facts and a different approach when presenting it to the foreman on the assembly line. Using an order based on what seems the most *logical* organization of the materials may not be successful with either.

Order will also be affected by the nature of a communication. A memo about a watchman's activities during his tour of duty and a memo on the growth of the aluminum industry will probably be ordered chronologically, a sales memo by geographical areas, a progress report according to types of problems met and solved, a personnel report by rank, salary bracket, or length of service. But the most effective order will always be the one which will be most useful to the reader.

4. Check Against Purpose

When the writer has determined the real purpose of a communication, gathered the materials, clarified his or her own thinking, and selected and ordered the materials, he or she should be ready to write. But if the communication problem is complex or delicate, the writer will do well to stop at this point and ask, "Will the plan I have formulated really do the job that I need to do? Will it satisfy the real purpose of the communication? Will it do the job in the most effective way possible?"

It is not easy to take this step. At this point the writer is "rarin' to go"— especially if he or she is ready with a thoroughly logical and interesting plan. But failure to stop for a check here is as dangerous as failing to check the gas supply before taking an airplane up. The plane may be properly fueled—but if it is not, the crash is likely to be spectacular.

5. Write

After the plan has been carefully checked and found suitable for the determined purpose, the writer is ready to prepare a draft. This should be done deliberately and according to plan. If there is any deviation from the plan, the writer will need to consider its impact on the ultimate effect of the communication. It may then seem appropriate to modify the plan, or strike out the deviating material and return to the original scheme. Whatever the course, the writer must be sure to know where the draft is going and why.

The language of the communication must also be keyed to the audience and purpose. Technical or esoteric terms are not likely to improve a communication to a manual laborer. Slang and a "clap on the shoulder" tone will probably not be appreciated by a company president if they come from a subordinate. The most carefully planned attack may lose all of its effect if the writer's language is judged by the reader to be frivolous or insulting.

6. Recheck Against Purpose

The draft of the communication does not complete the process. It must be carefully checked against the original purpose to be sure that the finished product will do the job that has to be done. Not only the overall effect, but also the effect of each paragraph, must be tested carefully. Where sentences, paragraphs, or sections do not appear to be suitable, they must be revised and the whole communication tested in its revised form. Only when every phrase is just right is the job completed.

THE VALUE OF METHOD

The procedure outlined above is admittedly an ideal one. It is, we believe, very effective for important communications which require care and precision. But frequently, as anyone in business knows, letters and memos must be prepared under great pressure. One might argue that to apply the procedure to such letters and memoranda would be bringing in a steamroller to crack a walnut.

There is a certain measure of truth in both of these objections. Our reply is simply this: those writers who have trained themselves to follow a procedure similar to the one outlined above prove most adept both at preparing and at writing communications of any kind. A quick review of the steps we have suggested may indicate why this is so:

1. Determine real purpose or function
2. Select materials
3. Order materials
4. Check against purpose
5. Write
6. Recheck against purpose

People who habitually use this procedure waste a minimum of time and effort. Hence they are well equipped to handle a rush job. Because they begin by thinking through to their real purpose, they soon know exactly where they are going. They will gather only materials that are pertinent to their purpose, automatically excluding all extraneous material. They will arrange their evidence in an appropriate order. Checking back to their purpose insures them against wasting time in writing up material which will ultimately prove irrelevant and against submitting a communication that does not do what is required. In short, they are professionals who can be counted on to act effectively and efficiently under any conditions; when an emergency arises, their trained reflexes automatically come into play and enable them to meet it effectively.

ILLUSTRATIVE MATERIALS

1.
Here is how a student who wanted to see a change in the college curriculum used the Lasswell formula to plan her strategy.

LASSWELL'S FIVE QUESTIONS	THE WRITER'S ANALYSIS
WHO	THE WRITER The writer chooses to use the voice of a concerned student rather than that of a complaining student, because she feels the former will be more persuasive.
SAYS WHAT	A CURRICULUM CHANGE IS NEEDED FOR THESE REASONS The student chooses the reasons she feels will convince the dean of the need for the change. Since she is addressing him in his official capacity, she decides to use a formal style.
IN WHICH CHANNEL	A LETTER Because the student has decided the receiver of her suggestion should be the dean, she chooses to write a letter with the hope that it will receive the dean's personal attention as well as serve as a record for later use. If she merely spoke to the dean instead of writing, he might forget some of the details.

81

TO WHOM

TO THE COLLEGE DEAN

The student writer feels that the dean of the college would have more immediate responsibility for changing the curriculum than the president of the university or any one professor of the college.

WITH WHAT EFFECT

TO HAVE THE CURRICULUM CHANGE ACCEPTED

2.

Here is a set of instructions designed for business people who dictate, either to a machine or to a secretary:

Two aims should be foremost in your mind when you dictate: (1) to produce as effective a communication as possible and (2) to help your secretary by providing clear instructions and clear dictation. The following suggestions will help you dictate well:

1. Before you begin to dictate

   a. *Assemble all necessary information.*
      Scrambling around for missing materials wastes time and will probably cause you to write an incoherent, disconnected sentence—or, worse yet, to make a mess of the whole communication.

   b. *Know what you want to say.*
      Too many dictators "think" their problems into a letter or memo. The result: much backing and filling by the writer; confusion for the reader.

   c. *Write down a plan.*
      If the communication is short, you may not need a complete plan.But if you expect to dictate more than a paragraph, you will find it helpful to jot down, either on the letter to be answered or on a pad, a carefully ordered list of the items to be covered. Use arrows to revise the order, if necessary.

   | Thanks |
   | Test-run results |
   | Pass along |
   | J's decision |
   | Looks good |
   | Hello, Tom |

   d. *Give your secretary the necessary information:*
      Are you about to dictate a letter, memo, or report?
      Rough copy or smooth?
      How many copies? Marked or blind?
      To whom do copies go?
      Any other special instructions?

2. During dictation
   a. *Start right in with some substance.* Avoid stock openings.
   b. *Follow your plan.*
   c. *Before you dictate a sentence, think it through to the end.* If you do, you can't dictate a sentence that is too long, and you won't tangle yourself in a grammatical maze.
   d. *Dictate at least a full clause at a time in normal speaking voice.* Be sure to modulate your voice so that the secretary will know where to insert minor punctuation. (Cigars, cigarettes, and pipes are major hazards. Keep them out of your mouth when you dictate.)
   e. *End with a specific request or suggestion.* If you do not have a real one, just stop. Whatever you do, avoid rubber-stamp conclusions. Nobody reads them anyway.

And there is always room for improvement.

1. *At least once a week read over a few of your letters. Try to spot clichés, words which you overwork, heavy phrasing, repetition, and confusing organization.*
2. *Work with, not against, your secretary. Talk things over occasionally. Encourage your secretary to ask questions when what you want is unclear, and invite suggestions for improvement. And don't forget that everyone appreciates a compliment now and then, especially for a job well done.*

MATERIALS FOR REVISION

A

Indicate the proper paragraph breaks in the following memorandum:

I feel that a person with both technical and administrative training, with the accent on technical, would be best suited for the position of production manager. Someone with plant background who also has training in administrative procedures here in New York would be preferable. Plant training is essential to this manager in order to best correlate sales programs with plant capacities and raw material availability. This person must supervise preparation of planning schedules to insure our making the best use of our plant facilities and must be familiar with our procedures and costs in order to protect profits. Therefore, the manager should have administrative ability to properly coordinate this phase of the department's work with the material allocation phase. Administrative training will also provide better appreciation of the problems of the other departments with which the manager must work closely. Someone with these qualifications would, in my opinion, be well qualified to handle this job.

B

The following business communications are poorly organized. Rewrite them.

1.   Dear Mr. Hood:

This letter is to report the progress of the subject job. The frame is completely built and ready for painting. The fenders, turret top, hood, and side and rear panels are all completed, ready for installation.

I doubt if I will be able to complete it by the end of the year but it will probably be the first week in January; however, I can report that most of the work is done. During this last two weeks other obligations will keep me from completing the job but I plan to have it by the first week of January.

As you have requested, I am sending a separate billing for this work.

Very truly yours,

Oscar F. Dutton

P.S. On the subject painting—I have your letter and instructions for painting. However, I wondered if you would care to have wheels painted a more contrasting color rather than the standard grey of the body. I would appreciate your comments on the painting of the wheels. I also am assuming that the body will be two-tone grey. If not, please advise.

2.   As you know, all sales to the Alpha Company are to be routed through the Sales Department of the Electrical Products Division and specifically to the attention of Mr. Deems.

There are occasional lapses in this procedure in the conduct of correspondence and in other details in regard to this matter, particularly those dealing with appliances.

Would you please emphasize to all your people that correspondence and official contacts with the Alpha Company are to go through the Sales Department, Electrical Products Division, Attention: Mr. Deems. Mr. Deems will see that all such matters receive prompt and adequate attention.

This is not meant to discourage informal contacts by any department with the Alpha Company. However, where any such informal contacts develop to the point where correspondence is initiated or sales are made, the correspondence or sales must be routed through the Electrical Products Sales Department, Attention: Mr. Deems, as outlined above.

3.   Construction Pollution
The following is a list of possible pollutants by the construction industry and how they can be reduced or eliminated.
A. Burning of vegetation and debris.
     Remedy—Use shredder to grind material and dispose of in landfill.
B. Air pollution—internal combusion equipment. (Diesel and gasoline.)
     Remedy—Minimize exhaust impurities by proper maintenance. This should result in lower operating costs and longer life.

    C. Noise pollution—from internal combustion equipment, air hammers, pile drivers, etc.
       Remedy—Use better muffler systems or electric drives.
    D. Air pollution—dust, dirt, and debris from spraying of insulation, and from refractory and poorly based roads.
       Remedy—Close in area for containment and treat surfaces to hold down dust generation.
    E. Stream and lake pollution—breaks in pipelines containing gasoline, oils, tars, acids, etc.
       Remedy—Properly prepare work before starting, so that spills are contained in the event of accidents.
    F. Dispersal of construction debris distributed to area surrounding site.
       Remedy—Do better housekeeping to collect and contain debris before it becomes spread over area.
    G. Erosion of cleared land into streams, lakes, etc.
       Remedy—Properly bench cuts, and treat exposed earth to hold material in event of hard rainfall.
    H. Pumping of pollutants from contaminated sources into lakes, streams, etc.
       Remedy—Pump to holding area until waste liquids can be properly treated.

D

Reorganize the following chart so that it can be appended to a report entitled "The Amount and Kinds of Communication Done by Engineers in Section K7."

Engineering Reports—Written Preparation of

Name and Position	Engineering Lab Work	Equipment & Design Specifications	Test Specifications	Equipment Progress Reports	Long Range Planning Reports	Overall Progress Reports	Conferences & Planning Meetings	Coordination of Personnel—Oral	Actual Design (Written)	Equipment & Hardware Follow-through	Total
Group Project Engineer	2%	10%	5%	3%	5%	3%	45%	15%	10%	2%	100%
Engineer	10%	25%	5%	5%	0	0	5%	0	45%	5%	100%
Engineer	15%	20%	0	5%	0	0	0	0	50%	10%	100%
Engineer	15%	5%	10%	5%	0	0	0	0	15%	50%	100%
Engineer	15%	20%	0	5%	0	0	0	0	45%	15%	100%
Engineer	15%	20%	0	5%	0	0	0	0	50%	10%	100%
Engineer	10%	15%	0	10%	0	0	5%	0	45%	15%	100%

PROBLEMS

1. Choose a problem in your department or at your college that you think needs to be remedied and plan an appropriate solution. Using the method of taking and organizing notes demonstrated at the beginning of the chapter, plan and write a letter to your department head or college administrator explaining the problem and proposing your solution. If you have access to a tape recorder or a dictating machine, you might try dictating the letter, using the procedure outlined in Illustrative Material 2.

2. You have been asked to explain in writing to someone assigned to take over a particular job you have done what its function is, what can go wrong if it is not done correctly, what aspects of it one must be most careful about, how to do it, and, if appropriate, how it relates to jobs performed by co-workers. Plan your explanation, using the method suggested in the chapter. Carry the planning up to the point where you are ready to write.

3. Do the planning necessary for one or more of the problems at the end of Chapters 5 and 6. Make your notes complete enough so that they will be useful to you in doing the writing necessary to solve the problem.

5

Letter Categories and Strategies I

In discussing the concept of audience and the principles of persuasion we have presented and analyzed a number of business letters. In this chapter we wish to look in a more formal way at certain types of letters which are produced by every business organization. They are usually thought of as "routine," but the way in which they are written can make or break a business. Thus people who can write them well are likely to be invaluable to the companies that employ them.

ROUTINE LETTERS OF INQUIRY OR REQUEST

We have already examined several instances in which routine letters of inquiry or request have caused problems. In Chapter 2, for example, we saw a letter in which John Larkin—not a businessman, but a student—asked a particular steel company to send him information and material that would be useful in writing a paper. (Larkin, we discovered later, had sent an identical letter to nine other companies.) What should have been a very simple, narrowly defined request, however, was a letter so pretentious and so poorly thought through that the steel company's Public Relations Department could not be helpful. Larkin should have decided to study a particular aspect of the steel industry before he asked for help. And before he sent the letter off, he should have asked himself, "If I received this request, what exactly would I send the writer?" If he had asked this question, he wouldn't have mailed the letter. Apparently it never occurred to him that requests and letters of inquiry should be specific enough so that the reader will know precisely what the writer wants.

Letters requesting references should also be specific. The following request is much too general to produce a useful reply:

Dear Mr. Alston:

Ms. Jane Stewart, who has applied for a position here, has given your name as a reference.

We would appreciate anything you can tell us about her.

Yours truly,

A more specific letter is more likely to procure a reply which contains the kind of detail that the letter writer will need in deciding whether to hire Ms. Stewart:

Dear Mr. Alston:

Ms. Jane Stewart, who left your employ last April to move to Chicago, has applied here for a position as assistant buyer in the toy department and has given us your name as a reference.

We are looking for a person who is responsible, intelligent, imaginative, and knowledgeable about toys. This is a particularly good job opportunity because our toy buyer will be retiring in ten months. On the other hand, the person hired could be in a difficult situation if she is not quite prepared to assume such responsibility.

From your experience with Ms. Stewart, what can you tell us that will help us to evaluate her potential for this position? Does she learn quickly? Is she creative? Does she enjoy responsibility? Will she grow on the job?

I apologize for putting you to all this trouble, but I am sure you will understand how important it is both to Ms. Stewart and to us that we find out whether she is really the right person for the position. We will be very grateful for your help and will look forward to receiving your evaluation.

Yours truly,

In the discussion of responses to requests for information about a new electrophotometer and about coal cleaning equipment we saw that even what seem to be routine letters of inquiry should not receive perfunctory replies. Even the most routine request may lead to a sale. Therefore, every response should be as specific as possible. Does the writer want to know about your water softeners? Send a brochure, but also offer to have a salesman call. And don't forget to mention your company's experience in solving water-softening problems for companies of similar size. Does the writer ask to have a paper on pollution control read by one of your staff at a professional meeting? Ask whether there are specific pollution problems that your company's expertise might help in solving. Does the writer want to know whether you sell wholesale as well as retail? If your reply is yes, describe the variety of products and brand names you sell, so that the inquirer will be sure to know all you have to offer. And emphasize any service you provide that may give your company an edge over its competitors. A few seconds' thought should always enable you to turn a routine letter of reply into a sales letter.

ESTABLISHING OR STRENGTHENING GOOD WILL

The thoughtful person in business can find—or make—opportunities to improve company good will. On the tenth anniversary of her joining Design Fabrics, for example, Mary Campanile, the company's sales manager, sent out a dozen letters like the following to certain Design Fabrics customers:

Mr. Joseph P. Blotner, President
Blotner & Sons
518 North End Avenue
Pittsburgh, PA 15206

Dear Mr. Blotner:

When I joined Design Fabrics ten years ago, one of the first orders I filled was from Blotner & Sons. Since then, of course, I've had the opportunity to fill many, many others.

My satisfaction with my position here comes largely from my being able to maintain Design Fabrics' record of service to its customers. So I thought I'd celebrate my tenth anniversary here by saying "thank you" for your continuing faith in us.

We value all of our customers, of course; but we feel a special responsibility to those whom we have served for as many years as we have served Blotner & Sons.

Sincerely,

Mary O. Campanile
Sales Manager

A company's tenth—or twenty-fifth—anniversary could provide a similar opportunity to thank its customers. **89**

Ms. Campanile also makes a point of personally acknowledging orders from new customers:

Ms. Jane Ordeville, Manager
Center City Upholstery
1376 Main Street
Mansfield, OH 44902

Dear Ms. Ordeville:

We are shipping today the seven bolts of 73-OR linen-finish material that you ordered. We think that you will be pleased with it, because our new Guard-All process makes it especially stain resistant.

I'm enclosing several swatches of the same material in other colors to show you the broad variety that we have available.

I hope that you will let me know the next time you come to Chicago, so that I can show you our full line. In the meantime, if you have any special needs please drop me a line, and I'll give your inquiry my personal attention.

Sincerely,

Mary O. Campanile
Sales Manager

If she hasn't heard from Ms. Ordeville in two or three months, Ms. Campanile will write again:

Dear Ms. Ordeville:

I hope that the linen-finish material that we sent lived up to your expectations.

Are many of your customers interested in an informal look? I'm enclosing swatches of a denim fabric that has worked particularly well for reupholstering furniture in summer homes and lake-shore cottages. It's just right for the relaxed style of vacation living.

Let me know if there are other kinds of fabric that you are specially interested in. I'll be happy to send you swatches.

Sincerely,

Mary O. Campanile
Sales Manager

SALES LETTERS

Presumably every product satisfies a need, or it would not be manufactured; and every service satisfies a need, or it would not be offered. Sales are made when potential customers need, or think they need, a particular product. A salesperson, therefore, will do well to convince potential customers of the need for a service or product before trying to make a sale. The problem is *how* to convince customers that they need the product or service.

A letter from a shoe store addressed to women on a mailing list obtained from a maternity hospital might begin:

> Whether this is your first child or your fourth, the new baby in your home has probably started you thinking about the additional responsibility you have just undertaken. A baby—small, helpless, and utterly dependent on those around it—generally makes even the most experienced parent feel just a little bit inadequate. The future will bring so many problems: health and growth, education and training, insurance, and a host of others.

> We'd like to help you with just one of these many problems—your baby's health. You know, of course, how important it is for a child to have healthy feet. Bad feet seriously handicap a child or an adult and can cause all sorts of other physical problems. Our shoes. . . .

A letter from the same shoe store to the parents of a boy in a nearby private school would take a different approach:

> Since you obviously are interested enough in your child to invest in a good education for him, you must also be interested in his health. We would like to offer our services in helping you to guard his health while he is away from home.

> Boys of your son's age grow quickly and in spurts. Thus the shoes that he started school with in September may be too small for him by November or December. Why not have him stop in to see us in a week or so? We know a lot about boys, and feet, and shoes. And we can give him the benefit of our thirty years' experience. . . .

Notice that the opening of each sales letter not only stresses the reader's need but also applies some of the other principles we have discussed in earlier chapters. Each is aimed at a specific audience. Each is worded positively. Each appeals to the feeling of parental responsibility. The second also appeals to the self-image of parents in a particular socioeconomic group: upper-middle-class and upper-class parents who can afford to pay for their children's education and probably tend to be a little self-congratulatory about it.

In these chapters we have deliberately avoided stating that a sales letter should begin with an "eye catcher." We have done so for two reasons. In the first place, the best way to get a reader's interest is to show that he or she needs what you have to sell—the approach which has just been demonstrated. Second, the phrase "eye catcher" focuses attention on the reader's *eye* rather than on the reader's *mind*. The result often is a search for the bizarre, which leads to the kind of openings featured in *The New Yorker* under the heading of "Letters We Never Finished Reading":

(from a magazine)

Dear Subscriber:

My wife did me a good turn last week. As I . . .

(from a department store)

Dear Busy Body:

You are a busy body, are you not? So much to do, so many problems . . .

(from a magazine)

Dear Sir/Madam,

Perhaps we have been a little hesitant in waiting a hundred years before introducing *The Squire's Calendar* to you . . .

(from a laundry)

Dear Friend:

If a tear rolls down the page as you open this letter, please forgive us. You . . .

Sometimes writers seek to arouse the reader's interest by what they think is imaginative use of language. Here is a letter from a management consulting firm to a potential customer:

Dear Mr. Johnston:

Today's greater need for cost control is rubbing salt into many open sores of impatience toward the slow pace of data processing improvements.

Harried internal staffs may not neglect normal service on existing operations, yet tabulating procedures resulting from spare-time planning need refinements with air-raid-siren urgency, and there is much need for a fair-minded understanding toward slow progress in implementing many of the benefits of mechanization originally contemplated.

Air-raid-siren urgency, indeed! The letter shrieks, but not in the way the writer intended it to. In the first place, the image of an open sore does not provide an attractive opening. The writer probably chose it on the theory that it would have impact. It does—the wrong kind. One may get potential customers' attention with a nauseating odor or by running them down with a truck, but that is hardly the way to *keep* their attention. Second, the two paragraphs quoted show the pretentiousness discussed in earlier chapters: "normal service on existing operations" (why not "regular service to customers"?); "tabulating procedures resulting from spare-time planning need refinements" (why not "tabulating procedures set up hurriedly must be reexamined"?); "a fair-minded understanding" (what does that mean?); "toward slow progress" (an anticlimax after "air-raid-siren urgency"); "in implementing many of the benefits of mechanization originally contemplated" (can benefits which have not yet been earned be "implemented"?). Neon lights or fireworks, used correctly, can be very effective. Used incorrectly, however, they simply illuminate incompetence.

Probably the most difficult kind of sales letter to prepare is the one aimed at a mass audience. With no specific group to write for, the writer often resorts to a gimmick, such as attaching a bit of colored string to the top of the letter and saying, "If you string along with us. . . ." Or attaching an untied miniature bow tie and inviting the reader to "Tie this if you can." If not too farfetched, such devices may win the continued attention of the audience. The writer should be careful, however, not to slip into pretentiousness, cuteness, or mawkishness, which are inappropriate for business.

In such sales letters it is often profitable to include a business reply card. The reader may simply check items in which he or she is interested, sign the card, and drop it in the mail. A potential customer who will not bother to write a letter for further information will often take the minute or two necessary to complete such a card. The last paragraph of the sales letter, of course, should invite the reader to use it.

Whether one uses a business reply card or not, the last paragraph should always invite the reader to take action: "Stop in next week . . ."; "Call 716-5320 . . ."; "Ask our salesman about TYREX the next time he stops in . . ."; "Take us up on this offer by sending. . . ." Certainly such endings say more than "Thank you for your courtesy. . . ." or "If we can be of any service to you, please don't hesitate . . ." They are positive. They are not rubber stamps. And they suggest action.

The body of the letter, of course, should supply the facts required to convince the reader. And here, more than in any other part of the letter, the facts ought to speak for themselves. Statements about quality of performance, comments by people who have used the product, a list of customers, information that will show the reader how and where to employ the product profitably— all of these may be useful, depending upon the circumstances. Once a writer has attracted the audience's attention, it is what the product has to recommend it that will determine sales. But a good writer will not retire after the initial fanfare. Difficult as it often is to get the attention of a busy executive, it is even more difficult to keep it. A reader will desert a writer much more quickly than a singer or an actor, and with much less reluctance. It only involves throwing the letter into the nearest wastebasket, for the reader has no investment in it— no time spent in preparation, no money spent for tickets, no commitment to pay attention.

GIVING UNWELCOME NEWS

Sometimes a person in business must send unwelcome news to a customer. Consider, for example, the following letter:

Dear Mr. Johnson:

A law recently passed by the state legislature requires that we change the Homeowner's Policy that you carry with us. All such policies, by law, now can cover only that part of a property loss over $100.

Since you have always chosen to carry a Homeowner's Policy without a deductible, I thought that I would call this to your attention now so that when your new policy arrives you will understand that we have not simply ignored your preference.

All of the other portions of the policy will remain the same; and our service, of course, will not be affected.

We are sorry not to be able to continue to write the kind of policy you prefer, but I am sure you understand that we must obey the law or cease writing policies in this state altogether. Naturally, we prefer continuing to serve you within the regulations set by the legislature for all insurance companies.

If this new regulation inconveniences you, you may want to talk with your state representative or senator to see whether the law can be changed. Because the state legislature is not in session now, many legislators are available in their local offices.

Sincerely,

John P. Arbendon
Vice President

An insurance company might send printed notices to most of its customers at policy-renewal time announcing the new state regulation. Certain special customers, however, might be candidates for personal letters of explanation like the one above. Such customers may carry large policies or several policies. Perhaps they have proven to be short-tempered, and a personal letter will forestall a long harangue over the phone or a nasty letter of complaint.

Here is an example of a letter that is carefully written to soften the unwelcome news that a company can not meet a potential customer's request for a "factory discount."

Mr. Fred A. Barbery
Barbery's Furniture
1809 Center Avenue
Wilkes Barre, PA 18701

Dear Mr. Barbery:

We appreciate your order for twenty sofas in our new Lounge-Away line. May we suggest that you send your order to:

Roger Williams Distribution Center
1422 Maine Street
Middletown, NY 10940

They distribute all of our furniture in the Northeastern part of the United States, and our agreement with them forbids our selling directly to anyone in that area.

I can't commit them on terms, of course, but I have written to Mr. Arthur Walenka, the Center's Sales Manager, to tell him that you have inquired about a large-order discount. You should hear from him soon.

In the meantime, you may be interested in the enclosed brochure on Lounge-Away furniture. The line includes not only the sofas you are interested in, but also sofa-beds and club and lounge chairs. The response to the new line has been very good. You may want to discuss with Mr. Walenka the possibility of a Lounge-Away exclusive in your area.

Thank you for writing. I can promise you that Mr. Walenka will do everything he can to meet your needs.

Sincerely,

Marc O. Stanton
Lounge-Away Sales Coordinator

In preparing a letter that contains unwelcome news, a writer can still demonstrate an understanding of the reader's problems and even, when appropriate, indicate sympathetic concern or suggest reasonable alternatives to what has been requested. No letter need say, in effect, just "We won't" or "You are wrong." Writers of letters bearing unwelcome news must pay particular attention to the last line of the Lasswell formula: With What Effect?

COLLECTION LETTERS

Writers of collection letters, too, should "consider the audience." A customer may simply have forgotten an overdue bill, or may be temporarily short of funds. To insult such a person is poor policy. Thus the first or second letter ought to be simply a polite reminder. The writer may also wish to inquire whether failure to pay the bill is in any way a result of poor service.

In later letters the writer will probably want to use some sort of appeal or suggestion that the customer is causing unnecessary embarrassment or expense for both parties:

Dear Mr. Williams:

We'd like you to help us save a customer—*you.* If you don't pay your bill, we'll have to send you more letters. That, certainly, will drive you away from us, a prospect we don't enjoy. So. . . .

Dear Mr. Samuels:

We don't want to turn your bill over to a collection agency. Neither you nor we will profit by that. . . .

The writer of a collection letter who understands the principles we have outlined earlier in the chapter can appeal to the customer's self-image:

Dear Mr. Peet:

As a competent businessman, you know that a company's credit rating is a major indicator of its success. . . .

Or the letter can attempt to invoke customs or rules of the business community to which the delinquent customer belongs:

Dear Mr. George:

The members of the Shadyside Merchants Association have established an excellent reputation for paying their bills. As you know, they are considered excellent credit risks and sometimes obtain terms not available to other merchants.

I am sure that as a member of the Association, you do not wish to risk the reputation of the entire business community. . . .

Or—in a last-ditch effort—the writer can appeal to the need for status and security:

Dear Mr. Frank:

We had hoped that by this time your account would be cleared up, but payment has not yet arrived. Needless to say, we have no desire to turn this account over to a collection agency, for we have found that such matters quickly become common knowledge, with unpleasant results for all concerned. . . .

Collection letters generally fall into classes or stages. A first letter assumes that the customer has simply forgotten about the bill or misplaced it. Frequently companies design for that purpose a letter that seeks to provide an excuse for the customer's failure to pay:

Dear Ms. Barber:

When I picked my phone bill off my desk last night, I discovered to my embarrassment that stuck to it was a bill from the electric company that was ten days overdue. Has the bill we sent you six weeks ago become attached by some accident to the back of another one—or been misfiled?

We find such an opening a little too obvious and recommend something simpler:

Dear Ms. Barber:

According to our records you have not yet paid your July bill. We would appreciate your checking to see whether we are correct.

If we are mistaken, please call me at 623-8875. If I am not in, the person answering the phone will take a message. If you have simply forgotten about the bill or misplaced it, we will appreciate your paying it promptly.

Since you are a valued customer, we want to clear up any discrepancies as quickly as we can.

If the customer ignores the first letter, a follow-up letter explains the seriousness of the situation and deplores the loss of a good relationship. Such a letter might open:

Dear Ms. Barber:

We hope that we are not losing you as a customer, but your bill with us is now two months overdue. And you haven't replied to the letter we sent you a month ago.

I will appreciate your giving me a ring so that we can discuss the problem. We would not want to cancel the charge card you have with us.

A third letter might set a date by which payment is expected:

Dear Ms. Barber:

Although we have sent you two letters requesting payment of your overdue bill, we have not yet received a reply. We must, therefore, send you this final notice.

We will expect payment in full on your delinquent bill within ten days of your receipt of this letter. . . .

And a fourth letter might resort to a threat:

Dear Ms. Barber:

Must we now turn your account over to a collection agency? . . .

Sometimes what we have indicated as stages three and four are combined in a single letter:

Dear Mr. Appleby:

If we do not hear from you in ten days, we will be forced to turn your account over to a collection agency. . . .

However long the series, the approach should move from understanding and sympathy to tactful analysis of the problem or persuasive appeal to self-esteem and image in the community (or both) and, finally, to suggestion of drastic consequences. At no stage will expressing anger or annoyance prove useful. Neither will help collect a debt. Intemperate language may simply provide the debtor with an excuse for becoming angry and feeling justified in not paying a company which hasn't the decency to treat customers politely.

CASE STUDY: A MATTER OF FORM

A large California utility company in a major metropolitan area has over 500 communicators in the customer communications sections of its four field divisions. Their responsibilities include sending letters to customers who have missed paying a bill and answering letters of complaint from customers about bills and deposits.

When a new head of Customer Communications asked to see the letters used by the communicators, she found a confusion of styles and forms. Some were left over from the time when all customer communications came directly from company headquarters. Others were forms devised by the field divisions themselves and stored in their own computer banks. The new head even discovered that communicators in one of the field divisions were using a form that was not consistent with company policy. Finally, she found that the style of the letters varied widely. Some were stuffy or curt. Others, especially handwritten "speed letters," were often too informal—and sometimes inaccurate or incomplete.

To remedy the situation, she set up a team of communicators to remove obsolete form letters, add necessary new ones, and improve the language used. Here, for example, is the form letter that had been sent to a customer who had failed to pay a bill:

Dear   :

After a careful search, we have been unable to discover any record of payment of the amount of $ from you for your bill dated

If you have paid that bill, would you retrieve your cancelled check or have your postal or bank money order traced. We will need a copy of that instrument in order to proceed with our investigation.

If you have neglected the bill, we would appreciate your prompt payment.

We hope for the courtesy of an early reply so that we can resolve this matter promptly. If you are uncertain about this problem, you may wish to call me at

Sincerely,

The team felt that the language of the letter was too old-fashioned, the instructions in the second paragraph not sufficiently clear, and the general effect of the letter not very courteous. They devised a new letter.

Dear   :

Although we have checked carefully, we can find no record of your having paid the $ due on your (electric/gas) bill dated

You can help us:

1. If you paid the bill at one of our division offices, just send us a copy of your receipt.

2. If you mailed us a check, please send us copies of both sides of the cancelled check the bank sent back to you with your monthly bank statement.

3. If you mailed us a money order, please ask the bank or post office where you bought it for copies of both sides of the cancelled order and send them to us.

4. If you simply forgot to pay the bill, please pay it now.

To make it easier for you to reply, I have enclosed a reply envelope. Please put this letter and either the necessary copies or the payment of the bill in the envelope and send it to us as soon as possible so that we can clear up your account.

If you have any questions, you can call me at

Sincerely,

The new letter is longer than the old one, but it is more likely to bring an appropriate response, because it is friendlier, more specific, and easier to understand.

Thanks to the new form letters, costs have been cut, all communicators use the same forms from a central computer, letters used in all divisions reflect approved company policy, customers receive replies faster, and customers who call in perceive the company as trying to be helpful.

ILLUSTRATIVE MATERIALS

1.

Here is a "sales letter" that, though certainly unorthodox, was successful. It is not a particularly polished piece of prose. It was obviously typed by the man who signed it rather than by a secretary, for the margins are ragged, there are several strikeovers, and several marks of punctuation are missing. (We have put them in and regularized the spacing to make the reading easier.)

Mr. E. E. Austin—Purchasing Agent
Johnson Manufacturing Co.
Lake Street
Milwaukee, WI 53202

Dear Mr. Austin,

I dislike annoying you again, but I am again asking why I have not had the pleasure of hearing from you in nearly 3 months. I have always been proud 99 of the fact that I had an account like Johnson Manufacturing Co., having built it up from nothing over a 20-year period, to a nice sizable account today. Now without warning I find I practically haven't the account anymore. This makes me feel terrible. Do you know, Mr. Austin, how impossible it is to replace a new customer? When I approach business firms, I usually get the standard remark, "We have to be loyal to those people who, during and after the critical war years, helped us out with merchandise hard to obtain." Of course, to this no one can give an adequate answer. Unfortunately, in many cases I was not so treated, Mr. Austin. In my place just what would you do in this matter? Please let me hear from you soon.

Very truly yours,

Nicholas Neustadt

What is the appeal of this letter? Would it have been successful with you? Would a letter of similar tone (although better written) have been appropriate from a large corporation? Explain your answers.

2.

Some companies use "gimmicks" in an attempt to get the customer to pay an overdue bill. What·effect would each of the following have on you?

(Attached to the top of this letter is a fish hook and fly.)

Dear Mr. Thomas:

Perhaps you know that the trout season opens next week. If you're a fisherman, we hope you'll use our fly and that you'll catch a lot of speckled beauties with it.

We're fishing too—for the $45.25 you owe us. How about sending a check before you leave for the trout streams?

Sincerely,

Dear Mr. Perkins:

> Roses are red
> Violets are blue
> We regret to say
> Your bill's overdue.

Amount $50.10.

Very truly yours,

3.

In their book Commercial Letters,[1] *John B. Opdycke and Celia A. Drew published this letter:*

THE BOOK OF KNOWLEDGE

THE CHILDREN'S ENCYCLOPEDIA

THE GROLIER SOCIETY

2 WEST 45TH STREET

TELEPHONE 200 BRYANT   **NEW YORK**

Feb. 2, 1917.

Mr. John B. Opdycke,
    139 West 72nd St.,
      New York.

Dear Sir:-

     I have your letter of Jan. 27th and it is encouraging to learn that you have a good opinion of some of our letters.   I am enclosing copies of some letters, which I trust will meet your requirements.

     Speaking of letter writing, I was engaged some years ago as correspondent by a concern which was going into the mail order business.   The head of this concern had no experience whatever in advertising or in sales correspondence, yet his letters were masterpieces, and I found that they were successful because he dictated his sales letters, then sent them out in quantities just as he dictated them, without revision.   If a criticism is appropriate, I think the fault with a great many sales letters is that they are rewritten and rewritten to such an extent that the human touch is taken completely out of them.   It is much like a very natural photograph which is retouched to such an extent in order to improve it, that any fair critic would say it was no longer life like.

            Yours truly,

            THE GROLIER SOCIETY.

HBK.HN

Opdycke and Drew said, "The comment on the refined *letter is interesting and strikes a responsive chord in many letter writers." To what extent do you agree with their implied approval of the method used by the head of the mail order concern?*

[1] New York: Henry Holt & Company, 1918.

PROBLEMS

1. Choose an advertisement for a camp, school, or workshop that would be of interest to you (for example: a tennis, golf, or weight-losing camp; a business or computer school; or a workshop on writing, accounting, or operations research). Write a letter asking for the kind of information that would help you decide whether to attend. Submit the ad with your letter.

2. You are the director of personnel for your university or company. Edwina T. Hall has applied for a position. (Select an actual opening that is being advertised by your institution or company.) Ms. Hall has given as a reference a previous employer: Advantage, Inc., 1850 Orange Street, Durham, North Carolina 27705, where her supervisor was Alberta S. Ober. Write a letter asking for an evaluation of Ms. Hall's competence.

3. From the newspaper, choose a bill that is being considered in either the Congress or the state legislature. Write to your representative explaining your position on the bill and asking how he or she plans to vote.

4. You are applying for transfer to another college or for admission to a graduate school. Write to a professor from whom you have taken a course, explaining the reason for your application for transfer or admission and asking him or her to send a letter of recommendation to the director of admissions at the appropriate college or university.

5. As the sales manager for your company, you have to reply to a letter from Mr. Ralph O. Triblenka of 2718 Warner Avenue, N.W., Washington, D.C. 20015, who asks what there is about your product or service that distinguishes it from similar products or services offered by your competitors. You are unable to discover anything about Mr. Triblenka. Write a reply. (If not currently employed, you may wish to choose a product discussed in *Consumer Reports, Car and Driver,* or some similar magazine.)

6. You have been asked in this course to write a report on forms and styles of business letters. Write a form letter which you can send to a variety of companies, asking for sample letters that you can use as examples.

7. You have been asked in this course to make a study of job application forms. Write a form letter which you can send to the director of personnel of a variety of companies, asking for sample forms that you can use as examples. (Or write a form letter to bank managers or managers of loan companies for examples of loan application forms that you can use in a study.)

8. You want to order for showing in your class or as part of your company's training program a film entitled *Effective Letter Writing,* provided free by the Northern Mills Paper Company, Appleton, Wisconsin 54911. Write to ask if the film is available on two particular dates three months from now, and if not, on what dates near the ones you have given you might show it.

9. You rent trucks. The Ace Delivery Service, 1782 Franklin Street, Philadelphia, Pennsylvania 19146, which up until now has maintained its own fleet of ten trucks, wants to sell them and rent from you instead. You know nothing about the company. Write to the president, Samuel E. Epstein, and ask him to fill in and return an enclosed credit form.

10. You are the manager of a store which has just completed its fifteenth year in business. Write a form letter which, with minor variations, can be sent to the store's best customers thanking them for their patronage. (Choose a store which you patronize.)

11. You are the sales manager of a new company which has taken over the stock and premises of a recently failed company. The previous company offered the same product or service that yours does. Write a letter soliciting the continued patronage of a customer of the failed company. (Choose a product or service with which you are familiar.)

12. You are manager of stockholder relations for your company. Beverly S. Flaherty writes to ask for a copy of the last annual report because she is considering buying some of the company's stock. Write the cover letter to go with the copy of the annual report you send. (If you are not currently employed or if your company does not publish an annual report, obtain one from some other company.)

13. Until recently, your company, Varico, has offered "cancel-proof" policies for automobile insurance to certain preferred customers. Company policy has now been changed to allow the company to cancel the policy:

    a. at the end of a premium period, or
    b. at any time if
       i. the premium is not paid on time
       ii. the policy holder's driver's license is suspended or revoked
       iii. the policy holder has concealed or misrepresented information which would have caused the company to refuse to issue him or her a policy if it had had that information.

    The company may cancel all or part of a policy by mailing a notice to the policy holder at his or her last known address. Cancellations as a result of failure to pay a premium will be dated fifteen days after the mailing of the notice. All other cancellations and announcements of intention not to continue the policy beyond the current premium period will be mailed to the policy holder thirty-five days before the effective date of the cancellation. Write a letter to be signed by the company president which will be sent to all individuals now having cancel-proof policies.

14. You are the sales manager of Alumilock, a company which manufactures aluminum siding with a special interlock feature. You guarantee the siding for twenty years only if it is installed by an approved dealer, but you allow those dealers to sell to a "do-it-yourselfer" if he or she reads and signs a statement saying that your company will guarantee only installations by approved dealers and that the

guarantee does not cover installations by the homeowner or by someone who is not on the company's approved list. You have received this letter.

32 Peachtree Way
Friendly, Georgia 30117
April 20, 19—

Sales Manager
Alumilock, Inc.
27 Hamlock Street
Athens, Georgia 30601

Dear Sir:

I bought your Alumilock Siding #706A from the Friendly Lumber Company and installed it according to your instruction booklet all along the back and two sides of my house two months ago, after taking off the shingles. We left the front alone because several big trees protect it from the weather.

During a heavy rainstorm last week, water came into our back bedroom on the second floor and ruined that floor and the ceiling underneath. What good is the siding if it doesn't protect the house?

I told Mr. Albert P. Ansley, a local contractor, to repair the damage and reinstall the siding so it doesn't leak and send the bill to you, but he said he would need your permission first. Please send the necessary letter. Better send it to me instead of Ansley in case he doesn't have time to do the work and I have to ask someone else.

I'd like the permission letter soon so that another rainstorm doesn't cause more damage.

Yours truly,

William A. Cubberly

A call to Mr. Ambrose J. Washburn, owner of the Friendly Lumber Company, where Cubberly bought the siding, reveals that Cubberly read and signed the statement saying that he understood that Alumilock would guarantee only Alumilock siding installed by approved dealers, not by anyone else. Furthermore, the instruction booklet that Cubberly followed to install the siding carries a similar warning.

Washburn is concerned, however, because Cubberly is a local politician of considerable influence in the county, and if he says nasty things about Alumilock and the Friendly Lumber Company, Washburn stands to lose lots of business.

Write to Cubberly.

15. You are opening a new store in a small town. Write a 200-word statement for a printed announcement to be distributed door-to-door. Choose the type of store you are opening and the town in which you will open it. When you turn in the announcement, attach to it a 100-word description of the town.

16. You are the new manager of a branch store in a shopping center on the outskirts of a city of 90,000 people. Write a letter that would be appropriate to publish as an advertisement in the suburban edition of the city's newspaper, announcing

yourself as the new manager. Choose the type of store you are opening and the city outside of which you will open it. When you turn in the letter, attach to it a 100-word description of the city and its suburbs.

17. You have been offered the position of manager of Culbertson's, a clothing store which caters to the relatively well-to-do in a medium-sized city in another part of your state. When you visit the store to look things over, you discover, to your surprise, that previous managers have allowed customers to run up large bills without having to pay any interest on their accounts. As the owner explains, "These families have been outfitted by this store for four generations. Our relationship is a tradition around here."

    The "tradition," however, requires the store to borrow regularly and, of course, to pay considerable interest. The result is that the store's prices are much higher than they should be.

    You agree to take the position if the owner will allow you to do away with the interest-free accounts. Before the owner gives you a contract, he wants to see the letter you will send to the store's customers announcing the new policy.

    Write the letter.

18. Mr. Culbertson has approved of your proposed new policy and of your letter and has given you a contract to manage his store. You know that it will take a while for your customers to get used to the new policy and that even after it is well established, some people will still not pay their bills on time—a problem everywhere, of course. Prepare the necessary series of letters so that they will be available after the new policy has been established.

19. You are the owner of a small business. Your biggest customer by far is the William F. Arnold Company, which has purchased from you for seventeen years. Mr. William F. Arnold, who at the age of fifty still retains control of his company but lives in Florida, has turned the day-to-day running of his business over to his son Carl. Knowing that you need his business badly, Carl pays you when he pleases, in complete disregard of your payment policies—a marked difference from the practices of his father, who always used to brag about how promptly he paid his bills. When you complain to Carl, he says that if you don't like it, he'll take his business elsewhere.

    First, draw up a list of assumptions about each business (size, products, location, etc.). Then draw up a "balance sheet" of reasons for and against writing to Mr. William Arnold and another for and against writing to Mr. Carl Arnold. Next, draft both letters. Finally, explain why you would send one of the letters, both of the letters, or neither letter.

20. You are the credit manager of Fruit-a-Month, Inc., which ran a large advertisement campaign last fall in anticipation of the Christmas season. The ads worked well and business boomed. Many of the new subscribers, most of whom gave the subscriptions as gifts, accepted your offer not to pay until January 15. You expect that, with the flood of new business, late payment and failure to pay will be a much larger problem than it has ever been. Prepare a series of collection letters to fit this situation.

21. You are the subscription manager of a trade or professional journal (choose a field or profession of interest to you). Failure of your subscribers to renew and pay on time has recently become a serious problem—not, as far as you can tell, because subscribers are not interested in renewing, but because people in general seem to be paying less and less attention to deadlines and closing dates. Your analysis of the problem suggests that a touch of humor would be more appropriate than a slap on the wrist. You decide, therefore, to design a new renewal notice and reply form, and a cover letter to go with them. Do so.

22. You are the president of Blake County Tech, a public community college which specializes in training technicians: automobile mechanics, TV repair people, electricians, plumbers, and so on. You have seen on the education page of *The New York Times* a short article on the need for trained technicians which you would like to put in a new brochure you are preparing to attract students. Write a letter asking for permission to reprint the article. You would rather not have to pay a fee.

6

Letter Categories and Strategies II

Like letters which give unwelcome news and collection letters, letters of complaint and adjustment letters are frequently difficult to write. People who write to complain are often angry because they feel misused or even cheated. People who write adjustment letters, on the other hand, sometimes feel that they have been attacked or that the customer is asking for something to which he or she is not entitled.

LETTERS OF COMPLAINT

Letters of complaint, which are usually requests for service or redress, should be specific. Here, for example, is a letter of complaint which is a request for immediate—and better—service:

Mr. Vincent Sanford, President
Vincent Sanford Auto Company, Inc.
Highland and Stanton Avenues
Pittsburgh, PA 15206

Dear Mr. Sanford:

I have always owned Borchard Automobiles and in the past have been pleased with both cars and service. But it's been something else with the Borchard Scat which I purchased from you on June 4.

Two weeks later I brought the car back with a list of problems that ran for a page and a half. When the head of your Service Department saw it, he said that he would have to keep the car for two full days to take care of all of them (7/18, 7/19). Several times since, I have had to ask for additional repairs under the warranty. However, when I ask to have a problem corrected, either the repair is not made or the problem recurs because the repair is not made properly. So far your shop has had my car for six days (7/18, 7/19, 7/25, 9/12, 9/17, 9/25), and my problems are by no means cleared up.

Let me give you some examples:

1. The first four times I brought the car in, I complained that it stalled when I started it in the morning. Evidently the fast idle isn't adjusted properly. After four trips to your shop, it *still* isn't working properly, despite supposedly very special attention to it. Now it also stalls when I go around corners and at traffic lights. Today my own garage man told me exactly what the difficulty is, and I'm sure he could fix it for me. (He has never failed to fix whatever trouble I bring to him.) Why can't your mechanics do so?

2. The second or third time I brought the car in, I complained that whenever I went over a bump I got a "pock" sound from the rear end. The difficulty was attended to, but now it is back, worse than ever when the weather is warm. Cold weather cuts it down some, but next spring it will be back in full force.

3. The second or third time I brought the car in, I complained about static on the radio; but it was not fixed. I finally brought the car in a sixth time specially to have the radio fixed, and the radio was replaced. I discovered last week, however, that it does not light up with the rest of the dashboard.

So after five visits to your service department and having my car tied up for six days in your shop, I am constantly reminded by the difficulty of starting the car in the morning and the pock-pock sound as I drive down the street that I've been had by both Sanford and Borchard.

Now two other problems have turned up. There is a knocking or ticking under the hood: either a valve tappet or the alternator. And when I turned the heater on the for the first time the other day, I discovered that the fan makes an annoying racket.

Bringing my car to your service department is extremely inconvenient. There is no public transportation available from your shop to my office, so I have to bother my friends or pay out money for a cab; and all this inconvenience and expense for nothing!

I will expect a call from you this coming week explaining exactly what you will do to solve my difficulties. My phone numbers are: 666-7489 (home); 543-9280 (office).

Exasperatedly,

Franklin A. Dusenberg

cc: Mr. George J. Byron
General Manager
Scat Division of the Borchard Motor Company

Mr. Dusenberg has been very careful to give full details about his problems with the car and his treatment by the Service Department. He is also specific about what he wants: a personal call from Vincent Sanford and a plan for solving his car problems.

Dusenberg's sending a copy of his letter to George Byron, General Manager of the Scat Division of Borchard, proved most useful. Someone in Byron's office called the head of the Service Department at the Sanford Agency and arranged to have a factory representative inspect Dusenberg's automobile. The details in his complaint had impressed the people in Detroit. Had Dusenberg given the impression that he was furious but cited no specific details about his experience, he would have evoked much less interest in responsible people at Scat Division headquarters.

By contrast, here is a letter of complaint that was much less specific than it should have been. Because he tried to seem reasonable in his complaint, the writer of the following letter never got around to explaining what he was complaining about:

T-Square Engineers, Inc.
829 Fifth Avenue
New York, NY 10021

RE: Georgia Screw Turner & Tryon Belt Tightener

Gentlemen:

In the past, our company has contracted with your firm for numerous design and detailing jobs. It is about two of these jobs in particular that I wish to write, namely the Georgia Screw Turner and Tryon Belt Tightener. Generally, the work was correct. Admittedly we all make mistakes, though a number of those that occurred in these jobs we feel were unnecessary. They resulted in considerable amounts of time and money expended by us.

We wish merely to point out these facts in the hope that those involved will become aware of their occurrence.

Very truly yours,

If he felt that "Generally, the work was correct," he should have gone on to explain specifically what went wrong and which "mistakes . . . that occurred in these jobs . . . were unnecessary." In trying not to seem unreasonable, he wound up writing a letter that was vaguely threatening but at the same time made him seem inept.

ADJUSTMENT LETTERS

Adjustment letters—letters which respond to letters of complaint—are of three general types: they agree with the claimant, they ask for further information, or they reject the claim. But whatever the type, they should be courteous. Whether or not the reasons given are valid, the person writing a claim letter is at least annoyed and possibly angry. In the adjustment letter any indication of suspicion or any unwarranted or ill-tempered suggestion that a claim is fraudulent will be sure to make the situation worse. The following letter does the required job:

Dear Mr. Potkin:

The rest of your order will be on its way this afternoon.

Although our shipping department mistakenly stamped the invoice "COMPLETE," a recheck showed that you are perfectly right. We still owe you ten dozen of No. 728.

We are sorry that you did not get all the towels you ordered last month. We hope that we have not unduly inconvenienced you.

Yours truly,

The letter is short and businesslike, but friendly and courteous. It does not go into long, involved explanations, apologies, or expressions of regret. It admits the error and indicates that steps have been taken to rectify it promptly. Notice how it differs from the following letter, which "says the same thing":

Dear Mr. Potkin:

We have your letter of June 17 in which you say that we still owe you ten dozen towels (No. 728) even though the invoice was stamped "COMPLETE." This is a most unusual circumstance. The people in our shipping department are very careful in making up and checking each order.

Our investigation shows that your claim seems to be valid. As a result we have directed our shipping department to send you an additional ten dozen of No. 728.

Yours truly,

This letter offers an explanation which turns into a statement of disbelief ("You *say* that we still owe you. . . . This is a most unusual circumstance") and suggests that there is still some doubt about the validity of the claim (it "seems" to be valid). It says nothing about when the towels are to be shipped. It offers no apology. The company may well lose Mr. Potkin's business.

A letter requesting further information should similarly avoid reflecting suspicion:

Dear Mr. Wilson:

We are sorry to hear that you are dissatisfied with your lawn mower. If you will give us the information requested on the enclosed form, we will send it to the authorized service station in your neighborhood. Our service agent will then call on you to discuss what should be done.

If you prefer, you may get in touch with one of our agents directly. You will find enclosed a list of those in your area.

The Roto-Cut Company feels that satisfied customers are its best advertisement, so naturally we want you to be pleased with your Roto-Mower.

Yours truly,

Notice the different effect of the following letter:

Dear Mr. Wilson:

We are surprised to hear that you are dissatisfied with your lawn mower and that the clerk in the hardware store where you bought it told you to write to us about it.

In order to evaluate your claim, we will need further information. Would you, therefore, fill in the attached form and return it to us? We will then send it to an authorized service station, where one of our service agents will check it.

You can save some time by consulting your phone book and getting the name of your local service agent directly, as the instruction booklet which came with your lawn mower directed.

Yours truly,

This letter suggests not only that the writer does not trust the claimant, but also that the claimant can't read. The whole approach is pointless. The first letter does not commit the company to any more than the second does. It took no longer to write. If a letter must be written, it might just as well be one that is pleasant.

The letter which disagrees with the claimant or denies his request is, of course, the most difficult to write. Take this one:

Dear Mr. Silvers:

This will acknowledge your letter of July 16. Company policy does not allow us to accept responsibility for failure of Roof-O-Spray applications not made by trained Roof-O-Spray workmen. All purchase agreements for Roof-O-Spray carry this stipulation. If you will check your original correspondence and your copy of the invoice, you will find that requirement clearly stated as part of the business agreement.

Yours truly,

Being a little more sympathetic will do no harm and may do some good:

Dear Mr. Silvers:

We are sorry that the Roof-O-Spray that you applied did not hold up as well as you expected.

111

Applying sealing sprays is a highly specialized job. The person applying the sealing material must be trained to adjust the viscosity of the liquid spray to the surface of the material being sprayed and to the ambient temperature. For that reason we urge our customers to use the services of the Roof-O-Spray agency from whom they buy the material.

Mr. Simpson of the Simpson Contracting Company, from whom you bought your Roof-O-Spray, tells me that he discussed the matter with you and pointed out that the purchase agreement stipulated that applications not made by trained Roof-O-Spray workmen were not guaranteed.

Perhaps you felt that this was an unwarranted requirement set up to provide more business for our agents. We have heard that some firms in other fields operate that way. I'm happy to say, however, that we do not.

We are sorry to have to tell you that we cannot assume responsibility for the application of Roof-O-Spray by your workmen, who have not gone through our training program. As an experienced businessman you will understand our position.

I have asked Mr. Simpson to examine the application without any expense to you. He may be able to suggest something that will help.

Yours truly,

The second letter will take a little longer to write than the first. But the extra investment of time and thought will certainly be worthwhile. It may make the difference between losing and keeping a customer. Note, too, that the second letter appeals to Mr. Silvers' image as a responsible, intelligent businessman, whereas the first letter attacks that self-image and suggests that Silvers is trying to "weasel" out of an agreement. The second letter also tries to be helpful instead of just leaving Mr. Silvers to solve his own problem—and nurse his grievance.

The best way to deal with a claim letter to which the reply must be "no" is first to be sympathetic (without accepting responsibility), next to explain as reasonably as possible why the claimant's request cannot be granted, then to say "no," and finally to be as helpful as possible under the circumstances.

Writers must remember always to check any tendency to be sharp in replying to a letter which seems unreasonable or which reflects badly on their company and always consider the reader, who may well have cause for complaint, or if not, may honestly not know it. And even if the person is consciously being unreasonable, a sensible, pleasant reply may well change that attitude. Replying to an angry claim letter with an angry adjustment letter may satisfy the self-image of the writer as an important person or help release the frustration that has been building up while dealing with other complaints, but it also damages the image of the company in the mind of the customer.

Sometimes, of course, a customer will complain about something for which

there is no remedy. For example, a major food company received a letter from a woman who had eaten—and evidently enjoyed—one of its products while she was in England. When she came back home, however, she was unable to find it anywhere. Furthermore, none of the storekeepers or supermarket managers had even heard of it. What kind of distribution system did the company have, she wanted to know.

Here is the reply she received from the national sales manager:

Dear Mrs. Parkinson:

Thank you for your recent inquiry about the availability of Curd-Cream, a product of our British organization. We have had similar requests from consumer friends who have used this product while visiting in England.

We regret that Curd-Cream cannot be made available here in the States. To import it would make the cost prohibitive to the consumer, and at present we do not feel that there is sufficient demand to produce it in the United States.

There are many factors to consider before we can market a new variety:

Will this variety find favor, nationally or sectionally?

How will its cost compare with that of other varieties in this same line?

Will its price be acceptable to the consumer?

How available are the raw materials?

Changing market conditions also play a large part in establishing new varieties.

Thanks again for writing to us. We are sorry that we cannot tell you that Curd-Cream will be available in the United States. But I am sure that you will understand that we can only market a new product in this country if we can be sure of a substantial sale.

Sincerely,

Charles Wrigley

Wrigley had to disappoint Mrs. Parkinson, but if she was a reasonable person, she would understand why and appreciate the care he took in replying.

CASE STUDY: "MY WORD!"

A touch of warmth and good humor can sometimes be very useful in replying to a complaint letter. It certainly got results for an executive in Simon Schuster's Puzzle Department. A friend of ours, a crossword puzzle addict, had purchased her thirty-fourth volume of *Crosswords from the Times* and found a portion of it so badly printed that it could not be used. She wrote a   113 mild but firm letter to the publisher pointing out the problem and requesting a replacement. A few days later she received the reply on the facing page.

Ms. Jones, as one might guess, was delighted to receive this letter and promptly began to show it to her friends. How often, after all, does one get such a pleasant letter of apology?

In dealing with the problem posed by Ms. Jones' letter, Fran Savage could have taken a modified Fred Peters approach (see pp. 33–35) and implied that somehow getting the defective copy was Ms. Jones' fault. Or she could have written a curt "We have received your letter of March 22. . . . We can assure you that such problems very seldom occur at Simon & Schuster. . . . Enclosed is a replacement copy of the book. Sincerely yours." A clear, cold unfriendly reply which would have made no friends. That is not Ms. Savage's way. She is not thinking of Ms. Jones as a nuisance who has to be placated, but as a crossword addict who has been sorely disappointed.

So she begins "MY WORD!!!"—certainly an unusual opening gambit, but appropriate for a letter about crossword puzzles, and one that forcefully expresses consternation at what has happened. She follows up immediately with a reference to the unhappiness of the reader, which she finds wholly justified: "You certainly have every right to feel put upon." *Put upon:* just the right word choice for the situation. How much better than *annoyed,* which might have faintly unfavorable connotations! In the same sentence, too, she agrees with Ms. Jones' argument that if you pay $3.95 for a crossword book, you ought to get one that is properly printed. She even goes further: you ought to feel unhappy about a poorly printed book *whatever* the price. But Ms. Savage doesn't linger on that potentially touchy subject. "Here's a nice clean copy," she says, ". . . to allow you to finish solving in peace."

Only after she has obtained the good will of her reader does she attempt to explain why Ms. Jones received a defective copy. But in doing so, she refuses to imply that such errors are all the fault of the system—an easy out, but one that has infuriated countless purchasers of defective goods. Even when you know that the books are printed many thousands at a clip, she suggests, "it's only *slightly* easier to understand that the occasional 'goof' gets through." And, from your point of view, that's no real excuse. Then she tells her reader about the positive action she is taking so that the problem will not occur again.

In concluding the long paragraph, Ms. Savage points out that the company does what it can, "but machines have a way of getting the best of all of us." Machines do indeed get the best of all of us all the time. One can imagine Ms. Jones recalling how her car failed to start last week, how the traffic light at the corner gets stuck on red every so often, how her vacuum sweeper always seems to break down just before a party. Then Ms. Savage expresses her appreciation for Ms. Jones's calling the company's attention to the "goof" and implies that her letter will make a real difference. It's not just that it will make them be more careful. They are already "vigilant"—an excellent word choice—but now they know *where* to be "extra vigilant."

The final paragraph is equally effective. It might well have read, "Thank you again for calling this matter to our attention," a good, standard, polite

conclusion. Ms. Savage does more. She uses her two sentences to thank Ms.

Simon&Schuster

March 27th, 1979

Dear Marjorie M. Jones,

MY WORD!!! You certainly have every right to feel
put upon to have bought such a badly printed puzzle
book -- for whatever price. Here's a nice, clean
copy of CROSSWORDS FROM THE TIMES 34 to allow you
to finish solving in peace - complete with single-
impression answers.

When you realize that these books are printed in
many thousands at a clip, it's only slightly easier
to understand that the occasional "goof" gets through
the inspection lines undetected; your samples are
being returned to the printer with our complaint
that his quality control has slipped up and (we hope)
will be prevented in future. We do make every
effort to eliminate all the errors, but machines
have a way of getting the best of all of us; we
appreciate your calling this to our attention so
that we know where to be extra vigilant.

Thanks for your mildly expressed frustration, too!
Not all of our puzzle fans would have been so
gentle with a reprimand.

Cordially, — *and Happy Solving!*

Fran Savage

Fran Savage
    Puzzle Department

ENCL: CWT34   Ms. Marjorie M. Jones
                    16 Brokaw Place
FS/   Appleton WI 54911
lom

Simon & Schuster Building
1230 Avenue of the Americas
New York, NY 10020
212 245 6400
A Division of Gulf & Western Corporation

Jones for the way *she* handled what for *her* was a frustrating situation and ends,
"Not all of our puzzle fans would have been so gentle with a reprimand."

End of letter? Not quite. "Cordially" she signs off (not "Very truly yours"
or "Sincerely yours"). But she again does more. As she signs the letter, she   115

adds in pen ''—and Happy Solving!,'' a final personal note which will surely be appreciated by her puzzle fan reader.

The situation in which Fran Savage found herself when she prepared to answer Ms. Jones's letter was not very unlike that which Fred Peters faced. But what a difference in the results! Ms. Savage, unlike Mr. Peters, had her reader clearly in mind: a lady who had bought a crossword puzzle book only to find that much of the text was unreadable; a lady who was irritated but who expressed her irritation in firm but reasonable language. Ms. Savage then prepared a response designed not merely to soothe her reader but to increase her loyalty to Simon & Schuster. In this she was wholly successful.

Although we have analyzed in some detail the sentences in this letter and the techniques they represent, we do not wish to imply that Ms. Savage planned out every detail. Like all true professionals, she did not need to do so. Having put herself for the moment in her reader's place and decided on a general strategy, she found, no doubt, that the right phrases ''just came to her.'' Training and instinct, working together, produced a model of graciousness and tact.

EFFECTIVE LETTERS

In our discussion of various kinds of business letters in Chapters 5 and 6, we have employed the principles we set out in Chapters 2 and 3. The reader who understands those principles and has followed our analysis of how they should be employed in typical letter-writing situations will be able to write not only the kinds of letters we have discussed, but any other kind as well. Whether one writes a letter giving welcome news or unwelcome news, granting a favor or asking a favor, praising or complaining, agreeing or disagreeing, the basic questions a writer must ask are the same: Who—Says What—In Which Channel—To Whom—With What Effect? There are no better guidelines for writing effective letters.

ILLUSTRATIVE MATERIALS

1.
Here is an exchange of letters about a serious blunder:

Magna Box Company
72 Franklin Street
Newark, NJ 07102

Attention: Mr. Paul Sully
             Sales Department

Reference: Complaint from your customer relations man regarding
             slow payment of your invoices totaling $1,900.00

Dear Mr. Sully:

Recently we received a letter regarding slow payment which we sincerely feel was sent injudiciously. The implication was made that we might feel "pinched" by having to pay $1,900.00 all at once. The treasurer of our company has assured me that invoices are paid promptly whether the amount is $190.00, $1,900.00, or $19,000.00. We have never had any vendors complain about our methods of paying invoices. We follow the same rules as all accredited firms in discounting our invoices, with net/30-day invoices being handled in the secondary cycle. In special instances where a vendor requests rapid payment of a bill, the Purchasing Department always sees that such a request is honored, if the request is bona fide.

Please understand that we do not mind your asking about an invoice that might possibly have gone astray, for we are anxious to clear such matters up as quickly as possible.

Yours truly,

ATLAS NOVELTY COMPANY

James L. McGee
PURCHASING AGENT

Atlas Novelty Company
1428 Navarre Street
Brooklyn, NY 11526

Attention: Mr. James L. McGee

Dear Mr. McGee:

When Mr. Sully showed me your letter, I was appalled. We have, as you know, thousands of accounts and many hundreds of letters going out of our Collection Department each week. I make it my personal task to review the letters each week to eliminate those which would be, as you say, "injudicious."

It was my fault for failing—through negligence, for that is all it can possibly be—to eliminate the letter you received from the run-of-the-mill collection reminders.

I do hope that you will accept my humble apology which I write with the utmost frankness.

Not only I, but every member of our company values your business, and more than anything, your good will. I know that you pay your bills most promptly, and in an exemplary manner.

Thank you for understanding.

Yours truly,

MAGNA BOX COMPANY

John F. Brindle
GENERAL CREDIT MANAGER

a. *How could the initial blunder have been avoided?*
b. *Is Mr. Brindle's reply a good one?*
c. *What are its strong points? What are its weak points?*
d. *Would you have written a similar reply or a different one? Explain.*
e. *How would you evaluate Mr. McGee's letter?*

2.
Here is an exchange of complaint and adjustment letters.

Mr. John T. Soames, President
Lavages, Inc.
2400 Ocean Avenue
Brooklyn, NY 11229

Dear Mr. Soames:

Three months ago our two sons, ages three and six, heard about your offer of cowboy scarves for My Bubbl-Bath boxtops. Although my husband and I do not succumb to such lures often, we bought two boxes of My Bubbl-Bath so that we could get a scarf for each boy, and, following the instructions carefully, mailed the two box tops to the proper address with the required dollar (fifty cents for each scarf).

Since then the boys have waited expectantly for each mail, predicting loudly each time that their scarves would arrive; and each time they have been disappointed—six days a week for three months. Surely that is cruelty to children.

Could we have our scarves right away?

Hopefully,

Anna S. Orlando

LETTER CATEGORIES AND STRATEGIES II

Dear Mrs. Orlando:

Mr. John T. Soames asked me to reply to your letter to him of June 7.

Lavages, Inc., regrets the reported inconvenience caused by the lack of response on our promotional offer of colorful cowboy scarves. We are indeed sorry and are forwarding to you today three boxes of My Bubbl-Bath in apology.

Yours truly,

John T. Quigley
SALES MANAGER

Dear Mr. Quigley:

Because the charm of bubble-bathing wore off very quickly (the bubbles interfered with the serious business of my sons floating their toy boats), we still have one and three-quarters boxes of My Bubbl-Bath. Now you threaten me with three more. If we have a leak that gets to all that powder we'd all be floated away in a torrent of bubbles.

Cowboy scarves, Mr. Quigley, not more boxes of bubble bath; and quickly, Quigley. I can't stand the daily disappointment on those two little faces.

Desperately,

Anna S. Orlando

Dear Mrs. Orlando:

Lavages, Inc., regrets the continued inconvenience of the non-arrival of the two ordered scarves. We have written to the supplier to urge that they forward them to you as promptly as possible.

Yours truly,

John T. Quigley
SALES MANAGER

a. *What can you tell about Anna Orlando from her letters? If you, as sales manager, received them, what would your reaction be?*
b. *From his replies, how does John Quigley strike you?*
c. *If you were Quigley, how would you have handled the situation?*

PROBLEMS

1. You have ordered from J. D. Orange, a reputable mail order firm in Aroona, Maine 04033, a Twill-Zip Jacket (#OF 7643), and enclosed with the order your personal check for $83.50. When the jacket arrives, you discover that the lining in the left sleeve is loose and the sleeve itself has been sewn into the shoulder improperly so that it hangs awkwardly when you wear the jacket. Write an appropriate letter to J. D. Orange.

2. While on vacation 450 miles from home, you saw a teak typing table for $150 which you liked. Since the table was available "knocked down" and packed neatly in a cardboard carton, you bought one and carried it home in the trunk of your car. At home you took it out of the carton, assembled it without any trouble, and put it in the den. You are pleased with the way it looks and functions. Two months after you assembled it, however, you notice that the veneer on one side panel of the table is coming loose. Since the table has not been exposed to any moisture or ill-treatment, you can not understand why the panel deteriorated. Write an appropriate letter to Modern Furniture, 13 Main Street, Wausau, Wisconsin 54401.

3. Last Saturday night you went to the largest movie theater in the city in which you live to see a film you'd been looking forward to. You were distracted by a raucous group of six or seven teen-agers who behaved noisily through the entire showing. No usher paid any attention to them, and after half an hour you asked them politely to quiet down. They not only responded with abusive remarks, but continued to make noise until the picture ended, at which time they trooped out noisily, jostling some of the other moviegoers who were also leaving. Write to the theater manager to complain.

4. You live in a farming community, population 450, several hours' drive from any city. Four months ago, you bought a vacuum cleaner from a door-to-door sales-man, who promised that his company would take care of any problems that might arise with the cleaner, at no inconvenience to you. As you were taking out the disposable paper bag inside the cleaner to put in a new one, the clip that holds the bag snapped off. Now when you try to use the cleaner, the bag will not stay in place and the inside cavity fills up with dirt. Write to Vacu-Sweep, 2218 High-land Avenue, Atlantic Highlands, New Jersey 07716.

5. While visiting a friend in Pittsburgh, Pennsylvania, you attended the Three Rivers Art Festival, where you bought a print for $75 from a printmaker who lives in Ohio. When you returned home and unwrapped the print, you discovered several flaws in the paper itself which you did not notice when you bought it. The flaws are too obvious for you to want to frame and hang the print. When the artist wrapped the print for you, he included his card. He is John A. Wisno, 43 Elm Street, Oberlin, Ohio 44074. Write an appropriate letter.

6. You have purchased a new watch with a variety of new features which you find not only fascinating but useful. Unfortunately, it beeps every hour on the hour, and you can find nothing in the two-color manual written in three languages to explain how to deal with the problem. You can't wear the watch to bed at night

because your spouse complains that it is disturbing. The owner of the store from which you bought it has not been able to help. Write to Techutron, 1832 N. Apple Way, Eugene, Oregon 97403.

7. You are the business manager of People's Electric Company, which has contracted with the Power Generating Service Division of Southern Electric to clean and repair a turbine generator at your main generating plant in Burlingame, California (PEC Order No. 57-2285, June 27, 19—). The project was not completed until two weeks after the completion date specified in the contract, and you want to invoke the penalty clause in the contract, which provides for a half percent reduction in cost for each late day. You attribute the poor performance to the inexperience of Southern Electric's project manager. Write to Philip A. Benswanger, Manager, Power Generating Service Division, Southern Electric, New Orleans, Louisiana 70122.

8. You are the sales manager of J. D. Orange (see Problem 1). Respond to the letter you have received. Give instructions for returning the jacket, and ask whether the purchaser wants a refund or another jacket. Address: August Johnson, 822 Arbor Lane, White Plains, New York 10605.

9. You are the owner of Modern Furniture (see Problem 2). You can offer two solutions. The complainant can disassemble the table and either ship the faulty panel to you or take it to a furniture store in a town ten miles away from her. The store owner is an acquaintance of yours. If there is no evidence of mistreatment, the panel will be repaired at no charge and shipping costs will be reimbursed. If the panel has been mistreated, the customer will have to pay for the repairs and shipping. Address: Maria Flower, 827 Mary Street, Ann Arbor, Michigan 48104.

10. You are the theater manager who receives the complaint written in response to Problem 3. On the night in question, you were attending the wedding of your son, and unbeknownst to you one of theater ushers called in sick at the last moment. The other one was kept busy in the lobby handling the crowds waiting for the next show. Write to explain. Address: one of your neighbors.

11. You are the sales manager of Vacu-Sweep (see Problem 4). Unfortunately, the salesman misled the purchaser of the vacuum cleaner. You can offer two solutions. You can send a new clip with simple instructions on how to install it (the only tools necessary are a pliers and a screwdriver), or she can bring the cleaner to The Fixit Store, Allentown, Pennsylvania, about seventy miles away, for repair. Write the reply. Address: Marian Ober, 13 Key Street, Mifflintown, Pennsylvania 17059.

12. You are John Wisno (see Problem 5). If the paper of the print is actually flawed, you certainly want to send a new print; but you want to be sure that you are not being cheated. Write a letter instructing the complainant to send you a large enough piece cut from the print to show the flaw and assure you that the piece does in fact come from your print. You will then send another copy. Address: Pierre Alonzo, 14 Mendicito Way, Palo Alto, California 94303.

13. You are the sales manager of Techutron (see Problem 6). The watch is flawed and must be returned to the factory for repair or replacement. Write the appropriate letter. Address: Jonathan A. Miller, 1217 Middle Way, Fort Smith, Arkansas 72901.

14. You are the manager of the Power Generating Service Division of Southern Electric (see Problem 7). When you receive the letter from the business manager of People's Electric, you talk to the project manager who led the generator repair team. He blames the late completion on lack of cooperation from People's Electric employees and offers some details. You need time to study the situation further, however. People's Electric is a long-time customer which gives you a lot of business. Write an appropriate letter to the business manager, whom you have never met. Address: Alice M. Prendergast, Business Manager, People's Electric Company, 73 Electric Way, Burlingame, California 94010.

MAJOR WRITING ASSIGNMENTS: THE REPORT

Planning

In discussing written communications in this book, we frequently distinguish between letters and memos on the one hand and reports on the other. The categories overlap considerably, however. A letter to a customer, for example, may be a report on how best to treat a particular machine to keep it from rusting. And most trip reports are written in memo form.

The distinction between the two categories, therefore, is frequently arbitrary. When a document will run to more than four or five pages, it is often typed up in report format, sometimes with a title page, and sent with a covering letter or a memo. If it will run only two or three pages, the document itself may well be typed up as a letter or memo.

STEPS IN PLANNING A REPORT

Since the distinction is more a difference in form than in substance, therefore, it is not surprising that the steps in planning and writing a report are the same as those in planning and writing a letter or memo.

1. Determine Real Purpose or Function

A report frequently has many more readers than does a letter or memo. Take, for example, a major report on a pilot plant study for removing oil from shale, written by the manager of the pilot plant and several of the engineers. The management group that is responsible for deciding whether to recommend commercial exploitation of the process to the board of directors will use the report in a variety of ways. Since the proposed venture not only will be expensive, but also may well determine the future of the company, each member of the group will probably read in the report to the extent that his or her expertise allows. The chairman of the management group will probably also send copies of the report to such other readers as the group's staff engineers or an appropriate consulting firm for a check on the soundness of the scientific and engineering principles employed in the pilot operation and the validity of the results; to the law department for an analysis of patent rights, antitrust implications, and other possible legal problems; to the real estate department for an exploration of sites available for such a plant, and later to the environmental engineering group for exploratory environmental impact studies of the three most likely sites; to a particular section of the marketing division for a comparison of the projected costs of retrieving saleable oil from a full-scale commercial operation, based on the pilot plant operation, with the costs of producing similar saleable oil from Nigerian crude and from coal; and to another section of that division for a recommendation as to which formulation from shale oil components would be most marketable and how best to maximize the use of the individual components.

The needs of each reader of the report will be somewhat different. All will want a good summary. Beyond that, in the management group, each will probably focus on a particular section and read to a different level in the report. Of the other readers, some will read the entire report, others the summary and all of the technical details in the appendices, still others the summary and the body of the report.

When the management group has received, discussed, and assimilated all of the reports it has asked for and reached a consensus, it will delegate to one or more of its members the responsibility of writing a report to the board of directors recommending action. The body of this report will probably be much shorter than any of the individual reports on which it is based; but an appendix will carry a list of those reports and short descriptions of each, in case a member of the board should want to read one. And, again depending upon his or her expertise, a board member may send for one or more of them.

The Audiences for Reports

The real purpose or function of a report, therefore, is determined by who will read it and how they will use it. Since any report may well be read at
several levels in the hierarchy of a company, no one set of prescriptions for

writing reports will be universally applicable. The soundness of the following generalizations, however, has been demonstrated by experience in business, industry, and government.

a. Reports that are written by members of a particular discipline or profession for members of that same discipline or profession are easiest to write, since the readers share a reasonably common technical vocabulary and set of concepts, and sometimes even common values. Thus if a report on the extraction of oil from shale written by a petroleum engineer is designed to be read by a variety of chemical engineers, it will be more difficult to write than if it is written just for petroleum engineers. If it is designed for a variety of chemical engineers, several accountants, and two lawyers, it will be still more difficult to write.

b. Reports designed to communicate from one level of the hierarchy of a company to another are frequently more difficult to write than those designed for one level. In planning its training programs, for example, the education department of one major firm distinguishes four levels of responsibility among its management people: professional personnel, first-level management, middle management, and upper management.

As one moves up the ladder, one's responsibilities and reporting activities change. The people at the professional level function largely in technical capacities: they are sales engineers, research scientists, accountants, technical information specialists. In their reporting, they provide the information that allows those at higher levels of management to monitor the operations of the company and to formulate new procedures, strategies, and policies. First-level managers tend to write largely about procedures, middle-level managers about procedures and strategy, upper-level managers about strategy and policy.

At the professional level, people are usually most interested in the details of the activities and procedures in which they are involved: the reasons for the success or failure of a particular machine or process, the data from a test, the purchasing record of an important customer, the language and design requirements for a new brochure. And that, typically, is what they report. A first-level manager, however, must look for patterns in the details, and the meaning behind them: is the failure rate of a particular type of motor cause for alarm, do the data from a particular test warrant recommending a pilot plant operation, does the record of major purchasers indicate a shift in interest from one type of product to another, is the in-house printing facility adequate for printing the new brochures being asked for? Where the professionals are frequently concerned with individual "trees," managers must understand what is happening to the "forest," so that they can report on what is occurring there. Immersed in the details of their activities, professionals see each detail as meaningful and thus may want to report it. Fearful of being so overwhelmed by details that they will not have time to determine how the details form patterns, managers press for meaningful abstracts and summaries in reports from professional personnel.

Similar differences in interest and need exist between all levels of management. People at one level have a reasonably good idea of the kinds of responsibility carried by others at their own level and the complexity or specificity of detail they need in order to function. But they often find it difficult to understand the interests and needs of people at other levels. Thus a research chemist may find it difficult to understand why the director of research will not read much more than the summary and introduction of his reports. On the other hand, the director of research, who frequently carries three or four such reports home with him of an evening to prepare for a meeting the next morning or to write a report of his own, cannot understand why the chemist writes such lengthy summaries and why he does not include in them his conclusions and recommendations.

At the very top of the pyramid sit the members of the board of directors, who read reports which interpret and analyze summaries of summaries of summaries. They must not allow themselves to be so enmeshed in the details that they cannot obtain an overview of company operations which will enable them to determine what goals to set and which policies to approve. The next chapter provides examples of how these principles operate in practice.

Considering the Purpose of a Report

Sometimes it is not immediately clear what the real purpose of a report is. A department head, for example, may call a meeting of the people who have worked on a particular project and say to them, "Before Bill [the project leader] starts to write this report, let's talk a little about what we want it to accomplish. Are we satisfied with the results of the project? Are we ready to recommend that the company adopt the procedure we've developed? Or should we ask for $5000 more and two additional months to explore the possibilities Mary raised in her memo of May 24? There may be other alternatives, too. What do you think?" Or the head of an advertising department may call together the senior members of her group and say, "The president wants a report proposing two possible sales campaigns for the new line of hosiery we'll be marketing next year so that she can choose one. Let's try to generate some ideas."

Such meetings are invitations to "brainstorm"—simply to pour out ideas without stopping to evaluate them. (People who call such meetings often signal their special character by announcing them in the meeting notice as brainstorming sessions.) After a broad variety of ideas has been proposed, the group can then explore and evaluate each. (An individual preparing to write a report can also brainstorm by writing down ideas freely, leaving their evaluation until later.)

When preparing to write a report, one can also generate ideas with the Lasswell formula:

Who

What stance do I assume in this report: technical expert, neutral observer, advocate of a particular position, manager, staff assistant?

Says What

Does the nature of the subject suggest an approach that would be useful?

In Which Channel

There is a meeting on October 10 at which I will report on this problem orally. Should I send a written report first to prepare the audience for my talk? Or should I design my oral report on October 10 to serve as preparation for their reading my written report, which I can distribute at the end of the meeting?

To Whom

What do I know about the people to whom I'm presenting this report? What are their technical and intellectual competencies? What levels of management do they represent? What will they want to know?

With What Effect

What do I want my report to do: inform, persuade, deter, challenge, encourage?

Such methods for generating ideas are frequently very useful. For other examples, see the Illustrative Materials section of this chapter.

2. Select Materials

All report writers realize that before they are finished they must have in hand the materials necessary to complete the job. But all too often people begin to compose communications before gathering *all* of the information. The inefficiency of this procedure can be observed in any large office a hundred times a day.

Let us take one example. Ben Wentworth has been out of town for a few days. When he arrives at his office he reads through the accumulation of mail and messages on his desk and then starts on the report that his supervisor expects momentarily.

He begins:

Plant management is reluctant to alter the proposed location of the catwalk above Vat No. 4 in the new facility. However, the safety department insists that the recommended design would produce a serious hazard to the operator from fumes. William Parsons of the Engineering Design Department has made a third suggestion which may satisfy both groups. He plans to move Vat No. 4 six feet to . . . .

Ben pauses and hunts through the piles of papers on his desk. Unable to find what he wants, he calls to his secretary, "Stella, where is the report we got from Parsons last week?" Stella thinks for a moment and replies, "You   129 didn't by any chance give it to Mr. Thomas, did you, Mr. Wentworth?" Light breaks over Ben's face. "No, I didn't. But I did lend it to Ted Garver. Just a minute, Stella." A phone call to Ted's secretary confirms the presence of the report in his office. "Stella, would you mind running over to Mr. Garver's office and picking up that report?"

Fifteen minutes after the interruption, Ben is ready to resume.

> He plans to move Vat No. 4 three feet closer to Vat No. 3. The catwalk can then go between the two mixers at that end of the building. The added cost involved will be nominal. The original estimate was . . . .

To obtain the necessary figure, Ben has to pull out and examine a report of over 100 pages, which he rapidly skims through. After much rustling of paper he finds the page he wants and continues:

> . . . original estimate was $89,920 for the whole unit. Parsons expects the new setup to run about a thousand more. When he first raised the question of moving the catwalk, I wrote to Lawrence Cotton at Purvis Chemical because I remembered his telling me about a similar problem.

"Stella, do we have Mr. Cotton's reply in the files? Could you dig it out for me? I'll need that to strengthen my argument."

We need not follow Ben any further. The point is obvious. Instead of gathering—or having his secretary gather—the materials he needed for the report, he began to write. Then he was forced to interrupt his writing to refer to other papers or send his secretary out for a report. As a result, therefore, his performance is dismal. It wastes his time and his secretary's time, disrupts his thought pattern so that his report may be incoherent, and frays both his nerves and Stella's. Unfortunately, far too many report writers compose in this harum-scarum manner.

CASE STUDY: A SITE ANALYSIS

Often after he has gathered a mass of material, the writer must select from it the information that he will use in his communication. How does he go about it? Let us take an example.

Bill Southworth has been assigned to investigate five possible sites for a small manufacturing plant which his company wishes to build, and to recommend the most feasible ones. He has coordinated the work of a staff of investigators who have studied exhaustively the potential of each site. He now has a drawer full of reports from his staff and must make his recommendations to his superiors. In his mind, all of the materials which have been submitted to him are carefully marshaled under headings: construction costs, transportation facilities, potential labor force, accessibility of raw materials, and so on. For each site, he can, if he wishes, compare in detail the probable construction costs, the transportation facilities, and the labor force available. But should he?

PLANNING

If he has thought carefully before preparing the report, he will have realized that his purpose is not to compare the sites: it is to provide useful information on which his superiors may base a decision involving millions of dollars. He must, therefore, select from the evidence available only that which will be genuinely useful to them for this purpose. As he looks over his materials, therefore, Bill Southworth begins to select. First, Site A. He has the fattest report on that one. His investigators have combed the area for him. He could write a detailed sociological study of it. At first this area seemed to be the most likely candidate, but the owner of the available site died suddenly, leaving the plot to the state as a wildlife sanctuary. In Bill's report the fat file on Site A will be reduced to a brief paragraph explaining why that site must be removed from consideration. The statistics so carefully arranged and interpreted will have to remain in the files.

Site B looks like an excellent candidate. Site C, however, does not. In many respects it would be ideal, but the source of raw materials on which the company is counting, although easily accessible, will be adequate for five years at most. Importing raw materials thereafter will not be economical, and no new sources are available in the area. Once again Bill consigns a mountain of information to the files and decides that for site C only the data on the inadequacy of the supply of raw materials are really needed for his report.

Bill's experience with Site D is similar. This time the labor force proves to be inadequate. Therefore, the bulk of his final report will consist of a comparison not of five sites, but of two—Sites B and E. The sections of the report on the other sites will merely record the reasons for ruling them out.

Although Bill Southworth's report was complex, his decisions were not difficult to make once he had his purpose clearly in mind. The temptation, of course, was to include all of the impressive statistics which he had obtained on Sites A, C, and D, despite the fact that they were no longer relevant. Frequently the effective selection of material for a communication involves the omission of available but irrelevant materials. The writer of a manual for servicing equipment will seldom need to include complete information on how the equipment is constructed or on the principles of mechanics that are involved, though he may be an expert on both subjects. A director of public relations, writing a report to be distributed to stockholders about a prolonged strike, will select from a vast amount of information only those matters which are of significant concern to them.

Here again we come back to the readers. Their needs govern what is included. The president who reports to department or division heads on a new law's significance for their company will select certain materials from a logically organized overall view of the situation. But when writing a memorandum for distribution to workers, the president must select other materials. A message to stockholders will require a third selection. In each instance, the purpose of the communication will determine the selection. The president may need to encourage department heads to consider means for taking best advantage of the law's provisions, to clarify for workers in the plant the company's attitude toward the law, to head off a demand by stockholders for increased dividends.

No one group can be effectively influenced by exhaustive analysis of a total situation. What concerns the stockholder may not concern the worker on the assembly line. And what affects the department head may not interest the stockholder.

The writer should not forget, however, to check that enough material has been selected to carry out the purpose and satisfy the reader. This is most important when writing to a reader less familiar with a situation than the writer. If a specifications writer, for example, does not indicate that copper wire capable of handling 2300 volts is required, the purchasing agent may order the wrong wire.

A writer must, then, consider the readers and the real purpose of a communication, and select only those materials—but *all* of those materials—that are needed to persuade the readers to think, feel, or act in a particular way. Materials which are not relevant to this aim must be discarded.

Sometimes the information or materials a writer should select will be obvious. In some instances, for example, the subject may dictate what must be included. At other times, however, the strategy to be employed must be the determining factor. A useful technique at this point is to stage a scenario—suggest an approach and then play out the scene in one's mind: "How would they react if I gave short shrift to the arguments against and dwelt mostly on the arguments for? Jones knows about that competing process over in Sweden. Koskiosko may, too. Do I need to put in a paragraph about it to help persuade them that I know what I'm talking about, or are my arguments strong enough to do that? GAF 72 is a long, narrow room. Should I use visuals for my talk, or should I use the blackboard? In my written report, how full a set of statistics do I need in the tables to make my argument clear?" Visualizing how one's readers or listeners will respond to particular information or materials can help one decide what to use.

3. Order Materials

The proper selection of materials will not automatically guarantee an effective communication, however. One may collect the finest building materials obtainable, but still not have a house until the materials are fitted together to form a carefully articulated whole. The parts of a watch spread out on a table do not communicate the hour of the day; they must be carefully put together before accurate communication is possible. So it is with verbal communication. J. C. Smith, in Chapter 4, had all the material he needed to write his memorandum about the salvage of the damaged barge and its cargo. But, as we have seen, he still wrote an ineffective communication, because he did not put the material in appropriate order.

Order, like selection, depends on the purpose and on the reader. For example, when explaining why a machine has been modified, an engineer not only will select different information but will also use a different approach and
132 a different ordering of that information in presenting his case to his department

head than in presenting it to an operator on the assembly line. If he uses an order based on the most logical organization of the materials in his own mind, he may not be successful with either.

Order will also be affected by the nature of the communication. A routine report of a watchman's activities during his tour of duty and a report on the growth of the aluminum industry will probably use chronological order. A sales report may use a geographical order. A progress report may be organized according to types of problems met and solved. A personnel report may be organized by rank, by salary bracket, or by length of service. But always the most effective order will be the one which will be most useful to the reader.

Staging a scenario is also an effective method of testing different ways of ordering information and materials. "Persuading Garibaldi that the strategy I propose will be effective is my biggest problem in this report. How will he react if I begin by attacking the strategy he proposed last week? What if I merely mention it in passing after I propose my strategy?" Playing that scene out in one's mind can be helpful in determining both order and emphasis. A similar technique is actually putting oneself into Garibaldi's shoes to try to determine how he will react to the different orderings and emphases.

4. Check Against Purpose

5. Write

6. Recheck Against Purpose

We need say no more about the last three steps here, since what we said about them in discussing the planning of letters and memos (Chapter 4) is equally applicable to reports.

FLEXIBILITY IN PLANNING

In actual practice, the planning and writing of a report, even by competent writers, is seldom as tidy as the progression of our six steps suggests. Sometimes, for example, the process of ordering materials (step 3) will disclose a gap which will send a writer back to look for missing information (step 2). Checking against purpose (step 4) or rechecking against purpose (step 6) may reveal a similar gap, or a flaw in the structure of an analysis or an argument that may require a different ordering of materials (and thus a return to step 3). The purpose of steps 4 and 6 is precisely to catch such problems before the document is sent out.

Experience has shown, however, that the writer who recognizes the function of each of the steps and moves through them in as orderly a way as possible can control the materials and thus fashion a piece of writing to fit the purpose in a way that a writer who is less orderly cannot.

ILLUSTRATIVE MATERIALS

1.

A group of engineering educators has formulated the stages which they feel are essential to the solution of a problem in their profession. Compare the stages listed below with those we have suggested for preparing a communication.

Stage 1. Define the problem.
Collect and analyze the facts in relation to the original question in order to fully discover and define the problem.
Stage 2. Plan its treatment.
Determine what values, principles, attitudes, and basic practices are applicable to the problem. Plan the means of dealing with the facts in the light of these ways of approach.
Stage 3. Execute the plan.
Carry through the plan so as to reach a decision, product, or result. (Often the decision does not end the problem but clarifies or changes the issue so that the problem is started over in a new aspect.)
Stage 4. Check the work as a whole before using the solution.
Go over the results, first systemically, then realistically in terms of use, and at last with reference to the general knowledge and experience of that field.
Stage 5. Learn and generalize if possible.
Take thought to find what can be learned that may be of use in future problems.

Note also the following comments on the list:

These stages cannot be considered a rigid sequence to be followed in handling any problem. Often the solver first must go through the problem roughly in order to discover its essentials before attempting a thorough treatment. Often also he may have to return to prior stages, or even repeat them all, as he gains enlightenment in the course of developing the problem. And whenever appropriate, one or more of the following functions must be performed in connection with any stage, or in connection with the problem as a whole.

Function 1.   Simplification
a.   by restricting assumptions;
b.   by condensed, exact statement in words or in symbols.
Function 2.   Alternation between analysis and insight.
Function 3.   Checking validity, both systematically and realistically in terms of use.

Function 4.   Using all that can be learned by experience as the solution proceeds as a basis for correction and as a guide to future steps, even if this involves radical change in the problem or its treatment.[1]

2.

Below is a statement by Richard I. Felver, a professor and consultant in industrial design, in which he indicates how he and his colleagues solve their problems.[2] *Compare his statement with that of the engineering educators and with our suggestions for solving a writing problem. What elements do the three statements have in common? Where do they differ? Why?*

In the design of practical things we have a more or less professional system that we follow. Usually there is a statement of the problem, but this, even when stated clearly, is usually wrong or inadequate. A problem arises from a conflict between criteria and a situation. Here we start. We study the situation: the background of the problem. This may be called a study, a survey, an analysis, or the like. It is essentially an orderly observation. Next we find that some things are related to other things and in particular ways. We begin to structure the situations. Now it is time to investigate the criteria. These too we order into a structure. Gradually the real problem comes to light. Sometimes cold hard logic may solve the problem, but we cannot trust this answer. We question if a better, more significant, or more effective solution is possible. This is the agony of integrity. If we do not arrive at this point and pass through it, we are at best intelligent, competent hacks.

We continue our work. Our real answer must come to us with its own authority. It is more than logically right; there is conviction—it is creative! This creative answer may come in a series of little insights or may burst perplexingly into our consciousness. It may take its own good time—hours, days, months, yes even years! We must, if necessary, wait in humble deliberation. If we have completed our study, checked it carefully, and explored all possible avenues to the true answer and nothing comes, we quit, rest, try something else. Then in the black deep inside of us, there seems to be a rearranging, a changing, a gradual reorganization going on without our conscious awareness. Then when awakening, shaving, lifting a piece of food to our mouth, or rising from a seat in a street car, we suddenly know the true answer, and we may excitedly say to a stranger, "That's right, right, right." He looks at us as if to say, "You are mad, mad, mad."

We are not finished yet. These flashes of insight can be wrong or only partial. Now we are back in the light, however, and we can use our tools of logic and common sense. We check our solution against the situation. Most likely, even when we are most clearly creative, there is quite a bit of

---

[1] We are grateful to Professor B. Richard Teare, Jr., for permission to use his statement.
[2] We are grateful to Professor Felver for permission to use his statement.   **135**

adjusting to do. Sometimes the necessary adjusting ruins the solution, so back into the well we go again.

Eventually through faith we get the job done. The client asks sometimes, "How did you come to think of that?" And we may reply, "Only God knows!" He laughs, thinking it a joke. He doesn't know that it is the truth.

3.

The following flow charts describe the process by which a document is designed.[3] The first chart, prepared by American Institutes for Research of Washington, D.C., describes the general process for all documents. The second describes how one type of document, a proposal, is prepared in a division of a large American industrial firm.

Document Design as a Process*

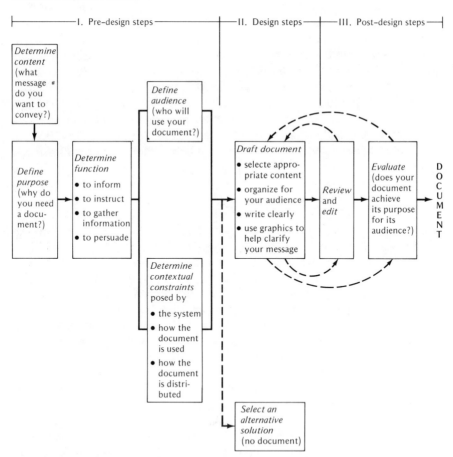

*Reprinted with permission of American Institutes for Research, Washington, D.C.

[3] "Document design" includes both the writing and the visual design of letters, memos, reports, proposals, and other business and government documents.

Proposal Process

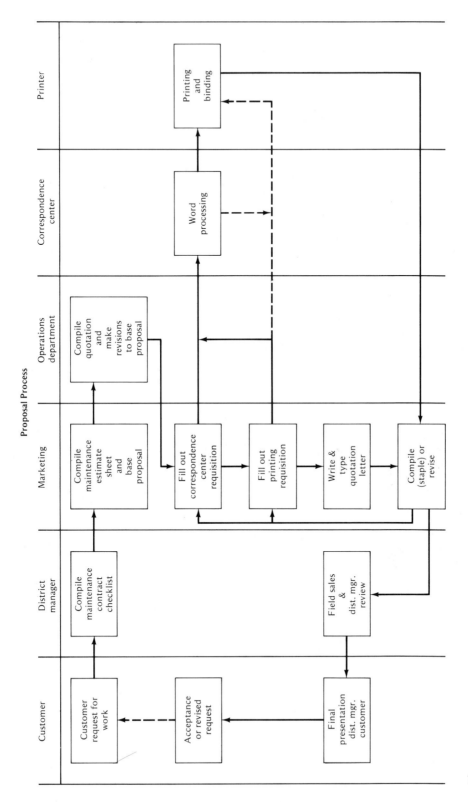

PROBLEMS

Do the planning necessary for one or more of the problems at the end of Chapter 8. Make your notes complete enough so that they will be useful to you in doing the writing necessary to solve the problem.

8

Ordering and Presenting Information

In this book we return again and again to a single concept: a communication—written or oral—can be judged only by how well it achieves the results desired by the writer or speaker. One cannot measure the effectiveness of a piece of writing without considering the writer's purpose and the reader for whom the communication is intended.

HOW MANAGEMENT USES REPORTS

How will its readers use a business report? Let us take a specific example from a large corporation: a report on the building and testing of a solid-state DC amplifier. The distribution list shows that it went to the vice-president for engineering, to the assistant to the vice-president for home products, to the manager of the patent department, to three staff engineering managers, to personnel in two research departments, and to line personnel in fifteen different operating departments.

The vice-president for engineering receives dozens of reports of this kind every day. Even if he did nothing else, he would not be able to read them all. And he has many other things to do. Still, he must be informed about new possibilities. In today's highly competitive market, corporations spend huge sums preparing for the future. They must make the most of the products of research and development.

To keep up with engineering activities in his own company, therefore, this vice-president and his staff must be highly efficient. Each morning his secretary gives him a list of the reports which have come in the day before. She gives him many other things at the same time: the rough drafts of two speeches he is to give the next week, a batch of letters to be answered, the information that he will need to take to a meeting with the president, management-development forms on which he has to rate several of his assistants, the testimony of the president of a competing company before a House of Representatives subcommittee inquiring into monopolistic practices in industry, a series of new regulations from the Patent Office in Washington, a report on an equipment failure which stopped production for three hours in a plant with 2500 employees, and a schedule of appointments and conferences which leaves him about forty minutes of reading time. Unforeseen problems that arise during the day will probably cut into even that short period.

The vice-president reads quickly down the list, pausing occasionally to put a check beside the titles of those reports he wants to see, among them "A New Breed of Solid-state DC Amplifier." His secretary then brings him the checked reports. Opening the one on top of the pile, he glances through the abstract on the title page: ". . . capable of accepting a number of isolated DC input signals and providing these with a power gain of approximately 105 . . . time of response . . . 3 milliseconds . . . quite stable . . . less than .5-percent drift . . . power gains . . . 108 . . . input level of 10-6 watts. . . ." The abstract concludes: "The amplifier can be used in a wide range of industrial applications when high performance solid-state nonthermionic reliability is needed." Turning to the distribution list, he notes who has received copies. Then he says to his secretary, "Send a memo to A. V. Smith in Product Development asking her if the amplifier described in development report 703-21-49 (3) will solve our problem at Cleveland. She has a copy of it. Then call Development and have them send a copy to Will Frank at Brownsville. I think he'd be interested in it." Before handing the report back to the secretary he glances down the table of contents and looks at the name on the front cover: "Milligan? Must be new."

The next report that he picks up is entitled "Heat Sinks." He had checked it on the list because he knew that the company was having difficulty cooling power transistors in several new products that it was developing. Opening the cover, he finds text: no title page, no identifying report number, no abstract— not even a heading; just 28 lines of type, which begin:

The purpose of the work described was to achieve two goals. The first goal was to learn. . . .

Thinking that he can find out something by checking out the conclusions, he flips through the report looking for them. He stops turning pages to look at a photograph immediately following page 5. Beneath the picture he reads:

Plate I

Photograph of several heat sinks and surface finishes that were tested. (Refer to "Heat Sink Designations.")

Top row, left to right: 1c, 1d, 1p.

Middle row: 2b, 2c, 2g, 2f.

Front row: 3a, 3b, 5c.

He turns back to page 5, but finds nothing helpful there. The items described on page 5 are 5d, 5e, 5f, 6, 7a, 7b, 7c, 7d, and 7e. He finally finds 1c described on page 2. Item 1d is also described on page 2; 1p on page 3; and 2b, 2c, 2g, 2f, 3a, 3b, and 5c on page 4.

More and more irritated at not being able to get what he wants from the report, he resumes his hunt for the conclusions. Since the body of the report is not separated in any way from the appendices, he has difficulty in locating the end of it. Finding at last what appears to be the first of many graphs, he turns back to the preceding page, page 14. No heading indicates *Conclusion,* so he turns to page 13, and then to pages 12, 11, and 10. Failing to find a *Conclusion* section, he moves to the end of the text and begins to read in the middle of page 14: "The fabrication of the sink discussed above was a preliminary step toward a final design being developed by F. E. Jones of this department." Since that paragraph obviously does not contain the conclusion, he goes on to the next: "It appears that the Redding sink is about as efficient a design as can be made practically. . . . Some improvement . . . ; this test was planned but not completed."

Looking at the end of the report for the distribution list, the vice-president does not find one. Returning to the cover, he notes that there is no identification number. He looks at the name of the author: Taylor. Thoroughly annoyed, he snaps on his dictating machine and dictates the following memo:

Subject: Reporting in the Development Department

To: Robert M. Hogan, Manager, Development Department

From: Arthur M. Greenberg, Vice-President, Engineering

Eubank Taylor has been with us long enough to have learned how to write a decent report. But his recent opus on "Heat Sinks" is a mess:

1. The title is too general: what, specifically, about heat sinks was he looking into?

2. The report has no: identifying number
    abstract or summary
    headings or subheadings
    tabs to separate sections
    distribution list

3. If the report has conclusions and recommendations, they are well hidden.

I assume that since you assigned the investigation, it was important. Please have Taylor rewrite the report so that I can tell *quickly* what the problem is and why it is important, what he found out, and what he recommends. This sort of thing gives me heartburn.

Fortunately Milligan's report on "A New Breed of Solid-state DC Amplifiers" worked as an antacid. It told me succinctly everything I wanted to know. Is he a new man? I'd like to meet him.

The two reports that we have discussed are not fictitious. We have them in our files. The first was arranged so that the vice-president could find what he wanted in less than two minutes. The second was not arranged. The material was presented in a solid mass. The vice-president spent almost five minutes looking for what he wanted and did not find it. If he hadn't asked for a revision, the report would eventually have been filed somewhere without ever having been considered by the person who might have used it to solve a crucial problem plaguing the company's new products.

There are other ramifications, too. Both Milligan and Taylor made an impression on the vice-president. The episode that we have just described is a vivid demonstration of the truth of the statement "Every report is an application either for promotion or demotion." Taylor's research may have been every bit as significant and as skillfully carried out as Milligans's; but his only reward is a black mark against his name in the vice-president's book.

Milligan's report on the solid-state DC amplifier was sent to many other people besides the vice-president. The assistant to the vice-president for home products examined it in much the way that the vice-president for engineering did. Two of the three staff engineering managers skimmed the full report, read the conclusions carefully, and passed it on to subordinates for more careful reading and evaluation. Someone in the patent department read the abstract and table of contents, skipped the introduction, read the sections on switching principles and circuits, and examined parts of two of the three appendices carefully. In the research department the abstract was read and the report filed.

In one of the operating departments, the engineering manager read the entire report carefully, appendices and all; then he reread it and gave it to his assistant, who also examined it minutely. The two men then discussed it and passed it on to a subordinate for a cost analysis. He examined the appendices even more minutely. Two people in Product Development also read the report from cover to signature and studied the appendices.

THE PARTS OF A REPORT

A report should be so constructed that readers can pick it up and get what they need from it: the title only, the abstract, the summary, the whole report, or the whole report with supporting materials. A good report moves in several stages from the very general (the title) to the very specific (the appendices). Each appendix is full of detail; the report itself will contain some detail from the appendices but is primarily devoted to generalizations based on precise results recorded in them; the summary, the abstract, and the table of contents all cover the same ground as the report, but each is more general than the body of the report. Most general of all is the title.

The report, then, can be thought of in terms of an abstraction ladder:

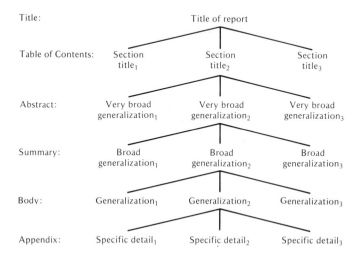

The number of items which make up each level decreases as we go up the ladder.

1. The Title

The "title of report," then, is a single abstraction based upon hundreds, or even thousands, of specific details in the report itself. The whole report is structured like a pyramid.

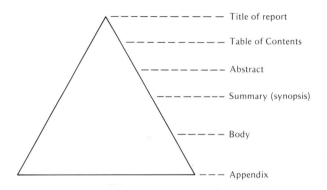

Even at the very top of the pyramid, however, the report writer must be careful not to be too general, too abstract. If the title is so general that it does not indicate the precise subject covered, the report may not be read at all. Thus a title should not read "Ultra-high Vacuum Valve" but "Electromagnetically Operated Ultra-high Vacuum Valve"; not "Molded Plastic Parts" but "Dimensional Stability of Molded Plastic Parts"; not "Sales Personnel" but "An Analysis of the Management Potential of 42 Staff Sales Personnel at Pittsburgh"; not "Polyethylene Marketing" but "A Program for Increasing Polyethylene Sales in the Next Five Years."

2. The Abstract

The level below the title is the abstract, a very brief summary of the report's contents. An abstract can either describe or inform. A *descriptive abstract,* which merely gives topics and subtopics, is likely to be awkward and does not give much information:

> The history of the study of cavitation is surveyed. The necessary preconditions of cavitation are discussed, and cavitation initiation is presented. Cavitation collapse and bubble oscillations are then considered. Finally, some of the effects of cavitation are explored.

An *informative abstract* is much more useful. It states the problem, briefly explains how the investigation was conducted, and mentions important conclusions and recommendations.

> The Fine Point Jewelry Company withdrew their advertising from *Suburban Life* magazine on the grounds that the stories in it were not of the type to appeal to readers who would buy their jewelry. A recent study by Muller indicates a positive correlation between the socioeconomic status of magazine readers and the socioeconomic status of the characters they generally read about. An analysis of the stories appearing in *Suburban Life* for the past year showed that the characters were largely from the international set rather than from suburban areas and were more often in the $200,000-a-year bracket than in the $40,000–$50,000 bracket. Thus our study indicates that *Suburban Life* is not appealing to the market that it was designed to reach. Interviews of a random sampling of subscribers support this conclusion.

An abstract is generally held to 100 or 125 words. If it is longer, it ceases to serve its purposes. Many companies type abstracts on index cards for filing in a central catalog. Others circulate a weekly bulletin composed entirely of the abstracts of reports published during the week. In some companies, top management personnel regularly see only these bulletins. If they want a report, they send for it.

A good abstract is also very useful to the company librarian, who is responsible not only for the reference library but also for the file of company reports. He or she cannot possibly read all the reports written in the company if it is of any size, but can keep up with the abstracts. A librarian who knows what is in a report can bring it to the attention of those to whom it may be useful and thus can give it wider circulation and increase its usefulness.

3. The Table of Contents

At about the same level of abstraction as the descriptive abstract is the table of contents. An outline of the report, it contains major headings and subheadings. For long reports it will also list sub-subheadings. Thus the reader may use it not only to find the various sections but also to see how the report is organized. The table of contents almost always follows the abstract, but usually precedes the summary. It may be supplemented by special tables of contents for illustrations, figures, or charts. A look at the front of this book will show how helpful a detailed table of contents for a longer document can be. Even for a report as short as twelve pages, a brief table of contents can be quite helpful.

4. The Summary

Since very little can be said in a 100- or 125-word abstract, reports which contain more than a hundred pages usually require a summary as well. Introductory summaries serve a double purpose. They provide a reasonably complete resume of a report for those who cannot read it all. They also help the person who *will* read the entire report. In any complex mechanism the function of individual parts is difficult to discover unless one understands the operation of the mechanism as a whole; thus the function of individual parts of a complex report may be difficult to follow unless one is given an overview of the entire report. A good summary provides such an overview.

Rules for the length of summaries vary. Some companies insist that they be held to one page. Others suggest that they should be from 2 to 5 percent as long as the report itself. A company's rules probably reflect the kind and size of the typical report prepared for its executives and the ways in which it is used.

A summary reproduces the main points of the report. It should be so written that it can stand alone. Like the abstract, therefore, it must include conclusions and recommendations if it is to be useful. In long technical reports, and frequently in technical books, a summary usually appears at the head of each chapter.

5. The Body of the Report

The report itself is at the next lower level of abstraction. It supplies more detail than the abstract, summary, or table of contents. Its first section is generally an *introduction,* which discusses the purpose and background of the   145 study which has been made. It tells not only what the problem was and why the study was undertaken, but also what limitations, if any, were imposed. Where relevant, it also includes a history of the problem, a short summary of earlier studies, a summary of the required technical background, and a definition of the way each important term will be used. When the report does not include a separate section on procedure, a brief discussion of that may also appear in the introduction. In short, the introduction should give the reader the background needed to understand, evaluate, and use what follows.

About the *discussion* section, the heart of the report, we need say little. Everything in the preceding chapter about organization is relevant here. Special attention should be devoted to the use of appropriate headings and subheadings to emphasize the organization of the material, as we have done in this book. Thus a reader who merely thumbs through a report looking at the headings is able to obtain a clear picture of how the materials are organized. In long reports where the subsections are also long, the author can help the reader further by placing at the top of each page the title of the appropriate section or subsection.

A section devoted to *conclusions* or *recommendations,* or both, generally follows the discussion section of a report. Here all of the separate conclusions recorded in earlier sections are brought together, usually listed in decreasing order of importance. They may be analyzed briefly, if necessary, so that readers who are interested *only* in the conclusions are not left with a mere listing which they must organize into a meaningful whole. The recommendations section indicates action that should be taken on the basis of the study being reported. In this section both conclusions and recommendations should be dealt with in fuller detail than in the abstract and the summary.

Certain reports may also call for a *bibliography,* which lists sources of information relevant to the study.

6. The Appendix

The appendix, always the final section, represents the next and lowest level of abstraction. Here the interested reader can find the wealth of detail which supports the writer's conclusions and recommendations. It may contain charts, graphs, tables, drawings, pictures, glossaries of terms, or any other materials required for a full understanding of the situation covered in the report. If it contains many items, the appendix should carry its own table of contents.

A perennial problem is how much of the supporting evidence (tables, graphs, and so on) should appear in the text and how much should be relegated to the appendix. One useful generalization we can offer is that the text should be as uncluttered as possible. There are, of course, always special situations. One company president we know, who was originally an accountant, can read tables of statistics much more easily than prose. He complains continually that he doesn't get enough figures in his reports. His subordinates face an unusual hurdle—but one which they cannot ignore.

Another useful generalization is that the more technical the report, the more

tables and graphs will be required in the text. One would expect, for example, that the body of a report on a new distillation process would include more tables and graphs than would that of a report on a proposed new corporate identity program.

Most of us prefer to have generalizations presented in words. Graphs and short tables, of course, help a writer to buttress arguments. But if there are too many, they will not only break up each page, making it harder to read, but also lengthen the report. Furthermore, fitting them into a page of text or placing large ones so that they are on the page facing the appropriate text is costly. By packaging a report so that readers can examine text and appendices at the same time, the writer can move many such materials out of the text and still allow readers to examine text and data together. In the next chapter we will suggest methods for facilitating such parallel reading.

7. The Distribution List

The distribution list does not fit into the pattern that we have been describing. It is a device for directing the report to the proper readers and for letting everyone who sees the report know to whom it is being sent. If it is short, it may appear on the cover letter or memo, or on the title page. If it is long, it will probably appear at the end of the report, after the appendix.

ORGANIZING AN EFFECTIVE REPORT

A good report, then, is built up in layers or levels of abstraction. The farther one gets into it, the more details one finds:

First level	Title
Second level	Abstract and Table of Contents
Third level	Summary (if any)
Fourth level	Body of Report
Fifth level	Appendices

Some specialized reports carry additional sections. These are easily fitted into the pattern described above. To determine where a section belongs, one need only think of its purpose, its relation to the rest of the report, and the use to which it will be put.

Reports are best written backwards, that is, built up from the lowest level of abstraction. Before any writing starts, a great deal of research will naturally have been done. The information gathered will ultimately be presented in the appendix. When the data begin to take some form, work on the report itself may begin. As we have suggested, it helps to start planning before all research and experimentation have been completed: planning often brings to the surface significant gaps in thinking or in data. When all the materials have been gathered, the writer can begin on the body of the report in earnest. Once that is completed, the summary can be written, then the abstract. Some people save the highest level of abstraction, the title, for last, using only a working title while the report is in progress.

After a report is completed, the writer still has one more device for making sure that a particular reader does not miss any part that may be especially useful. A cover letter summarizing briefly those aspects in which that individual will be most interested can direct attention to the pertinent passages. The writer should be sure, however, that he or she knows the recipient's interest well. It would be much better not to write such a letter at all than to cause the recipient to waste time on irrelevant materials or to skip over something important.

ORDERING THE SECTIONS OF A REPORT

Inexperienced report writers frequently ask about the "proper" order for the sections of the report. There is no one best sequence. Every aspect of any communication is governed finally by the material to be communicated, the person or group communicating, the audience at which the communication is aimed, and the real purpose which it is designed to serve.

In one company, for example, the development laboratory has issued an instruction sheet for report writing which states that its reports should contain most of the following elements, in the order listed:

1. Abstract (not more than 50 words)
2. Summary of report
3. Statement of problem
4. Analysis of critical elements
5. Analysis of possible approaches
6. Statement and justification of approach selected
7. Experimental technique employed
8. Experimental data obtained
9. Results of experiments
10. Analysis of results
11. Appendices

The research laboratory of the same company organizes its reports in this way:

1. Synopsis
2. Introduction
3. Conclusions, or Summary
4. Recommendations
5. Experimental procedure
6. Results
7. Discussion
8. Appendices

A section of the company's computer department issues the following instructions:

1. Title page, including a one-sentence description of the report
2. Table of contents, generally reserved for reports of 25 pages or more
3. Body of report

The format for the body of the report is left up to the writer; however, the following principles are to be employed. Our reports will be read and acted upon by men who will probably not have time to delve personally into the details of the report but may wish to assign subordinates to do so. Therefore, the report should be divided into three parts.

    A. Abstract, one-half page or less

The abstract should contain enough information so that the executive, if he so desires, can take action without reading the rest of the report.

    B. Text

The purpose of the text is to explain in detail to someone who is an experienced engineer (but not necessarily an expert in the subject of the report) the nature of the problem and its solution. Since we work closely with other organizations, this section should acknowledge the help of persons in other groups who have contributed to it.

    C. Appendices

These should contain sufficient supporting information so that all the work reported may be checked.

4. Distribution list

One of the major automobile companies suggests that its technical report writers follow this outline:

INTRODUCTORY SECTION

    Title page; Preface; Table of Contents

SUMMATION SECTION

    Subject; Object; Conclusion; Recommendations

TECHNICAL SECTION

    Parts or Materials Tested; Apparatus; Procedures; Results; Discussion

GRAPHIC-AIDS SECTION

    Tables of Data; Curves; Drawings; Photographs

SUPPLEMENTARY SECTION (APPENDIX)

    References; List of Symbols; Sample Calculations

The company's technical-report manual recommends this general organization "for major, minor, and one-page reports," but adds that the "length and complexity of the report" will determine how many of the headings should be used.

Another major producer of automobiles recommends: a preface, if necessary; a table of contents; a list of illustrations; and the body of the report, which should include an introduction, conclusions (recommendations or findings), a discussion, and appendices, in that order.

Such different instructions, even within one company, do not necessarily mean disagreement about what makes a good report. They indicate, rather, differences in material, purpose, or audience. What is just right for one department or company may not be quite right for another. Each, therefore, works out a format which will be effective for the particular type of reporting it does.

IMPROVING REPORTS

Report writers are showing more and more ingenuity in communicating their information. The research laboratory of one company, for example, recently introduced magazine-like spreads of pictures in its annual report to highlight certain parts of its story. The technique was so successful that the laboratory manager plans to use it more extensively in his next annual report. The manager explained his interest in such matters by saying, "Our only product is reports. If we don't produce readable ones, we'll go out of business." His attitude has spread through his department, with excellent results.

The attitude of supervisors is always very important. Not only can they impress on their subordinates the value of reports, but they can also help them to prepare good ones. When supervisors press their subordinates to turn reports out rapidly so that they can move on to the next job, management is likely to complain of poor reports. The report writers then find themselves in an impossible situation because, as we have just seen, the report may be their major—if not their only—product.

Management can also take active steps to improve reports. The head of one development department, concerned because her people were not writing enough of them, decided to make reporting easier by breaking it down into steps. Accordingly, she set up three methods of communicating engineering information: information statements (nicknamed "Infos"), engineering memoranda, and engineering reports. Infos are brief notes about interesting developments which occur while a project is being worked on. They do not have to be approved, have no special format, should not take much time to prepare, and are distributed only within the department. Engineering memoranda are informal engineering reports distributed within the development department and to selected engineering personnel in the operating divisions. Written periodically (although not necessarily at regular intervals) during an investigation, they generally include some of the following:

1. A statement of the problem
2. The approach taken
3. Results of experiments

4. Preliminary conclusions
5. Possible applications
6. Future work planned

The formal engineering report, written when a project is completed, tells the whole story and has all the customary paraphernalia.

The development department manager feels that by encouraging her engineers to begin with Infos, which they can dictate, which are relatively short, and which require no red tape, she can help them get going. Several Infos lead up to a memorandum, and the memoranda on a project give engineers a good start toward writing a formal report.

A supervisor can also make it routine to discuss reports briefly with new or relatively inexperienced subordinates before they write them. Young men and women just entering the business world have little conception of where reports go or how they are used. Thus they cannot write for an audience, even if they understand that they should do so. Instead they tend to set their ideas down as they would organize them for their own use. Needless to say, the result is inadequate communication. If a supervisor devotes a few minutes to describing the persons to whom a report is going, their positions, and what they will want to know, the young writer will be encouraged to write with those persons' needs in mind. After several brief discussions with the supervisor, he or she should be able to prepare good reports. But the instruction must begin before the report is written, rather than after. The writer who has begun to put material on paper may well interpret well-meant suggestions at that stage as unfavorable criticism.

Using the positive approach—helping a person to do a job properly instead of correcting his or her mistakes afterwards—will save time and energy for both the supervisor and the writer, establish a better relationship between them, and save money for the company. The same results may be obtained from discussions between a supervisor and an experienced writer who has taken a new job.

Convinced of the economy of preventing rather than curing error, one supervisor regularly sits down with each subordinate who is about to start work on a report. Together they draw up a tentative distribution list. As each name is added to the list, the supervisor mentions the person's position and the reasons why he or she may be interested in the completed report. Thus he establishes a painless routine for ensuring the necessary discussion of the audience without giving the impression that he is "riding herd" on his subordinates.

Management, then, may establish a favorable environment and sound procedures which produce good report writing; on the other hand, it may unknowingly cause poor report writing. One irate division manager showed us a report which could only be called a monstrosity. It was three inches thick. It had no table of contents, no appendices, no summary—nothing to help the manager find his way through it. In order to get anything out of it, he would have had to read the whole report, an eight- or ten-hour job. When we talked 151 with him, he was going to fire the writer of the report. But after a little investigation, we had to tell him that he would have to shoulder at least part of the blame.

Several months before, he had called his department heads together and told them that the company might profit by securing a license to produce in the United States a new building material developed in England. He asked each of them to write a report on the effect that obtaining the license would have on the operations of his department. One department head was assigned, in the manager's words, to "coordinate" the various reports and "pull them together." When they arrived, the coordinator didn't know quite what to do with them. Though some overlapped, as a group they did not give a complete picture. There were big gaps, some of which he tried to fill by inserting materials that he obtained from the licenser in England. These supplied much of the missing information; but since they were designed for other purposes, they increased the overlapping. Furthermore, the English materials were on different levels of technical complexity: some were technical reports, some were technical news releases, and some were advertising brochures. Written over a period of five years, they sometimes presented conflicting information. The coordinator tried to fill some of the remaining gaps by writing several sections himself. When finally gathered between covers, the "report" was a massive collection of undigested materials.

Why was the division manager at fault? He had given the department head an impossible task. He had not asked the department head to write the report. (As he well knew, the busy department head had no time to do the whole job.) He had asked him to "coordinate" the studies of a group of men at his own level. Understandably, the department head was reluctant to tear their reports apart and rewrite them, even if he had the time to do so. The result was a sorry compromise.

What should the manager have done? He should have selected a member of his staff, perhaps a young man or woman with promise, given him or her time to *write* (not coordinate) the report, and asked the department heads to supply the writer with appropriate *materials* (not reports). Thus the writer, with adequate time to do this important job, could have shaped the materials into a meaningful, coherent study of the potential effect of adding the new product to the division's line.

The coordinator, of course, was also partly at fault. When he received the assignment, he should have said immediately that he would call a short planning session later at which each of the department heads would stake out the area his material would cover. Thus the obvious gaps and overlappings, at least, would have shown up immediately and could have been eliminated. He should also have asked that each person include an informative abstract from which he could build an introductory summary. He should have provided a table of contents to guide the division manager through the report. He might also have provided tabs or sectional dividers. He would still have put together a clumsy report, but at least he would have done his best with the time and

means at his disposal.

OTHER TYPES OF BUSINESS COMMUNICATION

We have demonstrated above in some detail how the concepts we developed in earlier chapters can be applied to the formal report. We could apply the same approach to other forms of business communication which we have not discussed in any detail: memorandum reports, research memoranda; papers for professional societies and journals; articles for business and industrial magazines; engineering data letters; instruction manuals, specifications, maintenance standards; proposals. If we were to do so, however, we should have to cover much the same ground for each. As one can see by comparing Chapters 4 and 7, the same basic principles apply to them all. The reader who understands these principles will have no difficulty in applying them to the preparation of any type of communication. Some of the illustrative materials which follow will help in making these applications.

ILLUSTRATIVE MATERIALS

1.

Many companies are interested in improving the reports that their professional people write. In seeking a solution to this problem, the Westinghouse Electric Corporation conducted a study among its management personnel to find out "what management looks for in engineering reports." The results of that study appear on page 154.

2.

As we have seen in Illustrative Material 5 of Chapter 2, the United States Army recommends the writing of "performance-oriented" rather than "topic-oriented" training literature. Topic-oriented writing, says its Guidebook for the Development of Army Training Literature, *"places heavy demands on the reading, studying, and conceptualizing skills of the user"; performance-oriented writing, on the other hand, minimizes such demands. The following statements explain the difference between the two.*

WHAT IS TOPIC-ORIENTED WRITING?

Topic-oriented writing focuses on the generalizations and concepts which constitute a body of knowledge—it tells "about" a subject area rather than telling "what to do" or "how to do it."

Topic-oriented manuals do not identify a particular user audience. A topic-oriented manual is frequently described as a general reference text, intended for anyone from Private to General.

Topic-oriented writing does not identify subject-related duties and tasks, who might be expected to perform them, or how any given user might perform them. The description of the "body of knowledge" may carry im- 153

Fig. 1 How Managers Read Reports

FREQUENCY OF READING

SECTION OF REPORT

SUMMARY — INTRODUCTION — BODY — CONCLUSIONS — APPENDIX

Table I Questions Asked of Managers

1. What types of reports are submitted to you?
2. What do you look for first in the reports submitted to you?
3. What do you want from these reports?
4. To what depth do you want to follow any one particular idea?
5. At what level (how technical and how detailed) should the various reports be written?
6. What do you want emphasized in the reports submitted to you? (Facts, interpretations, recommendations, implications, etc.)
7. What types of decisions are you called upon to make or to participate in?
8. What type of information do you need in order to make these decisions?
9. What types of information do you receive that you don't want?
10. What types of information do you want but not receive?
11. How much of a typical or average report you receive is useful?
12. What types of reports do you write?
13. What do you think your boss wants in the reports you send him?
14. What percentage of the reports you receive do you think desirable or useful? (In kind or frequency.)
15. What percentage of the reports you write do you think desirable or useful? (In kind or frequency.)
16. What particular weaknesses have you found in reports?

Table II What Managers Want to Know

Problems
What is it?
Why undertaken?
Magnitude and importance?
What is being done? By whom?
Approaches used?
Thorough and complete?
Suggested solution? Best? Consider others?
What now?
Who does it?
Time factors?

New Projects and Products
Potential?
Risks?
Scope of application?
Commercial implications?
Competition?
Importance to Company?
More work to be done? Any problems?
Required manpower, facilities and equipment?
Relative importance to other projects or products?
Life of project or product line?
Effect on Westinghouse technical position?
Priorities required?
Proposed schedule?
Target date?

Tests and Experiments
What tested or investigated?
Why? How?
What did it show?
Better ways?
Conclusions? Recommendations?
Implications to Company?

Materials and Processes
Properties, characteristics, capabilities? Limitations?
Use requirements and environment?
Areas and scope of application?
Cost factors?
Availability and sources?
What else will do it?
Problems in using?
Significance of application to Company?

Field Troubles and Special Design Problems
Specific equipment involved?
What trouble developed? Any trouble history?
How much involved?
Responsibility? Others? Westinghouse?
What is needed?
Special requirements and environment?
Who does it? Time factors?
Most practical solution? Recommended action?
Suggested product design changes?

what to report

Westinghouse ENGINEER

plications for duty and task performance for everyone from the Private to the Unit Commander. However, it's left up to the reader to deduce from this description what duties and tasks should be performed, how they should be performed, and who should perform them.

WHAT IS PERFORMANCE-ORIENTED WRITING?

Performance-oriented writing focuses on the duties and tasks a user is expected to perform and the information he needs in order to perform these duties and tasks—it tells the user "what to do" and where possible, "how to do it."

Performance-oriented manuals identify a particular user audience. To write performance-oriented literature you start by identifying who you expect the major user to be and the subject-related duties and tasks this user will perform. You then translate your knowledge of the subject area into the information and directions this user will need to learn and perform the duties and tasks you have identified.

In performance-oriented writing, information is selected from the "body of knowledge" and organized to place major emphasis upon its application to duty and task performance. It "talks" directly to the user, the duties and tasks he is expected to perform, and how he can perform them. As a result, performance-oriented literature has greater relevance to a job training or job performance setting than topic-oriented literature. The reader does not have to strain the information he needs out of the general pot of knowledge and then wrestle with the "so what should I do about it" question.

3.

How a writer organizes a message should depend upon the needs of the reader, as the following distinction between writer-based and reader-based prose makes clear.[2]

1. DEVELOP A RHETORICAL STRATEGY

Developing a rhetorical strategy necessarily involves a wide range of skills and methods, from the sophisticated ones of Aristotle to simplistic formulas for packing three examples beneath every point. Rather than review some of these familiar methods we will focus here on a new heuristic based on the cognitive needs of the reader. The goal of this heuristic is to transform Writer-Based prose and its typical structures into Reader-Based prose. This rhetorical strategy is designed to help the reader comprehend more of what the writer has to say.

Writer-Based Prose. Writing is inevitably a somewhat egocentric enterprise. It is always easiest to talk to ourselves, and we naturally tend to express ideas in the same patterns in which we store them in our own mind. But if our goal is to communicate to someone else, those patterns in our own

[2] Linda S. Flower and John R. Hayes, "Problem-Solving Strategies and The Writing Process," *College English* 39 (December 1977), pp. 459–460.

head may not be particularly clear or effective for a reader. The writer's job is to translate his/her own train of thought into a rhetorical structure. That is, s/he must translate his/her own egocentric or writer-based organization of information into a reader-based structure that meets the practical and cognitive needs of a reader.

Writer-Based prose is often the natural result of generating ideas; it borrows its structure from either the writer's own discovery process or from a structure inherent in the material the writer examined. For example, papers which start, "Shakespeare wrote three kinds of plays . . ." or "In the economy a business cycle is defined as . . ." often let the writer "print out" his stored knowledge about the subject instead of reshaping that information to a purpose. Writing which depends on a textbook or list structure often buries its point in a mass of related information. Because the writer failed to restructure information to support a conclusion, the job is left to the reader, who may be unwilling or unable to undertake the task.

A second, even more compelling, way to organize a paper is to simply follow the pattern of your own discovery process. ("In studying the stress patterns in this design, the first thing to consider is . . ." or "If income level, then, is a strong indicator of energy consumption, we can start to develop a predictive model which will. . . .") This pattern has the virtue of any form of drama: it keeps interest by withholding closure, if, that is, the audience is willing to wait that long for the point. Unfortunately, most academic and professional readers are impatient and tend to interpret such narrative, step-by-step structures as either wandering and confused (does he have a point?) or as a form of hedging.

Both of these examples of Writer-Based prose have advantages—for the writer. They are an easy and natural way to express one's thought. Furthermore, it is often most efficient to generate ideas in this form. The point is that in constructing a paper, a writer must recognize his/her own use of code words and Writer-Based structures and try to transform them to meet the needs of his/her reader.

Reader-Based Prose. There are many ways to write with a reader in mind. We will offer two heuristics well suited for analytical papers. The first is to set up a paper around the problem it is intended to solve and the conclusion you intend to argue for. Papers organized around problems not only focus a reader's attention, they help the writer subordinate his information to his goals and draw conclusions.

A second technique is to organize ideas in a clear hierarchy or tree. In composing, writers often work from the bottom of a tree up to more inclusive concepts. But readers understand best when they have an overview, when they can see an idea structure from the top down.

2. TEST YOUR RHETORICAL STRATEGY

If you are lucky, you can test the effectiveness of your rhetorical structure on a live reader. Ask someone else to read your writing and to tell you in his own words what he thought you were saying. Use this feedback to compare what you intended with what you actually communicated.

If your friends seem to disappear when they see you coming, you can substitute a Highlight Test which simulates the comprehension process of a typical busy reader. With a highlighter in hand, go through your paper isolating the titles, headings, and topic sentences and conclusions to which position or convention give special significance. These major organizing elements should correspond to the top of your tree structure. They should form a capsule statement of the information you want your reader to focus on and retain. If they don't, you will be giving your reader loud but incorrect cues.

PROBLEMS

1. Until now, proposals made by the Engineering Service Division of the Argonne Construction Company were written by the manager of that division. Because business has increased considerably, however, that responsibility is to be assumed by the division's senior engineers.

   To make sure that the new writers understand both the principles and the process involved, the manager has asked you to write a manual for proposal writing. Using the two flow charts in Illustrative Material 3 of Chapter 7, write the manual (essentially a report on how proposals are written for ESD).

2. At the direction of the president of your company, you made a study of how managers in your company use reports. The facts of the study are outlined in Illustrative Material 1 of this chapter. Using those facts and the principles set out in this chapter, write a report to the president on the results of your study which concludes with a recommendation of a standard report format for the company.

3. Ask a friend to attend a meeting of an organization with you. Each of you should take notes and write up a set of minutes. Compare your minutes and determine the strengths and weaknesses of each.

4. Study the brochures of such government agencies as the National Science Foundation, the National Institute of Education, the National Institutes of Health, or the National Endowment for the Arts or the Humanities. Develop a research project that interests you, and, using the appropriate agency's guidelines, write a research grant proposal.

5. If you are studying for a license, certificate, or degree, write a progress report to your advisor reporting on the work you have completed and what you have still to do. If you are working, write also a report to your supervisor on your progress toward the license, certificate, or degree.

6. If you are currently involved in a project in a course or on the job, write a progress report for your instructor or supervisor.

7. Obtain samples of automobile accident report forms from several insurance companies. For the state insurance commissioner, write an analysis of the similarities and differences in the forms and what you think a complete form should contain.

8. Analyze the parking problems of the commuting students at your college or of your fellow employees and develop a car pooling plan. Write up the plan for presentation to the dean of students or the director of personnel.

9. Your supervisor has asked you to survey *The Wall Street Journal* for the last year and write a report for him on one of the following: changes in government regulations that affect your industry (if you are a student, choose an industry that interests you); recent trends in retailing or marketing; the impact of new scientific discoveries or engineering procedures on your industry; or recent economic trends. (If you prefer, you may choose the trade paper or journal of a specific field or industry instead of *The Wall Street Journal*.) Write the report.

10. Study the photocopying needs in your departmental office and then survey the costs and capabilities of the three or four best photocopiers. (Your Purchasing Office at college or the company at which you work can either provide you with the necessary brochures or help you obtain them.) Do a cost-benefit analysis and write a report to the department head laying out that analysis and recommending a particular copier for office use.

11. Find in a recent issue of *Consumer Reports* a major report on a product that interests you (like sports cars, washing machines, tape recorders, or air conditioners) and write a two-page, double-spaced summary (500 to 600 words) for someone interested in purchasing that product. (Choose a particular person so that you can determine his or her specific needs, and write a report focused on those needs.)

12. Study the availability of beverage and snack machines in a building in which you take classes or work, and survey the interest of your fellow students or fellow workers in the availability of such machines and what they should contain. On the basis of what you discover, write a report recommending the use and placement of such machines. Include in the report a recommendation for a pricing policy. Should prices cover only the cost of the beverages or food, or that cost plus the cost of the necessary electricity; or should they be designed to make a certain profit to be used to support a particular charity?

13. Choose a business, civic, or educational leader to whom you think that your college or the one from which you graduated should give an honorary degree. From the various biographical reference books in the library and as many other sources as you can find (newspaper articles about the person or stories in trade or professional journals) obtain as much information about the person's career and accomplishments as you need to write a persuasive statement to the college's director of public relations proposing that the college honor him or her. Include in your proposal the sources of your information to help persuade the director that the person you are recommending is indeed widely known and respected.

14. Prepare an annotated bibliography of at least ten items on a topic of interest to you, using the following format:

ORDERING AND PRESENTING INFORMATION

Schutte, William M., and Erwin R. Steinberg, *Communication in Business and Industry* (New York: Holt, Rinehart and Winston, 1983)

The authors, college professors of English and communications consultants in industry, "focus on those fundamental principles of communication that a person must master if he or she is to be able to write or speak well in the world of business and industry." The major sections of the book are: Context and Principles (The Climate of Business, Communication Theory, Considering the Audience, and Writing to Inform and Persuade); Writing Letters and Memos; Major Writing Assignments: The Report; Economy, Clarity, and Unity; Reading, Listening, and Speaking; and Applying for a Job. The book will serve best those who have already taken a course in freshman composition.

9

Designing the Page, the Figure, and the Report

In later chapters, we will examine ways in which grammar should reflect meaning to facilitate a reader's understanding of a message. Good layout will also help.

USING LAYOUT TO FACILITATE UNDERSTANDING

The following passage, for example, is reasonably clear:

Unusual maintenance expenses—replacing tires on lift truck and equipping with LPG fuel, $700; restocking machine shop with valves, fittings, etc., $400; cleaning septic tank, $150; and buying slag for yard, $300—increased the total of this category by $1,550.

The same information can be laid out on the page in tabular form to make it even clearer:

Unusual maintenance expenses:	
Replacing tires on lift truck and equipping with LPG fuel	$ 700
Restocking machine shop with valves, fittings, etc.	400
Cleaning septic tank	150
Buying slag for yard	300
Increase in Total	$1,550

In the revision the position of the phrases and the numbers on the page reflects—and thus reinforces—the structure, which was itself designed to reinforce the meaning of the message. Without reading any of the words, one can recognize how the various parts of the revision relate to each other:

Xxxxxxx xxxxxxxxxxx xxxxxxxx:	
Xxxxxxxxx xxxxx xx xxxx xxxxx	$ xxx
Xxxxxxxxxx xxxxxxx xxxx	xxx
Xxxxxxxx xxxxxx xxxx	xxx
Xxxxxx xxxx xxx xxxx	xxx
Xxxxxxxx xx Xxxxx	$x,xxx

The indentation of lines 2–5 indicates that the top line is a comprehensive statement explaining the four indented lines, which in themselves are parallel in meaning and importance. The column on the right provides costs for each line and a total, which is identified, and perhaps characterized, by the statement to the left of the total figure. The layout makes the statement not only easier to read and understand, but perhaps even easier to remember. Certainly the reader can more easily pick out a particular item and its cost from among the four indented items.

Other configurations signal other relationships. Thus in the following table there are two main sets of items, the first with two subsets, the second with three:

Xxxxxxxxxx	
xxxxx	432
xxxxxxxx	685
Xxxxx	1,117
Xxxxxxxxxxxxxx	
xxxxxx	928
xxxxxxxxx	44
xxxx	326
Xxxxx	1,298
XXXXXXXX	2,415

Each of the subsets carries a figure in the column to the right indicating the total number of items in the category involved. Each of the two main items has a subtotal, and there is also a grand total.

BEING CONSISTENT

Every letter, memo, or report should be consistent throughout in use of capitals, lower case, number of spaces for the first identation and succeeding identations, placement of columns, and designation of numbers or letters for main sections and subsections. Thus, for example, if in one section the information is laid out in table form using A, 1, a, (1), (a), the next section should not use I, a, 1, etc.

FURTHER EXAMPLES

A glance at any random sampling of business letters, memos, and reports will demonstrate that writers of such documents too seldom consider how a page will look—too seldom make a page inviting by opening it up for easy reading and comprehension, too seldom use layout to signal and reinforce meaning.

The difference between the versions of the memo about the *Robert Slack* in Chapter 4 tells a worse story than do the revisions of the statement on unusual maintenance expenses. The original is so badly organized that it is difficult for a reader to follow, let alone understand. The revision, of course, is much better organized. But beyond that, it is set down on the page in such a way that the layout alone shows Tom Morton and other readers the relationship of the various parts. Even a quick glance, therefore, gives them information that allows them to move through it efficiently, understand it, and remember its essence. Furthermore, the layout will later enable them to retrieve any particular piece of information quickly and easily.

The writer of the quotation below obviously determined what items were most important to his reader: specifications of the transformers, price, terms of payment, and shipping time. By indenting them, he makes them stand out. Indeed, so effective is the layout that one cannot avoid looking at them first when one glances at the letter. The very look of the letter reveals an understanding of the principles of design, a careful sense of organization, and an awareness of the needs of the customer—all characteristics that a high-technology company in a competitive industry wishes to reflect.

ABC Corporation
123 Kensington Avenue
Houston, TX 77002

Attention: Mr. L. B. Jones, Director of Purchases

Gentlemen:

Reference: Your Inquiry I-2984

Thank you for your inquiry. After careful examination of your requirements, we are pleased to quote the following:

Specifications: Two (2) 10,000 KVA, oil-filled, self-cooled, outdoor transformers, 3 phase, 60 cycles, 55 degree C rise, 22,900 volts delta high voltage to 480 volts wye low voltage, with two 2-½% full capacity taps above and below 22,900 volts.

These transformers will be provided with DEFENDRA, which offers many insulation advantages (see Bulletin 58–454 attached).

Price:	$92,500.00 net each.
	F.O.B. point of shipment with freight prepaid to the common carrier point nearest the first destination and included in the price.
Terms of Payment:	Net within 30 days after date of shipment of each unit.
Shipment:	Both units within 22 weeks from the date of receipt of an order with complete information.

This quotation is subject to the Terms and Conditions on the back of this letter, except that the Warranty is superseded by the "Standard Warranty" contained in Otco Selling Policy 68–888 dated October 31, 1982, as found in your Otco catalog.

To give you some idea of how widely used these transformers are, I have enclosed pictures of four that we have installed in the last six months and a list of companies that now have similar transformers on order with us. We would also be happy to send you whatever performance data would be helpful. You can call me any time at (412) 779-8422 for further information—and to let me know of your decision to place your order with Otco.

Yours very truly,

E. W. Seuratt

Enclosures

FROM MEANING TO GRAMMATICAL STRUCTURE TO LAYOUT

We can demonstrate how the principles we have just advanced build on principles of organization discussed in earlier chapters by taking a poorly written paragraph through several stages of revision. Most of us would characterize the following paragraph as choppy—the sentences go bumpety-bump. The passage is ineffective, however, not because it is choppy but rather because it does not indicate adequately the relationship of its ideas. The choppiness is a symptom, not the basic problem.

TWX is a nationwide teletype system. It is similar to the telephone system in that any machine or group of machines may be called to receive a message. It differs from the telephone system in that only alpha-numeric information may be used. Characters can be sent on-line directly to the receiver. However, normally a tape is made off-line and then sent to the receiving unit at the rate of 106 character words per minute.

The paragraph is simply a collection of related units ordered in an elementary way.

A different organization of the first three sentences will allow the writer to move the reader more easily from the known to the less familiar:

> TWX is a nationwide teletype system, similar to the telephone system in that any machine or group of machines on it may be called to receive a message. It differs from the telephone system in that only alpha-numeric information may be used on it.

It is also possible to indicate to the reader the relationship between two ideas by using a subordinating conjunction to introduce the first of those ideas. Thus the last two sentences in the paragraph may be revised:

> Although characters can be sent on-line directly to the receiver, normally a tape is made off-line and sent to the receiving unit at the rate of 106 character words per minute.

The use of the word "Although" to introduce the statement lets us know right away that there are two ideas coming and what their relationship is. The writer does not wait to establish the relationship until the reader has arrived at the second idea.

With the two changes we have made above, the statement would read:

> TWX is a nationwide teletype system, similar to the telephone system in that any machine or group of machines on it may be called to receive a message. It differs from the telephone system in that only alpha-numeric information may be used on it. Although characters can be sent on-line directly to the receiver, normally a tape is made off-line and sent to the receiving unit at the rate of 106 character words per minute.

By focusing on how best to relate the ideas for the reader, therefore, the writer provides a statement much less choppy than the original one.

By stressing the parallelism of the ideas in sentences two and three of the original statement, the writer may achieve a different effect:

> TWX is a nationwide teletype system which resembles the telephone system in that any machine or group of machines on it may be called to receive the message, but differs in that only alpha-numeric information may be used on it. Although characters can be sent on-line directly to the receiver, normally a tape is made off-line and sent to the receiving unit at the rate of 106 character words per minute.

Once again, the revision relates the ideas in a particular way, but an important byproduct is the elimination of the choppiness.

We can use structure, therefore, to reflect and reinforce meaning. We can
also use layout to reflect and reinforce both meaning and structure:

TWX is a nationwide teletype system which:
a. resembles the telephone system in that any machine or group of machines on it may be called to receive a message; but
b. differs from the telephone system in that only alpha-numeric information may be used on it.

Although characters can be sent on-line directly to the receiver, normally a tape is made off-line and sent to the receiving unit at the rate of 106 character words per minute.

The pattern on the page communicates the relationship of the ideas even before the reader takes in the meaning of the words. Grammatical structure reflects and reinforces meaning; layout reflects and reinforces both. This version, therefore, will be easier to read than the preceding one, easier to understand, and easier to remember. We do not suggest such layout for all parallel statements. But where a passage is very long or difficult, because it either contains technical terminology or seeks to convey subtle or complex meaning, layout which accurately reflects meaning and structure will be very helpful to the reader.

In the following illustration, the writer has recognized the need for special layout, but has not used it effectively:

DESIGN CAPACITY OF TRANSPORTABLE LATHE

1. The lathe is designed to accomodate loads up to 200 tons.
2. The maximum diameter of a component to be machined is 18 feet.
3. The lathe is designed to handle components up to 50 feet in length.

An obvious improvement would be:

DESIGN CAPACITY OF TRANSPORTABLE LATHE

The lathe is designed to accommodate:
1. loads up to 200 tons
2. components (to be machined) up to 18 feet in diameter
3. components (to be machined) up to 50 feet in length

An even better solution, however, would be:

DESIGN CAPACITY OF TRANSPORTABLE LATHE

The lathe is designed to accommodate:
1. loads up to 200 tons
2. components (to be machined) up to:
   a. 18 feet in diameter
   b. 50 feet in length

Once again, the structure makes clear the principle behind the relationship of the ideas, and the layout reflects and reinforces the structure. 165

USING LAYOUT TO SELL A PRODUCT

In a document designed to sell or persuade, layout can be used to emphasize important facts or ideas. Here, for example, is the beginning of a widely distributed sales letter:

Dear   :

We appreciate the opportunity of talking with you regarding the maintenance inspection of your turbine generator. The decision you make in selecting the inspection contractor can have a significant effect on the overall operation and reliability of the entire power plant. Before this decision is made, we suggest that you consider the following factors:

(54 words)

(1) *Experience*
     Rolectric has over 50 years of turbine generator maintenance and inspection experience. During the past 9 years, we have obtained over 120 turbine generator maintenance contracts. We have completed an average of one inspection contract every three weeks for the past three years, and are the largest inspection contractor of Rolectric turbine generators in the United States! With the average size of the turbines erected today exceeding 500 MW, and the accompanying expanded technology, only Rolectric is able to offer the highly specialized skills that are required to effectively maintain and inspect these larger and more complex units.

(98 words)

The company has several significant records to brag about, but after the customer has read the paragraph, how much will he or she remember? How much do you remember? When you look back at the paragraph, what stands out? Compare the original with this revision:

Dear   :

We appreciate your invitation to talk with you about the maintenance inspection of your turbine generator. Since the inspection contractor you choose can significantly affect the operation and reliability of your entire power plant, we suggest that you consider our:

(40 words)

(1) *Experience*
     Only Rolectric can provide the highly specialized skills and necessary technology required to inspect and maintain effectively such large and complex units as today's turbines, which on the average exceed 500 MW. We have had:
     —Over 50 years' experience in turbine generator maintenance and inspection.
     —Over 120 maintenance contracts for turbine generators during the past 9 years.

—An average of 1 inspection contract every 3 weeks for the past 3 years.
We are the largest inspection contractor of Rolectric turbine generators in the
United States.

(86 words)

Which version more effectively communicates the company's record?

Letters, memos, and pages of reports that look dense and heavy are forbidding. Written communications that are structured and laid out with functional white space, on the other hand, invite both initial reading and later reference. Furthermore, they say to the reader, "The person who prepared this communication has taken the trouble to make it as easy to understand as possible." Such thoughtful concern for the needs of the reader also demonstrates the desire of the writer and the writer's company to please customers and meet their needs.

USING LAYOUT TO EMPHASIZE ORGANIZATION

As we have indicated, layout is also important in documents to which a reader may need to refer after the initial reading. Examine, for example, the following section from a long and very complicated proposal.

SINGLE INSPECTION CONTRACTS

Under this contract, the Corporation will be responsible during the inspection period for scheduling, planning, providing the necessary labor, specifying materials, and supervising work and start-up.

During the course of the inspection, the Corporation will perform routine corrections where required. A routine correction shall be an item of minor nature requiring only labor that can be performed during the normal course of work without appreciable increase in cost to the Corporation.

As the work progresses, it may be necessary to perform extra work not covered by this proposal. The Corporation agrees to provide labor to perform this extra work requested or required by the Purchaser. This extra work will be billed on a time-and-material basis.

After completion of overhaul and inspection, a written report of conditions as found, work performed, and clearances and test data recorded will be submitted and recommendations made for the purchase of renewal parts for stock.

The writer's basic plan is a good one. Each paragraph contains information about the Corporation's responsibilities and performance during a particular phase of the contract. In the first paragraph, however, the phrase "during the inspection period" is buried; and in the succeeding paragraphs the tags—the phrases which identify the various operations—do not stand out as clearly as they should.

167

The writer could have carried the plan one step further and enabled the reader not only to see at a glance what the proposal involves but also, when rereading, to pick out particular points.

SINGLE INSPECTION CONTRACTS

Under this contract, the Corporation will:

Throughout the contract period:	Schedule, plan, and provide the necessary labor; specify materials; and supervise work and start-up.
During the course of the inspection:	Perform routine corrections where required; a routine correction is an item of minor nature requiring only labor that can be performed during the normal course of work without appreciable increase in cost to the Corporation.
As the work progresses:	Perform necessary extra work not covered by this proposal when requested or required by the Purchaser; and bill on the basis of time and material.
After completion of overhaul and inspection:	Submit a written report of conditions as found, work performed, and clearances and test data recorded; and recommend the purchase of renewal parts for stock.

An alternate layout might be:

SINGLE INSPECTION CONTRACTS

Under this contract, the Corporation will, throughout the contract period: schedule, plan, and provide the necessary labor; specify materials; and supervise work and start-up. It will also:

During the course of the inspection:	*Perform routine corrections* where required; a routine correction is an item of minor nature requiring only labor that can be performed during the normal course of work without appreciable increase in cost to the Corporation.
	Perform necessary extra work not covered by this proposal when requested or required by the Purchaser; and bill on the basis of time and material.
After completion of overhaul and inspection:	In writing:
	Report conditions as found, work performed, and clearances and test data recorded.
	Recommend the purchase of renewal parts for stock.

In this version, the general responsibility of the Corporation throughout the contract period serves as an introduction to its more specific responsibilities during and after inspection. Like the labels or subheads, the italics identify the topic of each of the subsections in which it appears. It also further emphasizes the organization and allows the reader to return quickly to a desired portion of the statement.

HEADINGS, SUBHEADINGS, AND TABLES OF CONTENTS

In a long letter, memo, or report—or a book like this one—headings and subheadings can provide the reader with visual cues to the organization of the text. When the document is long enough and the headings are gathered together into a table of contents, they inform the reader at the very start how the materials are organized:

This table of contents tells the reader exactly how the report is organized. Within the report, the headings and subheadings, as they appear in the text and in running heads like the one at the top of this page, keep the reader oriented. A reader who has momentarily forgotten the structure of the report can return to the table of contents for guidance. Thus headings, subheadings, and table of contents interact to keep the reader oriented.

EXPLAINING AND INSTRUCTING BY TABLES, DECISION TREES, AND FLOWCHARTS

Recently there has been considerable experimentation with ways of providing explanation and instruction. The standard method, of course, is by prose statement. For example, a company whose headquarters personnel must frequently visit other company locations scattered over several Western states found that its single company plane and its fleet of cars were being used inefficiently. In response, it developed a new travel policy, a copy of which was sent to all headquarters personnel and to all plant managers:

INSTRUCTIONS FOR TRAVELING TO PLANTS

Our plants are either within 100 miles of our office or beyond 250 miles.

When visiting plants under 100 miles away, if the plant director has called for help in an emergency or if two or more people are going, headquarters personnel will take a company car. Otherwise, where practical they will take a commercial intercity bus. Our travel office has the latest schedules, and travel agents have careful instructions on how to choose between bus and car. (Because of the unusually convenient bus service from the terminal across the street to the gates of our plants at Owona, Towanda, Orinari, and Franklin, this new policy should save the company at least $82,000 a year with minimal loss of time to those traveling.)

When visiting plants 250 or more miles away, if the plant director has called for help in an emergency, headquarters personnel will take the company plane and arrange to be met at the airport. Otherwise, they will take a commercial plane and travel from the airport by cab.

Attached to the new statement of policy was the "Ready Reference Table" shown in Table 9.1.

Management expected that, especially in the first few months, company travelers would use the phrase "where practical" to persuade the company travel agent to allow them to take a company car instead of using the bus. To demonstrate the logic of the choice for each trip and the real savings involved, therefore, it had posted on the walls of the travel office two large decision trees, shown in Figures 9.1 and 9.2, and provided the travel agents with smaller

170

Table 9.1   Table of "Instructions for Traveling to Plants"

	Emergency	*Not Emergency*
Where trip is 250 or more miles	Take company plane; arrange to be met at airport	Take commercial plane, then cab
Where trip is 100 miles or less and only one person is going	Take company car	Take intercity commercial bus where practical (see agent for comparisons)
Where trip is 100 miles or less and two or more people are going	Take company car	Take company car

copies of them. It could also have had posted a flowchart as an alternative to a decision tree. (See Figure 9.3.) Flowcharts use symbols and procedures developed by computer scientists to analyze and solve problems. Upon entering the travel office, the traveler or the traveler's secretary could quickly see the logic behind the decision trees or flowcharts. In two or three minutes the travel agent could show whether taking the bus provided substantial savings for a minimal loss of time. The process would have been less complicated if the agent had simply consulted a schedule and told the traveler either "You will have to go by bus" or "You may take a car." Management felt, however, that

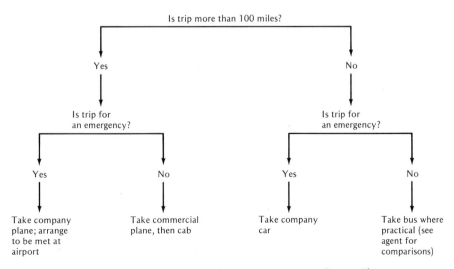

Figure 9.1.   Decision Tree: Instructions for One Person Traveling to Plants   171

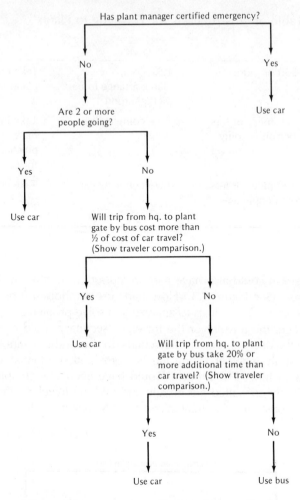

Figure 9.2. Decision Tree: Choice of Bus or Car for Trips of 100 Miles or Less

the traveler who had to take a bus would be more accepting if a few minutes were taken to make an individual decision and if both the reasons for the decision and the real cost saving were demonstrated. Secretaries who negotiated travel plans received from the travel agent copies of the decision tree and the notes on comparative costs and times to give to the traveler. The procedure was designed not only to make decisions rational, but also to be informative and, ultimately, persuasive.

Once headquarters personnel read and understood the new travel policy, they found it useful to keep the table in their desks for reference.

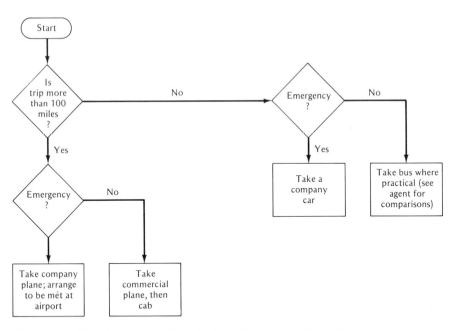

Figure 9.3. Flowchart: Instructions for One Person Traveling to Plants

GRAPHS

Writing is linear; and like all other Western European languages, English moves from left to right across the page. The right-hand margin, of course, signals the need for a return sweep to the left so that the left-to-right process can continue. Tables, decision trees, and flow charts, however, are generally multidimensional. That is, they work in at least two directions at the same time, normally both horizontally and vertically. The way they organize information on the page enables the reader quite literally to see, in a way that regular writing does not, how the various aspects of that information interrelate.

Graphs also function multidimensionally: they present numerical information visually, in drawings. The most frequently used today are bar graphs, line graphs, and pie (or circle) graphs. They are used to show relationships precise enough to be expressed, however roughly, in numbers.

Thus, for example, the following bar graphs indicate the number of operating and managerial personnel a company has employed over a five-year period. That same information can be presented in a single bar graph.   173

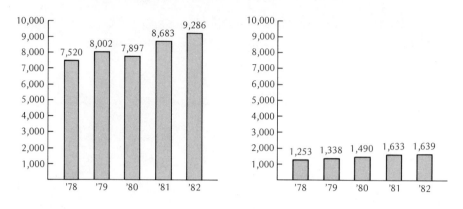

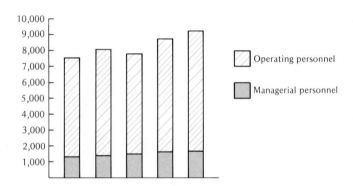

Figure 9.6. Operating and Managerial Personnel, 1978–1982

Bar graphs focus on quantity and changes in quantity. Line graphs emphasize movement or trends. Thus the information in Figure 9.6 could be presented in a line graph to show a little more clearly the rate at which company personnel is increasing (Figure 9.7).

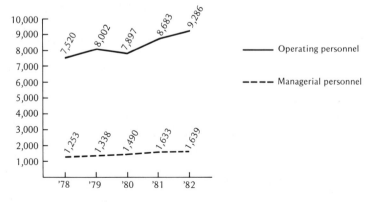

Figure 9.7. Operating and Managerial Personnel, 1978–1982

Pie graphs show proportions of a total (Figure 9.8).

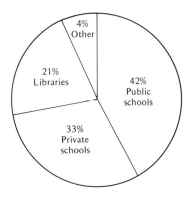

Figure 9.8. Book Sales for the
Current Year

Beginning at twelve o'clock, the segments are usually arranged in decreasing order of percentage, except that the "remainder" or the "all the rest" segment comes last, irrespective of its size. Shapes other than circles, of course, can also be segmented to show percentages (Figures 9.9 and 9.10).

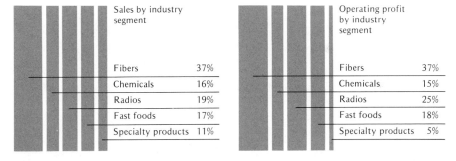

Figure 9.9. Sales and Profit by Industry Segment

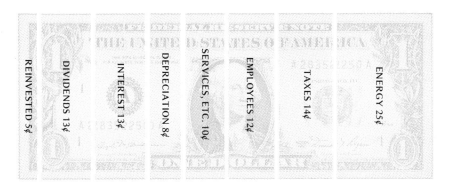

Figure 9.10. Where the Sampson Co. Dollar Goes

Each table or graph in a text should have a number for easy reference and a title which makes it understandable independent of the text. Columns, vertical and horizontal axes, and scales should be clearly identified so that quantities and relationships are quickly recognizable. A graph should not be so small as to be difficult to read or so large that a single glance will not take in its general contours.

Graphs are frequently hand drawn, but computer systems are available which present statistics in the form of bar graphs, line graphs, and pie graphs, not only as displays on cathode ray tubes, but also as hard copy.

GRAPHS THAT MISLEAD

Designers and statisticians warn that graphs can mislead in several ways. First, they can be so designed as to suggest differing interpretations of the same statistics. In Figure 9.11, for example, the overhead costs on Project Figura seem to have risen slowly over a six-year period, something to watch in future years, perhaps, but probably nothing to be alarmed about. Everything in the graph is in proportion because the bottom line is zero and the vertical axis

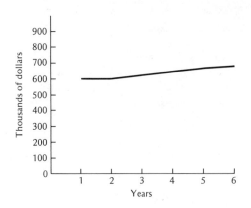

Figure 9.11. Overhead Costs on Project Figura

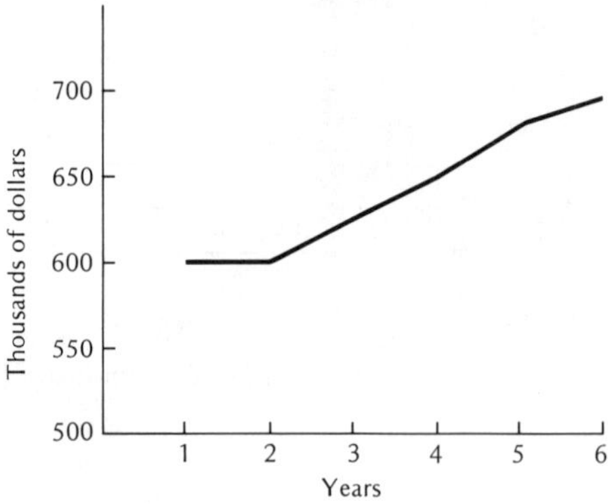

Figure 9.12. Overhead Costs on Project Figura

proceeds by identical intervals. The increase in overhead costs from $600,000 to about $680,000, about 13 per cent, looks like 13 per cent.

In Figure 9.12, however, the rate of increase of those same costs seems to be much more rapid because the designer of the graph has chopped off the bottom and increased the size of the vertical intervals. In Figure 9.13, the rate

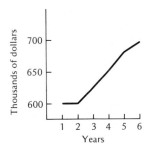

Figure 9.13.
Overhead Costs on Project Figura

of increase looks alarming because the designer has chopped off even more and has decreased the space between the horizontal intervals.

A second problem occurs when a graph designer attempts to show change by using comparable shapes other than bars. In Figure 9.14, for example, the circle used to symbolize oil and gas consumption in 1980 is almost twice as high as the circle used to show projected oil and gas consumption for the year 2000 because the designer wanted to show a proportion of almost two to one: 46 per cent to 24 per cent. The problem is, however, that in *area* the circle symbolizing the consumption for 1980 is three times that of the circle symbolizing consumption for the year 2000, and to the untrained eye looks even larger. The same difficulty occurs when designers use soldiers of different height to indicate the relative military strength of two countries or dollar bills of different length to indicate the percentage of total budget spent on research and development by two companies. Since each soldier or each dollar bill is drawn to scale, the reader notes not only the height or length of each, but also their area, and can thus easily misunderstand the true relationship.

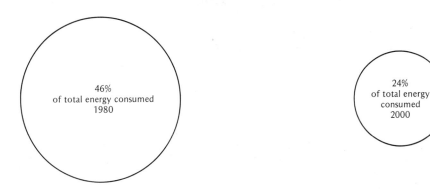

Figure 9.14. Domestic Oil and Gas Production as a Proportion of Total Energy Consumption in the United States

177

A third problem can occur when a reader tries to interpret line and bar graphs. In Figure 9.4, for example, one sees that the number of operating personnel in the company being described rose from 7,897 in 1980 to 8,683 in 1981 to 9,286 in 1982. These numbers represent the operating personnel on a particular day, probably the last day of the company's fiscal year. The top line graph in Figure 9.7, however, which presents comparable figures, may suggest to some viewers that the number of operating personnel rose from 1980 through 1982 in steady increments month by month and even week by week. Furthermore, a naive viewer might be led to believe that midway between 1980 and 1982 (whatever "midway" might mean) the operating personnel numbered 9,000. Such an interpretation, of course, would be incorrect. The line graph presents a single number for each year. The line between any two points simply indicates the direction and degree of change or continuity.

PACKAGING REPORTS

The principles of design can also be applied to the packaging of reports to make their contents more easily available to the reader. Most reports are bound, the various sections following each other in order. But such packaging can discourage a reader unnecessarily. The normal reaction to a report half an inch thick is to put aside what looks like an endless job. In fact, however, the body of such a report may be only six pages long and the rest appendix. Furthermore, in a report bound like a book it is difficult, while examining the text, to check facts or figures in the appendix. Flipping back and forth in order to compare text and data can be most exasperating.

There are several ways out of this dilemma. A report folder with a pocket on each inside cover can be used (Figure 9.15). The report itself may be placed in the left pocket, the appendix in the right. Upon opening the folder, the reader sees immediately that the body of the report does not bulk very large. After removing the text and appendix from the pockets, he or she can lay them out on the desk and use them together without inconvenience. If the pockets

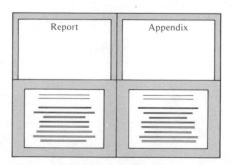

Figure 9.15

are deep enough, an appropriate table of contents for the report, and another for the appendix, can be pasted on them.

Another version of this folder has diagonal pockets which form a reverse V at the center fold (Figure 9.16). This type is particularly useful for a personally submitted proposal or bid. Open, its appearance is attractive, and the user can easily pull out the appropriate portions of the appendix (photographs, perhaps, or graphs) while talking to a client.

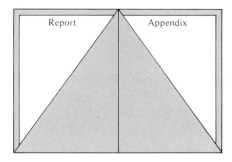

Figure 9.16

Report and appendix can also be separated by stapling the text to the top of one inside cover and the appendix to the top of the other (Figure 9.17). A person who reads while traveling or who customarily examines several reports at the same time may prefer this package. The sections cannot fall out or get mixed up, and the reader can move simultaneously through text and supporting appendices.

Figure 9.17

A fourth method requires a three-panel folder instead of the usual two (Figure 9.18). The text is bound between the first two panels in book fashion, either with staples or with a spiral plastic comb. The appendix is stapled to the top of the third panel, which may be folded in under the text when the report is not being used. Here too, the text is separated from the appendix, and they may be used together conveniently.

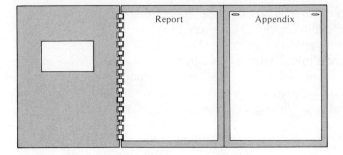

Figure 9.18

Sections of long reports can be marked for easy reference by inserting labeled dividers which extend beyond the right-hand margin or by attaching a gummed tab to the right-hand margin of the first page of each section.

ILLUSTRATIVE MATERIALS

1.

1. *In this chapter, we have provided a table (Table 9.1), a decision tree (Figure 9.1), and a flowchart (Figure 9.2) as alternatives to the prose statement of policy on methods that headquarters personnel should use in arranging travel to plants.*
   a. *Would you ever use one of the alternatives without the prose statement? If so, under what circumstances? Why?*
   b. *If you could use only two of the four methods (prose statement, table, decision tree, or flowchart) for a broadly distributed set of instructions, which two would you choose? Why?*
   c. *What are the strengths and weaknesses of each of the four methods of communicating?*
2. *Draw a flowchart as an alternative to Figure 9.3. Under what circumstances might you use it? Why?*
3. *Drug companies supply physicians with a variety of pamphlets and other aids to help the physicians, and sometimes their patients, understand the uses of a drug and the proper procedure for taking it. Following are two versions of such an aid: a set of instructions in prose for taking Tenelin and an alternate set in table form.*

Procedure for Each Day Until Next Visit

When you wake up in the morning, take your temperature. If it is normal (98.6°), take a glass of water. If it is above normal (higher than 98.6°), take one Tenelin. If at any time taking a Tenelin causes side effects (nausea, double vision, etc.), call the doctor.

Continue taking your temperature every three hours, following the same procedure as in the paragraph above:

If you are running a temperature, take one Tenelin.
If you are not running a temperature, take a glass of water.
If taking a Tenelin causes side effects (nausea, double vision, etc.), call the doctor.

Discontinue the procedure at bedtime. (Do *not* wake yourself up to take your temperature or your medicine.) Start the procedure again the next morning when you wake up.

PROCEDURE FOR EACH DAY UNTIL NEXT VISIT

		Yes	No
1	When you wake up in the morning, is your temperature over 98.6°?	Take 1 Tenelin	Take glass of water
2	Do you have any side effects (nausea, double vision, etc.)?	Call the doctor	Go to 3
3	After 3 hours from taking your pill or glass of water, is your temperature over 98.6°?	Take 1 Tenelin	Take glass of water
4	Do you have any side effects (nausea, double vision, etc.)?	Call the doctor	Go to 5

5 | Each 3 hours *until bedtime*, return to 3 , above, and continue down.

6 | At bedtime, discontinue taking temperature, pills, and water until next morning and go to sleep.

7 | When you wake up the next morning, start at 1 , above, and continue down.

a. *Do the two versions agree?*
b. *As a patient, would you prefer the prose statement or the table? Or would you like to have both? Why?*
c. *Draw alternative decision trees and flowcharts for the same set of instructions.*
d. *As a patient, which of the four versions or which combination of the four would you prefer? Why?*
e. *What are the strengths and weaknesses of each and of the various combinations?*

2.

The United States Army recommends the use of logic trees in its "performance-oriented" training literature. The Guidebook for the Development of Army Training Literature *says of the following narrative, "Decision points and instructions are buried in text. Difficult for user." Of the logic tree which it recommends to replace the narrative, also given below, it says, "Decision points, instructions, and warnings are clearly displayed for the user."*

Explosive Rounds in Hot Tubes

Explosive projectiles in heated tubes present an extremely hazardous situation. High rates of fire for extended period with high charges necessitate that the following precautions be observed:

a. Do not chamber the round in a weapon until immediately prior to firing.
b. A round that has been chambered in a weapon should be fired or removed from the weapon within 5 minutes.
c. If the round in a heated tube cannot be fired or removed within the 5-minute period, the following actions should be taken:

  (1) Where a misfire *is not* involved and in the event the round cannot be fired or removed within 5 minutes, the primer and propelling charge should be removed immediately, then elevate the cannon tube approximately 30° and evacuate all personnel to safe distance. Allow the projectile and weapon to cool for 2 hours.
  (2) After a 2-hour waiting period proceed as follows. Move the weapon carefully or relocate to a remote position. If relocating is necessary, the cannon tube should be lowered and locked in the traveling position. Waste will be placed in the chamber to cushion the projectile and to protect the face of the breech-block while the weapon is being moved. Request assistance from EOD personnel or request Direct Support Maintenance personnel with technical advice of EOD personnel regarding recognition of possible exuded explosive or other hazards to carefully remove the cannon tube (with stuck projectile) at a remote location away from buildings and occupied areas. The cannon tube containing the stuck projectile should then be released to EOD personnel.
  (3) For separate loading ammunition involved in a misfire:
  (a) Wait for 2 minutes from the last attempt to fire before removing the primer. If the primer has fired, personnel should be evacuated to a safe distance for a 2-hour waiting period without removing the propelling charge. After the 2-hour waiting period remove the propelling charge and follow the guidance outlined in (2) above.
  (b) If the primer has not fired after the 2-minute waiting period a new primer will be tried or the faulty firing mechanism corrected.

DESIGNING THE PAGE, THE FIGURE, AND THE REPORT

Then should the weapon not fire within a total elapsed time of 5 minutes, the propelling charge will be removed and personnel should be evacuated to a safe distance for a 2-hour waiting period. The guidance outlined in (2) above should then be followed.

HOT TUBE MISFIRE PROCEDURES

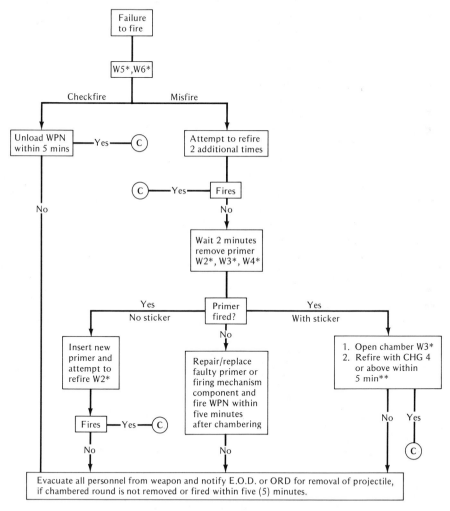

*Warnings:

1. Use CHG 1 in combat EMG only
2. Hangfire
3. Stand clear of recoiling parts
4. Sticker
5. Cook–off times apply
6. 5 minute time limit w/hot tubes
7. 50 foot lanyard used

Legend: (C) weapon cleared

**NOTE: No loss of range is expected after a sticker is fired with new charge

3.

These graphic design criteria have been developed by Siegel & Gale, a design and language simplification firm, for their own use in developing and preparing documents for their clients.

Our experience has shown that the following criteria have been very successful in improving readability, comprehension, overall impression and function.

- Limit the number of type styles
- Limit the number of type sizes
- Limit or avoid the use of all caps
- Limit the number of signals for heads, i.e., differences such as bigger, bolder, all caps, italic, color, underline, etc.
- The longer the line, the more leading is necessary
- Either indent paragraphs or skip space (1 line, ½ line, etc.) but never both
- Avoid justified columns
- Do not try to balance column length
- Never use rules except where they are functional
- Avoid vertical rules where possible
- Limit the weight of rules to no more than two
- Avoid "near-miss" type wherein one size is only a little different from the next weight, i.e., skip a weight where possible
- Avoid inconsistencies in vertical alignment
- Never mix centered material with flush left material
- Use typographic elements (boxes, bullets, etc.) in consistent styles and sizes
- Avoid leaders except where absolutely necessary in certain tabular materials
- Never "box" typographical material
- Use color only in a purely functional way in which it enhances understanding

PROBLEMS

1. Choose some process in your college (like admissions or registration) or in your company (like developing and issuing specifications or preparing an advertising or recruiting brochure). Describe the process by a flowchart *and* a decision tree. Then write a prose statement describing the process to accompany the visuals. The audience for the graphics and prose statement is someone who must administer the process.

2. Draw a flowchart or decision tree that maps the process by which you decide what sort of vacation to take, if any, or what make and model of car to buy (or clothes washer or dryer, or any other relatively expensive piece of equipment). The audience is your boyfriend or girlfriend, husband or wife.

3. Choose a patient package insert from some patent medicine and redesign it to make it easier for the user to read and understand. Submit the original with your revision.

4. Choose a news story with an accompanying graph and, using the ideas demonstrated by Figures 9.11, 9.12, and 9.13 (and the accompanying text), revise the graph to change the perception of the situation portrayed. If possible, choose a graph describing a problem and then experiment with two types of changes: first those that will suggest that the problem is more critical than the newspaper graph indicates; and then those that will suggest that the problem is less critical than the newspaper graph indicates. Submit the original with your revisions.

5. Choose three or four pages of a report, preferably one you have written, and redesign them to improve their readability. If the text does not have headings and subheadings, add them. Submit the pages of the original report with your revision.

6. Choose a set of statistics (for example: a baseball player's batting average for the past five years; the number of freshmen enrolling in your college and their SAT scores, or average starting salaries of graduates adjusted for inflation—for the past ten years; the sales and profit figures for your company for a significant period). Draw a graph representing those statistics, and write an accompanying news story for an appropriate news medium (for example, the sports page of a newspaper; your college newspaper; your company's paper for its employees). Submit the original set of statistics with your problem solution.

7. Compare for readability the "Nutrition Information Per Serving" panel on the sides of three boxes of different dry cereals. Consider such matters as layout, color, type face, and other typographic elements such as boxes and bullets. Write a statement awarding "Best Design" to one of the three and explaining in detail the reasons for your choice. Submit the panels with your statement.

8. Compare the graphic design of the annual reports of three different companies. Consider such matters as layout, color, type face and other typographic elements, pictures, and charts and graphs. Write a statement awarding "Best Design" to one of the three and explaining in detail the reasons for your choice. Submit a photocopy of at least two pages of each annual report with your statement.

9. Compare in two different newspapers the page or pages which carry the television listings and accompanying analyses of programs for that day (sometimes titled "Today in Preview" or "Today's TV Highlights"). For the editor of the television page of a newspaper who is considering revising the page, write a comparative analysis of the television pages of the two newspapers, explaining which you find more readable and why. (Choose two pages sufficiently different to allow you to write an analysis that will be helpful to the editor.) Submit the pages analyzed.

10. Consider item D in Materials for Revision of Chapter 4. Then write an analysis of it that would be useful to add as an example of how to organize statistics for a "Manual on Report Writing."

MAJOR WRITING ASSIGNMENTS: THE REPORT

11. This chapter has a section entitled "Explaining and Instructing by Tables, Decision Trees, and Flowcharts," accompanied by Table 9.1 and Figures 9.1, 9.2, and 9.3. Using that material, write for the transportation manager of the company concerned an analysis of the problems involved and the solutions proposed in the table and figures.

12. Figures 9.3, 9.4, 9.6, 9.7, and 9.9 give details about the Multi Corporation. Other relevant details are:

	Sales	Profits (after taxes)
1976	$4,828,973,000	$253,521,000
1977	$4,917,800,000	$251,791,000
1978	$4,600,220,000	$225,410,000
1979	$5,723,119,000	$343,387,000
1980	$6,150,217,000	$387,463,000

	Sales by Industry Segment					Operating Profit by Industry Segment				
	'76	'77	'78	'79	'80	'76	'77	'78	'79	'80
Fibers	35%	36%	37%	36%	37%	36%	36%	35%	37%	37%
Chemicals	12%	13%	13%	15%	16%	10%	9%	13%	14%	15%
Radios	28%	23%	21%	20%	19%	25%	26%	26%	26%	25%
Fast Foods	7%	10%	12%	15%	17%	5%	8%	12%	16%	18%
Specialty Products	18%	18%	17%	14%	11%	24%	21%	14%	7%	5%

From all the figures, the chairman of the board of the Multi Corporation can see the trends. He would like a summary report, however, explaining what happened in the corporation each year, so that he can attempt to relate operations each year with management decisions made over the five-year period. Write the year-by-year summary for him.

IV
ECONOMY, CLARITY, AND UNITY

10

Conciseness

READER REACTION TO WASTEFUL PROSE

As we have suggested in previous chapters, too many words are more likely to cause confusion than too few. By clogging the communication channel, verbiage makes it difficult for the receiver to interpret what is being transmitted. The reader (or listener) is forced to do two jobs at once: to winnow the unnecessary words and, with what is left, to try to piece together the message. The result is often annoyance and frustration.

Understandably, most people dislike frustration. Therefore, whether consciously or not, they develop mechanisms to avoid it. When they receive wordy communications, they soon begin to skip-read, trying to pick out important points without reading the rest of the material. Many business people have told us that after receiving a few letters from any correspondent, they know whether they can afford to skip or not, and often what sections they can omit.

Such individuals would much prefer not to have to skip, and they resent being forced to do so. Some of their resentment is certain to be transferred to the people responsible, as well as to their departments or companies, for, 189 as we have seen, people *are* judged by their writing. Blown-up phrasing suggests an inefficient, pompous windbag. We groan when we see a communication from such a person. If it asks for a favor or for information, we are tempted to brush it off as quickly as possible.

To be sure, our correspondent may not really *be* a windbag. Personal contact does sometimes modify opinions based on letters and reports. But damage has been done. We are never likely to feel quite at ease with such a person. Although initial impressions of this kind may be unfortunate, and in a sense unfair, the responsibility for them is the writer's, not the reader's. The reader can only react to the evidence; the writer supplies it. Anyone who wishes to be thought a friendly and efficient person must take pains to project that image by writing friendly and efficient communications.

CASE STUDY: A WEIGHTY MEMO

Here is the opening paragraph of a memorandum from the president of the Lofton Company to one of his vice-presidents:

> We received a telephone call from Mr. Herbert J. Jones of the Barton Aluminum Company late this morning, in which he reported among other things that he and various other Barton people have been carrying on a series of discussions with one Dr. Nash of one of the firms in the field of investments from Los Angeles. Dr. Nash was quoted as having said that he was interested in Lofton but also that he would very much like to be introduced to certain important people from Lofton in various areas so that he could discuss certain matters with them, all leading to the possibility, he hoped, of learning more with reference to this company than he now knew, and that at first-hand rather than from our publications or from written reports or the usual financial statements and analyses.

At first glance one might think that the writer had produced a message of weight and moment. But the weight is in the language, not the content. In the first sentence, for example, why did he have to stipulate that the call came "late" in the morning, that Jones reported "among other things" "that he and various other Barton people have been carrying on a series of discussions," or that Dr. Nash is "of one of the firms in the field of investments"? Most of the material in quotation marks is unnecessary. Why say that "Dr. Nash was quoted as having said"? Surely there are no grounds for libel here. Why must the president be so careful?

Placing a rewritten—and much improved—version alongside the original shows how windy the writer really is:

> This morning Herb Jones of Barton Aluminum called to say that they have been talking with a Dr. Nash from a Los Angeles investment firm. Dr. Nash has expressed interest in Lofton and would like to meet some of our key people to learn a little more about us firsthand.

CONCISENESS

The paragraph has been reduced from 138 to 50 words, an obvious improvement. But more important, the two versions present two different personalities. The original suggests a person who tries to make his every little act seem important, who needs fanfare and trumpets when he enters a room, and who wastes the time of everyone with whom he deals. The rewritten version, on the other hand, suggests a person who is efficient without being cold, who gets right to the point without being curt, who is sure enough of himself and his staff to be friendly and at ease. Other things being equal, which memo suggests the better administrator?

WORDINESS

One difficulty with the president's original memorandum is that it is just plain wordy. Whole phrases, as we have seen, can be omitted without loss. Throughout business and industry, writers suffer from this fault. Here are some further examples. The brackets enclose words that could have been left out.

[Regarding the question of the action of] the mixture of hydrofluoric and perchloric acid [on the gold dishes, we wish to advise that this mixture] will attack the gold dishes.

[It is the intent of] these regulations [to] describe a new accounting procedure.

[In order] to expedite [receipt of] purchase orders [at the earliest possible date], please mark them for the attention of H. O. Jones.

HEAVY PHRASING

An allied writing problem in the paragraph about Herb Jones' telephone call is heavy phrasing: using eight words where five would do, or big words for more common ones. Instead of saying that Jones has been "discussing" matters with Dr. Nash, the president says that Jones has "been carrying on a series of discussions" with him. Jones cannot just "say" something; he must be "quoted as having said" it. Dr. Nash does not wish to speak with "key people" but with "certain important people in various areas."

ELEGANT VARIATIONS

The heavy phrases we have just examined represent one form of a bad habit which has been known for more than half a century as "elegant variation": the use of a synonym, whether a word, a phrase, or a clause, for the word usually chosen to communicate a particular idea. Sometimes such words are selected in a misguided attempt to soften the impact of the term. Thus we have 191 golden agers instead of the elderly, and sanitary engineers instead of garbage men. People are not fired: they are "let go" or "terminated" or (in Britain) "made redundant." Sometimes elegant variations are used because the writer thinks they sound better. Thus people may be "assisted" rather than helped, they "proceed" rather than go, and they are "involved in interpersonal relations" rather than speaking or working with others. And sometimes elegant variations are the end product—not the result—of a teacher's arbitrary rule that no word is *ever* to be repeated in a sentence, or in succeeding sentences, or in a paragraph!

From time to time all of us use elegant variations for special reasons in special situations. But if we are to write or speak effectively, we must learn to avoid them wherever possible. If we allow ourselves to become enslaved by them, we may find ourselves writing like the president of the Lofton Company. (A list of elegant variations frequently used in business writing will be found in section 2 of the Illustrative Materials at the end of this chapter.)

HEAVY CONNECTIVES

The same paragraph also contains two special types of overblown phrasing: heavy connectives and piled-up phrases. A good example of the former is the president's reference to Dr. Nash's wanting to learn "more *with reference to* this company" when he means "more *about* this company." Heavy connectives are unnecessarily wordy phrases which some writers find "appropriate" in business to connect parts of a sentence or to relate the ideas in two sentences. In fact, almost always one or two words will serve better. Thus

> We will not approve HardRok for use *in conjunction with* our bonded roofs *due to the fact that* it is too light.

could have been written

> We will not approve HardRok for use *with* our bonded roofs *because* it is too light.

Heavy connectives have come into general business writing from several different sources. *In the amount of* instead of *for* probably comes from the accountants:

> We have billed you *in the amount of* $6,723.

Its use in business is now widespread. *With respect to* and *in the order of* are favorites of the engineers:

> The barge *with respect to* over-all length is 70 feet.
> The over-all length of the barge is *in the order of* 70 feet.

Many people have thoughtlessly adopted these circumlocutions, ignoring their deadening effect on writing. In section 1 of this chapter's Illustrative Materials we have listed some of the more common ones. All should be carefully avoided; all have more lively substitutes.

PILED-UP PHRASES

The president of the Lofton Company provides us with yet another example of ineffective phrasing. He tells his associates that Dr. Nash is "of one of the firms in the field of investments from Los Angeles," five phrases piled one on top of the other: of one . . . of the firms . . . in the field . . . of investments . . . from Los Angeles." All of these phrases may readily be replaced by one: "from a Los Angeles investment firm."

Anyone who surveys incoming business correspondence will rapidly discover that the president of Lofton is not alone—that most writers tend to pile up phrases. Here is another example:

> It is my belief that on the question of making use of the facilities at Johnstown for the running of the tests in June, the decision of the committee is in error.

Seven phrases in a row: on . . . of . . . of . . . at . . . for . . . of . . . in . . . And we should not be too surprised to find them in a sentence which begins "It is my belief that." If we ask what the writer wants to say here, we will come up with something like:

> I believe that the committee's decision to use the Johnstown facilities for the June tests is wrong.

Once again a writer has failed to make a direct statement. Instead, the words "on the question of" trigger a long series of phrases which bump along like the cars of an ancient freight train and require the reader to keep track of seven qualifications before coming to "is in error." A whole paragraph of such sentences would be extremely difficult to follow. It would also be extremely dull. Such sentences have neither shape nor emphasis. They irritate the reader by piling up unnecessary obstructions in the communication channel.

THE NATURAL REDUNDANCY OF ENGLISH

Why do so many people, in business and elsewhere, use so many unnecessary words when they write? In part, perhaps, it is because so few of them realize that the structure of the English language often requires us to use more words than are strictly necessary to communicate with each other. In other 193 words, it requires us to be somewhat redundant even when we write well. Here is an ordinary statement that might be found in a business letter:

> Therefore, we suggest you ask the Bork Company immediately to inspect the plated parts.

The sentence is clear, precise, and easily understood. Strictly speaking, however, even fourteen words may be more than required to do the job. We could strike out every other word and still leave enough information to get the message across:

> Therefore, — suggest — ask — Bork — immediately — inspect — plated —.

Or we could leave out all the vowels in the message:

> Thrfr, w sggst y sk th Brk Cmpny mmdtly t nspct th pltd prts.

Even if we struck out every other word *and* left out the vowels, the message might still get through:

> Thrfr sggst sk Brk mmdtly inspct pltd.

We do not recommend this procedure, and it will not work with every sentence. But it should suggest that adding words to straightforward prose will not improve it. We may wonder, then, why an executive would write, as one actually did,

> Therefore, it is our suggestion that the Bork Corporation be contacted in the immediate future regarding the important matter of inspection of plated parts so that they may be advised of our desires concerning this matter.

If we compare this sentence with the original,

> Therefore, we suggest you ask the Bork Company immediately to inspect the plated parts,

we discover that it is not only less efficient—36 words instead of 14—but also less informative. The original sentence refers to a specific action to be taken. The executive's version says that Bork is to "be contacted . . . regarding the important matter of" the inspection and "be advised of our desires." The verb forms "contacted" and "advised" are not only vague in meaning; they also suggest that two steps are involved. About the meaning of "we suggest you ask," there can be no question.

The discussion of this example should confirm the observation at the beginning of this chapter that spare, functional prose will best convey a message and that cluttering it up with verbiage will only *reduce* the chances of its being understood and acted on.

CONCISENESS

ELIMINATING VERBIAGE

All of us are affected by the environment in which we live. All of us develop bad communication habits. We begin to pick them up as soon as we start speaking. We develop them in school and college and on the job. Eliminating them is therefore a very difficult task. As soon as we seem to have conquered one, another pops up to take its place—as professional writers know all too well. However, conscientious effort to develop appropriate attitudes and to learn certain danger signals can produce great improvement over a relatively short period. Eliminating wasteful language is among the less difficult and more satisfying improvements one can make in one's writing.

How, then, should one approach this task? We suggest the following procedure.

1. Adopt the appropriate attitude: Say it directly!

By "it," of course, we mean "what has to be communicated." Think about the Shannon-Weaver diagram: transmitter—noise—receiver. Work at reducing or eliminating noise in the channel. If one conscientiously attempts to speak directly to the reader, many of the problems we have discussed in this section will begin to disappear. The person who is determined to get a message across directly will not begin a letter "We have received your letter of May 16 concerning . . ." or a memo "We received a telephone call from Mr. Herbert J. Jones of. . . ." Instead he begins with the real message: "I see no reason why we cannot ship" or "This morning Herb Jones called to say. . . ."

2. Take a red pencil to a sample of the mail you have received recently or to a textbook that you find difficult to read:

a. Cross out every unnecessary word or phrase. (A very satisfying procedure!)

b. Go through again, looking for heavy connectives. Cross them out and replace them with shorter ones.

c. Underline all phrases which still remain. If two are used together (*in the latter part of the afternoon*), try to eliminate one (*in the late afternoon*). If three or more are together, work even harder to reduce them.

d. Go through one more time. Look for wordy phrasing not yet found; replace it with direct phrasing.

e. Count the words in the revised version and compare with the number in the original.

If you follow this procedure for a few days, you will become "sensitized" to wordy prose and will begin to eliminate it from your own writing. If you have been religiously crossing out "in connection with" and "due to the fact that" in other people's prose, you are not likely to use them in your own. And in everything you write, you should find yourself thinking automatically about avoiding waste.

CAUTION: This process must be repeated regularly. We strongly suggest repetition after one month, three months, six months, a year, and thereafter as often as seems 195 desirable. Each repetition should include a careful analysis of incoming business correspondence, and also of one's own communications written a month or more previously. Looking at your own writing enables you to spot problems that require particular attention.

ILLUSTRATIVE MATERIALS

1.

Listed below in the left column are most of the popular heavy connectives. Now and then one must use them. Usually, however, the effective connective in the right column can be substituted.

HEAVY	EFFECTIVE
as regards	about
as related to	for, about
along the lines of	like
after this is accomplished	then
as to	on, about (*or nothing*)
by means of	by, with
due to the fact that	because
for the purpose of	for, to
for the reason that	since, because
in accordance with	by, under, according to
inasmuch as	since, because
in case	if
in conjunction with	with
in connection with	of, about
in favor of	for, to
in the light of the fact that	since, because
in order to	to
in reference to	about
in regard to	about
in relation to	with, about
in terms of	in, about
in the amount of	of, for
in the case of	for, by, in, if
in the event of	if
in the event that	if
in the instance of	for
in the majority of instances	usually
in the matter of	about, in
in the nature of	like
in the neighborhood of	about
in the order of	about

CONCISENESS

in the order of magnitude of	about
in the time of	during
in view of	because of, since
in view of the above	therefore, hence
in view of the foregoing circum- stances	therefore, hence
in view of the fact that	because, since
on a few occasions	occasionally
on behalf of	for
on the grounds that	since, because
on the part of	for, among, by
pertaining to	about
prior to	before
subsequent to	after
to summarize the above	in summary, thus
with a view to	to
with reference to	about
with regard to	about
with respect to	about, of
with the exception of	except
with the result that	so that

2.

One effective method of reducing the number of elegant variations in your writing is to make a collection of them from incoming communications. A few of those commonly used in business are:

ELEGANT	EFFECTIVE
Nouns	
aggregate	total
assistance	help
discrepancy	difference
modification	change
objective	aim, goal
obligation	debt
utilization	use
Verbs	
advise	say, tell, inform, report
ascertain	find out, learn
contribute	give
construct	build
demonstrate	show
effectuate	carry out
encounter	meet

197

endeavor	try
facilitate	make easy
forward	send
initiate	begin
occasion	cause
proceed	go
procure	get
purchase	buy
reimburse	pay
terminate	end
transmit	send
utilize	use

Modifiers

approximately	about
equivalent	equal
initial	first
optimum	best
presently	now
subsequent	next
sufficient	enough

3.

Elegant variations have been popular in all ages. During the sixteenth century in England, for example, inkhorn terms—words "Englished" from foreign languages—were much in vogue as substitutes for standard words. Thomas Wilson, in his Art of Rhetoric *(1553), attacks the users of inkhorn terms and gives as a "horrible example" a clergyman's letter of application for a vacant benefice. It was written to "a gentleman that waited on the Lord Chancellor." Most of the elegant variations, as one would guess, are words concocted from Latin.*

Pondering, expending, and revoluting with myself your ingent affability and ingenious capacity for mundane affairs, I cannot but celebrate and extol your magnifical dexterity above all others. For how could you have adepted such illustrate prerogative and dominical superiority if the fecundity of your ingeny had not been so fertile and wonderfully pregnant? Now, therefore, being accersited to such splendente renoun and dignity splendidious, I doubt not but you will adjuvate such poor adnichilate orphans as once were condisciples with you, and of antique familiarity in Lincolnshire. Among whom I, being a scholastical panion, obtestate your sublimity to extol my infirmity. There is a sacerdotal dignity in my native country, contiguate to me where I now contemplate, which your worshipful benignity could soon impetrate for me if it would like you to extend your sedules and collaude me in them to the right honorable Lord Chancellor. . . . I obtestate your clemency to invigilate thus much for me, according to my confidence, and as you know my condign merits for such a compendious living. But now I relinquish to fatigate your intelligence with any more frivolous verbosity, and therefore he that rules the climates be evermore your beautreux, your fortress, and your bulwark.

MATERIALS FOR REVISION

Here are some sentences which contain errors discussed in this chapter. Revising them will reinforce your understanding of the problems involved and your ability to recognize them in your own writing.

A

1. Refrigerator sales were down largely due to the fact that other manufacturers were offering extra discounts which the division generally did not meet.
2. Financial studies were made of a number of companies with respect to possible acquisition by Thompson.
3. In view of this experience, it is recommended that this limitation of the test be recognized.
4. During January this procedure was in the process of being evaluated.
5. I called on the subject company with regard to their inquiry on aluminum panels.
6. Also attached is a Performance Bond in amount of $5000 and a Payment Bond in amount of $1000.
7. Should you have questions in regard to the above, we will be glad to go over them with you.
8. At the present time the baking time is 10 to 13 minutes.
9. We will not approve GeeRock for use in conjunction with our bonded built-up roofs due to the fact that it is extremely light in weight.
10. As you will note, the sulfur contents of the acids are all in the order of about 0.004%.
11. Pliagloss can be expected to leave the furnace in the neighborhood of 600°F.
12. A meeting was held at the New York studios for the purpose of determining the new price ranges required as a result of the increase in the cost of film.
13. We wish to thank you for your letter of June 21 in reference to the three books which we sent you.
14. In such an organization almost daily conversations are held with the laboratory technicians in regard to the engineer's project.
15. At the same time the engineer must confer with the sales engineer in regard to customer specification problems.

B

1. During the month of January this product was being evaluated.
2. It was at this point that this office wrote a letter to Mr. M. Smith in Los Angeles.
3. Recently our New England representative, Roger Bacon, called at your office but was unable to see you inasmuch as you were not there when he called.
4. We have been informed by the Carryall Agency that they are holding the above order due to the fact that upon its receipt it was refused by you. The reason for this was no doubt due to the express COD charges involved.

5. Please let me have your comments as early as possible in order that I may be in a position to total shipments made to Hoboken on the exchange agreement for the month of April.

6. Under additional information on this credit memorandum, you state that you actually received 353 tons. When issuing this credit memorandum, you failed to show also the number of tons ordered to date. We are withholding process on this memorandum until you supply us with the number of tons ordered to date.

7. It will yield an oxide equally as active as the original preparation.

8. The current situation with respect to tests of this substance is that it is being investigated in at least ten laboratories in this country, and six other papers concerning its properties are known to be in the process of being written.

9. On the question of making use of television spot announcements, we do not know the reasons for trying to obtain time for such announcements at this time since it is the current policy of this company to restrict the advertising on BX-16 to the medium of radio.

10. In regard to the test results to be obtained by your laboratory, it is requested that a statement of these results be forwarded to us.

11. The filling out of the personnel forms was accomplished by this office without delay.

12. We are pleased to advise that we expect to make shipment of your truck by the middle of December.

13. Additional interviews with potential customers are currently in progress which will provide more useful customer data. These interviews will be completed in a period of approximately two months.

14. Mr. Brown indicated that it is his information that it requires $700 per trainee for equipment to train each individual under our present method of operation.

15. This is a four-week school which is supposed to introduce us to the basic fundamentals of the art of salesmanship as it is practiced in the company.

16. Will you please advise us as to your recommendation regarding the continuation of these interviews.

17. There is a negative opinion in regard to this theory among the majority of economists.

C

1. The current situation with respect to X-2 transistors is such that our entire production is being consumed in the domestic market.

2. It appears that Remco Standard is in line for a credit in the amount of 2000 pounds.

3. With respect to the use of No. 6 Filament, it is my understanding that this supply is preempted for light bulb manufacture.

4. The Construction Division, in addition to its unexpected new business, also has benefited from favorable upward revisions to the profits on four contracts.

5. With respect to the improvement of chicken pie quality, it is important that a small amount of thyme and rosemary be incorporated in the gravy before it is poured over the meat so that the resultant chicken pie will be more satisfactory to the taste.

6. We wish to thank you for your letter of September 21, in reference to Pliaform for Italy.

7. It should be noted in explanation, however, that the increase in earnings due to the replacements is approximately $10,000.

CONCISENESS

8. Exhibit 2 is a letter which is in response to a one-sentence assignment in the minutes of the July 1 Division Operating Committee meeting.
9. We cannot find any reference on your order as to when shipment is required.
10. It is anticipated that these units will be replaced on the basis of being worn out by next winter.
11. The new-formula Pliafilm 32 is very superior to the old formulation in stability.
12. In the future, we would appreciate it if you would show under additional information if the prepaid freight bill is to be attached to the invoice.
13. In summary, we suggest that all branches be immediately contacted regarding the matter of inspection of inventory reports so that they may be advised of our desires.
14. In regard to the affidavit to be executed by Rivers & Martin, it is requested that one executed and sworn copy be returned to us.
15. We are now trying to establish whether or not the two 30 H. P. electric motors for which it was necessary to cancel our order with Reddy Electric can properly be considered as specialties, and we are currently awaiting an answer from Reddy Electric to our most recent communication with it on that subject.
16. The activities of our group during the month were concerned with the annual closing of the company records.
17. Of the remaining property, that on Webster Avenue is in the process of being acquired by the Jones Realty Company.
18. During January representatives of this section visited three plants for the purpose of performing audit functions. In addition to performing audits at company plant and contract locations, personnel of this section audited various buildings submitted by subcontractors and other vendors.
19. Fabricators in turn are faced with the condition where their anticipated fourth quarter orders have been reduced as much as 35%, with more likely to come.
20. The property of anthracene which makes it desirable in this use is the fact that it forms a eutectic mixture with TNT.
21. This assignment of four weeks' duration terminated last Friday.
22. The system can be modified to bring it into line in the cost area to the extent that the savings in the area of energy will be able to offset the additional cost of the conversion.

11

Directness

As we have seen in the preceding chapter, all communications in the world of business and industry should put a message across as concisely and forcefully as the nature of the audience and the topic allow. In most situations informal language will do that best. "We will cut production by 50 percent next month" conveys a clear, unequivocal message. "Under existing circumstances it is the opinion of this office that there is no alternative at the present point in time to a reduction of normal production by 50 percent" leads us through a maze before getting to what we really want to know. The source and the precise nature of the message are not clear. There are too many words clogging the communication channel.

CLOGGING THE CHANNEL

In this chapter we will be talking about the need for direct statement in business writing. For reasons which we will examine in some detail in Chapter 13, most people find themselves using clear, direct statement when they are sitting around a conference table, or talking to a colleague, or even speaking at a convention. With the audience before them—whether it numbers one or a thousand—they feel a need to communicate, to get their message across. When the message is written, however, the audience tends to recede into the far distance, perhaps because there is no immediate feedback. As a result, for many writers the need to communicate effectively seems less pressing. When the audience is a woman you have never seen, who as you draft your communication is 3,000 (or even only 20) miles away, it is not so easy to concern yourself with her attitudes and her needs. There is a strong temptation to forget her humanity and write as if she were an object, to rely not on personal communication but on formulas, on stock phrases which can be plugged into the communication process wherever they seem appropriate.

A "TYPICAL" BUSINESS LETTER

In order to see how stock phrasing normally functions, let's look at the type of business letter which reaches thousands of persons in America every day. This one was written by the personnel manager of a small manufacturer of Christmas decorations.

Dear Mr. Askew:

This letter will acknowledge receipt of your communication of December 16, which has been referred to this office for a reply.

It is our understanding that you are interested in obtaining employment in our Sales Department.

We regret to report that due to the fact that our business is seasonal in nature, we are unlikely to be in a position to offer employment in our Sales Department in the near future. In the event that you should desire employment at a later date, however, please be advised that this office will accept applications after June 1.

Thank you for your interest in our company. We trust that you will understand our inability to provide a positive response to your application at this time.

Yours sincerely,

Helen S. Purdoe
Personnel Department

Anyone who regularly receives business letters will recognize that this one is "typical." It says the usual things in the usual way. To Paul Askew, who spent several hours working on a letter to the company's sales manager and on a resume of his experience, it was irritating. Despite the offer of possible employment in six months, it struck him as patronizing and unfriendly, though he couldn't say just why.

ENSLAVEMENT BY STOCK PHRASES

To a more experienced observer, the reason would be clear. Ms. Purdoe's letter is almost entirely constructed of phrases that have been used over and   203 over again in business communications. These phrases she has stored away in her head. When she needs a phrase to do a job, out pops the appropriate one: "This letter will acknowledge receipt of . . . your communication of . . . referred to this office for a reply . . . It is our understanding that . . . obtaining employment . . . We regret to report that . . . due to the fact that . . . in nature . . . unlikely to be in a position to . . . offer employment . . . in the near future . . . In the event that . . . desire employment . . . at a later date . . . please be advised . . . this office will accept applications . . . Thank you for your interest . . . We trust that . . . our inability to provide . . . positive response . . . at this time." Twenty-one of them! With all of these rubber stamps in her head, Ms. Purdoe didn't have to think about Paul Askew as she wrote this letter. She did not need to consider what his reaction might be. She could just "fill in the blanks." And that, presumably, is why she squirrels away stock phrases.

HOW NOT TO BEGIN

How does Ms. Purdoe prepare her letters? Probably she dictates—though the process is the same whatever her method. Holding her microphone with her thumb on the switch, she plucks a letter off the pile to be answered. First problem: How to start? Obvious solution: Grab an appropriate opening gambit from her collection. In this situation she has a wide choice:

In reply to your letter of . . .
This is in reply to your letter of . . .
In answer to your letter of . . .
With regard to your letter of . . .
In reference to your application of . . .
Reference is made to your letter of . . .
We have before us your letter of . . .
We are in receipt of your letter of . . .
We acknowledge herewith receipt of your letter of . . .

These are only a few of the many available to her. Any one of them will get her started. And as she continues to dictate, she is able to find a stock phrase for almost every situation.

Our point here is not that one should never use stock phrases—though obviously one should try to avoid them—but that one should not become enslaved by them. The reason is clearly indicated by Askew's uneasiness—his dissatisfaction—with Helen Purdoe's reply to his carefully phrased letter.

The rubber stamp user is a person who writes without bothering to think, especially when writing or dictating the parts of a letter which are most difficult to compose. In her desire to get Askew's letter out of the way and move on to other tasks, Ms. Purdoe failed to put herself in Paul Askew's shoes, to ask herself what he wanted to know and how he would be affected by what she was writing. Thus she created a certain amount of ill will toward herself and

her company.

DIRECTNESS

AN EFFECTIVE LETTER

So much for what Helen Purdoe failed to do. How would a more thoughtful member of the Personnel Department have responded to Paul Askew?

Dear Mr. Askew:

Our Sales Department has asked me to reply to your inquiry of December 16.

I am sorry to have to tell you that since our business is seasonal, we will have no openings in Sales for the next six months. In the summer, however, when we mount our Christmas sales campaign, we may be able to use a person with your qualifications.

We will keep your letter and resume on file. If you are still interested, just send me a note around June 1, and we'll reconsider your application.

Sincerely yours,

Janet Foxgrover
Personnel Department

Ms. Foxgrover, unlike Ms. Purdoe, is not a rubber stamp addict. She writes to Askew as if she were speaking directly to him. Her language is clear, direct, and friendly. Although his application has not been accepted, he will have a good feeling about both Ms. Foxgrover and her company.

Much of the effectiveness of her letter comes from the straightforward language she uses. In addition, because she is not simply arranging rubber stamps, but actively and sympathetically thinking about her reader, she gives him much more explicit—and hence much more useful—information. Instead of the cold "In the event that you should desire employment at a later date, however, please be advised that this office will accept applications after June 1," she says, "In the summer, however, when we mount our Christmas sales campaign, we may be able to use a person with your qualifications. We will keep your letter and resume on file. If you are interested, just send me a note around June 1, and we'll reconsider your application." The first version is impersonal: "In the event that . . . desire employment . . . please be advised that this office will accept applications. . . ." The words seem to have come out of a machine—as in a sense they have. On the other hand, Ms. Foxgrover's friendliness comes out in such phrases as "We may be able to use a person with your qualifications" and "Just send me a note." (Not "this office" but "me." In a somewhat larger company, she might have said "us," but one cannot imagine *her* using "this office.")

Furthermore, although her letter is a a good deal shorter, she provides more specific information than Ms. Purdoe. Paul Askew learns *why* he should write around June 1. And he will be pleased to know that he will not have to submit a new application. He-is also spared Ms. Purdoe's perfunctory last paragraph and her statement that she "trusts" that he will understand her position—which seems to imply that he is likely not to do so.

205

TOWARD EFFECTIVE OPENINGS

The opening of any communication is of special importance because it establishes a relationship between writer and reader. If it contains what the reader perceives as a possible insult, nothing the writer says later on will be seen as well-intentioned. On the other hand, if the opening suggests that the writer is friendly and sympathetic, the reader may overlook an unfortunate bit of phrasing later. Consider, for example, how the opening of the Fred Peters and Fran Savage letters (in Chapters 2 and 6) must have struck their audience:

Dear Mr. Crosby:

With reference to your letter of March 1 in which you inquired as to the approximate cost for reconditioning the thermostat assembly supplied with your order No. A-626 for a specially designed cooling system for the Short Beach Chemical Company Laboratory, we have contacted the factory from which we obtained the assembly and they advise that they do not wish to have anything to do with repairing it, due to the fact that it is not practical and the expense would be exceedingly high.

Dear Marjorie M. Jones,

MY WORD!!! You certainly have every right to feel put upon to have bought such a badly printed puzzle book—for whatever price.

As we all discover, the opening is frequently the most difficult part of a letter to write. How does one begin? We have already seen a list of a few standardized openings, all of which are awkward and wordy and all of which refer to the date of the communication to which the writer is responding. These openings have an obvious attraction: they get the letter started. They help the writer warm up to the subject. However, as we have observed, they inevitably set the tone for the rest of the communication. Therefore the temptation to use them must be avoided. Individuals just starting a career will not find it as difficult to do so as those who have fallen into bad habits. But even the latter can break away from rubber stamps, if they are willing to work at it.

How can we find a satisfactory opening? A few seconds' thought will almost always produce a friendly and courteous way into a letter or memo. At the very least we can thank a correspondent for his letter instead of merely "replying" to it or "acknowledging" it. Instead of

In reply to your letter of June 20 . . .
We wish to acknowledge your letter of June 20 . . .

we may use the more natural

Thank you for your letter of June 20.

DIRECTNESS

But even such an opening, courteous though it is, does no more than say: "I am about to answer your letter of June 20. Are you ready?" Furthermore, there are common openings for which a simple "thank you" cannot appropriately be substituted. For example,

> In accordance with our telephone conversation of June 30, there is forwarded herewith one (1) copy of our Drawing #654123.

Here a direct conversational approach will have a good effect:

> Enclosed is (or Here is) the copy of our Drawing #654123 that I promised you over the phone on June 30.

The revision includes the date of the telephone conversation, which should perhaps be recorded. However, it does not give it undue prominence by building a platform of prefabricated wooden phrases under it.

Most openings can be made to move even more quickly. Instead of

> This is in reply to your letter of January 6 regarding the Burden fuses which you supplied on the above purchase order. I wrote to our customer in an effort to have him reconsider and accept this material.

the writer may say

> When we received your letter of January 6, I wrote to our customer and asked him to reconsider and accept the Burden fuses which you supplied on the above purchase order.

Certainly a sales letter which begins

> We wish to acknowledge your letter of March 6 regarding the availability of Stolene Lubricating Oil. We can ship the thousand gallons you need on March 20.

might better begin

> We can ship on March 20 the thousand gallons of Stolene Lubricating Oil about which you inquired in your letter of March 6.

Note that the first three words give the reader the news he really wants. He is likely, therefore, to be pleased that he is dealing with an efficient and reliable company.

Here is another awkward opening:

> We have before us your letter of June 20, relative to the sample of Towanda Brick which has been sent to you for examination. In the last paragraph of your letter, you tell us that you would like to know the temperature to which the brick is heated, and we are informed that it is retained in the oven for a period of 70 hours at a temperature of 1250 degrees C.

This passage might be rewritten far more simply:

> The Towanda Brick about which you asked in your letter of June 20 is baked for 70 hours at 1250 degrees C.

One more example will show the extent to which unthinking reliance on rubber stamp openings can be carried:

> In reference to a recent letter from Mr. Zaroff of Zaroff Engineering in Chicago concerning the subject heat control, he has informed me that your company handles heat controls.

This opening refers to a letter which the reader has never seen and has no interest in.

THE MARATHON OPENING SENTENCE

Not only do rubber stamps make us sound like unimaginative—and un-friendly—clerks; they also tend to force us to summarize in long opening sentences everything said in the letter we are answering or everything that took place at a meeting or in a telephone call. Here is an example:

> In reply to your letter dated January 3, and in confirmation of the agreement reached with your Mr. Bach by phone today, it was agreed that we would accept billing in the amount of $1,808.72, which is the total amount of the costs incurred by you in installing the replacement gear on the first of the two grinders which we furnished under the subject contract, but that the costs which will be incurred by you at a later date in the replacement of the ring gear on the second grinder will be divided equally between French and Brindley.

Without the rubber stamp we could say the same thing more simply:

> By phone today, your Mr. Bach and I discussed the problem you raised in your letter of January 3. We agreed that:
> 1. Brindley will pay the $1,808.72 cost that French incurred in installing the replacement gear on the first of the two grinders we furnished under the subject contract;
> 2. French and Brindley will share costs when the ring gear on the second grinder is replaced.

"SUBJECT" AND "REFERENCE"

One way to avoid a rubber stamp opening is to use a subject heading, a device sanctioned by most companies for letters and built into virtually all memo forms. It eliminates the need for most of the awkward openings we have been discussing and allows the writer to get down to business right away. For "We are in receipt of your letter of April 22 and are investigating the matter of diesel replacement parts," we may substitute:

SUBJECT: Diesel Replacement Parts
         Your letter, April 22

Another type of heading is

REFERENCE: Graham Winch Company
           Order #601–362

And off we go into the meat of the communication.

Subject headings do, however, require a little thought. They should contain all the information needed to identify the subject precisely. Consider this opening:

SUBJECT: Bordentown Plant

Dear Sir:

This letter is to report progress on the subject plant. Johnson and Company have sandblasted. . . .

Here the heading does only half of its job. If it had been written

SUBJECT: Progress on Bordentown Plant

the writer might have started with his second sentence.

REPLIES USING SUBJECT HEADINGS

When replying to a letter or a memo containing a subject heading, however, one should use the same basic heading as the original. Otherwise the recipient will not immediately recognize what subject is being referred to, and the letter may not wind up in the same file as the original. Therefore, many companies insist that the first line of subject headings not be changed. However, there should be no great problem in providing a useful heading. If, for example, a company's Bordentown plant has been severely damaged by a tornado, the president may issue a directive asking for weekly reports on repairs to each building, using the heading

SUBJECT: Bordentown Plant Repairs

A report to a plant manager by the person supervising the work on a single building might carry the heading

SUBJECT: Bordentown Plant Repairs
Progress Report on Building "C," June 7–13

In most instances the subject or reference entry should contain only one or two short lines. The former summarizer, denied the lengthy opening sentence, should not take refuge in a bulky heading, a case history in outline. Concise identification of the real subject of the communication—short enough to be taken in at a single glance—will do the job best.

POSITIVE BEGINNINGS

If we look at the effective openings in the preceding sections of this chapter, we should be able to derive a general rule for starting a letter. What do we find?

Thank you . . .
Enclosed is . . . that I promised . . .
When we received your letter . . . I wrote . . .
We can ship . . .
The Towanda brick about which you asked . . . is baked . . .
By phone today, your Mr. Bach and I . . . agreed . . .

In each instance, the letter begins with a clear, direct statement and on a positive note. All but the first one report action taken or to be taken by the writer or the writer's company. That, after all, is what interests the reader, who will appreciate having the answer in the first few words of the letter—but will *not* appreciate having to wade through a lot of unnecessary words to find it.

Insofar as possible, therefore, every letter or memo which is a reply to a request for action or information should begin with a clear statement of what has been, is being, or will be done. Only in exceptional cases—as when the writer feels obliged to explain the steps leading up to a decision or action *before* stating what that decision or action is—should this rule be violated.

When a communication initiates a correspondence, the same general principle applies, though the strategy used may on occasion have to be somewhat less direct. The considerate writer will normally open up the subject in the first sentence. A vice-president for manufacturing might write to a manager in a supplier firm:

Dear Joe,

As I am sure you know, we are well satisfied with the way in which our arrangements with your company are working out. However, at a staff meeting yesterday our people came up with suggestions which they feel may eliminate a few minor bugs in the system. Why don't you talk to your people, and then. . . .

Or the sales manager in a home office might write to a district representative:

Dear Pat,

I have just learned something that may be useful in your dealings with Thompson Electric. Tom Brady stopped by yesterday and told me that. . . .

Or a small manufacturer might write to a representative of a marketing corporation:

Dear Sarah,

I wonder if you could drop by here sometime in the week of October 13. We have designed a new product which is a bit out of our usual line and would like to consult you about possible markets for it.

In each case the opening is clear, informal, and informative. There are no rubber stamps, and the tone is casual and friendly, even if, as in the first letter, the writer may know that some of the changes proposed will probably not be acceptable to the reader's company.

STOCK CLOSINGS

For many of us, finishing off a letter is almost as difficult as opening it. When we have stated our business or asked our questions, we feel a need to round things off with a compliment of some sort. If, for example, we have asked a favor, we may be tempted to conclude with one of these sentences:

Thank you in advance for your cooperation.
Thank you for your assistance in this matter.
Thank you for your consideration and cooperation.
Your cooperation will be appreciated.
Your prompt (or fullest) cooperation will be greatly (or deeply) appreciated.

Clearly these are rubber stamps—and there are dozens of additional variations on the formula. They are interchangeable, and they say virtually nothing. One glance will tell even the inexperienced reader that there is no need to read them. Therefore, they serve no function, and the time spent in dictating and typing them is wasted.

Nor are these the only stereotype endings. Each type of communication has its own set. To take just one other example, the unimaginative person who provides a reader with information will use one of these—or some variant of them:

> If we can be of further service to you, please do not hesitate to call on us (*or* write us, *or* let us know, *or* let us hear from you, *or* get in touch with us).
>
> May we have the pleasure of serving you further?
>
> If we can be of further service to you in any way, we will be happy to hear from you.
>
> Please do not hesitate to notify us when we can be of further assistance.

What, then, should you do when you have said what you have to say? If you have really said everything, you should simply stop. You should certainly resist the temptation to attach a rubber stamp. The complimentary close ("Yours truly," "Sincerely yours," "Cordially," etc.) is quite sufficient for saying good-bye.

BEING SPECIFIC

Sometimes you may find it necessary to end with a request. If so, you should be as specific as possible. If you want an early or immediate reply, you may say, "I will appreciate a reply by July 1, the beginning of our next accounting period" or "Could you let us have the measurements as soon as you have heard from your customer?" If you want other action, you should be equally specific:

> Therefore, we will appreciate your submitting future orders on the enclosed forms.
>
> I hope you will be able to reschedule your shipments to help us solve the traffic problem in our warehouse.

If you have provided information, you may wish to say:

> We will be happy to send you information about any of our future specials in which you may be interested.
>
> If you will send us details on your other flow processes, we may be able to recommend additional money-saving equipment.

A rubber stamp ending, then, contributes nothing and often suggests that the writer wants only to finish the letter and move on to more interesting matters. On the other hand, a specific ending suggests a writer who is alert and concerned enough to stay with the subject to the end.

A SAMPLING OF OTHER RUBBER STAMPS

There are other stock phrases that cannot be classified as easily as openings and closings. In some companies writers habitually use "it is to be expected" or "it is to be anticipated" instead of the simple "we anticipate" or "we expect." Instead of saying "probably," they use "it is not improbable" or "it is not unreasonable to assume"—perhaps on the theory that a double negative is more discreet or more impressive than a direct statement.

The word "advise" has been so misused and overused in business that it has almost lost any real meaning. These days one seldom says, or replies, reports, states, suggests, ventures, or even tells. Instead one advises.

> We are pleased to advise that our credit memorandum No. 47/12 was issued to you yesterday.
>
> The warehouse has advised that they have only six bolts of this material in stock.
>
> Mr. Faber will follow this and advise us as to whom they give the contract to.
>
> I would like to be advised as to your comments providing clarification of your position on this change.

As the last two examples indicate, rubber stamps often produce additional problems. Because "advise" is frequently followed by "as to," both writers wound up with virtually unreadable sentences. They might better have said:

> Mr. Faber will follow the negotiations and tell us who gets the contract.
>
> Please tell me how you clarified your position on this change.

As practitioners of special disciplines like engineering and computer science move into management positions, they bring with them additional stock phrases which are often adopted by their colleagues, especially if they seem to add "distinction" to language. Some engineers seldom say that a piece of equipment weighs "about" twenty tons. For them it weighs "in the order of" or "in the order of magnitude of" or even "in the order of magnitude of about" twenty tons. The rubber stamp engineer finds it impossible to say, "The temperature of the mixture is 300 degrees C." He will say instead, "The mixture with respect to temperature is 300 degrees C."

Why do people persist in using these rubber stamps—heavy phrases that have become institutionalized, circumlocutions that have become fads, old-fashioned habits of writing, and turns of phrase derived from popular culture? Some people, no doubt, really are pompous stuffed shirts: such expressions suit their taste and reflect their personality. Some people think these expressions are polite, or discreet, or proper. Some have been instructed to use them by a superior and stick to them when they find that no one seems to object. But probably most people use them simply because they see them so often on incoming correspondence, in the writing of their associates, and in the newspapers, advertisements, magazines, and other communications which surround them. We have even heard them warmly defended by a businessman who insisted that he preferred *not* to have to think when he wrote a letter!

Some individuals are vaguely aware that rubber stamp phrasing is inefficient, but nothing they see around them suggests that they need do anything to   213 eliminate it from their writing. Others understand the problem but find little encouragement—and sometimes active opposition—if they attempt to break away from stock phrasing. Still others, however, more sensitive to the sound of words and more individualistic in nature, recognize its deadening effect and avoid it. And because they concentrate on what they want to say, the audience they are addressing, and the effect they wish to produce, they communicate. Their writing is as direct and as well adapted to their audience as their speaking. It accurately reflects their personality. Their letters and memos are likely to be fresh, imaginative, attractive, and lively—qualities which are almost always, in our experience, to be found in the writing of people who reach the highest positions in a business organization.

ILLUSTRATIVE MATERIALS

1.

Every office worker, of course, knows about (or "is not unmindful of the fact that there are") rubber stamps. Executives enjoy passing around sheets which deride them. Here, for example, is a jingle which points up the lack of imagination and humor that distinguishes the rubber stamp wielder.

> We beg to advise and wish to state
> That yours has arrived of recent date,
> We have it before us, its contents noted,
> And herewith enclose the prices we quoted.
> Attached please find as per your request
> The samples you wanted, and we would suggest,
> Regarding the matter and due to the fact
> That up until now your order we've lacked,
> We hope you will not delay it unduly,
> And beg to remain yours very truly.

2.

Here is a memorandum of which the writer was very proud. Read it once at your normal reading speed.

To:	Mr. T. J. Mason, President
From:	Surplus Product Sales Department
Subject:	XYZ Company

1. Your note of January 5 about the XYZ Company has been received and we wish to advise that we concur on your opinion that a similar arrangement as undertaken by Underwood Company has no particular interest to this department. However, provided the circumstances are extenuated, it is apparent that some special credit arrangements could

be made. We have a particular and definite interest in this customer, which is identical with other concerns with which we do business and that is to increase our sales, when and if the availability of accumulations warrant doing so, consistent with the demands and policies as set forth by your office.

2. Unfortunately, we are not in a position to give any assurance of what might be available in the way of secondary products, as our offers and sales will fluctuate with the availability of the product, consistent with other demands placed before us, together with obligations incurred with other customers. It is, however, assumed that, in the event a plan can be worked out with this customer, it would not involve future inventories being held at our plant, as this would not be possible, since all the available warehouse space we have is limited and is used exclusively in the preparation and shipment of prime products.

3. Since we are unable to forecast what may be available in the future in the way of sizes and classifications of secondary products, we believe that it can reasonably be assumed that due to our expansion program the amount of off-grade products encountered in producing primes will increase proportionally—or at least we expect that they will. We might say further that this condition was rapidly developing prior to the current stoppage, and it can reasonably be assumed that when operations are resumed, or soon thereafter, a marked increase, certainly a noticeable one, of secondary products will occur. Therefore, for this reason, we anticipate an increase in our future offerings to this customer.

4. In view of the foregoing, and as soon as we are in receipt of the additional information and data required, we will be in a situation to make a prompt and complete analysis of our position; and we will inform you of our findings as well as of our decision.

J. C. Johnson

a. After reading this memo once, what impression do you have of Mr. Johnson? Do you know what he has told his president? Without looking back at the text, try to jot down the points he made.
b. Now go back and study the memo carefully. Can you rewrite it so that it will give Mr. Johnson's opinions clearly and concisely?
c. What have you omitted in your revision? Why is it difficult to understand the original?

3.
In this chapter we have mentioned the jargon of the engineer. Every field has its own jargon. Here, for example, is a composite financial newsletter, each sentence of which is based on one that we have seen in print.

ECONOMY, CLARITY, AND UNITY

That the nature of the economy is changing is a widely accepted premise. The difference to date has been generally psychological other than in the sometimes barometric stock market. The extent of what is likely to follow in both degree and duration now, as always, must be a matter for conjecture. On the basis of present indications, however, and especially if consideration is given to last month's slight gains, there seem little grounds for undue concern. Aside from seasonal factors, the indication is strong that the downturn has been scraping bottom.

However, it is probably as well to recall at this time that basic premise which states that no more dangerous pastime can be indulged in than trying to guess the bottom of bear movements. In some quarters there is a strong feeling that the November-December lows will hold on a number of stock situations.

Generally the outlook for significant upward revision of the economy this year is still uncertain and seems to hang on the extent to which customer buying is revived. Along this line there has been a considerable increase in the liquidity of retail business.

Under these confusing circumstances, it would be our opinion that a meticulous view should be taken of fundamental business developments and the technical performance not only of the list but also of various groups and individual issues. Broadening strength on the upside can be judged by ability to better fourth quarter highs; on the downside by resistance in the neighborhood of last year's lows.

a. *After reading this report once, do you know what the writer has said?*
b. *Try rewriting the passage in clear, direct prose.*

4.
Whenever we walk into a business office we run into a man named Bob (or Pat, or Bill, or Mac—the name does not matter), a man whose warmth and friendliness immediately put a stranger at ease, who makes customers feel that it is great to do business with his company, who can talk easily to crane operators about baseball and to vice-presidents about golf, a man whom one could classify only as a fine fellow. But if you talk to the plant superintendent in Wichita (or Hartford, or Sacramento, or Duluth) who has never seen Bob but receives a memo from him once a week, you discover that Bob is a cold fish and a stuffed shirt, a guy the superintendent hopes will never turn up at his plant.

What makes this difference? The answer is simple: when Bob writes, he puts on an entirely new personality, one he has pasted together out of letters his first boss wrote, a feeling that business letters should be "dignified," and his high school English teacher's insistence that he use a "formal" style in his themes. This is a Bob none of his friends at the home office would recognize.

What would happen if Bob talked about business the way he writes about it? Well, let's listen in on a conversation in his office. A visitor has just entered:

DIRECTNESS

TOM: H'ya, Bob!

BOB: Why, Tom Smith, you old coot! How're they treatin' you? Haven't seen you since we tied one on that night at the last State reunion. How's Sally and the kids?

TOM: Fine, Bob. Say, you're lookin' great.

BOB: You too! Seen Charlie lately?

A few minutes of idle conversation and soggy memories follow. And then . . .

BOB: Whatcha doin' at Acme Electric, Tom?

TOM: Well, Bob, Thornburg Products sent me down here to find out if you fellows can give us a little help in working out a schedule which will guarantee us a thousand electric fans a week in May and fifteen hundred a week in June.

BOB: With reference to your request, Tom, I regret to inform you that as of this date it is not to be expected that there is likely to be a significant upward revision in our production of electric fans, which will result in any expectation of our being in a position to insure delivery of fans as of a particular date.

TOM: You mean you aren't making enough fans.

BOB: It is expected, on the other hand, that in view of the fact that our Sergovia plant is in a position such that in connection with electric fans there is a potentially favorable outlook with respect to production . . .

TOM: Sergovia may produce more fans.

BOB: . . . it is estimated that there is a possibility that summer production may be expected to be in excess of ten percent of that obtaining as of the present month.

TOM: Perhaps ten percent more, eh?

BOB: With respect to your inquiry, therefore, it cannot be assumed that this company is in a position to—

TOM: Thanks very much, Bob. You can't up production more than ten percent, so you can't guarantee delivery. Well, it never hurts to try.

BOB: On the basis of the evidence at hand, it would be my opinion that that is a sound conclusion.

TOM: So long, Bob. Thanks again.

BOB: If we can be of further assistance to you in this matter, please do not hestitate to call upon us.

Try rewriting Bob's statements so that he will sound like a human being rather than a cliché machine.

5.

Still another approach to the rubber stamp problem is one devised by Philip Broughton, a former manager in the U.S. Public Health Service. He provides 217 a set of thirty much used "buzzwords," twenty adjectives and ten nouns, placed in columns:

COLUMN 1	COLUMN 2	COLUMN 3
0. integrated	0. management	0. options
1. total	1. organizational	1. flexibility
2. systematized	2. monitored	2. capability
3. parallel	3. reciprocal	3. mobility
4. functional	4. digital	4. programming
5. responsive	5. logistical	5. concept
6. optional	6. transitional	6. time-phase
7. synchronized	7. incremental	7. projection
8. compatible	8. third-generation	8. hardware
9. balanced	9. policy	9. contingency

To use his "Systematic Buzz Phrase Projector" one chooses any three-digit number and then selects the corresponding buzzwords from the three columns. Number 438 will produce "functional reciprocal hardware," a phrase which can be slid into your reports to impress readers with your expertise. "No one," says Broughton, "will have the remotest idea of what you're talking about. But the important thing is that they're not about to admit it."[1]

6.

Rubber stamps, of course, are not confined to business writing. As we have suggested, they are all around us. In order to increase your sensitivity to them, we suggest that you seek them out in other areas.

a. Select a kind of writing to which you are regularly exposed. Examples: textbooks (in general or in a particular field); legal documents; romantic novels; college and university catalogs.
b. Make a list of all of the rubber stamps you find in an extended sample of the writing you have chosen—at least 20 pages. After each rubber stamp write an appropriate substitute.
c. Write a brief report for your instructor in which you compare the types of rubber stamps you have found with those discussed in this chapter and illustrated in the Materials for Revision.

MATERIALS FOR REVISION

Here are some sentences which contain rubber stamps and other types of wasteful prose discussed in this and the previous chapter. Revising them will reinforce your understanding of the problems involved and your ability to recognize them in your own writing.

[1] Newsweek, May 6, 1968, p. 104. Copyright 1968 by Newsweek, Inc. All rights reserved. Reprinted by permission.

DIRECTNESS

A

1. We are in receipt of your letter of April 27 with regard to the color charts on the machinery enamels.
2. This is to advise you that on the recent sample of Pliaform coating for which you sent in a sample order for the subject company, we wish to give you the following information.
3. With reference to your recent advertisement in the *Chemical and Engineering News,* please send your Bulletin D-56 on "Controlling River Pollution."
4. This is in regard to complaints by the subject company on application of Protecto floor covering to floors in their Plainfield offices. They should be referred to Tom Neal in Baltimore.
5. With reference to your letter of June 30 we wish to inform you that the Acid Pump sent us for repairs against your purchase order No. 54-5614 has already been repaired by the factory and returned to you within the past week.
6. With reference to your letter of April 13 under the above subject, we wish to advise that all the district offices of our division have been canvassed for their opinions as to whether the Rite-Right or Rite-Well trademarks should be retained by our company.
7. In your letter of May 25 you requested permission to return 4 only T-417 Separatory Funnels, 4000 ml., and 4 only T-422 Separatory Funnels, 6000 ml., for credit. You have our permission to return these funnels to our Cleveland office prepaid, and upon receipt and inspection we will issue you full credit.
8. This is to acknowledge your letter of March 12, and thank you for calling to our attention the Federal Transportation Tax billed in error on our invoice K16-390.
9. Reference is made to your letter dated February 20. We have complied with Items (1) and (3) of your letter by adding an expansion joint and changing the gauge.
10. Your letter of August 8 regarding the necessity of grinding down camshafts when several are employed in parallel has been received. While your inquiry was directed to our Machinery Division Detroit Office, it has been forwarded to this office for response. Without presuming to write a book on the subject here, under the conditions you described and assuming that the camshafts are capable of withstanding a little grinding, we would not recommend grinding the camshafts.
11. Referencing your memo of August 20 to B. Boles mentioning it will be impractical to clean out the duct through the access doors, I also agree.
12. This letter is written to inform and summarize to you my understanding of our previous discussions and meetings regarding the status and actions to be taken on particular engineering items which will affect the present scope of work for the terminal and also additional scope of work items which affect the target price.
13. Please be advised that per my letter to Gorman Industries dated November 28, 1979, the following settlement has been reached relative to the claims against Gorman Industries, Inc.
14. Reference your letter dated September 18, the following samples are hereby submitted.

B

1. With regard to our contract on the San Francisco installation, we wish to herein outline our understanding of the agreement reached during our recent discussion in your office concerning payment for work performed.
2. On the matter of the $500 overrun for the first quarter, this seems to be very high. 219

3. I would like to be advised as to the equipment that was removed from our sand blast generator so your remote control feature could be installed.

4. Our equipment foreman, Mr. Tom Rand, is driving a truck to the site and it is anticipated he will arrive by March 22.

5. As far as the shipment of an 8000-gallon tank car for May 1 is concerned, we feel certain that we will be able to make this shipment.

6. With reference to your letter of December 20, we are pleased to advise that our Credit Memorandum 472/14 in favor of your company in the amount of $48.82 is enclosed.

7. The column with respect to its size is thirteen and a half feet high.

8. Attached hereto, is our brochure on Priam Sealing Compound which we trust that you will find of interest and considerable assistance to you.

9. Such publications afford the interested reader the opportunity to scrutinize the market carefully and with a minimum of expenditure of his time and energy.

10. We are expecting a return on investment in the order of $200,000.

11. We have taken your request under consideration, and although we cannot now give you a favorable reply we will communicate with you on the matter as soon as is practicable.

12. The Lorightstown Papers Project is nearing completion. Could you please tell me if any disputes or problems exist which may cost us financially?

    If you anticipate a satisfactory termination to this venture, it is necessary that I also know that.

    Please advise me on this matter as soon as possible.

13. Please return to me as promptly as possible the application, assignment, and receipt. Your early attention to this matter is appreciated.

14. For any further information, kindly contact Mr. George Owen or the undersigned. Thanking you in anticipation of your response.

15. We hope the above and attached proposal will meet your requirements and we are looking forward to receiving your written order.

    Thank you for your consideration. Should you in the interim desire any additional information, please don't hesitate to contact us.

12

Sentence Sense

In discussions of writing, one occasionally meets an old saw: if a sentence (or paragraph, or letter, or report) is confusing, it is because the writer was not sure what he or she was trying to say. Like any other half-truth, this one can be very irritating. It is often pronounced with great solemnity and just as often received with frustration. Annoyed listeners, although they may accept its validity as a general proposition, recall situations in which they knew exactly what they wanted to say but couldn't seem to figure out how to say it. Most of us have on occasion turned to a friend or associate and said, "Now, what I want to tell her is . . ." or "What we ought to tell him is . . ." and then, "But how do I [or we] say it?"

The old maxim might better read: a poor sentence (or paragraph, or letter, or report) *may* be the result of the writer's not being sure of what he or she is trying to say. Or better still: a person who is not sure what he or she is trying to say will probably write poorly. The causality indicated by the original statement is not always correct. Take, for example, the following:

Upon receipt of your June 23 invoice covering this transaction we were given only a 30 percent discount rate as I believe we were entitled to enjoy a 35 percent   **221** discount due to the fact that I requested on our confirming order to kindly group our order No. V-4817 with another mechanical convection oven, namely Model 43X appearing on our purchase order No. V-4816 of the same date.

The man who wrote this sentence knew what he meant, as a careful reading will show. The point is that many people (particularly those who pronounce the old saw) do not realize that there are two important aspects to writing:

1. Knowing *what* one wants to say, and
2. Knowing *how* to say it.

Weakness in the first almost always leads to ineptness in the second. But the inept statement of an idea does not necessarily indicate failure to understand *what* to say.

The second aspect of writing, knowing *how* to say something, involves some understanding of how the English language works, of how to put words together so that readers or listeners will understand exactly what we are trying to say. Fortunately, by listening to and reading the words of others, most of us have learned ways of getting our message across. When we talk with our friends over lunch, we can make ourselves understood, and when we write to our families about what we are doing or to a company to praise or complain about a product, we usually get the results we want. Still, some of us communicate better than others, probably because some have a better "ear" for the rhythms and the structures of English.

Grammarians, of course, have devoted their lives to studying the structure of the language, and have produced, like students of other fields, a complex terminology to describe every facet of the way we speak or write. Some knowledge of the essential elements of grammar is certainly useful, and a good handbook is a very helpful tool for anyone who wishes to communicate. Here we cannot deal with these matters in detail. However, we will attempt to suggest in this and the next two chapters how an understanding of some patterns of English usage may be employed to express ideas with accuracy, precision, and force. Here we will consider some problem areas in business communication which concern the structure of individual sentences. In Chapters 13 and 14 we will see how the proper use of formal and informal diction and the active and passive voice can help a writer to present ideas clearly.

ARRANGING THE SENTENCE

When we talk about a "good" sentence, we mean a sentence that conveys an intended meaning through an effective arrangement of its parts: its individual words and the larger units of which it is constructed. The key words here are "effective arrangement." We shall examine their meaning shortly, but first we should be sure that we know what a sentence is.

SENTENCE SENSE

A sentence is defined by grammarians as a group of words containing *at least* one independent clause—a group of words containing a subject and a verb: *Thompson* (subject) + *spoke* (verb)—which may stand alone as a statement or a question or an exclamation. It seldom, of course, consists of two words only. These words may be modified and their meaning sharpened by other words and groups of words:

> Then, after a long pause, *Thompson,* the central figure in the merger, *spoke* words that his hearers would never forget.

The added words fill out the bare bones of the original sentence. *Then* relates the sentence to the preceding narrative, as in a different way does *after a long pause. The central figure in the merger* defines Thompson's role and tells us why his words were important, and *words that his hearers would never forget* suggests the impact of what he said. These words, phrases, and clauses all modify and particularize the simple *Thompson spoke*—and they do it in such a way as to produce a particular effect.

Clearly the writer of the account from which we have taken this sentence is about to describe the climactic moment in a board meeting. The sentence leads into a historical pronouncement—at least as far as one company is concerned. The writer might have arranged the ideas differently.

> Then Thompson, the central figure in the merger, spoke, after a long pause, words that his hearers would never forget.
>
> Then Thompson, the central figure in the merger, after a long pause, spoke words that his hearers would never forget.
>
> Then the central figure in the merger, Thompson, after a long pause spoke words that his hearers would never forget.

Or slightly different wording might have been used:

> There was a long pause. Then Thompson, who was the central figure in the merger, spoke words that his hearers would never forget.
>
> Thompson was the central figure in the merger, and after a long pause he spoke words that his hearers would never forget.
>
> Thompson was the central figure in the merger, and after a pause he spoke, and his hearers will never forget his words.

There are many other ways in which the writer might have led up to Thompson's words. But even the seven possibilities we have presented are likely to produce varying reactions in a reader. Most of them convey something of the drama which the writer clearly intended to bring out. But the last two in the second group are obviously less successful than the other five. Neither sentence comes to a climax, and the last one with its *and . . . and* is just a dull statement of facts. The other five versions, each in a different way, preserve the climactic

223

effect of the original. Which of them one might choose would depend on *how* dramatic one wanted to be and on the style and content of the surrounding sentences.

The point we would make here is that most ideas, even simple ones, can be expressed in many different ways, even if one uses almost the same words. But some ways are better than others. Obviously the writer never has time to study all of the ways in which each of the sentences in a report or a letter might be written. Nor will every sentence be important enough to justify doing so. But some are, and they should produce the precise effect that the writer seeks. These are the sentences that good writers work over until they get them right. They know that to get their message across, to get readers to do or feel what they want them to do or feel, the choice and arrangement of words must be just right. *Almost* right is not enough.

COORDINATION

Working out a suitable pattern for a sentence is not usually a difficult task. Instinctively most of us recognize that some patterns are better than others, that they are more likely to elicit an appropriate response. There are, however, a few useful guidelines for producing effective sentences. The remainder of this chapter will be devoted to them. One of these concerns the use of coordination, one of the two basic ways in which relationships are suggested between the elements of the sentence—and sometimes between larger elements as well.

A little girl, when asked what she did today, will say something like this: "Mommy and I went downtown, and we went to the store, and Mr. Higgins was there, and he gave me an ice cream cone, and then. . . ." In the beginning, children use the simplest, most natural way to relate ideas. They simply add one statement to another in a long string connected with *ands*. They are using coordination.

Coordination is the basic pattern of all prose;[1] but as children develop, they find that it will not work for presenting complex ideas. They then begin to adopt the more sophisticated speech patterns of their elders. Still, coordination continues to be of fundamental importance in their speech, for they need it to join ideas of equal importance in a single sentence (using *and* to add one item to another and, later, *but, or, nor,* and *yet* to suggest contrast). They will also find it useful in suggesting relationships between larger units of speech or writing.

---

[1] Early English narrative prose was based largely on coordination, as this passage from Sir Thomas Malory's *Morte d'Arthur* will suggest:

So on a night he went to play him by the water side, for he was somewhat weary of the ship. And then he listened and heard an horse come, and one riding upon him. And when he came nigh, he seemed a knight. And so he let him pass, and went thereas the ship was; and there he alit, and took the saddle and the bridal and put the horse from him, and went into the ship. And then Launcelot dressed unto him and he said: "Ye be welcome."

EQUAL IMPORTANCE—EQUAL FUNCTION—EQUAL FORM

Children presumably string ideas on a chain of *ands* because to them each piece of information is of equal importance. Their minds simply add one thing to another. Occasionally they see a contrast and use a *but*. ("Mr. Higgins gave me a candy, but he didn't give any to Mommy.") They also use the same sentence pattern for each item: "Mommy and I went . . . and we went . . . and Mr. Higgins was . . . and he gave." Because for them each item has the same communication function, it is presented in the same form. Always it is subject followed by verb.

In adulthood the principles which govern children's use of coordination still apply. When we use a coordinating conjunction, it should join elements of equal importance and equal function, and they should be presented in the same grammatical structure:

Sales and *profits* are up.

Both *in sales* and *in profits* we have come out ahead.

Although *sales are up* and *profits are down,* we remain confident.

We have raised our interest rates, but *inflation has not been curbed.*

In each instance the items being added or compared are of equal importance and function and are in the same grammatical form. They should be, for we have come to *expect* that they should.

Here is the final sentence of a business letter that violates these principles:

Thank you for your letter of July 1, and we were pleased to have your Mr. Thorn visit us.

Why should the two clauses here be joined with an *and*? They are not really of equal importance, and they certainly have different functions. Presumably concerned that "Thank you for your letter of July 1" might sound too abrupt or impolite, the writer joined the two ideas in one very uncomfortable sentence. Clearly they belong in separate sentences:

Thank you for your letter of July 1. We were pleased to have your Mr. Thorn visit us.

These sentences say what the writer had in mind, and their simplicity suggests a sincerity completely absent from the distorted original.

HOOKS: MISLEADING COORDINATORS

Coordinating conjunctions used to yoke together ideas that really do not belong together we refer to as "hooks." Their presence usually suggests that **225** the writer (or speaker) is not *thinking* about the relationships between ideas. Here, for example, is a sentence in which *but* is used in this confusing way:

> We were careful not to discuss financial arrangements for obtaining the use of this equipment, but it is evident that we would like to do business with them, but we do not know how it can be accomplished.

This sentence is not merely very awkward: it is also an inaccurate expression of the writer's ideas. The first *but* implies a relationship between the first two clauses which does not in fact exist. It misleads the reader. Perhaps the writer was anticipating the appropriate *but* which comes later.

In support of our earlier contention that one writing fault often brings others with it, we should point out that there are other weaknesses in this sentence. It is wordy, and it is stilted. Compare it with the following revision:

> We were careful not to discuss how much it will cost us to use this equipment. We'd like to do business with them, but don't know how to swing it.

If the memo were going to someone not quite as close to the writer as the tone of this revision implies, it could be a little more formal:

> We were careful not to discuss financial arrangements for using this equipment. We would like to do business with them, but we do not know how to go about it.

Although the phrasing here is closer to the original, it is an improvement. Instead of a single long sentence, we have two shorter ones. Instead of 38 words, only 30. And instead of suggesting confusion, the revised statements reflect competence.

A hook can distort in still another way:

> The controls were moved forward and sales were found to rise.

The writer of this sentence has failed to express accurately the relationship between the two parts of the sentence. The two ideas in it are not of equal importance. Therefore, the less important one should have been placed in a subordinate clause.

> When the controls were moved forward, sales rose.

Or, with only a slight change in meaning,

> Because the controls were moved forward, sales rose.

Either revision expresses better the proper relationship between the two ideas.

Hooks, then, confuse the reader by signaling improperly in either of two ways: they may suggest a coordinate relationship which does not in fact exist, thus forcing the reader to discover the proper relationship before proceeding; or they may hook together separate ideas which should stand alone. In either case, clarity is sacrificed.

PARALLEL STRUCTURE

As we have seen, items joined by coordinating conjunctions must have a similar function. Furthermore, within a sentence, items with a similar function should have a similar structure. Thus we should not only join like things, but see that they have the same grammatical form; that, in other words, they have parallel structure.

Parallel structure is one of the most useful coordinating devices available to the writer who wishes to write clear, forceful prose. Here is the poorly worded original of a sentence we looked at in Chapter 9.

> Unusual maintenance expenses of $700 to replace the tires on a lift truck and equip it with LPG fuel, restocking the machine shop with valves, fittings, etc., amounted to $400, cleaning the septic tank cost $150, and slag for the yard totaled $300, increased this category total by $1,550.

About halfway through the sentence, readers are lost. Actually, they have been misled. Breaking the sentence up into its components will help to show what happened:

> Unusual maintenance expenses of . . . increased this category total by $1,550:
> —$700 to replace the tires on a lift truck and equip it with LPG fuel
> —restocking the machine shop with valves, fittings, etc., amounted to $400
> —cleaning the septic tank cost $150, and
> —slag for the yard totaled $300

There are many difficulties with the sentence. First, the reader must keep the subject in mind for 40 words before he finds the verb that goes with it. Second, the *of*, intended to introduce the series of expenses which follows, actually misleads by suggesting that $700 is the *total* maintenance expense. Only toward the end of the sentence does the reader discover that it is not. Third, three of the terms in the series are assigned three different verbs to indicate the same thing—*amounted to, cost,* and *totaled;* and the other term (the first of the series) uses a different approach altogether—*expenses of.*

But the most important difficulty is that after establishing a pattern, the writer reverses it without warning. The first phrase begins with a cost figure ($700), but in the other phrases the cost is at the end. The writer fails to use the grammatical parallelism needed to establish the relationship between the four terms in the series, all of which are equal in importance, parallel in meaning, and parts of a larger total. In tabular form, here is what the writer was trying to say:

Unusual maintenance expenses:

Replacing tires on lift truck and equipping with LPG fuel	$ 700
Restocking machine shop with valves, fittings, etc.	400
Cleaning septic tank	150
Buying slag for yard	300
Increase in Total	$1,550

Note that in listing the components of the series, we have used the same form of the relevant verb for each: repla*cing,* equip*ping,* restoc*king,* clea*ning,* and bu*ying.* Readers can move comfortably from one to the next without having to figure out where they are. In sentence form, a rewritten version of this material, with strengthened punctuation where necessary, might read:

> Unusual maintenance expenses—replacing tires on lift truck and equipping with LPG fuel, $700; restocking machine shop with valves, fittings, etc., $400; cleaning septic tank, $150; and buying slag for the yard, $300—increased the total of this category by $1,550.

Here, at least, there is no problem of comprehension, for the relationship of parts in the sentence is clear. However, basing the sentence too rigidly on the table produces an awkward solution with subject and verb still widely separated. Much more effective would be:

> Unusual maintenance expenses increased the total of this category by $1,550: $700 for replacing the tires on the lift truck and equipping it with LPG fuel; $400 for restocking the machine shop with valves, fittings, etc.; $150 for cleaning the septic tank; and $300 for buying slag for the yard.

Here subject and predicate have been brought together at the start of the sentence. We know precisely what we are dealing with. The colon after "$1,550" tells us that what follows will be the items that make up the total. Each is presented in an identical format: first the expenditure in dollars and then "for," followed by the nature of the expenditure. The sentence is easy to read, and the relationship of its ideas is never in doubt.

Parallelism is often important not only for the elements of a sentence but also for larger grammatical units. Note how difficult it is to follow these instructions:

> GENERAL SPECIFICATIONS. Outlined below are summaries of the specifications covering the shop or yard application of materials recommended for each use:
> *Use No. 1—Well-Column Piping*
>
> A. Interior
>   1. Clean by sandblasting.
>   2. One coat of "Primer X7."
>   3. Minimum 1/16 inch thickness of "Top Gloss," penetration 10 to 15.
>   4. Holiday-detect and touch-up.

B. Exterior
1. Clean by sandblasting.
2. One coat of "Primer X7."
3. Minimum 1/16 inch "Top Gloss," penetration 10 to 15.
4. Holiday-detect and touch-up.
5. Cut back six inches from ends.
6. Prime bare ends with one coat of "Primer X7."
7. One coat of whitewash to enameled surfaces.

The trouble, of course, is that the reader has to approach each item very tentatively, in order to determine its pattern.

The writer could have made it much easier for the reader by beginning each item in the same way:

A. Interior
1. Clean . . .
2. Apply one coat . . .
3. Apply a minimum thickness . . .
4. Holiday-detect and touch-up . . .

In the revised version the reader moves from one item to the next without hesitation. The parallel grammatical construction indicates the parallel function of the items in the instructions. The original specifications list at least gave the reader some help: the steps were listed in order.

In a sentence containing a series, one must be careful to provide consistent structure throughout. Try reading this sentence at normal speed:

A document should be developed that identifies the positions and titles of key personnel in the communication channels and their responsibilities for decision making, resolution of problems, for providing information, review of classifications, and for taking other action within the scope of the program.

One can figure out what the writer is trying to say, but the use of two different structures (*decision making, resolution,* and *review; providing* and *taking*) and the use of the word *for* with three items but not with the others makes for bumpy travel.[2] The writer might better have said "for making decisions, for resolving . . . , for providing . . . , for reviewing . . . , and for taking. . . ." The word *for* serves as a signpost which keeps the reader firmly on course throughout the sentence. One might, of course omit all but the first *for*—"for making . . . , resolving . . . , providing . . . , reviewing . . . , and taking. . . ." In this version the *-ing* ending would be the needed signpost. One might even try "for decision making, resolution of . . . , provision of . . . , review of . . . , and initiation of other action. . . ." A rather awkward, but not impossible, solution. What one must *not* do if one wants to keep the reader on the track is to use a combination of structures—as in the original sentence.

[2] One can only assume that the writer had been told in high school or college that his or her prose lacked variety. Perhaps it did. But the solution is not to vary sentence structure if to do so will confuse the reader.

SUBORDINATION

If coordination is one of the essential ingredients of English usage, subordination is the other. It is subordination in its many forms which gives English its infinite variety of tone, its subtle modulation of meaning. Without it we could do little more than catalog things; we could not reveal their relationships. Fortunately all of us use subordination all of the time. It is part of our heritage. But we can always refine the ways in which we use it. Certainly we should be able to distinguish it from coordination. Let's look at another sentence:

> Roger French is our representative in Canada and he has been working with us for the past year on a trial basis.

The *and* implies that the two clauses are equally important. The sentence appeared, however, in reply to a letter asking a company how long Roger French had been with them. Clearly, then, the information that French was the firm's Canadian representative was not as important to the reader as the length of time he had been their representative. If the writer wanted to mention French's job, the information should have been placed in a subordinate construction:

> Roger French, who is our representative in Canada, has been with our company for the past year on trial. (*relative clause*)

Or:

> Roger French, our representative in Canada, has been with our company for the past year on trial. (*appositive*)

If the questioner *had* been primarily interested in French's job, the sentence might have read:

> Roger French, who has been with our company for the past year on trial, is our representative in Canada. (*relative clause*)

Or:

> Roger French, on trial with our company for the past year, is our representative in Canada. (*prepositional phrase*)

A more neutral version might be:

> Roger French has been on trial as our Canadian representative for the past year.

The emphasis of even this version might be subtly changed by placing "for the past year" at the start.

It is not difficult to determine which is the main portion (*independent clause*) of a sentence. Reading aloud the groups of words below will reveal that each may stand as an independent clause:

the controls were moved forward
sales were found to rise
Roger French is our representative in Canada
he has been working with us for the past year on trial

Since each is an independent, or main, clause, it can function as a sentence.

Clarifying or supporting (*subordinate*) ideas should be put into subordinate constructions:

when the controls were moved forward
because the controls were moved forward
who is our representative in Canada
our representative in Canada
who has been with our company for the past year on trial
on trial with our company for the past year
as our Canadian representative for the past year

None of these word groups can stand alone as a complete sentence—except on the rare occasion when one may be used to simulate speech, as, for example, in a talk to a marketing department.

Why did we make so much money on our plastics this year? Because our new sales-incentive system is better for plastics than for cottons.

Even when used in this way, such a clause makes no sense unless it is obviously related to a main idea. The best way to indicate the relationship between such ideas is to keep them in the same sentence, using the proper subordinating conjunction.

DANGLING MODIFIERS

If a subordinate construction standing by itself is not meaningful, one incorrectly attached to a main clause may cause temporary or even permanent confusion. For example,

Confirming our recent discussion with Mr. Brown, Ms. Pope has requested a study to determine the level of investment required.

Who, one asks, has done the confirming? Presumably it is Ms. Pope. Her name follows directly the participial phrase with which the sentence begins. Actually the writer intended to indicate that *he* was confirming what *he* had already told Mr. Brown: that Ms. Pope had requested the study.

Another example may show more clearly what the trouble is:

Having made the required adjustments, the machine ran smoothly.

What does this sentence tell us? If the machine made its own adjustments, the sentence makes sense. However, the writer of this sentence intended to say that a *mechanic* made the adjustments, and readers were misled (at least temporarily) into thinking that the machine was able to make its own adjustments. Once again the participial phrase, "having made the required adjustments," refers to no word in the main clause.

Such phrases are usually called "danglers," because they dangle from the beginning or end of a sentence without referring to (or modifying) anything in it. The operative word in such a phrase is usually a participle, a verbal form ending in *-ing* or *-ed* which functions as an adjective to modify a noun or a pronoun. Our experience leads us to expect the noun or pronoun to come right after the participial phrase:

Confirming our recent conversation with Mr. Brown, *I* wish to report. . . .

Having made the required adjustments, the *mechanic* was able to. . . .

If we do not find it there, we are likely to be confused.

There are two ways of avoiding danglers. As we have just seen, we can make sure that the opening phrase actually modifies the subject of the sentence, or we can change the participial form to a verb and provide it with its own subject:

I'd like to confirm my recent discussion with Mr. Brown. Ms. Pope has requested. . . .

After the mechanic made the required adjustment, the machine. . . . *or* The mechanic made the required adjustment. The machine. . . .

The revisions avoid possible misunderstanding or amusing misstatement.

Throughout this chapter we have been talking about how writers should use the two most important structural patterns in English sentences: coordination and subordination. Underlying everything we have said here is the principle that grammatical structure should always reflect the relationship of the ideas to be communicated. Form must follow function. Usually the structure of our sentences naturally reinforces the relationships we are trying to convey to our audience. But if we fail to monitor our communications, we can quite easily fail to provide a noun or pronoun for a participle to modify, or neglect to use parallel structure for parallel ideas. As in most of our activities, the key to success is constant vigilance.

ILLUSTRATIVE MATERIALS

1.

Word order in English was not always as important as it is now. In King Alfred's time (A.D. 849–901), as Fries has pointed out, the sentence The man struck the bear *could have been written:*

Se mann þone beran sloh.
þone beran se mann sloh.
þone beran sloh se mann.
Sloh se mann þone beran.[3]

This randomness of word order was possible only because each word in Old English had an ending which indicated its relationship to the rest of the words in the sentence. Today, because our language has lost most of these case endings, the English sentence has a relatively fixed word order: subject—verb—object.

A good writer is aware of the finer points of word order. Examine several modern prose passages and consider these questions:

a. *What seem to be the normal positions of a noun and its modifier (or modifiers)?*
b. *Are there exceptions to your generalization?*
c. *What seem to be the normal positions of a verb and its modifer (or modifiers)?*
d. *Are there exceptions to your generalization?*
e. *How many ways does English have of indicating possession?*

2.

Examine this passage:

> The diggle woggles the sug. Then it fraggles a sig. When it lings, it fings. The sig's libid crimples. The sigs crimple too.

a. *In the first sentence, which word is the subject? The verb? The object? How do you know?*
b. *To what word in the first sentence does* it *in the second sentence refer? It in the third sentence? How do you know?*
c. *What is the relationship between the words* sig's *and* libid *in the fourth sentence? How do you know?*
d. *What is the difference between* sig's *in the fourth sentence and* sigs *in the fifth sentence? What gives you the clue?*
e. *Do you have to know the meaning of words in a sentence to understand their relationships? Explain your answer.*

[3] Charles Carpenter Fries, *American English Grammar* (New York: Appleton-Century-Crofts, 1940), p. 251.

3.

In writing headlines, editors often take liberties with sentence structure.

JUST NOT ENOUGH MEN,
   MACHINES TO CLEAR SNOW

DISTRICT ATTORNEY
   CANDIDATE SAYS LABOR
      RANK, FILE DELUDED

HE LOSES OUT TO WIFE, DAUGHTER IN COURT

a. *Each headline can be read in two ways. What are they?*
b. *What were the editors trying to do that caused the ambiguity?*
c. *What are the alternative readings for each of the following?*

JONES CHARGES ERROR

POLICE STILL CRYING

AGENT FOUND DOPE ADDICT

4.

One subordinating conjunction frequently gives writers a good deal of trouble. Read the following sentences:

The feeling is mounting trends in a number of directions must be viewed for their impact on the overall picture.

Preponderant thought continues the correction will be neither long nor severe.

More important, if the premise we are in a bull market is correct, we should not be overly concerned with intermediate movements.

a. *How far did you get in each sentence before you realized that something was wrong?*
b. *What is missing in each sentence and where does it belong?*
c. *Separate the main portion of each sentence (the independent clause) from the group of words which the missing word should have introduced. Does this procedure help to determine the meaning?*
d. *What function, then, does the missing word perform?*
e. *When can it be left out without confusing the reader?*
f. *In the first sentence does it make any difference whether the missing word is inserted before or after* mounting?

Now read these sentences:

Many people feel that if an article is advertised nationally that it is a good product to buy.

I was told that if I could supply the necessary benzine by July 3 that I could have the order.

How does the problem in these sentences differ from the problem in the above list?
Here is a further problem with the same word:

Jones should rerun the tests and try the new fuel. He can schedule Block C for the tests. That should be done by next Tuesday.

R. C. Donald became president and F. L. Grinnel was moved up to replace him. That means trouble for us.

a. *What causes the confusion in these sentences?*
b. *How can the confusion be avoided?*
c. *The writer might have used* this *instead of* that *in either sentence. Would the substitution have made either sentence clearer? What can be done to ensure that such sentences communicate effectively?*

5.

Here is the opening of a speech on corporate governance by Irving S. Shapiro, a former chairman of E. I. du Pont de Nemours and Company. Note how effectively Mr. Shapiro uses parallel structure. Try exploding the second and third paragraphs and study the parallelism in the others.

The proper direction of business corporations in a free society is a topic of intense and often heated discussion. Under the flag of corporate governance there has been a running debate about the performance of business organizations, together with a flood of proposals for changes in the way corporate organizations are controlled.

It has been variously suggested that corporate charters be dispensed by the Federal Government as distinct from those of the states (to tighten the grip on corporate actions); that only outsiders unconnected to an enterprise be allowed to sit on its board of directors or that, as a minimum, most of the directors should qualify as "independent"; that seats be apportioned to constituent groups (employees, women, consumers and minorities, along with stockholders); that boards be equipped with private staffs, beyond the management's control (to smoke out facts the hired executives might prefer to hide or decorate); and that new disclosure requirements be added to existing ones (to provide additional tools for outside oversight of behavior and performance).

Such proposals have come from the Senate Judiciary Committee's antitrust arm; from regulatory agency spokesmen, most notably the current head of the Securities and Exchange Commission, Harold Williams, and a predecessor there, William Cary; from the professoriat in schools of law and business; from the bench and bar; and from such observers of the American scene as Ralph Nader and Mark Green.

Suggestions for change have sometimes been offered in sympathy and sometimes in anger. They have ranged from general pleas for corporations to behave better, to meticulously detailed reorganization charts. The span in itself suggests part of the problem: "Corporate Governance" (like Social Responsibility before it) is not a subject with a single meaning, but is a shorthand label for an array of social and political as well as economic concerns. One is obliged to look for a way to keep discussion within a reasonable perimeter.

There appears to be one common thread. All of the analyses, premises, and prescriptions seem to derive in one way or another from the question of accountability: Are corporations suitably controlled and to whom or what are they responsible? This is the central public issue, and the focal point for this paper.

PROBLEMS

Below are several groups of phrases and clauses. They may be put together in various ways to fashion sentences which have roughly the same meaning but are likely to have somewhat different impact on a reader. Taking each group separately, work out sentences with as many organizational patterns as you can. (See pp. 223 and 230 for an example.) Then determine under what circumstances you might find each to be most effective: for example, if the reader were primarily interested in when the event happened; if I wanted to drive home the necessity of shopping around; if the reader were most concerned about where Shipton is located.

1. Those who can produce the pumps efficiently/companies with expertise and capital/ under these circumstances/with increasing regulation/only/can expect to show a profit.

2. When the matter was discussed in the committee/as Barnes pointed out/other than by looking at the balance sheet/there was no way to monitor the success of the program.

3. At the new plant/whichever incentive scheme we adopt/in the long run/profits are certain to increase/when we go into production next month.

MATERIALS FOR REVISION

The following items contain examples of errors discussed in this and the preceding chapters. Revising them will reinforce your understanding of the problems involved and your ability to recognize similar mistakes and to avoid making them in your own writing.

SENTENCE SENSE

A

1. The recent realignment of the Division has placed the Project Department and the Technical Department within the Development Department, and I understand that, in conformity with company organization terminology, these departments will in the future be considered as sections.
2. I have referred this case to our Insurance Section, and you will hear from us again in the very near future. (Closing sentence)
3. Will you please let me know when this sample has gone forward, and we will report to you on the results of our tests after they have been completed. (Closing sentence)
4. On July 13, it appeared that we would have difficulty moving some of our Buffalo stock and desired at that time, and still desire, to go into the winter at Buffalo with a minimum inventory.
5. We will, however, as indicated during our conversation today, endeavor to have this work completed so that I can give you the final figure by phone on Thursday, March 3, so that you can enter this on your books for the month of February.
6. It goes without saying, of course, that the sealed shaft precludes negotiating a curve, and we hope these comments are of value to you.
7. We have asked Eastern Refining Company to reserve their next car for your account, assuming you will need another one during the second half of October, so will appreciate your giving us the next estimated shipping date at your earliest convenience so we will know whether or not to continue to hold this car for you.
8. We want to call your attention to the compartment forward of the engine room which you showed as extending completely across the hull, whereas this compartment is only in the center portion of the hull and it extends forward of the oil-tank section.
9. We continued to improve and supervise the machine at Atlas and have recently appointed an independent committee to analyze and audit the past records and operation at Atlas and prepare a report recommending the future course to be taken in this field.
10. As you will note from the letter, your talk should last about one hour and the date is October 15.
11. The report I mentioned is not yet finished. I am waiting for some estimates from Barbara Hoffmann but a copy will be on its way to you as soon as it is off the press.
12. The general procedure was to show slides or movies about the products or in many instances the actual products themselves were brought along.

B

1. Under the best of conditions there exists a 215°F thermal shock and under the worst conditions the shock amounts to 480°F.
2. We are anxious to keep abreast of this situation and would appreciate your advising us as to when you now expect that these cars will be used and will you be able to release them for use in other sections of the country.
3. The pattern of new orders remained essentially unchanged. Increased orders were reported by 34%, and 48% reported their order books unchanged. 18% state new orders decreased. Of the members who responded to a special question, 52% say capital expenditures will be higher this year than last; 33% report they will be about the same, and 15% say less will be spent.

237

4. This statement is broken down into three categories. First, all items which have been set up in salesmen's and/or office quotas are shown in the first category. The second category covers district quotas not assigned to individual salesmen. Category three covers all items which are excluded from the incentive plan.

5. The sample is removed from the kiln. Allow to cool at least 12 hours. Apply two coats of .5 mil wet thickness each. Allow to dry at least 6 hours between coats. The finish coat is applied after 24 hours.

6. It can be used on all surfaces which are now hand brushed where it is possible to drive a truck within 50 feet of the area or in the case of a horizontal surface 100 feet would present no difficulty.

7. On costs for handling the shipment of this material we can give you the following estimates: drums will cost $6.16 each, our filling costs will run 1.4¢ per gallon, loading into trucks would cost .003¢ per gallon, and loading into box cars would cost .005¢ per gallon.

8. It is proposed to measure and record during each run:
   a. The vehicle will be traveling at full speed on level ground when it enters the course. Two satisfactory runs, with and against the wind, will be made.
   b. Time over the measured course traveling with and against the wind.
   c. Recording of the measured weight of the fuel used per hour by the main engines.
   d. Exhaust temperatures for each cylinder of the main engines.

9. Precautions:
   a. Make certain that temperature is below 300°F and that pressure is 45 psi or lower before starting.
   b. Initiate cooling methods if water temperature exceeds 300°F.
   c. System components may be damaged if overheated. Consult appropriate personnel if failure occurs.

10. For example, a project engineer spent 30% of his working time speaking and 15% in written communication.

11. Are you interested in determining the amount of compaction that occurs upon storage or is it to determine the "body" of the material?

C

1. On rechecking our field work performed at Southern Pipe, it was indicated that the bond on the interior of the pipe was completely satisfactory after several days.

2. Unlike a roof inspection, which can be rechecked by a local representative without the use of rigging and scaffolding, two skilled men, who are not normally available locally, are required to make the tank inspection.

3. Upon examination of the fabric which had been removed from the testing machine, there was a definite increase in wear noted on the untreated samples.

4. On drying, some cracks will appear, so it is necessary to fill these with the new compound and add another coat of paint.

5. When discussing the removal of solids from the gas, it was felt that probably fiber gas filters or electronic precipitators would be required.

6. Supplementing my letter of November 28 on above subject, the Department of Agriculture has indicated that farmers will purchase about 4 million gallons next year.

7. Although not being familiar with all the factors affecting the economics of the process, the following are valid observations of a general nature.

8. By knowing the speed ranges and maximum field currents for both the generator and the motor, the proper size rheostat can be obtained for each.
9. Having consolidated schools and no apprentice system, the young people are usually not qualified to work in our plants.
10. All defaulting should not occur among persons on welfare using the Madison study figures.

13

Tone and Style

Much of the worst writing in industry today comes from the attempt to be "proper." Many people feel that the writing they do on the job should be formal and easily distinguishable from spoken communication and from personal letters. The result is often what we may call pseudoformal prose, which we will discuss in this chapter. First, however, we should distinguish between formal and informal style and determine when each is appropriate.

THE WRITING CONTINUUM

The terms *formal* and *informal* are, of course, relative. When we use them we are thinking of areas on a scale or continuum, which is usually diagrammed in this way:

formal	informal	vulgate

Most prose can be assigned to one of the three major categories, but some seems to fall between formal and informal, some between informal and vulgate.

About vulgate we need say little. It is the language of the shop floor and the tavern.

> Tell ya, Sam. Trouble with old Tom is he don't keep his eye on the ball since his missus kicked the bucket. He didn't never used to be this way. Sure, he's tryin' all right. But every time he fixes a motor he gets a valve in backwards, or he don't tighten some bolt or somethin' an' the darned crate falls apart soon as we crank 'er up. An' I'll be a cockeyed so-and-so if last week he didn't strip one down ta put in a new gasket. An' what did he do? He puts the cracked one back in an' puts the whole thing together again. Honest ta God, Sam, you gotta do somethin' or we're goin' to go crazy.

This sort of language contains nonstandard structures and is often laced with profanity. Obviously, it is not usually appropriate to the executive or professional level in business and industry, though a manager may well use it from time to time when talking with machine operators or employees working an assembly line.

Formal prose—to move to the other end of the scale—tends to use complex sentences of considerable length and an "elevated" vocabulary. It is to be found at state funerals, in inaugural addresses, in lectures at gatherings of the learned, and on other solemn occasions. In the business world, it may be suitable for annual reports, some technical and scientific reports, and other reports designed primarily for outside readers. As the occasion becomes less solemn and ceremonial, writing tends toward the informal, which imitates the conversational style of educated persons. Its characteristics are moderate sentence length, casual tone, the use of contractions, and a less sophisticated and less technical vocabulary.

FORMAL PROSE

We have provided an example of the vulgate. It may be useful now to examine in some detail an example at the opposite end of the usage continuum: a paragraph of highly formal prose, well adapted to a particular audience and particular occasion.

> A constitution, a statute, a regulation, a rule—in short, a "law" of any kind—is at once a prophecy and a choice. It is a prophecy, because it attempts to forecast what will be its effects: whom it will benefit and in what ways; on whom its impact will prove a burden; how much friction and discontent will arise from the adjustments that conformity to it will require; how completely it can be enforced; what enforcement will cost; how far it will interfere with other projects or existing activities; and, in general, the whole manifold of its indirect consequences. A thoroughgoing and dependable knowledge of these is obviously impossible. For example, although we can anticipate with some degree of assurance who will pay a steeply graded income tax and in what amounts, there is no way to tell what its indirect effect will be: what activities of the taxpayers in the higher brackets it will depress; if they do not work so hard, in what way they will occupy their newly acquired leisure; how any new activities they may substitute will affect others; whether this will be offset by a loss of the mellowed maturity and the wisdom of those who withdraw. Such prophecies infest law of every sort, the more deeply as it is far-reaching; and it is an illusion to

ECONOMY, CLARITY, AND UNITY

suppose that there are formulas or statistics that will help in making them. They can rest upon no more than enlightened guesses; but these are likely to be successful, as they are made by those whose horizons have been widened, and whose outlook has been clarified, by knowledge of what men have striven to do and how far their hopes and fears have been realized. There is no substitute for an open mind, enriched by reading and the arts.[1]

To understand and appreciate this passage and its intended effect, we must examine Who—Says What—To Whom—In Which Channel.

Who

This paragraph was taken from a speech by Judge Learned Hand. When he delivered it, he was one of the most eminent jurists in the United States. He was eighty years old, had been a member of the bar for fifty-five years, and had just retired from the United States Circuit Court after forty-two years on the bench. In recognition of his accomplishments he had received honorary degrees from eleven colleges and universities in the United States and England. Thus, he was a highly educated and respected man, venerated for his years as a judge and public servant, for his legal knowledge, and for his wisdom. To many, he had become a symbol of the majesty of the law.

Says What

Judge Hand's topic was "Freedom and the Humanities," an inquiry into the "preparation of citizens for their political duties." The topic, then, was a very serious one and had important philosophic overtones.

In Which Channel

The address was presented orally on a highly ritualistic occasion from a podium behind which were ranged numerous individuals in full academic regalia.

To Whom

Judge Hand's audience at the Eighty-sixth Convocation of The University of the State of New York, the body that governs higher education in that state, represented a highly educated segment of the American population, one with diverse interests and occupations.

With such a speaker, topic, context, and audience, one would expect the message to be serious—even lofty—and certainly formal. And, indeed, the quoted paragraph has many of the characteristics that distinguish genuine formal English: the complex issues with which it deals, its vocabulary, the construction and length of its sentences and paragraphs, and even its punctuation. The issue discussed by Judge Hand in this paragaph is certainly complex: what is a just law? The vocabulary contains many words and phrases not found in

[1] The speech was reprinted in the *Bulletin of the American Association of University Professors* 38 (1952–1953), pp. 522–523.

242

everyday speech: *statute, regulation, prophecy, impact, anticipate with some degree of assurance, activities . . . it will depress, acquired leisure.* Some phrases even border on the poetic: *manifold of . . . consequences, mellowed maturity, horizons . . . widened.* Both vocabulary and phrasing are rich and dignified.

Some sentences in Judge Hand's paragraphs are unusually long and complex, as is the paragraph itself. The second sentence has 77 words and the fourth has 93. Though the paragraph includes sentences of 10 and 14 words, the average is slightly more than 43. Compare that average with those for newspapers and magazines of wide circulation—10 to 20 words; and with those in more serious books and periodicals, aimed at specific professional audiences—25 to 30 words. Similarly, the paragraph length of 303 words compares with an average of 76 in a lead editorial in *The New York Times* of the same period, 50 in a report in *The Wall Street Journal,* 56 in a *Reader's Digest* article, 85 in a *Time* news report, and 182 in a technical article.

The complexity of Judge Hand's punctuation reflects the complexity of the paragraph's organization, as shown in the following diagram. (We have substituted a slash mark for the period to make the sentence divisions more visible.)

```
____ , _____ , ____ , __ — ___ , __" __" __ — __/ ___ , ____ :
_____ ; _____ ; _____ ; ___ ; _____ ; _____ ; — , _____ ,
_____ / _____ / _____ , _____ ,
_____ : _____ ; _____ , _____ ;
_____ ; _____ / _____ ,
_____ ; _____/ _____ ; _____ ,
_____ , _____/ _____ , _____ /
```

The second sentence has eight major sections, seven of them in parallel construction. Although the other long sentence (the fourth) has few major sections (five, four in parallel construction), the sections themselves are complex, one having three parts. The unusually large number of semicolons reflects this complexity.

Adding to the density of the prose are smaller units arranged in formal patterns: *a constitution, a statute, a regulation, a rule; a prophecy and a choice; thoroughgoing and dependable; the mellowed maturity and the wisdom; formulas or statistics; hopes and fears.* Except in formal English, we seldom see so many balanced phrases. Their rhythm adds further dignity and formality to the style.

Simplifying Judge Hand's phrases and sentences would destroy the subtle shades of meaning in a carefully woven fabric. Complexity here is not the result of an attempt to impress. Rather, the phrasing and sentence structure accurately reflect a precise and subtle arrangement of ideas about a problem whose many aspects must be considered simultaneously in relation to each other. Cutting the sentences apart in an attempt to make them easier to read would only distort the message. Judge Hand was able to deliver such a complex message, of course, because he knew his listeners would be able to understand it. Had he had a less well educated audience, he probably would not have attempted such a subtly argued speech. He would, in other words, have moved across the continuum toward informal usage.

ECONOMY, CLARITY, AND UNITY

INFORMAL PROSE

On some occasions good formal prose is called for in business and industry, but usually the most appropriate level is the informal. Informal English has many characteristics of good speech. It uses conversational words and phrases if they communicate clearly. (Note, for example, the use of "called for" in the first sentence of this paragraph.) Its sentences are considerably shorter than those in Judge Hand's speech, usually averaging from 18 to 25 words in length, though an individual sentence may contain three words or 53. They are seldom as elaborately constructed as those in Judge Hand's paragraph. Most of our recommended versions of sentences, paragraphs, and memos are in informal English.

Here is a passage of good informal prose from a progress report:

> Our biggest problem has been the weather. Not only has it rained continuously since mid-January, but predictions early in February were that the rain would continue until the beginning of March. Had we decided to wait until then to start building the forms, we would have found ourselves four weeks behind schedule and headed for a heavy penalty at the end of the contract.
>
> Fortunately, Ralph Pinder kept his wits about him. During a two-day break in the weather he had a slab poured near the construction site and erected on it a 12' x 50' metal prefab that he had heard was available at Ringold. For almost a month now, the carpenters have been working inside the building on the forms needed not only for this job, but also the one at Portal. As soon as the rain stops, we will start pouring concrete at both sites, right on schedule.
>
> There is a bonus, too. The customer's local people say that they will be able to use the prefab. They have promised to buy it from us when we finish here.

Notice how the writer explains clearly, concisely, and authoritatively without the labored heaviness that makes for difficult reading in much business writing.

On occasion the writer uses phrases that have a slightly formal ring: *Not only has it rained continuously* and *Had we decided to wait until then.* But he also uses colloquial phrases: *headed for a heavy penalty, kept his wits about him,* and *right on schedule.* His sentences vary in length from seven to 33 words. Similarly, he employs a variety of sentence structures—simple, compound, and complex. But the sentences average only 20 words, and none is so involved that it is difficult to read. Just as his sentences are considerably shorter than Learned Hand's, so too are his paragraphs. Here, then, is the writing of an educated professional who treats his subject with both ease and respect and doesn't flaunt his expertise.

Engineers and other professionals are finding that a judicious use of informal phrases even in highly technical documents makes such documents more readable, more appealing to certain audiences—particularly those that are not as technically trained as the professionals who write them. Here, for example, is a section of a statement about the virtues of a software package for a new computer system:

> The operator is still needed to manipulate the model and interpret results, but much of the dog-work has been removed. The minicomputer now performs the searches for the maximum overvoltages by varying the breaker closing angles. The

time-consuming process of photographing individual cases is eliminated. Thus, there is a major improvement in study efficiency.

The problem with this setup arises when the operator has to perform a large number of repetitive tasks. If this occurs, the study becomes labor intensive and the operator does not find fulfillment in his job. Fortunately, there is a cure for this situation: it is called a digital computer. As we all know, digital computers just love to do repetitive tasks, and, contrary to popular opinion, they can be trained to perform some of the operator's judgment tasks.

Words like "dog-work" and "setup" add a touch of informality to what without them would be a heavier statement. And the last sentence in the second paragraph contains several informal phrases which establish a personal relationship between the writer and the reader. Such informality may not be appropriate with all audiences, but it does make communication friendlier—and easier.

FORMALITY AND INFORMALITY IN THE BUSINESS WORLD

We have, then, three types of writing, two of which—formal and informal— are appropriate to the business world. In the not-so-distant past, as we have seen, most business writing was in the formal mode—though never all of it, as a reading of the business correspondence of men like Henry Frick, Andrew Carnegie, and J. P. Morgan will testify. Still, most letters and reports were formal, as were the relationships between individuals. But things have changed.

The atmosphere in which we do business is everywhere more personal than it used to be. Many executives make a point of learning and using the first names of their employees. In meetings at which as many as five levels of authority are represented, all personal reference is likely to be by first name. Expense accounts attest to the amount of time business people spend with their customers in informal settings. Business dress has become more casual and more comfortable than the stiff-jacketed clothing worn in past generations. Business letterheads are simple and clean; one seldom sees formal script or Gothic lettering. Even the architecture and interior of office buildings reflect the trend. Clean lines, comfortable furniture, colored panels, and attractive landscaping have replaced the pomp of nineteenth-century neoclassicism with its impressive facades, friezes, and gingerbread. Inside, colorful floor tiles, pastel walls, and indirect lighting give an impression of warmth and friendliness.

PRESSURES TO PRESERVE OLDER FORMS

With all this movement toward informality in business and industry today, why do many people still feel that their writing should be formal? Probably most important is the feeling that, whereas speech is fleeting, a written record is permanent. On this record individuals may be judged by colleagues and superiors. Therefore it should represent their best. Subconsciously many feel that their best should be couched in prose that is weighty and "dignified." Our artists and artisans, however, have shown us that dignity can be achieved through simplicity, a lesson many letter and report writers have not yet learned.

A second reason for the continued insistence on formality goes back to what most of us are taught in school about writing. In too many high school class-rooms, the use of "proper English" was—and often still is—held up as a sacred duty for all who wish to write respectably. Quite literally, many students who do not use the standard formal phraseology, foreswear the use of "I," and refrain from beginning a sentence with "and" are made to feel somehow immoral. In an attempt to "maintain standards," many teachers have preached that only one variety of our native tongue is good—in other words, acceptable—English. Such indoctrination makes a permanent impression. Of course, every student knows from experience that effective *spoken* English is the English appropriate to the situation—that no one speaks to an elder the same way as to a child and people use one pattern of English in the ballpark and another in the law court. However, most students do not have enough writing expe-rience to know that roughly the same generalizations hold there too. So they have allowed themselves to be persuaded that all writing, except perhaps per-sonal letters, should be "formal."

Furthermore, most people find writing or dictating much more difficult than speaking informally. The very act of picking up a pencil, turning on a dictating machine, or calling in a secretary imposes a restraint, reminds us of prescrip-tions and taboos, and makes us self-conscious about what we are going to do. In short, we find ourselves in an unnatural situation. Most of us have been speaking since the age of two. Linguists tell us that we have mastered the major patterns of the spoken language by the time we reach five. Writing, however, comes much later and often involves clumsy grappling with intractable pens and pencils, assignments in which we have no interest, and teacher dis-approval. And no matter how much we write during our adult lives, we use the spoken language far more. Hence we will always be more comfortable with it.

WRITING AND SPEAKING

Writing also requires more careful attention than speaking. In conversation we can tell immediately what effect we are producing. A listener who does not understand will look puzzled and ask a question. We can then rephrase our message. If the listener frowns or smiles, we can temper our speech ac-cordingly. But when we write, we cannot count on such immediate feedback. Therefore, we must put our sentences together with care and try, as we have seen in Chapter 2, to anticipate the reader's reaction. If we fail to do so, our message will not get across. Additional letters, memos, or phone calls may be required. Worse yet, improper action may be taken, a customer may be lost (remember Fred Peters?), or serious delays may occur—with consequent loss of money to our company.

Writing, whether formal or informal, must be more precise, more accurate, and clearer than speech. It is also likely to be more concise, and it requires an appropriate vocabulary and style. Like the modern architect who allows a building's lines to reflect its structure, and the structure its function, the writer should adapt the design of each communication to the demands of the situation. The poetry of the George Washington Bridge is in the sweep of its cables and the obvious strength of its towers and supports. Its combination of ease and majesty reflects the ability of its designers to build functionally and with the greatest simplicity permitted by their materials and the gap to be spanned. Similarly, a piece of writing which perfectly reflects the content and organization of the thought it was designed to communicate is pleasing in itself. Ornamentation would only clutter it up.

Good business prose, then, is appropriate to the situation: its language and structure reflect its position on the usage continuum. Seldom, if ever, will a person in business use a style as formal as Judge Hand's or as folksy as that of the fellow talking to his foreman, Sam. Given the increasingly informal atmosphere in business, in many instances informal prose is replacing the formal style used a generation or two ago. But, as we have seen, in certain circumstances, which may differ from company to company, a relatively formal style is required. One should, therefore, know how to use that style when it is needed.

What business does *not* need is people who use the pseudoformal style—a bad imitation of the formal—which today clutters up much of the writing in business, in government, in the media, and in the academic world.

PSEUDOFORMAL WRITING

Here is a routine business letter:

Dear Ms. Rogers:

Subsequent to our recent discussion in your office, we have reviewed our present situation with regard to the possibility of our submitting a proposal for the Thomasville project about which you inquired and regret to advise that at this time we are unable to quote.

Our foregoing decision was reached after a thorough and complete study revealed that we are not currently in a position to be able to produce the engineering drawings within a period of time as indicated by you in your office to be acceptable.

We trust that we will continue to be favored with your inquiries and that we will be better situated in the future to undertake such projects as you would care to propose.

Here no complex ideas are being sorted out and evaluated. The reader-writer relationship is straightforward—if difficult. The writer has to tell Ms. Rogers that just now his company cannot take on a particular job, though in the future it will be able to do so. He would also, needless to say, like to ensure that Ms. Rogers will call on his company when her company next needs an addition to a plant.

Clearly the writer is in an awkward position. But instead of using clear, direct statements to explain his company's decision and the reason for it, he 247 employs the diction and phrasing of the pseudoformal style, presumably in an effort to make his explanation more palatable to the reader: *subsequent to our recent discussion, reviewed our present situation with regard to the possibility of, our foregoing decision, thorough and complete study revealed, to be favored with your inquiries, better situated in the future to undertake.* Of course, his use of the pseudoformal style is particularly inept. (Is a "complete" study not "thorough"? When other than in the future will his company be "situated" to "undertake" the desired task?) Whether consciously or unconsciously, this writer, like so many who are faced with a difficult situation, has tried to camouflage his message with meaningless phraseology. He may feel that doing so will somehow soften its impact. In fact, he is likely only to irritate his reader with his pomposity.

Compare his version with this alternative:

Dear Ms. Rogers:

After our recent discussion in your office, I checked with my staff to see whether we could submit a proposal for your Thomasville project.

A thorough study of our present commitments convinced us that no matter how we juggle them, we cannot produce engineering drawings for Thomasville by the date you have specified. I am very sorry, therefore, to have to tell you that we will be unable to quote.

I hope, however, that you will continue to call on us. After we expand our engineering department this spring, we will easily be able to handle a rush job like Thomasville without sacrificing the thoroughness and efficiency on which this company has built its reputation.

The difference in the effect of the two letters is striking. The revised version makes the original sound cold, pompous, and inefficient. Note, for example, the difference in the type of phrasing used:

ORIGINAL	REVISION
subsequent to	after
we have reviewed	I checked
with regard to the possibility of our submitting	whether we could submit
a thorough and complete study revealed that	a thorough study convinced us
we are not currently in a position to be able to produce	we cannot produce
within a period of time as indicated by you in your office to be acceptable	by the date you have specified
we trust	I hope
be favored with your inquiries	call on us

In each instance, the phrasing of the original is heavy and awkward, but that of the revision is forthright and informal, as it should be in a letter of this type. The original averages 40 words per sentence; the revision, 23. Because the original conceals information in an undergrowth of verbiage, it suggests that the writer is more interested in excusing himself than in helping to solve Ms. Rogers' problem. Furthermore, the revision, unlike the original, gives specific reasons why the writer is now unable to quote and why Ms. Rogers should ask him to do so in the future. The overall effect of the two versions is quite different: the original is likely to lose the customer, the revised version to keep her.

The two examples we have been discussing point up the difference between appropriately formal writing and pseudoformal business writing. Judge Hand's language was appropriate to himself, to the subject, to the audience, and to the occasion; the language of the original version of the business letter was not. Judge Hand's sentences were appropriately long and complex; the sentences in the business letter were long and complicated because they were artificially inflated. Judge Hand used "big" words because they were needed to say precisely what he intended; the writer of the business letter used them unnecessarily. Judge Hand's paragraph reflects sobriety and integrity; the business letter reflects pomposity and inefficiency.

When we run communication seminars for people in business, we try to demonstrate that, though they may not realize it, they can quite easily adjust the level of a message to meet the needs of a particular situation and that they can be formal without using pseudoformal phrasing.

One way we do so is by asking them to identify the informal words in the revised memo about the Thomasville project. Invariably they select those italicized below:

After our recent discussion in your office, I *checked* with my staff to see whether we could submit a proposal for your Thomasville project.

A thorough study of our present commitments convinced us that no matter how we *juggle* them, we cannot produce engineering drawings for Thomasville by the date you have specified. I *am very sorry,* therefore, to have to *tell* you that we will be unable to quote.

I hope, however, that you will continue to *call on* us. After we expand our engineering department this spring, we will easily be able to *handle* a *rush job* like Thomasville without sacrificing the thoroughness and efficiency on which this company has built its reputation.

When we ask them what words they might substitute if they wanted to make the memo more formal, they usually suggest the following:

INFORMAL	MORE FORMAL
checked	consulted
juggle	rearrange
am very sorry	regret
tell	inform
call on us	consider us
handle	undertake
rush job	emergency order

When they then read the memo that *they* have revised, they discover that they have made it as formal as the original, but truly formal, not pseudoformal:

> After our recent discussion in your office, I consulted with my staff to see whether we could submit a proposal for your Thomasville project.
>
> A thorough study of our present commitments convinced us that no matter how we rearrange them, we cannot produce engineering drawings for Thomasville by the date you have specified. I regret, therefore, to have to inform you that we will be unable to quote.
>
> I hope, however, that you will continue to consider us. After we expand our engineering department this spring, we will easily be able to undertake an emergency order like Thomasville without sacrificing the thoroughness and efficiency on which this company has built its reputation.

This exercise demonstrates that most people can sense the difference between formal and informal language and can be as formal as they wish without falling into "businessese." It also demonstrates that although in the course of their work people in business regularly use speech which covers a wide range of the language continuum, when they write business letters, memos, and reports most tend to aim at a single level, somewhere well above the informal. Although they can easily use this much of the continuum

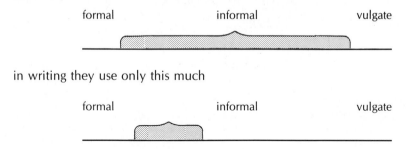

in writing they use only this much

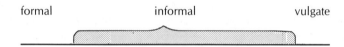

Further, as they move from communication to communication—from audience to audience, subject to subject, channel to channel—they should be using this much

formal   informal   vulgate

THE DANGERS OF PSEUDOFORMAL WRITING

One effect of pseudoformal writing was dramatized for us at the end of a communication seminar. The writer of a memorandum which the group had just analyzed approached us and announced that we had solved an important problem for him. He was the production manager of his division, which has plants in various parts of the country. He knew all of the plant superintendents well; they entertained him at their homes when he visited their plants, and he often invited them to dinner at his house when they came to the home office. When he discussed problems with them face to face or even over the telephone, he got along with them very well. His written communications, however, often produced irritated replies. "I couldn't understand," he said, "why the boys raised hell every time I wrote them a memo." The group's analysis of his memorandum had showed him the source of the irritation. While his speech and manner were easy and friendly, his memoranda were stiff and peremptory and had all the unnecessary heaviness of the pseudoformal letter analyzed above. "From now on," he said, "when I write to them, I'm going to use a more informal style."

Without realizing it, many people in business and industry give the impression of being two-faced. Talking to a customer or a subordinate, they are naturally informal and friendly. Writing to the same person, they too often slip into a pseudoformality that projects an entirely different, and often irritating, personality. The contrast can make a customer or a subordinate uneasy—without ever knowing why.

The tradition of pseudoformality in business letter and report writing leads to another difficulty, exemplified by this letter:

Dear Polly:

Your letter advising your desire not to return to work has been received. We have prepared and forwarded an EP-630. Hopefully you'll be getting your pension refund soon.

We have missed you this past month and are sorry you have decided not to come back to work, but we are also happy to hear that the Thomas family is increasing in numbers.

Joe requested (of course I concurred) that I inform you that your years of good work were much appreciated by all of us in the department.

Sincerely,

Here is a communication that can't make up its mind whether to be formal or informal. It is addressed to "Dear Polly," but the first and second sentences are couched in a highly stereotyped prose, the kind that might be expected from a computer rather than a human being. The third sentence is somewhat less formal, beginning as it does with "Hopefully you'll be getting," but it is insensitive, because it could suggest that sometimes the refunds are not sent promptly. The second paragraph is very friendly and personal, but in the third the writer drops back into the pseudoformality of "of course I concurred" and "your years of good work were much appreciated by all of us in the department." Nothing about how Polly completely revamped the department's cataloging system, about all the new employees she trained, or about how her smile charmed customers. Polly can certainly be excused if she feels that she isn't really being missed very much.

All of us have frequent occasion to use language at most points on the continuum. At a ballgame with our friends or with a customer we know well, we may use language closer to the vulgate than the informal. As a speaker at a testimonial dinner, we may use language closer to the formal than the informal—unless it is the kind of testimonial dinner known as a "roast," in which case the language used might move sharply toward the opposite end of the continuum. However, most of the language we use, both oral and written, will fall somewhere in the broad area called the informal. The exact level is determined in each situation by the position of our reader, our position, the subject matter, the result that we want, and the general background against which all of these variables must be seen.[2] To ignore these subtle relationships and attempt to solve all writing problems with the pseudoformal style is at best unproductive and at worst disastrous.

I—WE—THE WRITER

For two centuries scientists and technical writers have maintained that the use of the first person in reports of their experiments is inappropriate. Their readers, they say, are not interested in who does the experiments but in the technique or process used. Therefore, "I" and "we" are usually avoided.[3]

In the past a similar taboo was applied to business correspondence. The use of "I" was considered indecorous because it might suggest that the writer was vain or "pushy." Fifty years ago, therefore, the word was seldom to be found even in the most informal type of business communication. A young man was advised never to use that treacherous word, even when the situation made it perfectly obvious that he was not being egotistical. "Your letter of the 13th inst. received. It is regretted that the invitation to the Freemont Conference has not been replied to due to its being temporarily mislaid. It is a pleasure to accept the kind invitation of the committee to. . . ." Today the same letter might start: "I'm afraid that the invitation to the Freemont Conference got buried in my pile of correspondence. Of course, I'll be happy to accept the committee's invitation to. . . ."

The prohibition against "I" was also deemed useful for keeping a correspondence clerk from sounding like a vice-president. If the clerk received a complaint, he did not say, "I shall take steps to see that this error will not occur again." That, to be sure, is what he would do. But to be safe he stuck to the indefinite: "Steps will be taken to see that this error does not occur again." As he rose up the corporate ladder, he tended to retain the same style—sometimes even if he became president of his firm. "It is understood that . . . ," he would say. Or "The enclosed is transmitted for your inspection and comment." Or "It is intended to proceed to New Orleans on October 22."

[2] On certain occasions a phrase from one level may be used for a special effect when the bulk of the communication is on quite a different level.

[3] Although a ban on the first person in scientific and technical reports is still the general rule, there seems to have been some movement in recent years toward modifying it. This is especially true in the case of we in scientific papers (see pp. 270–271) and in the case of both "I" and "we" in informal reports to management.

TONE AND STYLE

If he were asked why he continued to avoid "I" in his correspondence, this president of the late nineteenth century would certainly have spoken about "the way things are done in the world of commerce" and about the "dignity required in carrying on matters of this sort." But he would not have felt at all defensive. After all, most of his business correspondents were doing the same thing. Fortunately this curious convention of business writing is slowly withering away. It is still strong enough in the public mind, however, to lead many young men and women to seek ways of avoiding "I" in their first job application letter.

One way of avoiding "I" is sometimes sanctioned—wrongly, we feel—by certain teachers in the schools: the substitution of "the writer." Other substitutes, more widely used in business than on the campus, are "the undersigned" and the archaic "your correspondent." All of these terms, however, fail to do the job expected of them. They merely call attention to the writer's attempt to avoid the first person and often lead as well into very awkward constructions.

Still another substitute devised by business to avoid giving the impression of vanity has developed into a business cliché, which unfortunately causes more problems than it solves. This is the use of "we" for "I." On the surface "we" appears to be an ideal solution. It allows the writer not only to avoid seeming egotistical but also to take shelter under the umbrella of corporate responsibility, to speak as the voice of the company or department instead of having to take personal responsibility for decisions.

The use of "we" is fine as long as the writer is in fact speaking for the company or department and the correspondent knows that. But when "we" is used primarily to avoid the first person singular, there are likely to be complications. Let us assume, for example, that a company has just lost a good customer. What is more, the customer has written to the president to complain about the inefficiency of the department with which he has been dealing. The president demands a full report from the young woman who has handled the account. What is likely to be his reaction to the following report? "We do not understand why Mr. Hunt has decided to withdraw his business from our company. We received his first letter on May 13, and after careful study we reported to him that . . ." The president knows who handled the account. He can hardly avoid concluding that the young employee is attempting to shift the responsibility to the department as a whole. And as the "we" is repeated again and again, the impression will be reinforced.

The use of "we" can also cause real confusion. What happens, for example, when the same young employee asks her supervisor for a June vacation? "If we take our vacation in the middle of the month," she says, "it will not conflict with other vacations in the department. Furthermore, since John Drew will be available as a substitute, it will not materially affect our ability to complete the experiments assigned to the department during those two weeks." Notice that in the first sentence the writer makes a clear distinction between "we" (the writer) and "the department." "Our ability" in the second sentence, therefore, seems to refer to the writer's ability. Not until the end of the sentence does it become clear that this time "our" refers to the department. The reader then has to go back and sort out the sentence. If the confusion between "we" the writer and "we" the department continues (with the probable addition of "we" the company), the supervisor will soon become understandably irritated by the difficulty of wading through the letter.[4]

Even more awkward is inconsistency in the use of "I" and the various substitutes for it. These two sentences are not untypical:

> If you could assist me in this endeavor of mine, the writer would be most pleased to send further details of my investigation so that you may be better aware of my needs. It will be most gratifying if you will provide us with your counsel and guidance, and this writer will be grateful for any materials which you can send.

In just two sentences, "me," "mine," "the writer," "my," "us," and "this writer" all refer to one person! One wonders, too, about the writer of the letter below, who forces the reader to try to figure out to whom the various pronouns and pronoun substitutes refer.

> Dear Ms. Pickett:
>
> Your letter of December 26 was read with a great deal of interest. We would be most happy to discuss with you our latest developments in coating materials and in return learn of new developments in converting machinery. We suggest a visit to our laboratory at a mutually convenient date.
>
> The laboratory is located outside the city. I am enclosing a road map showing its location in relation to the airport. We could arrange to meet you there and bring you to the laboratory if this would be more convenient.
>
> The writer plans to be in the laboratory most of January. However, in future months I will be doing considerable traveling, but I am sure that we can find a convenient time for your visit.

Perhaps "the writer" is Dr. Jekyll and the "I" is Mr. Hyde.

ILLUSTRATIVE MATERIALS

1.

In this chapter we discussed part of a definition of "a law" by Judge Learned Hand. Lawyers are always concerned with definitions. Another great jurist, Justice Louis Brandeis, in an article first published in the American Legal News,[5]

---

[4] An impressive illustration of the traps into which overreliance on "we" can lead one came from the correspondence of a business executive who flew from New York to California to discuss certain matters with the manager of one of his company's subsidiaries. His wife and a business associate accompanied him. On his return he dictated a letter to the manager, the last paragraph of which read: "Tom Stewart and the writer are very grateful to you for the opportunity to go through your plant, and we are especially appreciative of the many courtesies which you extended to our wife." For some reason wives and husbands seem to cause many problems in business correspondence. One letter writer wished to indicate that the husbands and wives of delegates to a convention were invited to a reception. He wrote: "If your spouse should be in New York at that time, that person, of course, is also cordially invited."

[5] 44 (January 1913).

attempts to define regulation. Compare the tone and style of the two definitions.

Regulation is essential to the preservation of competition and to its best development just as regulation is necessary to the preservation and development of civil or political liberty. To preserve civil and political liberty to the many we have found it necessary to restrict the liberty of the few. Unlicensed liberty leads necessarily to despotism or oligarchy. Those who are stronger must to some extent be curbed. We curb the physically strong in order to protect those physically weaker. The liberty of the merchant and manufacturer to lie in trade, formerly permissible, and expressed in the fine phrase *caveat emptor,* has yielded largely to the better business ethics supplemented by pure-food laws and postal-fraud prosecution. Formerly the interests of business and of the community were supposed to be best served by letting buyer and seller trade without restriction on native or acquired shrewdness. Those laws present examples of protecting those who, by reason of position or training are, in respect to particular business transactions, the weaker or unable to take care of themselves. Recognizing differences in position of employer and employee, we have similarly restricted theoretically freedom of contract by factory laws which prescribe conditions under which work may be performed and, to some extent, the hours of labor. Experience had shown that under the changed conditions in industry, it was necessary, in order that life and liberty of the worker be preserved, to put a restraint upon the theoretical freedom of the individual worker and the employer—the employer and the employee—to do as he chose in that respect.

The right of competition must be similarly limited; for excesses of competition lead to monopoly just as excesses of liberty have led to despotism. It is another case where the extremes meet.

2.

Some years ago President Douglas Knight of Lawrence University faced a task which most college and university presidents are called upon to perform: he had to speak for twenty minutes or so to the graduating seniors and their families during the Commencement festivities. But his was not the standard, cliché-ridden address. Note how, in the opening paragraphs, Dr. Knight set the tone for his remarks.[6]

Whatever it may be for you, Commencement Day is always a very special privilege for me, as it is for all of us who have worked with you, taught you, learned from you, put up with you these last four years. At the same time there is a quality of heartache that goes with the very real triumphs of this day; it grows in part from our sense of all that might have been done, all that still remains to do; but it grows above all from the high value we put on what you are and what you can be. We hate to let you go. It is heartache

[6] Printed with the permission of Dr. Knight.

without sentimentality, in short, an emotion which can justify itself in a harsh, uncertain and often terrifying time.

I do not really need to use phrases like the last ones when I talk to you. There is no need to load you further with the burdens of the world, as though it were some hideous disease which you must either defeat or succumb to. Diseased it often is, of course; but disease is not its nature any more than it is yours. If I am going to be of any use to you as you leave, I need to talk about the things that are truly and permanently at the heart of our world. Enough has been said about our nightmares; perhaps we need to look at our common life instead, asking ourselves what we are and also what we must do and be as educated people.

a. *What impression do you have of the speaker? What elements of the speech have helped you to form your opinion?*
b. *What does Dr. Knight seem to wish to accomplish in these opening paragraphs?*
c. *How would you characterize the tone of the paragraphs?*
d. *What functions does the first sentence perform? How about the next-to-last sentence in the first paragraph? And the first sentence of the second paragraph?*
e. *What other sentences seem to be especially effective? Why?*

3.

To produce memorable prose one need not necessarily have had a great deal of formal education. Bartolomeo Vanzetti, an immigrant from Italy, was largely self-educated, and his English was not always grammatically correct. With Nicola Sacco he was accused of murder during the post-World War I "Red scare." The two men, who were active in groups striving to bring about radical social change, were convicted on flimsy evidence. This is a short excerpt from his final statement:

I have talk a great deal of myself, but I even forgot to name Sacco. Sacco too is a worker, from his boyhood, a skilled worker, lover of work, with a good job and pay, a bank account, a good and lovely wife, two beautiful children and a neat little home at the verge of a wood, near a brook.

Sacco is a heart, a faith, a character, a man; a man, lover of nature, and mankind; a man who gave all, who sacrifice all to the cause of liberty and to his love for mankind: money, rest, mundane ambition, his own wife, his children, himself, and his own life.

Sacco has never dreamt to steal, never to assassinate. He and I have never brought a morsel of bread to our mouths, from our childhood to today, which has not been gained by the sweat of our brows. Never. . . .

Oh, yes, I may be more witful, as some have put it. I am a better babbler than he is, but many, many times in hearing his heartful voice ringing a faith sublime, in considering his supreme sacrifice, remembering his heroism, I felt small at the presence of his greatness and found myself compelled to fight back from my eyes the tears, and quanch my heart trobling to my throat to not weep before him—this man called thief and assassin and doomed.

But Sacco's name will live in the hearts of the people and in their gratitude when Katzmann's bones and yours will be dispersed by time; when your name, his name, your laws, institutions, and your false god are but a dim rememoring of a cursed past in which man was wolf to the man. . . .

If it had not been for these thing I might have live out my life talking at street corners to scorning men. I might have die, unmarked, unknown, a failure. Now we are not a failure. This is our career and our triumph. Never in our full life could we hope to do such work for tolerance, for justice, for man's understanding of man, as now we do by accident.

Our words, our lives, our pains—nothing! The taking of our lives—lives of a good shoemaker and a poor fishpeddler—all! That last moment belongs to us. That agony is our triumph.

MATERIALS FOR REVISION

The following items contain examples of certain errors discussed in this chapter, as well as some you have met before. Revising them will reinforce your understanding of the problems involved and your ability to recognize similar mistakes and to avoid making them in your own writing.

A

1. *Subject:* IMPLEMENTATION OF THE AUTOMATED PARTS AND SERVICE BILLING SYSTEM.

   As discussed in our meeting of June 2, enclosed is a list of what I feel are major tasks to be completed to implement this system. Please review this list and be prepared to discuss it at our next meeting.

   Please advise as to when you would like to schedule our next meeting.

2. *Subject:* ELECTIVE ALLOWANCE OF CREDIT TO LESSEE

   In general, any owner of Sec. 38 property who leases it to another may elect, with the lessee's consent, to have the investment credit on such property taken by the lessee. The election to pass on the credit may be made only with respect to new Sec. 38 property, and with respect to property which would be new Sec. 38 property if acquired by the lessee.

3. *Subject:* EFFECTIVE WRITING WORKSHOP

   As requested in O. Otterbein's memo of May 16, I am forwarding herewith a number of examples of my writing. I trust that this will satisfy Dr. Weinstein's request for preparation material.

4. Dear Mr. Phillips:

A review of our records shows that there are still two invoices unpaid, invoice #81-1756, in the amount of $186.90, and #81-0767, in the amount of $122.48. We have sent several letters inquiring into the status of the mentioned unpaid invoices, but to date have not been favored with a reply.

We are asking once again if you would please check your records and advise if the above-mentioned invoices have been forwarded to your bank for payment and when we may expect payment.

B

1. Philip Carey Mfg. Company
   1427 Owen Street
   Cincinnati, OH 45215

   Attention: Mr. E. F. Dittmar

   Gentlemen:

   After talking to you over the phone this morning, I checked our files regarding the special freight equalization on roofing pitch with Ironton, Ohio, on shipments into Cincinnati, Ohio. . . .

   The writer of this letter will call your office sometime during the week of June 2 to make final arrangements for the arrival of our crew.

   Very truly yours,

   John J. Jones

2. It is planned that we will arrive on September 30.
3. It was agreed by the committee to send the undersigned on the inspection trip he proposed.
4. After retirement in June, there will be no one to fill this position. We plan to leave the company on the last day of the month.
5. We just discovered that when we wrote the order the carbon underneath covered only half of the underlying sheet, so that only three of the four items you asked for appeared on it.

14

Active and Passive Voice

CASE STUDY: TURNING DOWN A SUGGESTION

To begin our consideration of the active and passive voices, let us look for a moment at two versions of a single memo written by a staff executive to a plant superintendent who had made a suggestion. Here is the first:

To: G. C. Downing, Plant Superintendent, Works No. 27

From: T. J. Helper, Synthetic Fiber Division

Subject: Inspection of Permalast Samples

This refers to your memo of October 6, in which it was proposed that the Sample Department be given responsibility for the inspection of Permalast samples.

It is true that the bulk of the inspection of samples can easily be accomplished by the Sample Department. On the other hand, if the matter is left entirely in their hands, only giving assistance when a question arises, the results are not likely to

259

be altogether satisfactory. The importance of a sample being right cannot be over-estimated. Therefore, it seems desirable that the responsibilities of the Quality Control Section should not be vacated, especially in view of the fact that Perma-last is our fastest-selling product.

By the title of the memorandum of October 1, it is indicated that the proposed relaxation of inspection by the Quality Control Section applies only to "Permalast Super" samples, until sufficient personnel are available to the section so that the job can be handled adequately. By maintaining a minimum amount of control of regular Permalast samples by Quality Control, inspection will not be left entirely to the workmen in the department in which the work is performed.

This is the other version:

To: Mr. G. C. Downing, Plant Superintendent, Works No. 27

From: T. J. Helper, Synthetic Fiber Division

Subject: Inspection of Permalast Samples
           Your Memo of October 6

Although I understand why you would like to have the Sample Department inspect all Permalast samples, I'm afraid that we cannot afford to bypass Quality Control. Charley Pratt and Tom Evans agree that we must take no chances on the quality of our fastest-selling product.

The division proposes to relax inspection on "Permalast Super" samples only until Quality Control has enough men to tackle the job.

If we apply the criteria which we have developed in preceding chapters, we will certainly agree that the second version of T. J. Helper's memo is more efficient than the first. It is also clearer. Although it uses fewer than half as many words, it does a better job, omitting nothing that is needed to transmit management's decision and the reasons for it. Furthermore, the second memo makes its point more firmly, but at the same time in a friendlier manner: "Although I can understand why you would like . . . ; I'm afraid that we can-not. . . ." Here we have an individual talking, one who is sympathetic, but also decisive in rejecting Downing's proposal—in short, one who has taken his audience into consideration. He is not attempting to persuade Downing to adopt management's point of view: the function of the letter is merely to inform him of the decision taken. Nevertheless, he has explained clearly and concisely the reasoning behind the decision and has stated that others with responsibility for product quality have concurred. The second memo also meets the criteria which we developed in the last four chapters. It is, as we have already said, concise; it contains no confusing phrasing; it is appropriately informal; and it makes use of no standard business jargon. It is an effective communication.

The original version of the Helper memo, on the other hand, is puzzling. Anyone in business will recognize that it is written in ordinary business lan-guage. Its message does come through: "We don't accept your suggestion."

But the writer takes a long time doing his job, and if the letter is not unfriendly, it is not friendly either. It may leave Downing dissatisfied, perhaps even disgruntled, at the insensitivity of "those guys up there."

Why is this letter basically unsatisfactory? A brief analysis will suggest the reason.

The first paragraph is a standard business opening of the type we have discussed in Chapter 11. It is unnecessary and can be eliminated if the date of Downing's memo is moved up into the "Subject." As it stands, this first paragraph may make Mr. Downing a little bit uneasy, though he may not be aware of the reason for his uneasiness. Helper talks about "your memo of October 6, in which *it was proposed....*" Presumably Downing himself made the proposal. He has not tried to duck responsibility for it. But the use of "it was proposed," which washes out the person responsible, suggests something vaguely illicit about the whole proposal. The opening of the second paragraph also has a vaguely suspicious sound. Instead of coming right out and saying, "The Sample Department can easily inspect the bulk of the samples," Helper worms his way into the sentence: "It is true that the bulk of the inspection of samples can easily be accomplished by the Sample Department." The next sentence requires a second reading for comprehension: "On the other hand, if the matter is left entirely in their hands, only giving assistance when a question arises, the results are not likely to be altogether satisfactory." Who is to give assistance to the Sample Department? Only the Sample Department has been mentioned. There is no way for Downing to know until he has read to the end of the paragraph, where he learns that the help is to come from Quality Control. Presumably Quality Control is the logical candidate, but he may wonder why Helper doesn't say so right away.

ACTIVE AND PASSIVE DEFINED

Before we go through the rest of the original memo, let's see why it has a faintly unpleasant flavor. Many readers will have recognized that all three of the sentences discussed above are in the passive voice.

The English language has only two voices—active and passive—and the distinction between them is easily made:

Active:	Tom	- - - - -	filed	- - - - -	the letter.
	(actor)		(action)		(acted on)
Passive:	The letter	- - - - -	was filed	- - - - -	by Tom.
	(acted on)		(action)		(actor)

Our "normal" way of expressing a thought is to use the active voice. It is more direct and more powerful than the passive. When we tell a friend what happened at a meeting, we are not likely to say, "A report was given by Bill, and his proposal was voted on by the committee." Instead we say, "Bill gave his report, and the committee voted on his proposal." In conversation we are more likely to say, "The Sample Department can inspect the samples" than "The samples can be inspected by the Sample Department."

You will have noticed that to communicate the same message, the passive voice always requires more words than the active. "Tom filed the letter" is four words; "The letter was filed by Tom" is six. Thus the passive tends to slow down reading. And because it provides more "filler" between the thing acted upon and the actor (in this case between "letter" and "Tom"), it makes misreading—and hence misinterpretation—easier. Furthermore, the passive reverses the normal order of ideas. It requires the reader to make a subconscious adjustment and thus cuts down on both reading speed and comprehension.

Another problem with the passive, as we shall see, is that sometimes it is used in a way that leaves out the people concerned. If it is important to know who filed the letter, the sentence "The letter was filed" is inadequate.

THE PROPER USE OF THE PASSIVE

What we have just said should not be taken to mean that the passive voice, like the human appendix, has no legitimate function. In fact, we cannot do without it.

Often neither we nor our audience are at all interested in the person or thing that performs an action. We say, "The equipment was shipped" or "The case was closed." We may or may not know who shipped the equipment or who closed the case. Even if we do, in many situations there is simply no point in mentioning the actor. In such instances, the passive is appropriate. We use it, in other words, whenever our interest is primarily in the action performed and in the person or thing receiving the action.

Scientists and engineers are particularly prone to using the passive; it dominates all their reports. Here is a brief example, written by an engineer:

> The ore, as mined, *is received* at plant battery limits from an overland conveyor at an average rate of 1,544 short tons per hour. Depending upon the operational status of the downstream equipment, the overland conveyor empties into one or the other of two bins.
>
> Under normal operating conditions, the ore *is discharged* to the first bin, *is passed* through an ore feeder at the bottom of the bin, and *is loaded* onto the in-plant conveyor which transfers the ore to grinding.
>
> When an upset occurs downstream, the in-plant conveyor empties the ore into the second bin, from which it *is fed* to an emergency stack-out conveyor discharging onto an emergency pile. Capacity for eight hours emergency storage *is provided*. Reclaim rate for the emergency stack-out pile is 500 tph.

This passage contains a good mixture of passive and active voice. Most of the passives, which we have italicized, indicate what happens to the ore as it is handled. There is no point in telling who or what receives, discharges, passes, loads, or feeds it. On the other hand, the person who wrote this description is not addicted to the passive. We hear of two conveyors emptying into bins, of another transferring the ore, and of an upset occurring—all in the active voice. The verbs *empties, transfers,* and *occurs* give the passage life.

Still, the basic mode of the passage is passive, for the engineer's readers are concerned not with *who* is handling the ore but with *what* is being done, and *how* it is done.

ACTIVE *OR* PASSIVE

To see the problem more clearly, compare the following descriptions of the same procedure, the first simply describing the procedure, the second explaining a jurisdictional dispute between labor unions which arose as a result of the procedure.

> The kryptoma *is brought* in on the railroad spur and *is unloaded* on Unloading Dock #1. From there it *is trucked* through the east gate to Warehouse #1, where it *is stored* until it *is needed*. At appropriate times, it *is carried* by conveyor belt to the East Processing Plant, where it *is used* in the manufacture of fertilizer.

> When the kryptoma is brought in on the railroad spur, members of Local 726 of the Laborers Union *unload* it on to Unloading Dock #1. They then *transfer* it to trucks for transportation to Warehouse #1, where members of Local 19 of the Warehouseman's Union *unload* and *store* it. At appropriate times, members of Local 19 *place* it on the conveyor belt, which *carries* it to the East Processing Plant for use in the manufacture of fertilizer. Last week the the business agent for Local 32 of the Trucker's Union *told* management that the loading and unloading of the trucks should be the responsibility of the members of his union and that he *will ask* for arbitration in the matter.

The first version is appropriately passive because the focus is on how the kryptoma *is handled* (passive), that is, on the material and the procedure. Who does what is irrelevant. In the second version, however, who does what is all-important. It causes a jurisdictional dispute. The actors (i.e., the members of the three unions) become the subjects of the sentences, and the sentences become active. Thus, instead of the statement that the kryptoma *is stored* until it *is needed*, we find "members of Local 19 of the Warehouseman's Union *unload* and *store* it."

ACTIVE *AND* PASSIVE

The explanation could, of course, begin with the passive version, but it would have to move to the active to describe the problem. Thus the first version could serve as the first paragraph, but the second paragraph should shift to the active:

> Last week the business agent for Local 32 of the Truckers Union *told* management that the loading and unloading of the trucks should be the responsibility of the members of his union and that he *will ask* for arbitration in the matter. Members of Local 726 of the Laborers Union currently *load* the trucks at the Unloading Dock, and members of Local 19 of the Warehouseman's Union *unload* them at Warehouse #1.

There is no reason why a passage should not move from passive to active or from active to passive as appropriate. The reader may have noticed that although the second version above is largely active, it begins with a passive.

The legitimate use of the passive is not confined, however, to formal reports on technical matters. Let's assume that Tom and Helen Smith are walking down a street. Ahead of them they see Bob Preyer. Helen watches him for a moment and then says: "What's wrong with Bob? He looks so depressed today." How might Tom answer? He might say, "Ted Cook fired him yesterday" (active). If he does so, it is likely to be either because Ted Cook's role in the firing is important to him or because he thinks it will be important to Helen. On the other hand, Tom might answer, "He was fired yesterday" (passive). He may put it this way because he does not know who fired Bob; or, if he does know, because he feels that who did the firing is of no importance either to him or to Helen. Tom could, of course, have used a third variant: "He was fired yesterday by Ted Cook." This does the same job as "Ted Cook fired him yesterday," but it lacks vigor and directness.

OVERUSE OF THE PASSIVE

If we return now to the first version of the T. J. Helper memo, we may be able to determine why it is so unsatisfactory. We will discover that at least one verb in every sentence is in the passive voice. Actions have taken place, but the actors have all disappeared. Nobody is said to have done or decided anything. Nobody in particular is to give assistance when a question arises. Nobody in particular feels that Quality Control should remain responsible for sample testing: it just *seems desirable.* Nobody worth mentioning wrote the memorandum of October 6. Nobody is specified as being responsible for seeing that Quality Control maintains minimum control of regular samples. Nobody, in short, seems to be responsible for anything. The result is an overall impression, to use Helper's own words, of "vacated responsibility."

The alternate version of the Helper memo, however, gives quite a different impression. It is written in the active voice. Hence it is full of actors: *I, you, we, Charley Pratt and Tom Evans,* and *the division.* Here Helper is addressing Downing very much as if he were talking to him: "I understand," "you would like," "I'm afraid," and "we cannot"—all in the first sentence. The result, as we suggested earlier, is a forthright, friendly memo, one which will gain Downing's respect. Furthermore, when Helper uses the active voice, he automatically relieves himself of long, awkward constructions and frequent repetition. He can relax and be himself.

CASE STUDY: THE PUSSYFOOTER

The passive, then, tends to wrap everything in a cloak of anonymity. As a result, it can produce effects that the writer does not intend. We have sometimes handed to the members of a writing workshop this selection from a memorandum drafted by a department head for the signature of the manager of his division and asked them to read it once rapidly:

> It is now estimated that the proposed schedule change in production of brass items will affect the shipments to an extent which will make it necessary to cancel the existing plan. Until shipping schedules are brought into line, it is proposed to pay overtime to the crews in the warehouse insofar as it may seem desirable.
>
> There has existed the possibility of a force reduction in some of the warehouses, and it was planned to set forth these reductions for management's consideration. However, it is currently our opinion that no reduction will be required for some time. A detailed investigation will be conducted to test this opinion. It is felt that this investigation can be completed in two months so as to provide time for consideration of reassignments where desired.

When we ask the participants "On the basis of this piece of writing, what do you think of the writer?," we invariably get the same reactions:

> "He's afraid to take responsibility."
>
> "Doesn't know his own mind."
>
> "Pussyfooter."
>
> "Wouldn't trust him to clean out a wastebasket."
>
> "I'd hate to have to *talk* to that guy."

If the members of the group had met "that guy," they would have found him a pleasant, efficient, straight-talking fellow, not at all averse to taking responsibility—in fact, a man in a position of considerable importance. His report, however, gives a completely distorted impression of his personality.

What has this writer done to earn such unflattering comments from his business peers? Once again we find that the villain of the piece is an addiction to the passive: *is now estimated, are brought into line, is proposed, was planned, will be required, will be conducted, is felt, can be completed.* Nowhere in the memo is any individual mentioned. At no point is responsibility assigned for any action. The "passiveness" is further accentuated by the use of such expressions as *there has existed the possibility of, it may seem desirable,* and *it is currently our opinion.* Once again we do not know *who* estimates, *who* will bring the schedules into line, *who* proposes, *who* planned, *who* will conduct, or *who* feels. Nor do we know whether *"our* opinion" is that of the company president, some group, or just the writer of the memo.

IT IS AND THERE IS

A careful study of these two short paragraphs will reveal that many of the passive constructions are preceded by the word *it* and one by the word *there.* These two words, referred to by grammarians as expletives, introduce a large 265 percentage of the passives in business writing. They are the favorites of the person who hates to put anything on the line—the pussyfooter. Such a person will say, not "I believe," but "It is believed"; not "We will ship the bolts on Thursday," but "It is expected that the bolts will be shipped Thursday"; not "We may have to lay off some workers," but "There has existed the possibility of a force reduction" (or "A force reduction may be necessary").

On rare occasions, of course, a writer may wish to soften a blow or downplay his or her department's role in an unfortunate occurrence. But the way to do so is not to fall back on the type of evasions we have been discussing. To post a notice on the shop floor which begins, "It is regretted that in the next three weeks there is a possibility that the necessity of a force reduction may exist" will not mollify the workers. It will make them angry.

For many individuals, unfortunately, using *it* and *there* in this way is addictive. After being in business a few years—or sometimes even a few months—certain people begin to write everything in the passive and to pile *it* and *there* constructions on top of each other. Like the man whose paragraphs we have been discussing, they become so conditioned to using the passive that they find it actually painful to write active sentences—though they do use them more easily in conversation. The young person who is starting in business should always be aware of this danger and keep reminding himself or herself to avoid the way of the pussyfooter. Few people have ever made a success in business by evading—or *seeming* to evade—responsibility.[1]

KEEPING VERBS STRONG

A related tendency, which is found not only in business but in virtually all writing today, also helps to undermine the effectiveness of our prose by reducing the impact of our verbs—the words which give action to our speech. Over the years business people, like other writers, have compiled an extensive collection of verb substitutes which seem to have a glamor not associated with the strong verbs they replace.

The man who sees a thief make off with an automobile will shout to the policeman, "He turned left on Main"; but when he writes a report of the incident he is likely to say, "He made a left turn on Main Street." Instead of saying, "Fasten the assembly to the frame with a No. 3 bolt," he will write "Use a No. 3 bolt to fasten the assembly to the frame" or even "Make use of a No. 3 bolt to fasten the assembly to the frame." In each instance here, the writer substitutes for a vigorous action verb a wordy dilution of it:

make a turn instead of *turn*; *use . . . to fasten* instead of *fasten*.

---

[1] We would caution, however, that we are recommending clarity, not brashness; straightforwardness, not arrogance. We have characterized the revision of the Helper memo as "a forthright, friendly memo, one which will gain Downing's respect." One earns respect by being neither a pussyfooter nor a know-it-all.

Other examples of similarly diluted verbs come readily to mind:

WORDY DILUTION	VIGOROUS ACTION VERB
Research resulted in the production of improved surface quality.	Research produced improved surface quality.
This company arrived at its decision to increase its contribution only after it gave careful consideration to other alternatives.	This company decided to increase its contribution only after it carefully considered other alternatives.
At our Paris shop, we experienced a sales drop.	At our Paris shop, sales dropped.
The workman has put the new equipment to use in bending wire.	The workman bends wire with the new equipment.
The Art Department gives assistance in the preparation of these displays.	The Art Department helps to prepare these displays.
It is currently our belief that adjustment of inventories should be accomplished by the Chicago warehouse.	We now believe that the Chicago warehouse should adjust its inventories.

If we isolate the verb forms we can easily see what is happening:

resulted in the production of	produced
arrived at its decision	decided
gave . . . consideration to	considered
experienced a . . . drop	dropped
has put . . . to use in bending	bends
gives its assistance in the preparation of	helps to prepare
is . . . our belief that	believe

In each instance, the action verb has been converted into a noun (*production, decision, consideration, drop, bending, assistance, preparation, belief*), which is preceded by a colorless and, in context, almost meaningless verb (*resulted, arrived, gave, experienced, put to use, gives, is*). In addition, two or three articles or prepositions are usually required to fill out the phrase.

In some situations using the passive voice is not only useful but necessary. Occasionally—very occasionally—*it is* or *there is* may be helpful. However, we can think of no instance in which diluting a vigorous, active verb will improve a sentence. "We are instituting a slash in prices" has none of the force of "We are slashing prices." "Our business is returning to normal" is certainly preferable to "Our business is experiencing a return to normal." Whatever glamor diluted verbs may have is cosmetic. A good writer, whether a novelist, essayist, historian, or business executive, will do everything possible 267 to keep verbs at full strength. Effective writing is active writing, and verbs are the most important source of strength in any passage. They do not deserve to be diluted.

SIDE EFFECTS OF OVERUSING THE PASSIVE

The person who habitually uses the passive rather than the active voice will also fall easily into the habit of using diluted verbs, standard business jargon, overformal openings, and heavy phrasing. Take, for example, the following memo written by a member of a seminar for middle-management people:

> It was requested by Management Systems that a list be submitted by this department of the department's project's recurring reports. Monthly Assessments, Critical Items, and Project Commitment Reports have been recognized as regular items; however, there are other such recurring reports that are regularly submitted by individual subdivisions which have not been so identified or, if identified, with which the writer is not fully familiar. The Proof-of-Breeding Report is an example of such a recurring report.
>
> It would be appreciated, therefore, if any such recurring reports the preparation of which is regularly undertaken by the personnel under your cognizance be listed by job and that that list be returned by you to the undersigned as soon as it is possible to do so.

We presented this message to the group during a discussion of the passive and asked them to revise it. They spotted the passives quickly enough: "It was requested by Management Systems" instead of "Management Systems requested"; "that a list be submitted by this department" instead of "that this department submit a list"; and so on.

In addition, however, they picked up a variety of other problems, such as unnecessary detail and wordiness. Soon the person who had written the memo decided that it really wasn't necessary to list writers of recurring memos "by job." The group then went on to agree that "regularly" was redundant and that "not fully familiar" didn't say any more than "not familiar." In cutting down "as soon as it is possible to do so" to "as soon as possible," they recognized that they had laid hands on a rubber stamp and substituted the more specific "by June 15." They then found another rubber stamp, "It would be appreciated," and threw it out.

They discovered the diluted verb in "the preparation of which is regularly undertaken by the personnel under your cognizance" and cut it down to the more functional participial phrase "prepared by the people under your supervision." (We would have preferred "prepared by the people under you," but they considered the simpler statement indelicate.) And they laughed away "the writer" and "the undersigned" as overcautious modesty and replaced them with the "I" and "me" the writer would have used in speaking.

268

The result was not only a much shorter memo (72 words compared with the original 127), but also "a forthright, friendly memo, one which will gain the readers' respect"—to return to a criterion we used earlier in this chapter.

> Management Systems requests that we submit a list of our project's recurring reports. I am aware of the Monthly Assessment, Critical Items, and Project Commitment Reports; however, there are reports submitted by individual sub-divisions with which I am not familiar. The Proof-of-Breeding Status Report is one example.
>
> Will you please, therefore, list any recurring reports prepared by people under your supervision and return the list to me by June 15.

The problem with the passive or the rubber stamp or any other element of "businessese" is that one breeds another. The passive tends to breed rubber stamps—and vice versa. Admit a diluted verb, and with it come other forms of wordiness, like the shy "the writer" and the obsequious "the undersigned." Together they produce unreadable prose, not a commodity much appreciated in today's business world.

On the other hand, a person who adopts an active approach to writing and speaking will not be tempted to use unnecessary passives, standard phrasing, diluted verbs, wordiness, and circumlocution. He or she will recognize them as inappropriate for a person who wants to be forthright but friendly and to earn the respect of the audience.

AN ACTIVE APPROACH

Clearly people who spend a significant portion of their working hours in writing or speaking to a variety of audiences—and this certainly includes the business executive—should develop a style which will get results. Ideally it should also always represent them at their best. It should be a firm, active, and flexible instrument, adaptable to any situation and any audience.

Developing such an instrument is not easy, and few individuals, if any, achieve perfection. Furthermore, we come to serious writing with varied background and training. Whether we learn to write well or to write inefficiently will depend in part both on how alert we are to the effect of words in their various combinations and on how hard we work at the job of writing.

But most important, as we have suggested elsewhere, learning to write well depends in large measure on our attitude toward our writing. If we are content to "play it safe," to hide behind barricades of unnecessary words and passive constructions, we cannot expect others to take our talents seriously. But if we begin with an active approach to our writing and speaking, as well as to our job, we can ensure that our words will have a genuine impact, that people will not only listen to them but also act on them. People may not, of course, always accept our recommendations or our point of view: they may actively oppose both. Some who prefer not to risk anything will not hesitate to attack   269 us for the manner in which we speak and write. But in the long run we should succeed because we will project ourselves as people who know where we are and where we are going.

ILLUSTRATIVE MATERIALS

1.

In these two selections of technical writing, both active and passive constructions are used.

It was suggested by Tammann in 1922 that the different rates of oxidation exhibited by iron crystals of different orientations can best be explained by a fixed orientation relationship between the lattice of the iron crystal and the lattice of the oxide film. During the succeeding years, fixed orientation relationships have been demonstrated for reaction products of many kinds, such as recrystallization structures, products of transformation in the solid state, Widmanstätten figures and others; in view of the general occurrence of such orientation relationships, it now seems more than likely that oxide (and other) reaction films grown on metal crystals will upon analysis also be found to exhibit them. Indeed the results of Finch and Quarrell, published during the course of our work, seem to prove that films of zinc oxide on zinc, and magnesium oxide on magnesium possess such a relationship, though the analysis does not seem to be complete. We have been successful in demonstrating a fixed orientation relationship for wüstite ("FeO") films grown on iron, and for cuprous oxide films grown on copper. . . .

In another experiment, cuprous oxide was grown on a single crystal of copper by oxidation in air. This film is almost entirely cuprous oxide, for only an extremely thin film of cupric oxide is formed. Simultaneous determinations of the orientation of the underlying copper crystal and the cuprous oxide film showed that the cube axes in both crystals lay accurately parallel. The copper atoms in cuprous oxide form a face-centered cubic lattice, and the oxygen atoms form an interpenetrating body-centered cubic lattice; the side of the unit face-centered cubic lattice of copper atoms in cuprous oxide is 4.26A., whereas that in pure copper is 3.61A. In this case, therefore, the oxide film is formed merely by an expansion of the copper lattice without change in orientation. Thus only one orientation of cuprous oxide will form on a single crystal of copper. The orientation relationship described is the more nearly perfect the thinner the film; as the film becomes thicker, the perfection in orientation is progressively lost, owing largely, no doubt, to distortion effects coming from the large difference in volume. At a thickness of 0.002 in., little evidence of preferred orientation remains. Even in the thinnest films there is evidence of lattice distortion, coming probably from the necessity for adaptation in lattice dimensions at the interface, similar to that found by Finch and Quarrell for metallic films deposited on platinum.

How useful these orientation relationships may be in explaining the differences in rates of oxidation on different crystal faces is at the moment quite uncertain. Work now current in our laboratory may, however, lead to definite issue on this point.[2]

The atoms at the top of the chromosphere rest on the weakened light which has passed through the screen below; the full sunlight would blow them away. Milne has deduced a consequence which may perhaps have a practical application in the phenomena of explosion of "new stars" or novae, and in any case is curiously interesting. Owing to the Doppler effect a moving atom absorbs a rather different wave-length from a stationary atom; so that if for any cause an atom moves away from the sun, it will support itself on light which is a little to one side of the deepest absorption. This light, being more intense than that which provides a balance, will make the atom recede faster. The atom's own absorption will thus gradually draw clear of the absorption of the screen below. Speaking rather metaphorically, the atom is balanced precariously on the summit of the absorption line, and it is liable to topple off into the full sunlight on one side. Apparently the speed of the atom should go on increasing until it has to climb an adjacent absorption line (due perhaps to some other element); if the line is too intense to be surmounted, the atom will stick part-way up, the velocity remaining fixed at a particular value. These later inferences may be rather far-fetched, but at any rate the argument indicates that there is likely to be an escape of calcium into outer space.[3]

a. *Ignoring the forms of the verb* to be, *make a list of all active verbs and another of all passive verbs. Does either active or passive dominate one or more of the long paragraphs? If so, is there a legitimate reason why it should do so?*
b. *Is there a significant difference in the overall effect of each paragraph? Explain.*
c. *Can any passive verbs in these selections be changed to active verbs without violating the intention of the paragraph in which they occur? If so, revise the sentences.*

2.

In writing this chapter, we have occasionally used the passive voice. Here is a list of passive verbs with the page and line where each will be found. In

[2] R. F. Mehl, E. L. McCandless, and F. N. Rhines, "Orientation of Oxide Films on Metals." Reprinted by permission from *Nature*, Vol. 134, p. 1009. Copyright 1934 Macmillan Journals Ltd.
[3] A. S. Eddington, *Stars and Atoms* (London: Oxford University Press, 1929), p. 75. By permission of Oxford University Press.

each instance, consider the reasons which may have led to the use of the passive rather than the usually preferred active.

VERB FORM	PAGE	LINE
is written	260	40
is moved	261	8
has been mentioned	261	22
is . . . made	261	32
is used	262	9
should . . . be taken	262	13
is handled	262	38
is being done	263	2
is done	263	3
is . . . confined	264	4
is said	264	21
is specified	264	25
is written	264	30
is . . . assigned	265	29
is . . . accentuated	265	30
are preceded	265	38
has been converted	267	29
are . . . required	267	33
will . . . be tempted	269	17

MATERIALS FOR REVISION

In the sentences below, replace awkward passive constructions with active ones, and make any other improvements you can.

1. A quantity of Pliafilm No. 80 for use as a dampproofing material was also offered by us at that time.
2. As you know, our company has a pipeline contract, which will be visited by our executive officers.
3. The list of potential items for manufacture has been thoroughly checked, and we will submit a report on each as it becomes available.
4. The sticking you observe can be eliminated by making the index scale more taut. This operation can be performed by you.
5. Your interest in our company products is sincerely appreciated, and we regret that some sort of arrangement cannot be made.
6. Since you are dealing with very small numbers of individuals, extreme caution must be taken in weighing each factor to be considered.
7. We have been advised today by Mr. Hart that reserve samples covered by 1718, 1928, 1654, 1698, and 1701 met specifications 100 percent.
8. In addition, when it is known that you will not be present to write your report, someone in your section should perform the task.
9. A copy of the pamphlet prepared by the State of Vermont may be obtained from the Payroll Branch if needed.

10. In this market, there is seen by Sales to be great potential.
11. By taking the trouble to notify these regulatory agencies in event of bona fide troubles, a favorable impression is created, since it indicates our desire to cooperate to a maximum degree.
12. If this is not successful, removal with a steam lance might be tried. As a last resort, the material might be carefully heated with torches and scraped from the surface while still in the molten or softened condition. Care should be taken in the heating, or the material may catch fire.
13. It is recommended, therefore, that a similar procedure be followed by Sales this year and that a list of suggested Research and Development projects be prepared by them as rapidly as possible.
14. We have received no adverse comments to date. It is understood, however, that some additional classifications and man-hours must be added to the final report.
15. It is certain that this proposal will be approved by management.
16. The assistance we received from Mr. Jones of your department in the preparation of this manual is greatly appreciated.
17. There is likely to be a downward turn in stock prices next month.
18. This material will be submitted by our Advertising Department for your approval before it is used in any form of publicity.
19. The problem of improving ignition in jet fuel systems is considered very important by the armed services.
20. The advisability of filing an appeal to the appropriate state court is being considered by Division Management.
21. There is an investigation of the elasticity of these fibers planned for next month by the Research Department.
22. According to my findings the amount and kinds of communication carried on by these persons vary over wide ranges. Within the sections the professional people holding managerial positions were found to communicate much more frequently than engineers, and a great deal of this communication was oral. With the engineers, however, much of the required communication was in the form of written matter, such as reports and letters. There was also found a distinct difference with whom those in managerial positions and those holding engineering positions communicated.

15

Special Problems of Technical and Professional Writing

We are all aware that the various academic disciplines and the various professions, in addition to using standard language, have developed special terminology. Only persons trained in a discipline or a profession are able to use its language fluently, and only they are really able to understand all of it.

ORIGINS OF TECHNICAL LANGUAGE

Special purpose languages—or professional languages—developed almost as soon as language itself. Aboriginal human beings, after inventing a crude bow, needed a word for it. As they began to use it, they must have needed a special terminology to identify what they did with it. To describe what happened when a person held it with one hand, inserted a notched arrow in the string with the other, pulled it, and let go, a word was needed. So someone coined the equivalent of "shoot." As new types of bow and of arrow were developed and new ways to use the weapon and a whole range of new hunting techniques were invented, a very considerable vocabulary came into being to describe all these things. This vocabulary naturally was used largely by the hunters of the tribe. To them it was meaningful. To outsiders—to women, children, agricultural workers, and artisans, as well as to members of groups which had not yet invented the bow—it meant less. The use of this special terminology gave the hunter a feeling of separateness, of prestige. He and his friends could talk shop without others being able to understand them. If others did begin to penetrate the secrets of their language, the hunters could always invent new terms to describe their activities and so maintain their solidarity and their prestige in the larger group.

THE ROLE OF TECHNICAL TERMS

Today the same motives—the genuine need to describe both new objects and new procedures and the desire for group prestige or group solidarity—still govern the linguistic activities of specialized groups. When metallurgists devised a treatment of the surface of iron-base alloys with air or steam at a particular temperature so that a thin blue oxide film would be formed on what was originally a scale-free surface, they needed a name for it. So they called it "blueing." Without that term they could not talk to each other about the process unless they went through some such description as we have given every time they wanted to refer to it. The term "blueing," then, is a metallurgist's shorthand identification for a rather complex process. In much the same way lawyers use the word *tort*, economists use *imputation*, fox-hunters use *drag*, physicians use *antihistamine*, and literary critics use *metaphor*. If we did not have such technical terms, every area of the world's work would operate much less efficiently, for no specialist of any kind would be able to confer satisfactorily with colleagues.

THE DESIRE FOR PRESTIGE

Technical terms have, then, a very important role to play. However, they can be used for purposes other than precise communication. When they are, a possible motive is the second one we have mentioned: the desire for prestige or solidarity. As the hunters in a primitive society used special terminology to obtain and then to demonstrate their superiority to those who were not hunters, modern specialists may use their terminology for the same purpose.

A hundred years ago the social sciences did not exist in the form in which we know them today. It has often been observed that as each of them moved toward acceptance by society as a genuine discipline, it developed complex technical terminology. Certainly each has needed a special vocabulary to speak more precisely about phenomena in its area, but the complexity of the terminology may have arisen in part also from a desire to make the discipline seem more "scientific," and hence more respectable. (Medicine, for example, has always derived prestige from its terminology, much of it stemming from Latin and Greek.)

Thus in certain instances grandiose terms seem to have been assigned to simple objects, acts, and phenomena. Having these terms enabled the adepts to act as if the new names defined objects, acts, and phenomena which the discipline had discovered and which only its members could possibly understand. To be sure, not all social scientists have followed this course or had these motives. Many of the important figures in each of the social sciences—like those in other areas—seldom use much technical jargon. Nor is the abuse of technical language confined to the social sciences. These days it is merely a bit more conspicuous there. It may exist in any field. Some physical scientists use language pretentiously, and so do some literary critics, linguists, and philosophers.

If people within a single discipline talked only to each other, perhaps no great harm would be done, and those who wanted to demonstrate their skill in manipulating the latest terminological fad could be left to do it in private or at professional conferences. Unfortunately, however, disciplines do not exist in isolation, especially in the world of business and industry, where in a single working day a plant manager or a vice-president for manufacturing may communicate with lawyers, engineers, sales representatives, psychologists, physicians, chemists, physicists, and other specialists. Almost any employee of a large company will have to communicate frequently with these people. Since neither managers nor foremen can be expected to understand the language of all of the specialists with whom they confer, there are likely to be misunderstandings.

PROVIDING TOO MUCH
INFORMATION

Another frequent cause of problems when professional people write for persons in business about their special area of competence is the temptation to supply more information than the reader needs or wants to solve a special problem. It is very difficult for any of us to put aside an opportunity to "clarify" a recommendation or decision by going into a thorough discussion of the basis upon which we make it. Somehow we feel that a simple statement of our conclusions is not sufficient. The psychologist who is asked by the president of her company whether her studies show that male consumers of a new product will be amenable to a particular kind of television advertisement will be tempted to explain what tests she has run, how they were administered, how the subjects were selected, and the probable accuracy of each test. It is hard indeed for the researcher to confine herself to a brief answer to the president's request. We all want to "show our stuff," to suggest how hard we have worked and how competently—even brilliantly—we have succeeded. If she succumbs to temptation, however, she will merely be adding to the huge pile of materials which the president has to go through each day. And unless she organizes her report so that the answers *he* wants are the first thing he sees when he picks it up, he will have to waste valuable time hunting for them.

276   The problems of professional overcommunicating can be seen in this ex-

ample from everyday life. A friend of ours, having just discovered that she was pregnant, wrote a note to her doctor as the hay fever season approached. She said she had heard that hay fever injections were dangerous during pregnancy. Should she, she wondered, have her usual series this year? This was the reply she received.

Dear Mrs. Johnson:

Opinion among allergists is divided as to whether or not the pregnant patient should receive injections. Personally, I suggest you avoid them until your pregnancy is completed. The course of allergic disease is often profoundly influenced by pregnancy. The effect is extremely variable. Some patients experience complete relief of allergic manifestations, some are improved, and others are unchanged or become definitely worse. We have observed several multiparous patients in whom the effect of pregnancy seemed to be related to the sex of the fetus, but we have been able to detect no constant relationship of this type between patients. Evidence that cortisone or a related substance may be formed by a placenta suggests an explanation for the effect of pregnancy on allergic diseases, although other factors also may be involved. Allergic rhinitis, bronchial asthma, atopic dermatitis, and urticaria are particularly apt to be alerted by pregnancy. These diseases usually revert to their original state within a few weeks after parturition. Occasionally the effect of pregnancy may be more sustained. Aside from strictly allergic disease, there is a vasomotor rhinitis of pregnancy which is practically indistinguishable from allergic rhinitis. Its presence may explain the apparent exacerbation of allergic rhinitis which is not infrequently seen during pregnancy.

Sometimes favorable results of treatment (allergic) have been obscured by complicating factors such as respiratory infections, emotional upsets, important food or animal allergies, or pregnancy.

Tolerance to allergenic extracts may diminish or increase markedly during pregnancy. Therefore, even when a woman has been accustomed to receiving a certain maintenance dose of allergen, it is advisable to reduce the maintenance dosage as soon as she becomes pregnant. A severe constitutional reaction might contribute to abortion through the strong uterine contractions thus produced.

Cordially yours,

James S. Bool, M.D.

P.S. Accordingly, I would appreciate your keeping me posted during the season if you have any symptoms of hay fever and after the baby is born.

Those of us who are not physicians should have no difficulty in seeing what the problems are here. First of all, the lady has asked a simple question: should she resume taking her shots? What she receives in reply is a brief scientific treatise on the relationship between allergies and pregnancy. Her question is answered in the second sentence. Then Dr. Bool goes into a lengthy dissertation. His motive is no doubt commendable: he wishes his patient to understand the basis for his recommendation. But as he begins to explain why it is   277 that allergists disagree, he warms to his subject and winds up giving her far more information than she could possibly need or want. Furthermore, what he dictated is badly organized, and his language—containing terms like "multiparous patients," "atopic dermatitis and urticaria," and "vasomotor rhinitis of pregnancy"—will send her to a dictionary. Fortunately our friend was not frightened by the long list of possible dangerous reactions, but found the letter amusing. A younger or more anxious person might not have reacted so sensibly.

Dr. Bool's letter, then, illustrates two of the major problems of professional technical writing: the twin temptations to say too much and to say it in confusing language. Why are specialists likely to say too much? Usually because they know so much about their subject and are so fascinated by it that they can't believe that everyone else will not want to know as much as they do. Why do they confuse readers? They use too much of the specialized terminology that comes so naturally to them.

TECHNICAL WRITING

When one suggests to some professionals that their writing should perhaps be less formal, they insist on the need for traditional language patterns. "For the ordinary business person, yes. No need there for a special kind of language. But in our profession. . . ." One hears such statements most often in the business world from engineers and scientists. However, we have found that the more observant professionals have long recognized that most of these arguments are specious. Read, for example, what one aircraft industry representative said a generation ago about training students in technical writing:

> Actually the models, the standards, and the requirements [for technical writing] should be identical with those that the graduate should expect to encounter in the field—with one important exception: the meaningless chestnut that technical writing is "different" from standard writing should be extirpated. This argument is usually advanced by engineers who cannot write standard English and need an excuse for the stuff they do write. Technical writing is standard writing plus a small special vocabulary appropriate to the topic under discussion. All else remains the same; the requirements for clarity, logic, readability, completeness, compactness, style are not changed.[1]

Directors of research often complain bitterly that their subordinates cannot write. They resent the time they have to spend sorting out and recasting reports before they can send them on, but, as one of them said to us, "If I didn't keep sending each report back loaded with questions and then working with the guy who'd done the experiments, management would never know what we're

---

[1] Other professions whose members sometimes claim such privilege are physicians, lawyers, and literary critics. But any group which adopts a specialized vocabulary will be tempted to make a similar claim.

doing down here." Frequently, too, we hear stories about good researchers who are not promoted because their reports do not make clear what they have accomplished. On the other hand, many engineers and scientists do write reports that are readily intelligible to anyone who knows their vocabulary and that contain conclusions couched in terms management can understand.

A HORRIBLE EXAMPLE

The "horrible examples" of unnecessarily complicated writing that engineers and scientists pass around among themselves show that they are not unaware of the problem. And the spoofs that appear frequently in their journals indicate that they understand which aspects of their writing cause the trouble. Here is a paragraph from one such caricature:

> Forty-one manestically spaced grouting brushes were arranged to feed into the rotor slip-stream a mixture of high S-value phenylhydrobenzamine and five percent reminative tetryliodohiexamine. Both of these liquids have specific pericosities given by P = 2.5C/n6.7 where n is the diathetical evolute of retrograde temperature phase disposition and C is Cholmondeley's annular grillage coefficient. Initially, n was measured with the aid of a metapolar refractive pilfrometer (for a description of this ingenious instrument, see L. E. Rumpelverstein in "Zeitschrift für Elektrotechnistatischs-Donnerblitze," vol. vii), but to the present date nothing has been found to equal the transcendental hopper dadoscope. (See "Proceedings of the Peruvian Academy of Scatological Sciences," June 1914).

The writer calls attention to several typical faults of technical writing: (1) overuse of highly specialized terminology; (2) long parenthetical interpolations; and (3) unnecessarily long sentences. The resulting pomposity is as ridiculous as the sign over a door in a Boston hotel: "This door is not an accredited egress."

CLARITY IN TECHNICAL WRITING

Scientific and technical writing need not confuse its readers. Although only a chemist could fully understand the following paragraph, anyone can recognize that it avoids pretentious, over-complicated posturing:

> The isolation of 3,5-dibromonitrobenzene (VI) as a by-product of the Ullmann reaction of I presents no new features. The hydrogenolysis of halogen from aryl halides by copper and organic acids and by copper and tetralin has been demonstrated. But substitution of aromatic halogen for hydrogen has also been observed when no obvious hydrogen source was present. Hydrogenolysis has been reported as a side reaction to Ullmann coupling in several cases when no solvent was used; indeed, in one instance some hydrogenolysis occurred in an "inert" atmosphere. The fact that VI was isolated from I in the present investigation even when the mixture was carefully dried and protected from atmospheric moisture indicates that the hydrogen

279

which replaced the iodine probably came from I or its products. It is significant, also, that the iodine atom of I was removed by hydrogenolysis, but no debromination product of I was detected.[2]

The sentences average 25 words, and none is so convoluted as to suggest a boa constrictor negotiating a maze. Beginning a sentence with "but" and using such words as "indeed" and "probably" lighten the style. Even without understanding it, a lay person can read the paragraph with meaningful expression.

Clearly the readers of a technical report or paper should not have to waste time scouting each sentence cautiously to discover what it is all about and make sense of its intricate twists and turns. Rather, they should find sentences short enough to be negotiable, language technical only where necessary, and "road signs" (but, indeed, even, probably, also) frequent enough to keep them from losing their way.

Here, for example, is a paragraph which in tone, vocabulary, and sentence structure would be appropriate for a report by a scientist to the management or the board of directors of an industrial concern. It is, in fact, the final paragraph of a short report published in Science[3] in which the author considers the biological significance of a study she has made:

> Biological significance. It is difficult for the lay person to understand uncertainties in science, yet it is imperative that scientists attempt to educate the nonscientist concerning the problems which arise when extrapolating from laboratory data to an assessment of risk in human populations. Stochastic events that occur after exposure to mutagens, clastogens, carcinogens, and teratogens are not easy to explain. Chromosome damage is only one indicator in a series of poorly understood biological events that occur randomly in cells (and therefore in individuals) as a result of an external environmental insult. We cannot equate a ring chromosome in a lymphocyte with a cleft palate in an offspring. We should recognize our ignorance and uncertainties and try to help the regulators as well as the human subjects to appreciate the concept of probabilities rather than certainties. In our democratic society, perhaps we will decide that 500,000 deaths per year is an acceptable price for toxic chemicals in our environment, just as we have decided that 50,000 traffic deaths per year is an acceptable price for automobile travel. On the other hand, we may decide that 5000 deaths per year is an unacceptable price for toxic chemicals. The scientists should provide the data and interpret the results; the public should decide.

Although this paragraph was written primarily for an audience of scientists, only one word in it is likely to give the educated person any real difficulty: stochastic, a word that has been traced back to 1662 by the Oxford English Dictionary and which seems to have been revived by scientists. It means conjectural or problematic. Otherwise, except for the series "mutagens, clastogens, carcinogens, and teratogens," the general meaning of which can be deduced

---

[2] Robert B. Carlin and Edward A. Swakon, "Anomalous Ullmann Reactions. The Unsymmetrical Coupling of 2,6-Dibromo-r-nitroiodobenzene," Journal of the American Chemical Society, 77 (1955), p. 969.

[3] Margery W. Shaw, "Love Canal Chromosome Report," 209 (August 15, 1980), p. 752.

from the presence of the widely known *carcinogens,* there are no problems of vocabulary. Certainly there are none with the structure of individual sentences or with the coherence of the paragraph. It moves smoothly from the problem of the lay person's difficulty in understanding uncertainties in science, through the scientists' difficulties in explaining the uncertainties, and finally to the conclusion that despite these difficulties, the scientist must provide full information so that the public can decide on the action to be taken.

Sometimes technical writers must write for a diverse audience. Many technical reports, for example, are read by several readers with different degrees of technical competence. Here is a section from such a report, written by a consultant to an electric utility company. Since he was recommending an expensive consulting arrangement, the writer knew that his report would be read not only by the utility's engineers, but also by its board of directors, many of whom were not technically trained.

Before proceeding to discuss techniques of transient analysis, let us first define the concept "transient" as it will be used in this report. By "transient," we mean:

a. passing especially quickly into and out of existence, and
b. temporary oscillation that occurs in a circuit because of a sudden change of voltage or of load.

Thus transients on electrical systems are short-term phenomena often lasting for only a few milliseconds.

Since programs for transient field measurement tend to be difficult and require a high degree of specialized knowledge, there are only a few organizations which are capable of conducting them. To see why this is so, let us look at a typical arrangement for such measurement.

Figure 1 is a single-line diagram of a substation where three voltages are to be measured. (For simplicity, only one of the three phases is shown.) The transient surge to be recorded is shown entering the station from the line on the left. Voltage transducers connected to the system are tied to a recording device which will preserve the transient waveform. It all sounds very simple until one begins the actual analysis. Then a series of problems presents itself.

Note how the consultant opens by defining his terms in such a way that his nontechnical readers will understand the nature of the problem but his technically trained readers will not feel that he is being condescending. In his second paragraph, he prepares his readers, technical and nontechnical, for the conclusion of his report. Not until the third paragraph does he begin to discuss the technical aspects of the problem.

In all three paragraphs he uses rhetorical devices carefully designed to move his readers into and through his analysis. In the first paragraph, for example, he could simply have begun, "In this report, by 'transient' we mean . . ." Instead he opens with a sentence inviting his readers to consider with him the meaning of the concept "transient," an effective introduction with a conversational tone. The second sentence in the second paragraph serves much the   281 same function: it leads from the short "introduction" (i.e., the first one and a half paragraphs) to the technical analysis. In the third paragraph, the writer uses the same conversational tone for the disclaimer in the next-to-last sentence and for the last sentence, which provides transition to further technical analysis.

The writer's consideration for his readers is also demonstrated by his using only those technical terms that are absolutely necessary and, although two of his sentences contain more than 30 words, by writing sentences that average only 19 words.

Compare the consideration for the readers in the opening of that report with this opening paragraph from the introduction to a proposal by the Customer Service Section of a large engineering firm:

> The Customer Service Section is a central and integral part of Otco Engineering with the fundamental and unique responsibility for determination, planning, and layout of all facilities in both the pre-order proposal stage and the post-order contract stage and for providing a complete range of plant layout and planning services for feasibility studies when such studies are requested. In the pre-order stage, the Customer Service Section interfaces with the customer's representatives to coordinate the customer's requirements with Otco's experience for an optimum design, especially with respect to technical expertise and economic considerations, using design concepts and engineering principles, to put into process flow-sheets, conceptual plant layout drawings, technical specifications and documents to be submitted to the customer as a proposal by Otco Engineering. Among other things, the Section determines the optimum location and orientation of plant facilities on the customer's property to take the maximum advantage of site conditions, access ways, and design considerations, always striving for the optimum overall layout of all facilities with respect to plant operations, economy, minimum maintenance costs, future expansion considerations, and other parameters. In the post-order stage, the Section combines the proposed pre-order conceptual plant layout, available and specially prepared equipment drawings, and other design concepts with the desired modifications and new requirements input during the period between proposal and contract before proceeding with the final definitive general arrangement drawings.

There is no consideration here for the reader, technical or nontechnical. The statement is wordy and unnecessarily heavy. Jargon abounds. Phrase piles on phrase until the sentences, which average 56 words, seem interminable.

LEGALESE

As a result of the proliferation of government legislation which applies to business and has generated vast quantities of regulations and forms, business people have become increasingly concerned in recent years about legal writing. As with technical writing, the problem here involves both lawyers writing for lay readers and lawyers writing for each other. Such writing, often called "legalese," sometimes makes unnecessary use of legal terminology where standard English would communicate better to the audience addressed. It is a variety of what we have called pseudoformal language.

SPECIAL PROBLEMS OF TECHNICAL AND PROFESSIONAL WRITING

Today legalese flavors much of the writing in business, industry, and government. Here, for example, is a statement of "Terms and Conditions of Sale" used by a major manufacturing company in its proposals:

> Rolectric hereby gives notice of its objection to any different or additional terms and conditions except for any such terms and conditions as may be expressly accepted by it in writing.

> Unless different or additional terms and conditions are stated or referred to in the proposal, in which event such different or additional terms and conditions shall be exclusive as to the particular subject covered, the terms and conditions stated below apply, and such terms and conditions supersede any prior or contemporaneous agreements or correspondence between the parties.

The argument for using this particular wording is that when proposals are accepted, they become part of a contract. Thus, as potential legal documents which may have to withstand the scrutiny of a judge and hostile lawyers in court, they must be written in time-tested legal language. Such a claim, in effect, removes the writing of proposals from the management's area of competence and makes it a specialists' problem, a lawyers' problem. Lawyers, after all, have been to law school and know how to use legal language; business people do not.

When we asked a group of executives at Rolectric about specific phrases and structures in this passage, we discovered that the lawyers present would not defend them. What, we asked, was the function of the phrase "hereby gives notice of"? Was it necessary? No, said the lawyers, probably not. Was it necessary for the second paragraph to be all one sentence? Could it not be broken in two? The lawyers agreed that it could. Eventually we proposed the following revision, which both the lawyers and managers accepted as an improvement:

> Rolectric objects to any different or additional terms and conditions except for any such terms and conditions as it expressly accepts in writing.

> If different or additional terms and conditions are stated or referred to in the proposal, they shall be exclusive to the particular subject covered. If not, the terms and conditions stated below apply and supersede any prior or contemporaneous agreements or correspondence between the parties.

The original has 88 words, the revision 68. The sentence length of the original averaged 76 words, of the revision just under 23. We suspected that we could make further improvements. Why not say, for example, "If other terms . . ." in place of "If different or additional terms . . ."? But we decided not to press too hard and left the passage with some flavor of legalese.

There are two easily identifiable problems with the original statement. The first is legal jargon, legal rubber stamps, which make the statement sound contract-like but which can readily be replaced by simpler phrasing: "Rolectric hearby gives notice of its objections" by "Rolectric objects"; and "unless . . . in which event" by "if." The second problem is the convoluted structure of the long single-sentence second paragraph.

CLARITY IN LEGAL LANGUAGE

David Mellinkoff, Professor of Law at the University of California at Los Angeles and a member of the California bar, cites many "continuously vague archaisms," which, he says, "have been used long and often, with never a healthy smell of precision about them. They are flabby words; and, in addition, many of them are treacherous, for . . . they are not obviously vague."[4] In his list, for example, is the word *hereby,* which appeared in the original version of Rolectric's "Terms and Conditions of Sale." "*Hereby,*" Mellinkoff says, "gives only the flavor of the law"; it is not a precise term. Furthermore, "Usually, no word need be substituted for *hereby.* It is just unnecessary. *I do hereby revoke* is not more precise than *I revoke.*"[5]

Mellinkoff also argues for brevity and shorter sentences: "As precision is the loudest virtue of the language of the law, so wordiness is its noisiest vice. Even the untutored can see that law language is too long, and some have not hesitated to say so." His solution: "There are only two cures for the long sentence: (1) Say less; (2) Put a period in the middle."[6]

The second paragraph of the original Rolectric statement is typical of much legal writing, which tends to back into assertions instead of making them positively. Often, too, successive negatives seem to change the direction of a passage several times. Here, for example, is a sentence from an instruction sheet issued recently with a stock purchase offer, a communication not between lawyers, but between a company and the stockholders of another company that it wanted to take over:

> *Guaranty of Signatures.* Signatures on Letters of Transmittal must be guaranteed by a commercial bank or trust company having an office or correspondent in the United States or by a firm which is a member of a registered national securities exchange or of the National Association of Securities Dealers, Inc. (an "Eligible Institution"), EXCEPT in cases where the Shares tendered are tendered (i) by a registered holder of Shares who has not completed either the box entitled "Special Payment Instructions" or the box entitled "Special Delivery Instructions" on this Letter of Transmittal or (ii) for the account of any Eligible Institution.

The statement means

> Signatures on Letters of Transmittal must be guaranteed . . . ONLY when Shares are tendered by a registered holder who *has* completed either the box entitled "Special Payment Instructions" or the box entitled "Special Delivery Instructions."

[4] *The Language of the Law* (Boston: Little, Brown and Company, 1963), p. 304.
[5] Mellinkoff, p. 314.
[6] Mellinkoff, pp. 399, 366.

To ferret out that meaning, however, takes several readings of the original, which changes direction twice: once at "EXCEPT" and a second time at "who has *not* completed."

Many lawyers, of course, recognize these problems. We have already quoted one. Here is another, Richard C. Wydick:

> We lawyers cannot write plain English. We use eight words to say what could be said in two. We use old, arcane phrases to express commonplace ideas. Seeking to be precise, we become redundant. Seeking to be cautious, we become verbose. Our sentences twist on, phrase within clause within clause, glazing the eyes and numbing the minds of our readers. The result is a writing style that has, according to one critic, four outstanding characteristics. It is: "(1) wordy, (2) unclear, (3) pompous, and (4) dull."[7]

You may have noticed that Wydick is not talking here about lawyers writing for laymen. He is talking about lawyers writing for lawyers. But, as Mellinkoff says, "If lawyers but concentrate on writing more intelligibly for each other, with the same strokes they will write more intelligibly for laymen."[8]

Elegant variations and unnecessary jargon, of course, are not peculiar to lawyers, although particular elegant variations and particular examples of jargon may be. Writers in all professions display similar tendencies. Instructions for drafting understandable legal documents, therefore, sound much like instructions for drafting understandable letters, memos, and reports. Wydick's chapter headings, for example, are a series of imperatives: Omit Surplus Words; Use Familiar, Concrete Words; Use Short Sentences; Use Base Verbs and the Active Voice; Arrange Your Words With Care; and Avoid Language Quirks.[9]

Students of legal writing clearly agree that "legalese" must go. It interferes with communication even between people well versed in the law. When non-lawyers in business, industry, and government adopt it in an attempt to be correct or formal or impressive, they inevitably produce quantities of unreadable prose—sand traps for unwary readers which slow down and sometimes stop progress toward solving problems.

ILLUSTRATIVE MATERIALS

1.

Galileo Galilei (1564–1642) was one of the founders of modern science and the inventor of the telescope, which enabled him to demonstrate the validity of the Copernican theories about the universe. Perhaps because he realized

---

[7] "Plain English for Lawyers," *California Law Review* 66 (July 1978), p. 727. See also Wydick's *Plain English for Lawyers* (Durham, NC: Carolina Academic Press, 1979). In this paragraph, Wydick, Dean of the School of Law at the University of California at Davis, is quoting Mellinkoff, whose *The Language of the Law* has become a classic.

[8] Mellinkoff, p. 436.

[9] Wydick, *Plain English for Lawyers,* Table of Contents.

*that his novel views on many subjects would be resisted by most of his con-
temporaries, he was also a dedicated student of communication. The historian
Eric Cochrane[10] discusses Galileo's attitude toward writing:*

> Galileo followed three simple principles. The first was clarity: he wrote
> "obscure" over every line of his favorite poet, Ariosto, that could not be
> instantly understood, The second was relevance: he constantly upbraided
> his least favorite poet, Tasso, for "filling up the page" when there was really
> "nothing more to say." The third was effectiveness; a period that was "cold
> and forceless," he insisted might just as well be left unsaid. Galileo thus
> learned to bridge the gap between literary and spoken language, to express
> the loftiest matters in the form of casual conversation. . . . Better yet, he
> learned to communicate his theses not just to the academic elite to which
> he belonged by vocation, but to the society of nonspecialized educated
> laymen to which he . . . belonged by birth and by choice.

2.

*As we have indicated, members of all professions have a responsibility to use
language effectively. Here a physician, Dr. Morgan Martin, talks to his colleagues about the importance of the language they use in speaking with their
patients.[11]*

> Physicians use words in various ways. They use them as tools to uncover
> diagnosis and as vessels to carry treatment and caring. As the physician
> explores the human condition, his English may be more meaningful than
> his biology or neurology.
> It is not that the medical man's English is especially bad, but that it is
> especially important for it to be good. Words carry weight, and those of the
> physician carry particularly heavy burdens. They influence not only how
> the medicine goes down but how the patient sees life and death.
> Some physicians use more words than necessary because they try to
> explain everything. This is understandable: first, there is the medical student
> who seldom hears "I don't know," and later there is the physician facing
> patients who hope against hope that the physician knows everything. The
> physician is sorely tempted to peddle personal prejudices or to play God.
> Yet some physicians, being what they are, accept the mysterious and feel
> no compulsion to explain everything.
> Novelists and poets describe people better than physicians, and the phy-
> sician who reads increases his ability to use words closer to life. To appre-
> ciate language, the physician must read nonmedical works, even poetry.
> And for deeper appreciation of words, he should try writing—that hard-bred
> child of reading.

[10] *Florence in the Forgotten Centuries, 1527–1800* (Chicago: Chicago University Press, 1973),
p. 168. The word *period* in line 5 refers to a formal, oratorical sentence.

[11] *Journal of the American Medical Association* 239 (June 30, 1978), pp. 2776–2777.

SPECIAL PROBLEMS OF TECHNICAL AND PROFESSIONAL WRITING

The physician must know words as he knows his other instruments—their history as well as how they work with one another in rhythm, melody, and alliteration. He must be sensitive to the rise and fall of sentences, including the long sentences he uses to comfort. If he wishes to be like Osler, or a Lewis Thomas, or, for that matter, William Carlos Williams, he must respect his words as worthy members of his available resources.

The exchange of words between physician and patient is complex: how to listen, how to talk, and how to think are vast subjects. Thus it is useful to focus on words apart from their producers, on words dwelling alone or in figures of speech.

Words have special problems. One is that they change with time. Another is that words are imprecise; perfect understanding is a fallacy. Words are imperfect instruments for expressing complicated concepts with certainty because each has "a penumbra of uncertainty." Since words are both transitory and imprecise, it behooves the physician, while striving for clarity, to make allowance for misunderstanding.

3.

In the *Illustrative Materials for Chapter 11*, you will have found Philip Broughton's "Systematic Buzz Phrase Projector." A similar device appears in The Phrase-Dropper's Handbook by John T. Beaudouin and Everett Mattlin.[12] It calls for using a four-digit number to construct an impressive-sounding sentence using the jargon of the computer expert. Why not try out a few of your favorite dates?

MODULE A	MODULE B	MODULE C	MODULE D
1. In particular,	1. a large portion of the interface coordination communication	1. must utilize and be functionally interwoven with	1. the sophisticated hardware
2. On the other hand,	2. a constant flow of effective information	2. maximizes the probability of project success and minimizes the cost and time required for	2. the anticipated fourth-generation equipment
3. However,	3. the characterization of specific criteria	3. adds explicit performance limits to	3. the subsystem compatibility testing
4. Similarly,	4. initiation of critical subsystem development	4. necessitates that urgent consideration be applied to	4. the structural design, based on system engineering concepts
5. As a resultant implication,	5. the fully integrated test program	5. requires considerable systems analysis and trade-off studies to arrive at	5. the preliminary qualification limit.

6. In this regard,	6. the produce configuration baseline	6. is further compounded when taking into account	6. the evolution of specifications over a given time period.
7. Based on integral subsystem considerations,	7. any associated supporting element	7. presents extremely interesting challenges to	7. the philosophy of commonality and standardization.
8. For example,	8. the incorporation of additional mission constraints	8. recognizes the importance of other systems and the necessity for	8. the greater fight-worthiness concept.
9. Thus,	9. the independent functional principle	9. effects a significant implementation of	9. any discrete configuration mode.
10. In respect to specific goals,	10. a primary interrelation between system and/or subsystem technologies	10. adds overriding performance constraints to	10. the total system rationale.

PROBLEMS

1.

Below you will find two versions of the same section of an automobile insurance policy issued by the Home Mutual Insurance Company of Appleton, Wisconsin. The first is the version used with minor alterations until recently. The second is from the company's new "Easy Reading" policy.

Version 1

PART III—PHYSICAL DAMAGE

Coverage D—(1) Comprehensive (Excluding Collision) (2) Personal Effects:

(1) To pay for loss caused other than by collision to the owned automobile. For the purpose of this coverage, breakage of glass and loss caused by missiles, falling objects, fire, theft or larceny, explosion, earthquake, windstorm, hail, water, flood, malicious mischief, or vandalism, riot or civil commotion or colliding with a bird or animal, shall not be deemed to be loss caused by collision. The deductible amount, if shown in the declarations, shall be deducted from the amount of each loss, other than loss by (a) fire or lightning, (b) smoke or smudge due to a sudden, unusual and faulty operation of any fixed heating equipment serving the premises in which the automobile is located, or (c) the stranding, sinking, burning, collision or derailment of any conveyance in or upon which the automobile is being transported.

(2) To pay for loss caused by fire, lightning, flood or explosion to robes, wearing apparel and other personal effects which are the property of the named insured or a resident relative, while such effects are in or upon the owned automobile.

Coverage E—Collision: To pay for loss caused by collision to the owned automobile or to a non-owned automobile but only for the amount of each such loss in excess of a deductible amount stated in the declarations as applicable thereto. The deductible amount shall not apply to loss caused by collision with an automobile owned by another person and insured by this company if such person is not a resident of the insured's household.

Coverage F—Fire, Windstorm, Theft and Transportation: To pay for loss of the owned automobile, caused by: (a) fire or lightning, (b) smoke or smudge due to sudden, unusual, and faulty operation of any fixed heating equipment servicing the premises in which the automobile is located, (c) the stranding, sinking, burning, collision or derailment of any conveyance in or upon which the automobile is being transported, (d) windstorm, hail, earthquake or explosion, excluding loss or damage caused by rain, snow or sleet, whether or not wind-driven, (e) loss of or damage to the automobile caused by theft, larceny, robbery, or pilferage.

Coverage G—Towing and Labor Costs: To pay for towing and labor costs necessitated by the disablement of the owned automobile, provided the labor is performed at the place of disablement.

Coverage H—Automobile Rental Expense: To reimburse the insured for automobile rental charges, excluding mileage charges, for a substitute automobile rented from a garage, auto body repair shop or car rental agency due to loss of use of an automobile by reason of a loss insured under the Comprehensive or Collision provisions of the policy. This insurance shall apply during a period of twelve (12) consecutive days commencing with the date and time of such loss of use, not to exceed Ten Dollars ($10.00) per day nor more than One Hundred Twenty Dollars ($120.00) as a result of any one loss. Such insurance as is afforded by this Coverage H does not apply to loss of use by theft.

Benefits in Addition to the Applicable Limit of Liability:

(a) To reimburse the insured for transportation expenses incurred during the period commencing 48 hours after a theft covered by this policy of the entire automobile has been reported to the company and the police, and terminating when the automobile is returned to use or the company pays for the loss; provided that the company shall not be obligated to pay aggregate expenses in excess of $10.00 per day or totaling more than $300.00;

(b) to pay general average and salvage charges for which the insured becomes legally liable as to the owned automobile being transported.

Definitions: The definitions of "named insured," "resident relative," "owned automobile," "temporary substitute automobile," "private passenger automobile," "farm automobile," "utility automobile," "automobile business," and "war" in Part I apply to Part III and under Part III:

"insured" means (a) with respect to the owned automobile, the named insured and spouse if a resident of the same household; any other person or organization, other than a person or organization engaged in the automobile business or as a carrier or other bailee for hire, maintaining, using or having custody of said automobile with the permission of the named insured; and (b) with respect to a non-owned automobile, the named insured and spouse if a resident of the same household provided actual use thereof is with the permission of the owner.

"non-owned automobile" means a private passenger, farm or utility automobile not owned by or furnished or available for the regular use of the named insured or a resident of his household other than a temporary substitute automobile, while said automobile is in the possession or custody of the insured or is being operated by him.

"loss" means direct and accidental loss of or damage to the automobile, including its equipment.

"equipment" means accessories permanently attached to the automobile including the spare tire, standard tool set and jack, tire chains, and two additional tires maintained for seasonal use on the described automobile, and unless endorsed hereunder, no more than one tape, wire, record disc or other medium for use with any device or instrument permanently installed in the insured automobile and designed for the recording, reproduction or recording and reproduction of sound.

"collision" means collision of an automobile covered by this policy with another object or with a vehicle to which it is attached or by upset of such automobile.

Exclusions This policy does not apply under Part III:

(a) to any automobile while used as a public or livery conveyance, or used for carrying persons for a charge, but the transportation on a share-the-expense basis in a private passenger automobile of friends, neighbors, fellow employees or school children shall not be deemed carrying persons for a charge;

(b) to loss due to war, declared or undeclared, or to confiscation by government or civil authorities;

(c) to loss to a non-owned automobile arising out of its use by the insured in the automobile business;

(d) to loss to a private passenger, farm or utility automobile or trailer owned by the named insured and not described in this policy or to any temporary substitute automobile therefor, if there is other valid and collectible insurance against such loss;

(e) to loss to an automobile owned by, or furnished or available for the regular use of a resident relative of the named insured's household;

(f) to damage which is due and confined to wear and tear, damage from chemicals and materials used on roadways, freezing, mechanical or electrical breakdown or failure, unless such damage results from a theft covered by this policy;

(g) to tires, unless damaged by fire, malicious mischief or vandalism or stolen or unless the loss be coincident with and from the same cause as other loss covered by this policy;

(h) to loss due to radioactive contamination or sonic boom;

(i) to loss due to secretion by any person in possession of the automobile under a bailment lease, conditional sale, purchase agreement, mortgage or other encumbrance, or to conversion or embezzlement;

(j) to loss to any automobile while used in an organized race or speed contest;

(k) under Coverage D, to breakage of glass if insurance with respect to such breakage is otherwise afforded.

Limits of Liability: The limit of the company's liability for loss shall not exceed the actual cash value of the property, or if the loss is of a part thereof the actual cash value of such part, at time of loss, nor what it would then cost to repair or replace the property or such part thereof with other of like kind and quality, nor, with respect to an owned automobile described in this policy, the applicable limit of liability stated in the declarations; provided, however, the limit of the company's liability for loss to personal effects arising out of any one occurrence is $200.

Other Insurance: If there is other insurance against a loss covered by Part III of this policy, the company shall not be liable under this policy for a greater proportion of such loss than the applicable limit of liability of this policy bears to the total applicable limit of liability of all valid and collectible insurance against such loss; provided, however, the insurance with respect to a temporary substitute automobile, a newly acquired automobile, or a non-owned automobile shall be excess insurance over any other valid and collectible insurance.

Version 2

COVERAGE D—CAR DAMAGE COVERAGE

We will pay **you** for **loss** to **your insured car**

(1) caused by **collision** (Coverage D-1); or

(2) not caused by **collision** (Coverage D-2)

less any applicable deductibles. The deductibles shall not apply to **loss** caused by a **collision** of **your insured car** with another vehicle insured by **us**.

We may pay the **loss** in money or repair or replace damaged or stolen property. **We** may, at any time before the **loss** is paid or the property is replaced, return, at **our** expense, any stolen property either to **you** or to the address shown in the Declarations, with payment for the resulting damage. **We** may keep all or part of the property at the agreed or appraised value.

You or **we** may demand appraisal of the **loss**. Each will appoint and pay a competent and disinterested appraiser and will equally share other appraisal expenses. The appraisers, or a judge of a court having jurisdiction, will select an umpire to decide any differences. Each appraiser will state separately the actual cash value and the amount of **loss**. An award in writing by any two appraisers will determine the amount payable.

ADDITIONAL DEFINITIONS USED IN THIS PART ONLY

As used in this Part:

(1) **"Collision"** means collision of **your insured car** with another object or upset of **your insured car. Loss** caused by missiles, falling objects, fire, theft or larceny, explosion, earthquake, windstorm, hail, water, flood, malicious mischief or vandalism, riot or civil commotion, colliding with a bird or animal, or breakage of glass is not deemed **loss** caused by **"collision".** If breakage of glass results from a **collision** however, **you** may elect to have it treated as **loss** caused by **collision.**

(2) **"Loss"** means direct and accidental loss of or damage to **your insured car,** including its equipment.

(3) **"Your insured car"** shall also include any other car or **utility trailer** not owned by or furnished or available for the regular use of **you** or a **relative.**

ADDITIONAL PAYMENTS

(1) If there is a total theft of **your insured car we** will pay up to $10 per day, but no more than $300, for the cost of transportation incurred by an **insured person.** This coverage begins 48 hours after the theft and ends when the car is returned to use or when **we** pay the **loss.**

(2) **We** will pay **you** up to $10 for the cost of substitute transportation in traveling from the place of a covered car damage loss to **your** intended destination.

(3) **We** will pay **you** for **your** reasonable and necessary additional living expenses if **your car** is disabled from a covered car damage loss. This benefit applies if we insure **your car** for both **collision** (Coverage D-1) and **loss** not caused by **collision** (Coverage D-2) under this policy. The **loss** must occur more than 100 miles from the place of principal garaging as stated in the Declarations page. **We** will pay up to $75 per day, not to exceed $150 per policy period.

(4) **We** will pay salvage charges for which **you** become legally liable because of transporting a **car we** insure.

(5) **We** will pay **you** up to $200 for loss of, or damage to, **your** clothes and personal luggage—including its contents. This benefit applies to loss or damage by theft from **your car,** provided there are visible marks of entry, or from any other direct and accidental loss of, or damage to, **your car** — other than by **collision.**

EXCLUSIONS

This coverage does not apply to **loss:**

(1) To **your insured car** while used to carry persons or property for a charge. This exclusion does not apply to shared-expense car pools.

(2) Caused by war (declared or undeclared), civil war, insurrection, rebellion, revolution, nuclear reaction, radiation or radioactive contamination, or any consequence of any of these.

(3) To any sound equipment not permanently installed in **your insured car** nor to one tape, record, or similar item used with sound equipment.

(4) To sound receiving or transmitting equipment designed for use as citizens band radios, two-way mobile radios, telephones, scanning monitor receivers, television sets, or their accessories or antennas, not permanently installed in **your insured car** in the dash or console opening specified by the manufacturer of the car for the installation of such equipment.

(5) To a camper body or **utility trailer** owned by **you** or a **relative** and not described in the Declarations. But, coverage does apply to a camper body or **utility trailer** ownership of which **you** acquire during the policy period if **you** ask **us** to insure it within 30 days after **you** acquire it.

(6) To awnings, cabanas, or equipment designed to provide additional living facilities.

(7) Resulting from wear and tear, freezing, mechanical or electrical breakdown or failure or road damage to tires. But, coverage does apply if the **loss** results from the total theft of **your insured car.**

(8) To any **car** not owned by you which is used in the business of selling, repairing, servicing, storing or parking **motor vehicles.**

(9) To any **car** used in preparation for any pre-arranged or organized racing, speed, demolition or stunting contest or activity, or used in the event itself.

LIMITS OF LIABILITY

Our limit of liability for **loss** shall not exceed:

(1) The lesser of (a) the actual cash value of the stolen or damaged property or (b) the amount necessary to repair or replace the property.

(2) $500 for a **utility trailer** not owned by **you** or a **relative.**

COVERAGE E—TOWING AND LABOR COSTS COVERAGE

We agree to pay up to the limit shown in the Declarations for towing and labor costs incurred each time **your insured car** is disabled. The labor must be performed at the place of disablement.

COVERAGE F—REIMBURSEMENT OF AUTO RENTAL EXPENSE

We agree to reimburse **you** for expenses **you** incur in renting a substitute car when there is a loss to **your insured car** which

(1) results in its withdrawal from normal use for more than 24 hours; and

(2) the loss is covered under Part IV of this policy.

This coverage does not apply in the case of the total theft of a car for which transportation expense reimbursement is covered under the policy. **We** will pay up to $10 per day only during that period of time reasonably required to repair or replace the car, but no more than $300 maximum.

NO BENEFIT TO BAILEE

This coverage shall not directly or indirectly benefit any carrier or other bailee for hire liable for **loss** to **your insured car.**

OTHER INSURANCE

If there is other applicable similar insurance on a **loss** covered by this Part, **we** will pay only **our** share. **Our** share is the proportion that **our** limit of liability bears to the total of all applicable limits. However any insurance **we** provide with respect to a vehicle **you** do not own shall be excess over any other collectible insurance.

The stated intention of the insurance company was to make its policy easier to read and understand.

1. How does the new format help to achieve this goal?

2. Some materials have been moved to different places in the section. Why has each move been made?

3. Compare the section "Exclusions" in the two versions. Which exclusions have been dropped? Compare those that remain with the similar items in the old version. How have they been altered? Why?

4. In the same way, compare the sections on reimbursement for auto rental, on other insurance, on towing costs, and on additional benefits.

5. On the whole, do you feel that the revision is a significant improvement over the original?

2.

Following are assembly instructions for two Log Storage Racks made by different companies.

LOG CRIB ASSEMBLY

Insert all the bolts with the heads to the outside of the crib, but do not tighten until the crib is assembled.

1. Fit four rubber caps "A" over ends of base tubes "B".

2. Use four bolts. Bolt cross tubes "C" to base tubes "B". Fit four rubber caps "A" over ends of cross tubes "C".

3. The two hoops "D" are made of two sections each. Fit them together so that the bolt holes line up. Note that each seciton has a smaller end, which fits into the larger end of the adjoining section.

4. Fit end caps "E" to the top of the two hoops "D".

5. Bolt two hoops "D" to the inside of the base tubes "A" and the cross tubes "C". Tighten all nuts and bolts.

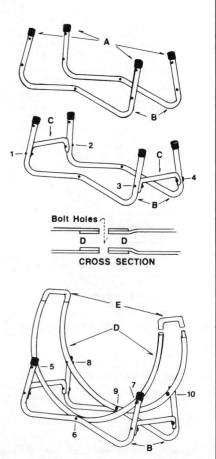

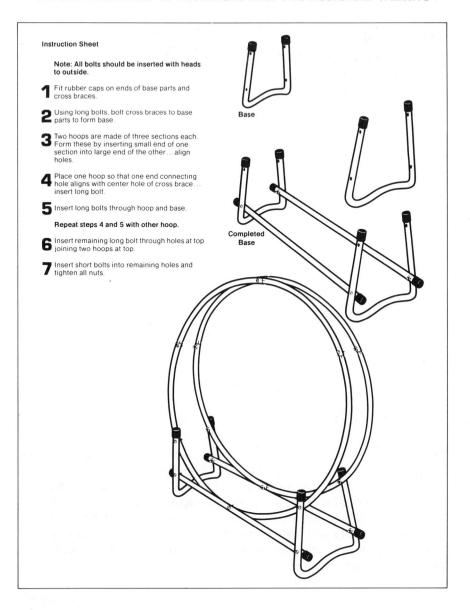

Instruction Sheet

Note: All bolts should be inserted with heads to outside.

1 Fit rubber caps on ends of base parts and cross braces.

2 Using long bolts, bolt cross braces to base parts to form base.

3 Two hoops are made of three sections each. Form these by inserting small end of one section into large end of the other...align holes.

4 Place one hoop so that one end connecting hole aligns with center hole of cross brace... insert long bolt.

5 Insert long bolts through hoop and base.

Repeat steps 4 and 5 with other hoop.

6 Insert remaining long bolt through holes at top joining two hoops at top.

7 Insert short bolts into remaining holes and tighten all nuts.

Base

Completed Base

1. How do the two sets of instructions differ?

2. Which of the two is likely to be easier to follow?

3. What changes would you recommend for improvement of each?

16
Coherence

In the first fifteen chapters we have often concerned ourselves with coherence—the way in which the elements of a sentence, a letter, a memo, a report are bound together into a unified whole. We have talked about the role of such devices as parallelism, subordination, and consistency in voice and tone in making sentences coherent, and we have seen how divisions, headings, and layout will perform the same service for major writing projects. However, we have not examined coherence directly. Here we will do so. And since coherence concerns not an individual segment of a communication but the relation among the parts, we will use this chapter and the next to demonstrate the interdependence of principles which we have already discussed individually and see how they function together in the communication process. Along the way we will also look at a few specific problems not yet discussed.

The word *cohere* derives from the Latin *co* (with) and *haerere* (to stick). The elements of a communication may be stuck together in either of two principal ways: by the appropriate choice of words (semantic coherence) or by the appropriate arrangement of words and other elements in sentences, paragraphs, and larger units (structural coherence). We will begin with the latter.

CONSTRUCTING A COHERENT PARAGRAPH

It will be helpful at this point to look at a paragraph of expository prose to see how coherence is achieved. Here is one from the middle of an article, "Advertising and Ethics," by Philip Nelson.[1] In the preceding paragraphs, Nelson has begun to consider laws designed to protect consumers against fraudulent advertising.

> I am not saying that these laws against deceptive advertising are pointless. I am only asserting that most people have missed the point. The virtue of these laws is not that they reduce deceptive advertising. Rather, it is that they can make more information available to consumers than they would otherwise receive. Take, for example, the law prohibiting the mislabeling of the fabric content of clothing. If that law is sufficiently enforced, consumers will believe that a clothing label is usually correct. This will provide an incentive for some manufacturer to mislabel—unless the law is enforced so vigorously that nobody gains from breaking it (a non-optimal level of law enforcement). In the absence of the law, no one could trust any clothing label that it was not in the self-interest of the producer to specify correctly. Hence, these clothing labels, though incorrect, would not deceive many people. This law is not reducing deception in advertising, but it is enabling consumers to determine in many instances the fabric content of their clothing from the label. Laws can achieve the objective of more direct information at the price of both enforcement costs and costs to the consumer of being deceived where otherwise he would be appropriately distrustful.

You will perhaps have noticed that Nelson uses some of the devices discussed in Chapters 10–14. Here we will concern ourselves with how he cements his ideas into a coherent, easily followed whole.

He begins this building block in his argument by referring to the subject of the preceding paragraph: "I am not saying that these laws against deceptive advertising are pointless." Thus he ties the two paragraphs together. Then he tells us what he *is* saying: that people have missed the point of the laws. Next, in two sentences we are told, first, what the virtue of these laws is not, and then, in a sentence beginning with *rather*, which signals a contrary opinion, what their virtue really is. "Take, for example" tells us that we are to be given an illustration, which is the law on labeling fabrics. "If *that law* is sufficiently enforced" leads into a brief discussion in which one sentence builds on another. Each contains words which tie it closely to those that precede it: *This . . . the law; the law; Hence; This law*. Note also that in each sentence appears some variant of the word *label: mislabeling, label, mislabel, labels*. The paragraph concludes with a generalization about what it may cost to achieve the objectives of a law.

[1] In *Ethics, Free Enterprise & Public Policy* (New York: Oxford University Press, 1978), pp. 193–194.

We do not wish to suggest that this paragraph is a meticulously crafted example of coherent exposition. It is not. It is a workaday paragraph of prose embedded in a twelve-page article. The point is rather that Nelson is a writer who, like all conscientious writers, makes a real effort to get his message across clearly, to be sure that his readers are never in doubt about where they are.

PRONOUNS AND ANTECEDENTS

Coherence works in many ways—as it must, since it alone can give meaning to individual words, the building blocks of language. Without it, meaning is blurred. In the business world one often meets sentences like these:

> This equipment would be furnished by Farco. It has great merit, not only in our contract business, but also as an aid in promoting paint sales. If this were considered possible, it would be necessary to bring in other members of management to discuss the most profitable way to handle it.

The sentences lack coherence because the writer, unlike Mr. Nelson, has not provided satisfactory connections between their elements. To what does the second *this* refer? The equipment can hardly be "considered possible." There is, in fact, nothing for *this* to refer to. Nor is it clear what the final *it* might refer to. The equipment? Promoting paint sales? Who knows?

A pronoun has a specific job to do. It stands in for a noun, which grammarians call its antecedent, so that we don't have to repeat the noun over and over again. As we read, we expect every pronoun to have an easily identifiable antecedent. The confusion created by a writer's failure to provide such antecedents for pronouns can be serious. Even when the confusion is brief, it breaks the reader's concentration and is certain to be irritating.

In the following sentence the difficulty caused by improperly related pronouns is confounded by a dangling participle:

> Confirming our telephone conversation of this morning, we have received word from Hancock Mills that they will ship the material by January 18.

The *our* refers to the reader and the writer. The *we* refers to the writer's company. A less confusing version would be:

> Confirming my telephone conversation with you this morning, I'd like to repeat that we have received . . .

The revision requires more words, but it eliminates any chance of confusion. The fuzzy overlapping of *our* and *we* in the original probably results from an attempt to avoid using *I* and *my,* a matter discussed in Chapter 13.

COLLECTIVE NOUNS

Another confusion involving pronouns arises from the use of collective nouns: *company, department, team, plant,* and so forth. Although each of these words refers to a group of individuals, that group is being considered as a unit. Therefore, the noun is singular and must be followed by a singular verb and a singular pronoun, if any.

The company *needs* additional financing. (not *need*)

The negotiating team, despite the varying views of some of its members, *approaches* its task with confidence that *it* will be successful. (not *approach* and *they*)

To refer to the individuals in a group, one should speak of *team members, company employees,* or *department personnel* and use the plural.[2] A similar problem frequently arises with *each, anyone, everybody,* and *everyone.* In everyday conversation many of us have fallen into the habit of using the plural pronoun with these words. However, the singular is correct and should always be used in business communications:

Everyone does her best under these conditions.
Each member of the team works smoothly with his partner.

An alternative, of course, is to use the plural throughout:

All people do their best under these conditions.
All members of the team work smoothly with their partners.

However, as is sometimes the case when one uses the plural to avoid the masculine pronoun, the change in the second sentence introduces ambiguity. It is not clear, as it is in the singular version, whether each member has one partner or more.

APPROPRIATE COORDINATION

A reader's attention may be temporarily diverted from the writer's message, with consequent loss of coherence, by careless use of coordinating and sub-

---

[2] The word *customer* makes trouble for business writers. We frequently see sentences like this:

The customer has asked us whether we can manufacture a collar for this product in stainless steel. We can, but the cost will increase by 46 percent. Therefore, I doubt that they will decide to make the change.

Here the writer starts out thinking of the customer in the singular, but by the third sentence is thinking of the customer as a group of individuals who will be making a decision. However, because there is no indication of the shift, the reader is confused. The writer should have been consistent and used *he* or *she* instead of *they.*

ordinating conjunctions. A letter which contains such a sentence as this one provides a minor puzzle:

> On July 9 we received 30 complete units, and we also received 60 extra units which we believe may have been packed with this shipment in error.

We can, to be sure, understand what is being said here, but we may well have to read the sentence twice before we are certain that we have everything straight. Why? Because the writer has not given us the right traffic signal. The "and we also received" coming directly after "we have received 30 complete units" seems to signal a routine addition. We are not likely to suspect that trouble lies ahead. Hence we plow on only to discover that there is a problem with the 60 extra units. Had the writer changed the conjunction to *but,* which signals a contradiction, there would have been some warning:

> . . . we received 30 complete units, *but* we also received 60 extra units. . . .

Even this revision, however, does not indicate adequately the proper relationship between the ideas. They are equal in importance, but the relationship between them is still not expressed exactly. Here is what the writer meant:

> On July 9 we received *not only* the 30 complete units we ordered, *but also* 60 extra units, which must have been packed with the shipment by mistake.

Laying out the sentence in outline form will show the function of the four italicized words:

> On July 9 we received
>   *not only* the 30 complete units . . .
>   *but also* 60 extra units. . . .

The emphasis here is on the equal and parallel importance of the ideas introduced by the pair of coordinators.

APPROPRIATE SUBORDINATION

Coherence may also be insured by using subordinate conjunctions meaningfully. There are many of them, as we have seen in Chapter 12, and each should contribute importantly to the precise meaning of any sentence in which it appears. "*When* the tests were completed, Patton left Milwaukee" does not mean quite the same thing as "*Because* the tests were completed, Patton left Milwaukee." The second sentence tells *why* Patton left Milwaukee; the first simply indicates a sequence of events. If the intent is to suggest that the completion of the tests caused Patton's leaving Milwaukee, the first sentence does not communicate effectively. The reader may be left wondering whether the completion of the tests actually *did* cause Patton's departure. And having to puzzle something out breaks the train of thought, which then must be picked up again.

PILED-UP MODIFIERS

Coherence can also be seriously disrupted by piling up modifiers behind a noun—a habit that seems to be showing up more and more frequently in business correspondence. Here are two sentences which exemplify it:

Bob Engel was invited to participate this month in a DKK academic community summer industrial NSF appointment planning meeting.

A conceptual reprogrammable electron beam scanned MOS memory array tube which uses this ionizing radiation induced predisposition is described as a memory design example.

How are we to unscramble these monsters? What goes on here? Even a physicist would have trouble with the second one. Each of them may sound impressive—and was apparently intended to—but, except perhaps for someone working very closely with the writer, no one could be expected to handle the second sentence without unraveling item by item the phrase *conceptual reprogrammable electron beam scanned MOS memory array tube*. And a reader who has taken the time to do that certainly has lost the thread of whatever discussion is being carried on. Coherence has gone out the window.

Why do people write this way? Partly, of course, so that their words will sound impressive, especially to the outsider. Partly, no doubt, because in some circles piling up modifiers is an "in" thing to do. So Bob Engel, who was invited to participate in a DKK fraternity meeting sponsored by the National Science Foundation to plan appointments of members of the academic community (i.e., college professors) to summer positions in industry, appears in a report of his department's activities as having been invited to a DKK academic community summer industrial NSF appointment planning meeting.[3]

SUPPLYING TOO MUCH INFORMATION

In much the same way as piling up modifiers or phrases, the inclusion of large amounts of unnecessary information may destroy coherence. All of us have received letters that rehearse every detail of a transaction before saying

---

[3] This problem is, of course, related to the piling up of phrases, discussed in Chapter 10, and to the desire to impress, discussed in Chapter 15.

anything new. Writers sometimes devote entire opening paragraphs to reviews of previous correspondence. Here is an example:

> In reply to your letter of July 19, in which you state that you received 2 only No. 608 bottles (blue) with white stoppers and 2 only No. 609 bottles (white) with blue stoppers, each pair of bottles packed and shipped separately, we have questioned our order and shipping departments closely to discover the reason for the bottles reaching you with the wrong stoppers and in different shipments, even though they were ordered by you on the same order for shipment at the same time by the same carrier so that you could most conveniently reship them to your customer as soon as they arrived without any loss of time or unnecessary confusion and without having to store one pair of bottles until the second pair arrived.

This writer not only tried to retell the whole story of the blue and the white bottles—and to do it in one sentence—but he also ensured that his lengthy summary will almost certainly not be read. Rather than assume that the summary is accurate, his correspondent will consult his own files for the details of the transaction.

Here is a slightly different example. First, the complete text of the letter to be answered:

> On May 20, our Freemont Plant shipped car COX 4702 containing Sodium Carbolate against your order BY 70–32.

> According to our laboratory report the salable acid content was 57.7%. The specific gravity was 1.096 and the car contained 7,855 gallons. Just as soon as your plant reports their analysis and gallonage, we can get together on settlement.[4]

Here is the beginning of the answering letter:

> With reference to your letter of June 2 covering COX 4702 containing Sodium Carbolate shipped by your Freemont Plant to our Meadville plant on May 20 against order BY 70–32, we wish to advise that we have received our plant report on this car.

> In comparing the gallonage, I find a difference which is substantially greater than we would normally expect to encounter. Remembering that this car. . . .

Note that in the reply the opening phrase of the first paragraph contains all of the information in the first paragraph of the incoming letter plus two additional items: "your letter of June 2" and "our Meadville plant." Certainly some of the information in the opening phrase is superfluous. Since there is a disagreement, the person to whom the answer is addressed will have to check invoices and laboratory reports. The date June 2, the words "Sodium Carbolate," and either the car number or the order number should be enough information to locate the right file. And a good subject heading would provide that.

---

[4] Note the use in this sentence of singular subject and singular verb followed by a plural pronoun referring to the singular subject, an error discussed a few pages back.

COHERENCE

Occasionally a letter writer feels obliged to summarize the letter being answered for the benefit of other people who should receive copies of the reply. Without such a summary, they will not be able to understand what is going on. The solution to this problem is to send the best possible letter—that is, one without an opening summary—and then either have a brief summary added at the bottom of the carbon copies or enclose a xerox copy of the letter being answered. Thus the customer will get an efficient letter, and those who receive the carbons will have all the information needed to understand the situation.

Another type of communication in which a writer often reduces coherence by supplying too much information is the report. Directors of research and members of management frequently complain that report writers clutter the body of a report with so many unnecessary details and so many excursions into matters of purely personal interest that their readers lose sight of the structure of their exposition.

A personnel man, for example, wrote an analysis of his management-appraisal program. It was intended primarily to inform the appraisers that the company was profiting from the work and the time they were putting into the program. Twelve pages long, the report discussed the purpose of the program, analyzed both the appraisal forms and the procedure which the appraisers used to fill them out, summarized the picture of management personnel given by the completed forms, and evaluated the entire program. The writer was crest-fallen when he learned that the personnel manager thought that the report was much too long and involved. It *was* long and involved. By the time she finished reading the twelve pages—if she ever did—the manager was so thoroughly entangled in scales and scores and other details that she remembered only dimly the purpose of the report. Furthermore, the intended readers, the appraisers, already were thoroughly familiar with much of the detail.

The report was eventually rewritten to make the important information in it more readily available. As a first step, it was shortened a page and a half by removing wordiness and unnecessary repetition. What was left was then rearranged so that the information of real interest to the readers was presented in three pages as the body of the report. The supporting details and paraphernalia, of interest only to some potential readers, went into four brief and well-organized appendices. Not only for the intended readers but for anyone else who picked it up, the rewritten report said what the writer intended to say far more clearly than did his original version.

Supplying too much information, then, can be as dangerous as supplying too little. In his now famous essay on communication theory, Warren Weaver discusses the danger in trying to force too much information over a communication channel. Then he goes on to say:

> A general theory . . . will surely have to take into account not only the capacity of the channel but also (even the words are right!) the capacity of the audience. If you try to overcrowd the capacity of the audience, it is probably true, by direct analogy, that you do not, so to speak, fill the audience up and then waste only the remainder

by spilling. More likely, and again by direct analogy, if you overcrowd the capacity of the audience you force a general and inescapable error and confusion.[5]

CONSISTENT WORD CHOICE

If coherence can be affected by the amount of material included in a communication—whether too much or too little—and by the way that information is used, it can also be affected by failure to maintain consistent choice in words. Here is a letter written by a man holding a responsible position in a large company:

Dear Harry,

We wish to acknowledge your letter dated December 29 and are glad to have the opportunity to give you a report on the picture currently displayed by our crystal ball.

There would seem to be little or no possibility of significant changes in the price structure between now and April 30, when the current government regulations expire. Whether or not Congress will pass legislation to extend these regulations beyond April 30 is the $64,000 question, with the pros and cons pretty well balanced. . . .

Please advise if the foregoing is in need of further clarification.

Very best regards for the New Year. Please say hello to Jeannie and the boys.

Yours very truly,

John F. Swinsel

Mr. Swinsel's analysis of the problem, which we have omitted, indicated an alert, perceptive mind. A personal interview supported that impression. His associates and superiors shared it. But the letter suggests a curious lack of sensitivity to language.

John Swinsel knows his reader well enough to call him by his first name, speaks of his "crystal ball" and the "$64,000 question"—a bit out of date, that!—and asks Harry to "say hello to Jeannie and the boys." It sounds as if Harry is someone to whom he would like to write a friendly, informal letter. But the overall tone of the letter is formal. It contains such stuffy rubber stamp phrases as "we wish to acknowledge your letter," "are glad to have the opportunity," and "Please advise if the foregoing is in need of further clarification," all of which sound as if they have been transferred from a thousand previous Swinsel letters.

[5] Warren Weaver, "Recent Contributions to the Mathematical Theory of Communication," in Claude E. Shannon and Warren Weaver, *The Mathematical Theory of Communication* (Urbana: University of Illinois Press, 1949), p. 116.

To Harry this must have seemed a very peculiar communication, with its mixture of breezy informality and stuffy pseudoformality. To anyone with a sensitivity to language, the mixture suggests that the writer is using a tool which he cannot really handle. His lack of control keeps the reader constantly off balance, not a pleasant sensation at any time.

Here the remedy should be obvious: maintain a consistent tone throughout. And if the relationship between the two men is friendly, as the salutation and the message sent to "Jeannie and the boys" suggest, the tone should be informal. Why not something like this?

Dear Harry,

We've been doing our share of puzzling over the problem that you posed in your letter of December 29. All I can say is that we do not expect prices to change before April 30 and that we have no clue to whether Congress will extend the regulations beyond that date. Actually, the evidence on Congress is contradictory and evenly divided. . . .

If there is any other way that we can add to your confusion, please let me know.

In any case, don't let the price problem spoil your holidays. Have a fine New Year. My best to Jeannie and the boys.

Sincerely,

John P. Swinsel

The problem here is essentially the one we have seen earlier in the "Dear Polly" letter (Chapter 13). And in each instance the solution is based on the premise that consistency in tone ensures coherence. Coherence, in turn, ensures that readers always know exactly where they are.

ILLUSTRATIVE MATERIALS

1.

Grammarians have identified four basic types of connectives: coordinating conjunctions, correlative conjunctions, subordinating conjunctions, and conjunctive adverbs. The simplest are coordinating conjunctions:

and   but   or   nor   yet

They connect parts of a sentence that are of equal weight or importance:

The pin is continually being immersed in water, *but* it never rusts.

Mr. Farren cannot collect the money due him in time, *nor* can he obtain a loan.   **303**

For and *so* have sometimes been considered coordinating conjunctions. However, *for* really functions as a subordinating conjunction, though it normally does not introduce a sentence-opening clause. ("The strike had little effect on production, for the men returned to work almost immediately." Compare: "The strike had little effect on production because the men returned to work almost immediately"; "Because the men returned to work almost immediately, the strike had little effect on production.") There is a subtle distinction between the meaning of *for* and that of *because*. Though each concerns cause and effect, *because* places stronger emphasis on it. *For* stands between the main clause, which receives most emphasis, and the causal element, which is slightly subordinate in importance. Almost always a comma precedes *for* when it is used as a conjunction.

So functions as a coordinating conjunction only in informal usage: "He worked hard, so he succeeded." Otherwise it is used between clauses as an adverb accompanying *and* ("He worked hard, and so he succeeded") or *that,* either expressed or implied ("He worked hard so that he would succeed"; "He worked hard so he would succeed").

Similar in function are the correlative conjunctions:

both . . . and	not only . . . but also
either . . . or	not so . . . as
neither . . . nor	whether . . . or

By using these paired coordinators to introduce groups of words which are in parallel structure, a writer can indicate that the ideas presented (1) are of equal importance and (2) stand in a particular kind of coordinate relationship:

We can *neither* hold the sale during the week of June 15th *nor* postpone it until September.
You must send *not only* the check *but also* the appropriate form.

A third group of connectives is called subordinating conjunctions. *They connect a subordinate idea to a main idea (a subordinate clause to a main clause) in such a way as to indicate the exact relationship between the two. Some of the more common are:*

Those expressing temporal relationships: after, as, as long as, as soon as, before, since, until, when, whenever, while
Those expressing place: where, wherever
Those expressing causal relationships: because, inasmuch as, in order that, since, so that, why
Those expressing other relationships: although, as if, how, if, though, unless, whereas, whether

Subordinating clauses may appear either before or after the main clause:

When subjected to high-vacuum sublimation, this form yielded another.
We cannot replace this machine *because* the warranty has expired.

COHERENCE

A fourth group of connectives is called conjunctive adverbs. *Unlike the conjunctions, they need not appear at the beginning of a clause. They may be used where needed not only to connect but also to give emphasis:*

He may have said that; *however,* he may not have meant it.
He may have said that; he may, *however,* not have meant it.

When a conjunctive adverb rather than a conjunction is used between two independent clauses in the same sentence, the clauses are separated by a semicolon, not a comma. It is very important, therefore, to be able to distinguish between these two types of connective. The easiest way to do so is to see if the connective can be used, as above, elsewhere than at the beginning of its clause. If it may be moved without essentially changing the meaning of the statement, it is an adverb; a semicolon must separate the clauses. If it may not be, it is a conjunction; a comma preceding it will do.

Here is a list of the more common conjunctive adverbs:

Those expressing temporal relationships: afterwards, eventually, immediately, meanwhile, meantime, then

Those which may express causal relationships: accordingly, certainly, clearly, consequently, evidently, obviously, otherwise, perhaps, possibly, predictably, presumably, seemingly, somehow, surprisingly, therefore, thus

Those which may suggest comparisons: admittedly, alternatively, conversely, correspondingly, equally, however, instead, likewise, nevertheless, nonetheless, notwithstanding, only, similarly

Those which may suggest amplification or generalization: altogether, basically, besides, chiefly, especially, essentially, furthermore, fundamentally, generally, indeed, moreover, overall, thus

Those which may suggest other relationships: again, certainly, even

Finally, in addition to the basic connectives, we have a great many phrases which serve to link ideas. There are so many that we will provide only a representative sampling: above all, after all, at any rate, comparatively speaking, even more important, even so, for example, in addition, in any case, in conclusion, in the first place, needless to say, on the one hand, on the whole, to sum up.

All of these connectives—and the many which we have no space to mention—help to hold together the writer's sentences and make it possible for the reader to follow an argument with ease and confidence. The writer who uses them effectively has a great advantage over one who does not.

2.

The paragraphs below are the opening of an essay, "Business and Technology," by Peter F. Drucker.[6] *Examine them carefully. List examples of the var-*

---

[6] From Peter F. Drucker, *Toward the Next Economics and Other Essays* (New York: Harper & Row, 1981), pp. 37–38.

ious devices Drucker uses to insure coherence. Then write an analysis of the passage based on your findings.

Technology has been front-page news for well over a century—and never more so than today. But for all the talk about technology, not much effort has been made to understand it or to study it, let alone to manage it. Economists, historians, and sociologists all stress the importance of technology—but then they tend to treat it with "benign neglect," if not with outright contempt.

More surprisingly, business and businessmen have done amazingly little to understand technology and even less to manage it. Modern business is, to a very considerable extent, the creature of technology. Certainly the large business organization is primarily the business response to technological development. Modern industry was born when the new technology of power generation—primarily water power at first—forced manufacturing activities out of home and workshop and under the one roof of the modern "factory," beginning with the textile industry in eighteenth-century Britain. And the large business enterprise of today has its roots in the first "big business," the large railroad of the mid-nineteenth century, that is, in technological innovation. Since then, the "growth industries," down to computer and pharmaceutical companies of today, have largely been the outgrowth of new technology.

At the same time, business has increasingly become the creator of technology. Increasingly, technological innovation comes out of the industrial laboratory and is being made effective through and in business enterprise. Increasingly, technology depends on business enterprise to become "innovation"—that is, effective action in economy and society.

Yet business managers, or at least a very sizable majority of them, still look upon technology as something inherently "unpredictable." Organizationally and managerially, technological activity still tends to be separated from the main work of the business and organized as a discrete and quite different "R & D" activity which, while in the business, is not really of the business. And until recently business managers, as a rule, did not see themselves as the guardians of technology and as concerned at all with its impact and consequence.

MATERIALS FOR REVISION

A

1. If your customer is in need of bearings and you care to give us their name, we will be pleased to communicate with them.
2. Since our conversation last week, we have received several inquiries about this clause in the contract.
3. We are aware that shipping the exact amount requested is sometimes difficult, but not knowing how close the customer orders to his requirements, it is best that we supply them with a little more than they asked for rather than short change them.

4. These accounts, which remain unpaid, were discussed at length in our letters of April 21, May 16, June 7, and July 3. It was also the subject of our telephone call last week.
5. On arrival here we entered the first phase of this orientation program and then worked in the mill. This lasted for two months.
6. Confirming our telephone conversation of this morning in regard to the above customer, we have received word from Chicago that they will have the material by January 17 or 18.
7. In accordance with our recent telephone conversation, we have checked with our Newark plant to obtain further information.
8. On March 15 we issued an additional billing for 490 gallons on our invoice 86-9090 in the amount of $106.33. This should now be in your possession. On this invoice you will note that payment is to be made in 10 days.
9. We are attaching our Invoices 589/66 and 589/67. These invoices cover additional prepaid freight charges on Barge XYZ 273 and Prince 479.
10. The second major classification would be interdepartmental memorandums. This is a letter that distributes and requests information.

B

1. Following the acquisition by private companies of the five large government-owned synthetic rubber plants, Oxene purchase agreements were negotiated with the new owners.
2. The schedule for increased salaried employees' group-life insurance will be offered to salaried employees.
3. There seems to be ample market to support a 24,000,000- to 30,000,000-pound per-year sale in New York State.
4. The survey of the organizational and procedural problems of the Jones and Warfield Chemical Division's district sales offices was continuous during the month.
5. The result of the recent extensive evaluation of the use of this new low-molecular-weight bulk polymer have shown this new product to be preferable.
6. The 60-ampere unused disconnect fused switch is convenient.
7. The plastic fire clay-burner eye liners are crumbling.
8. You were sent advertising copy covering the above subject: semimonthly long-range tooth-paste vs. tooth-powder saturation ads for the Chicago papers.

17

Punctuation

O ne element of composition which is indispensable to coherence is
punctuation. It guides the reader through the maze of words. What
pitch, tone, and volume do for spoken words, punctuation does for words in
print. Without it we would have great difficulty in determining which words
go with which, which words should be emphasized, or how words and word
groups relate to each other.

"Punctuation? That is an easy one," we have been told. "All you need is
a good secretary." In the best of all possible business worlds, this solution
might sometimes be satisfactory. In routine matters a secretary may handle
punctuation. But anyone who writes important letters, reports, and memoranda knows that punctuation has a large and sometimes subtle effect on
meaning; it is too important to turn over to anyone else. Only a thorough
understanding of the function and conventions of punctuation and of how to
put them to work will enable the executive to be sure that each communication expresses accurately what is intended.

THE FUNCTION OF PUNCTUATION

A mark of punctuation serves much the same function as a road sign. It tells
the reader when to stop, when to slow down, and sometimes what road con-

ditions to expect immediately ahead. Read the following sentence at a normal pace.

> The product pattern of this plant has changed requiring the installation of the column and allied equipment and space availability is such that congestion cannot be avoided.

This sentence—on the fourth page of a report to management—stopped a vice-president cold. By the time he hit it, he had gathered considerable momentum in his reading and was moving along at a good clip. For the vice-president, meeting this sentence at this point was like driving into a brick wall. His reaction was in direct proportion to the shock he received.

Why did the vice-president have this reaction? First of all, he had begun to read the sentence rapidly: "The product of this plant has changed requiring the installation. . . ." *Whoa!* he subconsciously told himself. *That doesn't make sense. Let's try it again.* "The product of this plant has changed [pause] requiring the installation. . . ." *Now I'm on the track again.* ". . . requiring the installation of the column and allied equipment and space availability. . . ." *Whoa again! We can't install space availability.* Again he had to go back, to put in an even longer pause after "equipment." Finally he had the meaning of the sentence clearly in mind. But he had twice been misled by the writer's failure to tell him when to pause, and each time he had to back up and retrace his steps. Understandably, he was not pleased.

The writer could easily have prevented his annoyance—with a few road signs:

> The product pattern of this plant has changed, requiring the installation of the column and allied equipment; and space availability is such that congestion cannot be avoided.

Here the punctuation indicates very clearly both where and how long he should pause as well as the relationship between the ideas. Lack of proper punctuation, on the other hand, wastes valuable time. It forces the reader to stop and then attempt to organize what appears to be merely a string of words. If such interruptions are frequent, the letter or report may be tossed aside in irritation or frustration.

However, punctuation marks are *not* exact equivalents of pauses in speech. It is true that one can generally tell whether what one has written is an intelligible sentence by reading it aloud. But it is emphatically not true that a comma should be used wherever one would pause in speaking. These days good writers tend—except where certain conventions are involved—to use the minimum amount of punctuation that will assure exact communication. Interrupting a sentence with a series of unnecessary commas ("hiccuping commas," one of our colleagues calls them) misleads the reader and disrupts the train of thought.

PUNCTUATION IN THE PAST

The tendency to cut down on punctuation derives in part from our using simpler sentence structure than we once did. Over 300 years ago Isaac Newton wrote these three sentences in his *A New Theory about Light and Colours,* published in 1672:

> In the year 1666 (at which time I applied myself to the grinding of optick glasses of other figures than spherical) I procured me a triangular glass prism, to try therewith the celebrated phenomena of colours. And in order thereto, having darkened my chamber, and made a small hole in my window-shuts, to let in a convenient quantity of the sun's light, I placed my prism at its entrance, that it might be thereby refracted to the opposite wall. It was at first a very pleasing divertissement, to view the vivid and intense colours produced thereby; but after a while applying myself to consider them more circumspectly, I became surprised to see them in an oblong form; which, according to the received laws of refraction, I expected should have been circular.

Here is the punctuation pattern of the passage:

    _____ (_____)
    _____ , _____ / _____ ,
    _____ , _____ , _____ ,
    _____ , _____ / _____ ,
    _____ ; _____
    _____ , _____ ; _____ ,
    _____ , _____ /

Some of Newton's punctuation is required by the complicated sentence structures that he uses. Much of it, however, simply reflects the heavier punctuation that writers used in his time. Today, Newton's second sentence, whose structure is not particularly complex, would probably look like this:

> And in order thereto, having darkened my chamber and made a small hole in my window-shuts to let in a convenient quantity of the sun's light, I placed my prism at its entrance that it might be thereby refracted to the opposite wall.

Two commas instead of five!

PUNCTUATION TODAY

Unfortunately, vestiges of the comma-sprinkling days remain. Here are two sentences from a recent report:

> The main purpose of having a prescribed amount of Xeno in a phenol mix for use in resins, is to delay the set or hardening time. The reason for this is that Xeno is not nearly as reactive as Emeno, or 3,5 Artite.

PUNCTUATION

There is no logical reason here for defying the convention of not separating the subject from the verb with a mark of punctuation. The comma after *resins* does not clarify the meaning of the first sentence; it actually misleads the reader by suggesting that an interpolation is to follow. Instead comes the verb. Only in rare instances is a subject so long or heavily modified that it must be followed by a comma before the reader can proceed.

Nor is the comma necessary between *Emeno* and *or* in the second sentence. Here the chance of confusion is even greater, since the comma between the 3 and the 5 is necessary. The added comma suggests a series that is not intended, grouping the *or* with the 3, and pulling the 3 away from the phrase in which it belongs—*3,5 Artite*. If one were not a chemist, one might very well think that 3,5 Artite was another name for Emeno.

Obviously, leaving commas out of sentences where they belong and putting them into sentences where they do not belong can cause real trouble. What can be done about it? Let us see how punctuation *should* be used.

One useful way to look at the major marks of punctuation—the comma, the semicolon, and the period—is to recognize that they stand for increasing degrees of pause or separation. They are, in fact, members of an even larger series of devices used to indicate divisions in works of prose. If we begin with the indicator for the least significant pause, we have

comma
semicolon *and* colon
period *and* question mark *and* exclamation point
paragraph
chapter
section *or* book

In ordering the materials in this book we have used all of these devices. We have discussed the last three in Chapter 8. Here we shall look at those associated with the sentence. However, we should always keep in mind that the paragraph, chapter, and section also serve to indicate breaks in the narrative.

THE COMMA

The comma is used to mark minor separations within the sentence. In a compound sentence it separates independent clauses.

Jack and Pete will be in Washington, but Tom will be available.

The long-term benefits may be substantial, and the short-term ones should be spectacular.

If the clauses in a compound sentence are very short, the comma may be omitted.

Commas may be used between the items in a series of words, phrases, or clauses:

Let us eat, drink, and be merry.[1]

We discussed advertising techniques used in local papers, on the radio, and on television.

January 16 came, the offer expired, and we no longer were able to supply the spoons as premiums.

after an introductory (subordinate) clause or long phrase:

Because we can expect a return of 19.2 percent, this will be a good investment. By acting as promptly and as vigorously as possible, we should be able to close the deal before Jones can disrupt our plans. Now as we all know. . . .

around words or phrases that interrupt an idea:

I submit, therefore, that we have proven our case.

Items IV and V, both products of unsymmetrical Ullmann couplings, were combined in 24 percent yields.

around nonrestrictive phrases and clauses (explained more fully below):

Jones, an importer of diamonds, will join us.

Gilson's sketches, which I have mailed separately, will show you exactly what I mean.

in·certain places established by convention:

November 15, 1920
72,436,519
Pittsburgh, Pennsylvania
John E. Frank, Jr.

and wherever separation is needed to eliminate possible confusion:

In proofreading, reports to be sent to top management should be carefully scrutinized for coherence. [If a comma had not followed *proofreading* the reader would not have realized that he was off the track until he reached *should*.]

There are other uses of the comma, but these are the most important.

---

[1] Some writers do not insert a comma before the *and* which precedes the last item in a series. This practice, however, is dangerous because at times it can cause temporary confusion: "What we received were the wool trousers, heavy sweaters, winter coats and jackets designed for the summer season." A writer who always uses the comma before the *and* need never worry about possible confusion.

PUNCTUATION OF MODIFIERS AND APPOSITIVES

Most inexperienced writers find the punctuation of modifiers and appositives very confusing indeed, because it requires what seems to be a subtle distinction between those which are "restrictive" and those which are not. Actually the distinction is not so very difficult to understand.

Let's start with an example:

Our enamel paint Hyglow would be best for your purposes.

As punctuated, this sentence indicates that the company involved makes more than one brand of enamel and that the word *Hyglow* is included to tell the reader *which particular brand* of enamel the customer should choose for the job. *Hyglow* identifies the one brand among two or more that the writer has in mind. It is restrictive. On the other hand, the sentence

Our enamel paint, Hylgow, would be best for your purposes.

indicates that the company manufactures only one kind of enamel: Hyglow. The word *Hyglow* (set off by commas) does *not* serve to distinguish one enamel from another: there *are* no others involved. It simply names the paint already identified. It is nonrestrictive.

For longer appositives and modifiers the same rules apply.

You should send your letter to the department which fills orders for medical books.

Here the subordinate clause (*which . . . books*) is clearly restrictive, for, once again, its function is to identify the one department (among several) to which the letter should be sent. Therefore, no comma is used. On the other hand, if we write the sentence

You should send your letter to Department G, which fills orders for medical books,

the function of the clause is not to identify the department. "Department G" does that job. The clause is useful, to be sure, but here it explains rather than identifies.

Since the concept of restriction can be confusing, perhaps we should look at another example:

Ms. Pacelli should visit Denver, where she can confer with the Superintendent, and then move on to the Harrison plant, where she can see the machine in operation.

In this sentence neither of the "where" clauses restricts the noun it modifies. The words *Denver* and *Harrison plant* are assumed to provide adequate identification for the reader. The "where" clauses tell the reader what Pacelli will   313 *do* in each place; they do not identify either of them. Therefore, commas are used to set off each clause. (Normally commas are used before and after such a clause, but when it is at the end of a sentence, the end punctuation—period, question mark, exclamation point—supersedes the second comma.)

One should always remember that *the writer* has to determine whether commas are needed and must do so on the basis of whether or not the modifier—which may be a clause, a phrase, or even a single word—serves to identify. If it does—no commas. If it does not, set if off!

THE SEMICOLON

The semicolon is used when, for reasons of style or meaning, we need a heavier mark of punctuation than the comma. In a compound sentence it may suggest a greater distinction between two coordinate items which normally might be separated by commas:

> There is no question about our commitment to develop new routes; but each route must be carefully designed to serve a constituency large enough to insure at least 25 percent ridership.

A semicolon is always used when a conjunctive adverb introduces the second of two main clauses in a sentence:[2]

> This may well turn out to be a losing proposition; however, we must undertake it.

We may, if we wish, substitute a period for the semicolon. If we move the conjunctive adverb into the second clause, we must always do so:

> This may well turn out to be a losing proposition. We must, however, undertake it.

When submembers of a series are separated by commas, semicolons will provide the necessary clarity:

> Attending the meeting will be: Gruber, Stein, and Schmidt of Glockenfabrik; Moroni, Berlanguer, and Pinelli of Altobelli; and Mason, R. Jansen, LeFevre, and Berger of Colloco.

Here the semicolons clearly separate the representatives of the three companies so that there is no possibility of confusion.

---

[2] The distinction between conjunctive adverbs and conjunctions is discussed in Illustrative Materials 1 of Chapter 16.

THE COLON

The colon has roughly the same "weight" as the semicolon but functions very differently. It is a mark of anticipation, indicating to the reader that what is to follow explains a statement just made. Take the following sentences:

Presented below is an idea believed to have great economic potential. This idea is application of Paulson cost-accounting to the coal-hydrogenation process.

The second sentence contains an awkward repetition, the result of a clumsy attempt to relate the two sentences. A colon would have done so more clearly:

Presented below is an idea believed to have great economic potential: application of Paulson cost-accounting to the coal-hydrogenation process.

This revision avoids the awkward repetition. It also presents the relationship of the ideas dramatically and forcefully. Letter and report writers should use the colon in this way much more than they do.

The colon may also, of course, introduce a list:

Under the circumstances, we hope that you will provide us with these items as soon as possible: 600 gross of No. 2 pencils, to be sent to Mr. Murphy; 30 reams of typewriter paper, 20-pound weight; and 45 B&B combination bicycle locks.

THE DASH

To use the dash properly requires understanding of its legitimate functions. Too many people, especially those who are unsure about the accepted patterns of punctuation, confuse their readers by substituting it indiscriminately for the comma, semicolon, or colon. But the dash is not an all-purpose punctuation mark. It should be used sparingly and only when appropriate.[3] Properly employed, it can be very helpful.

In certain specific situations a pair of dashes may serve as a strong pair of commas or a single dash as a weak colon. A pair may set off a phrase or clause which the author wishes to emphasize:

The time will come—and it may come soon—when we will be looking desperately for customers.

They insist—though I can't imagine why—that they must have the shipment by Thursday.

---

[3] Most authorities suggest that its effect is diluted if it appears more than once on a page. As our examples suggest, it is most often used in informal prose. In formal reports and professional papers it is used sparingly.

Definitions or lists may be similarly set off:

> What you need is a bulk spreader—a machine for transporting and spreading materials—if you want to do the job efficiently.
>
> Shellfish—oysters, clams, crabs, shrimp, lobsters—must be transported with care.

When used at the end of a statement to point up an observation added for emphasis or to expand an idea, the dash acts more like a colon:

> We can no longer ignore the problem that Brown raises—that the Poli-plane line is losing money.
>
> Brown and Smithson have provided what we need—the answer to the constantly increasing overhead.

It may also be used after an opening series which precedes a summarizing main clause:

> To direct, to lead, to persuade, to encourage—these are the functions of a supervisor.

MULTIPLE PUNCTUATION

A problem which plagues letter and report writers is the position of quotation marks in relation to other marks of punctuation:

> I doubt that it was marked "office copy only."
>
> I doubt that it was marked "office copy only," for Jones is always very careful about confidential information.
>
> I doubt that it was marked "office copy only"; Jones is always very careful about confidential information.
>
> I doubt that it was marked "office copy only": Jones is always very careful about confidential information.

In standard American usage, the period and comma are always placed *inside* and the colon or semicolon always *outside* the quotation mark. In neither case is any consideration given to where they logically "ought" to go.

The question mark and exclamation mark, however, are placed inside or outside the quotation mark depending on whether they belong with the quoted matter or with the whole sentence:

> Jack said to me, "Do you want 100 gallons?"
>
> Did Jack say, "I want 100 gallons"?
>
> Jack shouted, "I want 100 gallons!"
>
> Jack couldn't have said, "I want 100 gallons"!

PUNCTUATION

The punctuation of the third sentence indicates that Jack put a lot of power behind his demand for 100 gallons. The punctuation of the last sentence indicates that the writer is surprised or even shocked that Jack should have asked for 100 gallons; Jack himself may have made his request in the quietest and most reasonable manner.

American printers have found that a period or comma inside the quotation marks minimizes the white space following and produces what they feel is an attractive page. The practice, therefore, is based not on logic, but on esthetics. In Great Britain, on the other hand, esthetic considerations are ignored: there a comma or period almost always goes outside the quotation mark. Unfortunately, many Americans see this British usage just often enough to pick up what is in the United States an unacceptable practice.

Probably because punctuation is so frequently misused, the courts have long held that:

> In a document which contains punctuation marks, the words, and not the punctuation, are the controlling guide in its construction. *Lambert v. People,* 76 N.Y. 220, 32 Am. Rep. 293. Punctuation is no part of the English language. It is always subordinate to the text. . . . *Ewing v. Burnet,* 11 Pet. (36 U.S.) 41,54, 9 L. Ed. 624. Punctuation in writing, therefore, may sometimes shed light upon the meaning of the parties, but it must never be allowed to overturn what seems the plain meaning of the whole document. *Osborn v. Farwell,* 87, 29 Am. Rep. 47.[4]

Although a grammarian might question the statement "Punctuation is no part of the English language," he would probably agree that a court should attempt to determine what was intended by a whole piece of writing; it should not allow justice to be frustrated by a carelessly or ignorantly placed comma.

This ruling, however, does not justify the careless use of punctuation. A wholesaler who offers a haberdasher an exclusive on a new line of "ties, shirts, wash 'n' wear slacks and suits" may well be in trouble. What if the haberdasher refuses to pay the bill because the suits he receives are not wash-and-wear? He is not likely to be satisfied by the wholesaler's explanation that only the slacks are washable and that there should have been a comma before the *and* in his offer. The wholesaler could take the matter to court and perhaps get a favorable judgment. But that would certainly lose a customer. Our wholesaler is fictional, but mistakes of this sort occur in business every day. They do not win friends.

Punctuation, then, should be a matter of real concern to all of us if we wish to get results with our writing. To punctuate accurately we need not memorize a book of rules. We do need, however, to understand certain conventions. More important still, we need to understand the function of punctuation—

---

[4] *Travelers' Insurance Co. v. Pomerants et al.,* 207 N.Y. Supp. 81 (Supreme Court of New York, New York County, 1924).

rendering accurately the relationships between words and groups of words—and to use this understanding in selecting and placing commas, semicolons, colons, and other punctuation marks.

ILLUSTRATIVE MATERIALS

1.

The Inventor of the Period[5]

By K. Jason Sitewell

Soon there will occur an event of profound importance to the literatures of all languages. I refer to the 2500th birthday of Kohmar Pehriad (544-493 B.C.), inventor of punctuation in written language. . . . Pehriad was the leading literary figure of Macedonia in the pre-Christian era. His writings ranged from poetry to speculations on astronomy and physics. Few of these writings remain. What does remain, however, is his successful reform of written language in virtually all tongues.

In those days written language was continuous. There were no sentence or paragraph breaks. Pehriad's own writings represent the first recorded use of the small round dot to indicate the end of a completed unit of expression. More important than that is the fact that he gave thirty years of his life, traveling throughout ancient Greece, Rome, Persia, North Africa, and Asia, in the effort to obtain local acceptance of the small dot that has since done so much for literature.

His first great success outside his country came when he was able to persuade some Greek scholars to issue a complete version of Homer's *Odyssey* and *Iliad*, with the small round dots in the proper places. Up to that time Homer had had a limited following in Greece. With the reformed version, however, his work gained widespread acceptance. Pehriad's next success came in Constantinople, where he was directly responsible for the first manuscript of the Hebrew Torah containing periods.

As he traveled from place to place the logic of Pehriad's argument became increasingly accepted. It was not necessary, he reasoned, for each language to devise its own mark to denote a proper pause. The small round dot could be used in all languages. The stark simplicity of this idea, amounting virtually to genius, is doubtless responsible for the fact that every written language in the world today uses the small round dot. Thus, Pehriad's contribution is not only to his own country but to mankind.

Pehriad's reward, of course, is that the small round dot has been named after him, our spelling of his name having been anglicized. Even in a country

[5] From *The Saturday Review of Literature*, March 24, 1956, pp. 15–16.

as remote as Nepal the influence of Pehriad today is to be found in the fact that the sentence dot is called a "puhyed." In China it is called a "pi-yen." In Malaya, "pee-yeed." In New Guinea the capital *P* is used as a gesture of respect to the inventor of its word "Peeliod."

Pehriad's efforts did not stop with the period. He was also concerned with the need for an appropriate marking that might correspond to the pause in a person's speech in the middle of an incompleted sentence. This led him to devise what we now know as the comma, also named after him (Kohmar). It is interesting to read in his *Journal* that he later felt he had made a mistake in not using the comma marking instead of the period and vice-versa. "The dot with the curved tail is the more impressive and visible mark and should therefore have been used for the more important purpose of indicating the end of a sentence," he wrote. "The dot slows up the reader and should therefore have been used to indicate a pause." Pehriad, in his declining years, sought to bring about this shift in comma-period usage, but by this time the custom had hardened.

It remained for Pehriad's son to devise yet other markings for the purpose of strengthening the written language. Apos-Trophe Pehriad felt that the comma was adaptable to a wide variety of purposes, so long as its position could be varied. He used it inside a word to denote the abbreviation; at the end of a word to denote possession; in tandem to denote quotation. As in the case of his father, his invention bears his name.

PROBLEMS

1.

Punctuate this passage.

SECOND QUARTER RESULTS

Smith Dexters estimated net income in the second quarter of the year totaled $1065 million $2.11 per share net income was up 11.0 percent from 968 million $1.78 per share in last years second quarter and up 13.9 percent from $932 million $1.61 per share in the first quarter of this year all per share amounts reflect the two for one stock split effective May 15 1982 in the second quarter of the current year the U S dollar weakened against most foreign currencies as it had in the first quarter this weakening resulted in two significant but opposing effects on net income a positive impact of indeterminable amount on operating earnings due to reduction in foreign affiliates operating margins and a negative impact from translation of the corporations net foreign currency debt into more lower valued U S dollars in the last quarter there were transition losses of $223 million which followed gains of 258 million in the first quarter of the year in contrast the considerable strengthening of the U S dollar in the third quarter of the last year resulted in translation gains totaling $255 million and a favorable impact on the operating earnings of that quarter

2.

Here is a one-sentence paragraph of 188 words.[6]

To consider the world in its length and breadth, its various history, the many races of man, their starts, their fortunes, their mutual alienation, their conflicts; and then their ways, habits, governments, forms of worship; their enterprises, their aimless courses, their random achievements and acquirements, the impotent conclusion of long-standing facts, the tokens so faint and broken of a superintending design, the blind evolution of what turn out to be great powers or truths, the progress of things, as if from unreasoning elements, not towards final causes, the greatness and littleness of man, his far-reaching aims, his short duration, the curtain hung over his futurity, the disappointments of life, the defeat of good, the success of evil, physical pain, mental anguish, the prevalence and intensity of sin, the pervading idolatries, the corruptions, the dreary hopeless irreligion, that condition of the whole race so fearfully yet exactly described in the Apostle's words, "having no hope and without God in the world"—all this is a vision to dizzy and appal, and inflicts upon the mind the sense of a profound mystery, which is absolutely beyond human solution.

We do not recommend such paragraphs. But when a good writer like Cardinal Newman uses one, it is instructive to examine his punctuation.

a. *How many different punctuation marks does Newman use?*
b. *How does he organize for the reader the subsections which precede the dash?*
c. *How would substituting commas for the semicolons affect the reader's ability to understand the passage?*
d. *What is the function of the dash?*
e. *Newman was a great religious thinker and a famous preacher. The passage above is from his spiritual autobiography. Does it reflect in any way his long training as a preacher? If so, what is the effect on the structure of his sentence and on its punctuation?*
f. *What changes would you make if you wished to modernize Newman's nineteenth-century punctuation?*

MATERIALS FOR REVISION

In some instances you may wish to modify the wording as well as the punctuation of a sentence.

A

1. As problems arose, several were assigned to the Research Department. These included the effects of impurities in the raw materials, analytical methods for raw material control, and methods of product evaluation.

[6] John Henry Newman, *Apologia pro Vita Sua,* 1864 (New York: Longmans, Green and Company, 1908), p. 241.

PUNCTUATION

2. Sales for January dropped 3 percent below expectations as the Road Construction and Bridge divisions both failed to meet the month's goals.
3. Sales of the newer products have also been disappointing and in October were in total $150,000 less than planned for.
4. The demonstration was presented to approximately 40 interested persons representing the three major manufacturers of antibiotics, namely Crown, Brumpf, and Gordon Laboratories.
5. Presented below for your consideration is an idea believed to have great economic potential. This idea is proper application of aptation to the coal-hydrogenation process.
6. The types of communication between engineers can be divided into three general categories for simplification, speaking, writing, and reading.
7. This sample was prepared by Jones and the writer to contain 9.0% binder; sample 1 represents a portion of Priam Mix manufactured by Parco on May 17 to contain 9.0% binder; sample 2 was prepared in the laboratory with the Parco aggregate and made to contain 9.0% binder.

B

1. Automobiles, which are gas-guzzlers, are hard to sell these days.
2. We should certainly plan on making a profit which we can hardly do without.
3. As I mentioned before this was a four-week school.
4. Experienced sales personnel who are hard to find should be paid premium salaries.
5. We have obtained varying melting points here at Merrivale which seem high if air currents are present, and low if a shield is placed before the oven, or if air currents are absent from the laboratory.
6. Although he has three brothers, his brother, John, is the only one who sought employment here.
7. Please forward this item to New York City where our Complaint Department will take care of it.
8. As you will note, there is only one retirement in this survey which was a typewriter handled under the blanket exchange.
9. John F. S. Drew Sales Manager for Pulham and Company will arrive by plane today.

C

1. The planned increase in the work force is 40 per month, however, many problems arise in securing trained personnel, and we doubt that over 30 per month will be hired.
2. The square-foot surface in each stove is approximately 7600, consequently our price for blasting bare surface is $.435 per square foot.
3. Each of the men who is employed in this work has more than ten years' experience, nevertheless we discussed the safety procedures on a few points.
4. It will be necessary for these orders to be filled by April 30, therefore, please notify us as soon as possible if you need additional materials.
5. I presume that you would like Mr. Frank or Mr. Roberts to go in and give Mr. Owen this information, however, I would be more than happy to do anything that I can to aid the cause.
6. Since this item is manufactured by only one company in California, its availability in the East has been limited, thus most companies have turned to other sources of supply.

ECONOMY, CLARITY, AND UNITY

D

1. In this school we were told that the company produces some 750 different products, this information I found very interesting.
2. The product pattern for this plant has changed requiring the installation of the column and allied equipment and cannot be avoided.
3. Please order: 200 reams of ditto paper, 20 boxes of stencils, and 10 gallons of fluid, 120 reams of stationery, 20 boxes of carbon paper, 2000 large, 2000 small, and 500 kraft envelopes, 15 typewriter ribbons, 10 desk blotters, and 2 pairs of scissors.
4. The number of issues of "Development News" per year varies with the number of new products introduced, as many as four issues have been produced in one month.
5. Please pass on the following information: when we call in periodically, as is now planned, we will report temperatures, when we discover the fault, during the peak load period, we will ask for a reading on the meters and a time check and when we have to remove the shaft and examine the socket, we will ask for an immediate shutdown of power.

E

1. I can report the good news, and I feel that it is very good, that Johnson and Company will announce its acceptance tomorrow morning.
2. I need only tell you the following—that T. C. Williams and Sons is after the same contract, that the longer we wait the higher our costs will be, and that Johnson would prefer to deal with us.
3. Short of taking a loss on the job—we will do everything we can to remain competitive.
4. We cannot release our stock into the current market; a market already badly depressed.
5. Johns will arrive on Tuesday—I will arrive on Wednesday—and Green will arrive on Saturday.
6. The manufacturer, the wholesaler, the retailer, the consumer, none of these wants a price increase.

V

READING, LISTENING, AND SPEAKING

18

Reading
and Listening

Throughout this book we have stressed the importance of the five elements in the communication process: source, message, channel, receiver, destination—who/says what/in which channel/to whom/with what effect? But we have assigned the primary responsibility for the success of a communication to the writer or speaker. In this chapter we wish to consider the responsibility of the reader or listener, for as Thoreau said, "It takes two to speak truth—one to speak and another to hear."

"TO WHOM?"

Much has been written in recent years about the responsibilities of the writer and the speaker: the writer of letters, reports, advertising copy, memoranda, or any of the many other types of communications which pass into, through, and out of a business organization; and the speaker at board meetings, banquets, group conferences, or training sessions. Certainly the writer and the speaker are primarily responsible for making a communication effective. They must do everything possible to capture and hold their audience. Until recently, however, very little attention has been given to the responsibilities of the reader

325

and the listener. Yet it should be obvious enough that even the most carefully planned and executed report, the most clearly written letter, or the most efficient memorandum will be useless if it is not read with thoughtful attention. The finest speech will not inform an individual who either cannot or will not listen attentively to what is being said.

Obviously if a receiver is turned off completely, communication will not take place. However, this situation seldom occurs when we are reading or when we are listening. Usually, inefficient reception occurs because the human receiver is not tuned in properly or is operating only intermittently.

WHY WE ARE POOR RECEIVERS

Investigators who have studied the human brain do not agree on the detailed operation of its 13 billion cells, but most do agree that it functions at very great speeds and that one of its most important uses is to process language. Although thoughts may pass through our brains "like lightning," in any given length of time the number of words our eyes can read and the number of words our lips can form are limited.

In one minute the average American can speak between 125 and 150 words or read about 300 words. But the brain, psychologists tell us, is capable of functioning much more rapidly: at most, it needs only one-fourth as much time to receive and encode an oral message as it takes a speaker to deliver it. Thus we have a situation not unlike that of the proverbial hare and tortoise. But our hare, the human brain, is in a much less comfortable situation than the hare in the fable, who could have gone ahead if he had wished, and scampered across the finish line. The brain cannot do so: when receiving, it is forced to dawdle along at much less than its optimal speed. It usually can move toward the finish no faster than the eye can read or the ear can pick up a message.

It is not surprising, therefore, that the human brain, capable of very rapid thought and prevented from moving more rapidly than the slow rate at which information is normally transmitted and received, tends to imitate the hare. It may either take a nap or—more likely—wander off on a variety of excursions. From these side trips it will return now and then to check on the progress of the "tortoise" before taking off again.

Anyone who has listened to a speech will recognize this process. During a fifteen-minute talk on economic conditions in South America, we may find ourselves daydreaming about the beach at Waikiki, what we will say to our son if he brings home an undistinguished report card, what we should have said to the rude cashier in the department store, whether we should get a haircut tomorrow or next week, how to keep the dog from breaking off the branches of the little azalea plant by the porch steps, and so on. All the while, we assure ourselves, we have been listening to the speaker. We know roughly what was said: Brazil is on its way up; conditions in Argentina are uncertain; Bolivia is seeking American capital. But if we are pressed for details, we may be in trouble. Here and there an isolated fact may have penetrated—probably because it has some direct bearing on our life. Having had an argument a night or two ago about the price of coffee, we may prick up our ears when the speaker says that coffee is in abundant supply and that Brazil is selling it for 15 percent less than last year. But most of the details, many of them bearing directly on the speaker's argument, may be lost to us as soon as they are voiced. We simply may not take them in.

THE NEED FOR TRAINING

On the job, however, such inattention is dangerous. Today, according to recent studies, the average manager spends about 70 percent of the working day in some communication activity. Of that 70 percent, speaking and writing account for only about 40 percent, reading for about 15 percent, and listening for about 45 percent—almost half. And as M. Lee Goddard has pointed out, "Only a glimpse at predictions of things to come in the communication field between now and the turn of the century provides convincing evidence that listening will occupy an increasing amount of everyone's time regardless of occupation or profession."[1]

Certainly we can no longer afford to neglect training in reading and listening, activities which take up 60 percent of our communication time and 40 percent of all the time we spend on the job. The need is especially great because so many of us are both poor listeners and poor readers. Since both activities are "receptive processes," similar skills are needed to master them, and improving one tends to improve the other also.

INCREASING EFFICIENCY

The obvious way to increase the efficiency of our reading or listening—and each of us can improve these skills—is to harness the nine-tenths of the brain's activity which is not needed for receiving the message and to put it to constructive use. Like the waters of a great river, thoughts must be channeled if they are to be productive. The result is intellectual power, the ability to assimilate and synthesize what we read or hear.

But how is this to be done? We must learn to rescue our brainpower from aimless daydreaming and train it to concentrate on the subject at hand; or, to put it more simply, to fasten our complete attention on what a writer or speaker is saying. We must keep the hare out of the thickets and teach it to stay close to the tortoise, studying its progress and its method in moving toward the finish line.

[1] "Listening: Forgotten Skill in Effective Communication," *Business Education Forum* 30 (January 1976), p. 19.

ESTABLISHING USEFUL HABIT PATTERNS

Once we have recognized the importance of skill in receiving communications, our next step in becoming good readers and listeners is to establish useful habit patterns. When we pick up a report or a book, we should pause briefly to consider why we are about to read it. Are we after answers to specific questions? If so, what are they? We may even jot them down, leaving room for brief notes on what we discover in the text. Such stock-taking is very useful, for we are likely to read better when we read for a clearly defined purpose.

Before beginning to read a book or report, we should examine the materials which surround the text—the table of contents, the preface or abstract, the appendices, the index, and similar materials. They help to determine what ground the report covers and how it is organized. And they enable us to read quickly and comfortably instead of having to feel our way.

An examination of a report's introductory materials, for example, may reveal that instead of being forced to wade through hundreds of pages—a task seldom approached with enthusiasm—we may have to read only fifteen or twenty to obtain the information we need. If the report has been organized so that one can enter it at one of several levels of complexity, we may be able to read selectively. Even if it is not well organized, we may still be able to save time by using as our guides to relevant materials the table of contents, chapter headings, subheadings, and other indications of organization. If conclusions are not presented at the beginning of the report, we may look for them at the end before beginning to read: with the conclusions firmly in mind, we will be prepared to consider the validity of the writer's way of getting to them.

Effective listeners will make similar preparations for a speech or a meeting. Each will ask questions. Who is the speaker? What is his or her background? Affiliations? Qualifications for discussing the announced topic? Probable or possible prejudices? The auspices under which he or she is appearing? What should I expect to hear? What do I want to learn from the talk? What answers should I expect it to provide for me? Asking these and other questions will give us a framework for listening. If we expect to receive answers to specific questions about the subject to be discussed, we will do well to have them written on a sheet of paper, with space for notes under each. Whatever our interests, we should certainly have paper and pencil to jot down points to remember.

As good listeners and readers, we have yet another responsibility. When we actually begin to read a report or a book, participate in a board meeting, consult with a subordinate, or listen to a speech, we must concentrate only on the matter at hand, consciously rejecting all present and potential distractions. Our attention must be riveted on what is being said.

Since we need only a small portion of our brainpower to take in a message, we can use the remainder to increase our understanding of what we are reading, seeing, or hearing. These are some of the operations involved:

1. Sorting out and grouping the materials presented, looking always for significant patterns of organization;
2. Isolating the central theme as soon as possible and considering how various details are related to it;
3. Trying to determine the goal toward which the writer or speaker is moving;
4. Constantly reading between the lines of the message in order to pick up subtle implication and innuendo;
5. As the argument moves from one major point to another, reviewing the essential elements so far presented in order to better understand those which will follow;
6. With our own prejudices put firmly to one side, analyzing and weighing the evidence presented and implied to determine how well it supports the conclusions being drawn;
7. At the end, trying to recreate the structure of the completed argument and carefully evaluating the conclusions which have been put forward.

Most of us perform all of these operations intermittently. The good reader or listener performs them both consciously and conscientiously.

PSYCHOLOGICAL DETERRENTS

In addition to the inability to see and evaluate the structure of ideas, the most powerful deterrents to efficient reception are emotional filters, external distractions, and the tendency to daydream. The last two can be overcome by an effort of will—and *only* by an effort of will. We must simply train ourselves to close our ears and eyes to any movement or noise which might distract us and to pull firmly on the checkrein at the first sign of daydreaming. The ability to see and evaluate the structure of ideas may be developed by performing the operations indicated in the preceding paragraph.

Of all the elements which undermine good reading and good listening, emotional filters are probably the most severe, most persistent, and most difficult to overcome, for they condition all messages coming into the brain. It has been repeatedly demonstrated that we tend to distort or reject without thought not only ideas which run counter to our prejudices but also any facts introduced to support them. A Democratic candidate in an election-year speech—no matter how carefully constructed his arguments or how valid a dispassionate examination would find them—will not convert a confirmed Republican member of the audience. Nor will a Republican fare better with a group of confirmed Democrats. Furthermore, what a Democrat actually hears when a candidate speaks sometimes differs considerably from what a Republican hears. Their emotional filters make this not only possible, but inevitable. 329

Confirmed Democrats and Republicans are even more likely to disagree completely on what candidates *mean* by certain things they say. Their differing interpretations are usually caused by the common practice of permitting the mind to lie in wait for a statement which can be either vigorously attacked or staunchly advocated. Fastening on such a statement, partisan listeners use it to fan the flames of their righteous indignation while they ignore the rest of what is said. By the time a speech is over, they are prepared to demonstrate their loyalty in no uncertain terms.

Most of us will readily agree that there are people who act in such an irrational way. But we are sure that *we* do not do so. In reality few, if any, of us are exempt. On any subject about which we have firm convictions or in which we have been deeply involved, we have an overpowering tendency to pander to our prejudices. We allow our brain to filter out everything that we do not wish to hear and to retain only what seems to support our convictions. If you do not believe that you are subject to this temptation, you should listen to a discussion of an issue on which you have strong beliefs. You should then analyze your reactions to determine exactly how dispassionate they have been.[2]

Or play this amusing parlor game: Take five or six pictures from a magazine, cutting off any accompanying text, and mount them individuallly on pieces of cardboard; then hold them up one at a time and ask all those present to write down the "story" they see in the picture. The wide variety of interpretations almost always surprises the players. A picture of a dog nosing about rows of cases in a warehouse, for example, elicited these descriptions:

He's a trained police dog looking for hijackers hiding in the building.

The warehouse is his home. He's a watchdog, about to settle down for the night. He's just looking for a place to go to sleep.

He's lost and lonesome—looking for a friend.

The scene described by the first person is tense and exciting; by the second, warm and comfortable; by the third, sad and bleak. Similarly, a picture of two boys in a boat, one standing and the other halfway over the side, meant entirely different things to two observers. The first said that the standing boy had pushed his companion; the second, that he was about to jump in to save him.

This discrepancy in interpretation holds not only for what we see with our eyes, but also for what we read and hear. Psychologists have shown conclusively that the way people "see" the world is determined by their background and their inner needs. This concept—projection, as it is called—is so thoroughly established that psychologists use variations of the parlor game described above to identify people's attitudes and personality traits.

---

[2] As one might imagine, the ideas a closed mind will uphold or attack are likely to be very abstract—"self-determination of nations," "back to normalcy," "the Century of the Common Man," or "the Great Society," to mention only four which have been rallying cries in the past.

READING AND LISTENING

THE ROLE OF PREJUDICE

The subtle and frequently inadvertent distortion of messages is perhaps the most dangerous cause of communication failure. Such distortion may occur without our recognizing it. Though we all consider ourselves reasonably broadminded, even the most broad-minded of us have our quirks and prejudices. Often they concern individuals. Some of us dislike brash, loud-talking people and find it difficult to listen to them dispassionately. When we encounter a man of this type in our office, in a conference, or on the shop floor, we feel irritated, our blood pressure seems to rise, we become tense. The minute he opens his mouth, we begin to think how dreadful he is. Instead of listening to what he is saying, we notice the way he pounds the table, his pronunciation of "New York" or mispronunciation of "circuitous," the flamboyant tie he is wearing, the way spittle sprays from his mouth when he is excited, his rudeness in replying to an objection, and dozens of other mannerisms which irritate us and prevent us from giving his *ideas* a fair hearing.

Others, of course, may be irritated by different personal characteristics. Some of us, though we would never admit it to ourselves, dislike quiet people, people who *don't* pound the table and *don't* love a good argument. Others of us feel uncomfortable with supervisors of the opposite sex and in our subconscious—or even conscious—mind tend to deprecate whatever they say. A worker with a high school education may resent a college graduate supervisor; the latter may feel that the former doesn't have the capacity to understand instructions. The range of potential prejudice in business, as anywhere in life, is unlimited. None of us is exempt. What we must do is to bring to the surface all of our prejudices, analyze them, and determine to put them aside in our dealings with individuals. When we listen, we must resolve to concentrate on the message and ignore the personality of the speaker. When we read a report or a memo, we must not allow a picture of the writer to form in our mind's eye and distract us from what is said on paper. Only by isolating and understanding our own prejudices and then carefully neutralizing their effects can we make full use of the talents and energy of the people around us.

SHUTTING OFF NEW IDEAS

In the world of business, prejudice of another sort can lead to disaster. As we grow older and acquire a fund of experience, we inevitably tend to feel that we have *the* solution to certain problems. Henry Ford, to take a conspicuous example, created a revolution in automobile production with his Model T. He knew what the American people wanted, and he gave it to them. But as the years went by, people's desires changed, the economy changed. Ford's associates pleaded with him to pay more attention to passenger comfort. They pleaded with him to produce the Ford in a variety of colors. To both requests he turned a deaf ear. He *knew* what sold cars. To the demand for color he replied, "They can have a Ford in any color they like—as long as it's black." 331

Not until Chevrolet had taken away from him a large share of the low-price market did Ford grudgingly give way. By then, his company had lost its position of leadership in the industry.

Many executives have their own ideas about how things should be run. Such a person may encourage the younger people in his department to bring their new ideas to him. In some areas he may enthusiastically put his subordinates' suggestions into operation. But in other areas, perhaps those with which he is most intimately acquainted, he may resist novelty. A young woman comes to him to suggest packaging a product in round rather than square containers. By the time she has finished her first sentence, the department head has stopped listening. He knows enough about morale, of course, to *pretend* to hear her out, but his thoughts have turned to speculating about the best time to take his vacation. After all, he has been through the mill on the round-container business. He had the same idea himself a few years ago—and got his fingers badly burned. The round containers proved to be too expensive and too easily damaged in transit. So, as he thinks about his vacation, he simply does not hear the woman point out that by using a newly developed plastic the company can obtain round containers that are less expensive and far less likely to be damaged than the square cardboard ones currently in use. Since he does not really hear these facts, his convictions remain unchanged. When the woman hands him the detailed memorandum she has prepared, the boss smiles and says: "That's a very interesting suggestion, but it presents some practical difficulties. Let me have the report. I'll study it carefully and talk with you again. At the moment I'm afraid I have an appointment with Mr. Barstow." So the report sits on his desk for a couple of weeks. Then it is returned, still unread, with the notation: "Excellent idea, but it doesn't seem practical at this time. J. C. M." And so a good suggestion dies.

These filters operate wherever self-interest or prejudice exists—and often we do not ourselves know that it exists. Because each individual in a business organization has his or her own picture of how the company operates and of how it should operate, any communication that is passed along from one person to another is unconsciously adapted—and usually distorted—to fit that picture. Thus what begins as a complaint by a group of machinists to their foreman about the relationship between wages and productivity may gradually be modified as it moves up the chain of command until the president of the company hears that the machinists are pleased with their working conditions. By the time a worker's reasonable request for an essential testing device reaches an assistant plant superintendent, it may be transmuted by unsympathetic supervisors into a demand for unnecessarily elaborate equipment.

THE RESPONSIBILITIES OF THE AUDIENCE

As these illustrations suggest, the recipients of reports, whether written or oral, must fulfill certain responsibilities if their company is to receive full value from the work that went into them. After all, every report involves a considerable investment by the company. The person or persons who prepared it may well have spent many hours analyzing a problem, probing for solutions, discussing alternatives with people who would be affected by changes in procedure, and digging up data to support the recommended solution. For this reason alone, the report deserves a thoughtful, sympathetic hearing.

Evaluating with Care

Wise supervisors, therefore, make a point of seeing that they are undisturbed while reading or listening to an important report. Knowing that one cannot do justice to any report if one has to read it a little at a time or cannot adequately digest its contents, they allow plenty of time for a careful consideration of content, concentrate their attention, and perform the seven operations listed on p. 329.

After thoughtfully reading or listening to the report and refusing to allow preconceptions to distort its message, these supervisors will have a clear picture both of the conclusions reached and of the reasoning which supports them. They will have been measuring the argument against their own experience, reading between the lines both for unstated assumptions and for prejudices that may have led to the rejection or downplaying of material tending to refute the writer's argument. Having spotted each potential soft spot, they are ready almost immediately to begin asking important, searching questions—not to embarrass the writer, but to be certain that no consideration has been dealt with inadequately.

Taking Prompt Action

Every supervisor, whether foreman or president, has three additional responsibilities toward communications which call for action. The first is not to sit on them. Nothing is more frustrating to a subordinate (or a colleague) than to send a message and have to wait weeks or months for a reply. If unable to read a communication promptly, the recipient should send a note to explain why—and more important, to tell the writer when to expect a reply. "Dear Jim: I am leaving for New Mexico in a few minutes. I'll read your progress report while I'm there and let you have my comments on Monday morning." Or, if a secretary handles the matter, "Dear Mr. Stroud: Ms. Thomas is now in New Mexico, but I will have your report on her desk when she returns on Monday. She will be very busy the early part of the week, but I should think you could expect to hear from her by Friday." Such a note assures the recipient that the communication will not be lost in "the pile on top of the desk." Needless to say, the manager must see to it that she does give Jim her comments on Monday morning and that Mr. Stroud does hear from her by Friday.

Some executives are so impressed with the importance of not letting cor- **333** respondence pile up on desks that they have established routines to guard against it. In one company, for example, a person who does not answer a letter or memorandum within three days must explain the delay to his or her supervisor. In another, trip reports and field-trouble reports are circulated by a central department, which logs them in and out and makes sure that delay in answering questions raised by reports, in prescribing remedies for breakdowns, in taking required action, or in filling requests is justified. A manager we know gathers up everything on the top of his desk before he leaves for the day and puts it in a drawer. This procedure forces him to sort the material the next morning. In his office, nothing can be buried at the bottom of a pile.

In many companies, the top echelons of management have been forced to develop methods to cut down on the amount of reading required and at the same time ensure that vital information is not overlooked. Some managers, for example, have trained a subordinate to summarize in two or three sentences the problems raised in an incoming letter and to indicate what decisions are involved. The summary and any materials needed to make the required decisions are clipped to the letter. If there is a file of previous correspondence, it too is attached. Thus the manager may act on the summary and vital materials alone, may go on to read the letter, or may dig further into the problem by studying the file. Other executives train their assistants to go over incoming mail and to indicate by notations in the margins specific sections that they should read. At least one extremely busy—and extremely fortunate—manager relies on his secretary to go through *The Wall Street Journal,* marking in red those items that will interest him. Since such secretaries are often harder to find than good managers, this procedure is not likely to become widespread.

But whatever the procedure they set up to help them, all supervisors are responsible for communications addressed to them. Whether they handle them all personally or assign others to help them, they must see that their mail is answered as rapidly as possible.

DEFINING THE RESPONSE CLEARLY

Another of the supervisor's responsibilities is to be certain that the subordinate who has submitted a report knows precisely what action is being taken on it. If a recommendation is rejected, the supervisor should state clearly and specifically the reasons for its rejection. The subordinate who is told only that a proposal is "impractical at this time" is left to wonder not only why what seems so practical to him or her seems impractical to the boss, but also what "at this time" may mean. On the other hand, a message like the following will have positive results:

Bob Vincent says that Sales has given your proposal a great deal of thought. They agree that the change in design would be attractive to our customers, but not enough so to offset the added 10 percent on the retail price. If we can figure out a way to manufacture the new design as inexpensively as the current one, we'll be in business. Can you solve that one?

This message not only makes it clear why the proposal is being rejected but also challenges the subordinate to try a new approach to the problem.

If the supervisor, after reading the report we have been discussing, should decide to take some other action—to refer it to another department or to recommend the proposal to top management—the subordinate should be informed. Once again we return to a matter we have discussed frequently in this book—consideration of the other person. The good supervisor knows that the longer subordinates have to wait to learn what has happened to a suggestion or report, the more they will worry, the more resentment will build up, and the less efficiently they will perform other tasks. So the supervisor makes every effort to keep them informed. After all, one can hardly be expected to maintain interest in one's work when report after report disappears into the void "upstairs" and is never heard of again.

PROVIDING GUIDELINES

One other responsibility of persons receiving communications which call for action is frequently neglected in the business world. Too many managers who are annoyed by reports that seem to be inadequate, and sometimes incompetent, simply fume and fuss and sputter. When we have suggested that they do something about the problem, they have sometimes replied: "My job is to make decisions. I haven't got time to sit down with my department heads and teach them how to prepare their reports."

Managers, of course, should not have to teach the fundamentals of report writing. But they can and should make clear what kind of reports they find most useful. This they may do in a group conference or by writing judicious comments on individual reports. The latter will achieve considerable circulation, and before long all subordinates will know that "Ms. Stavik wants profit and loss figures broken down by . . ." or "J. B. likes to have engineering drawings of new motors in a folder attached to. . . ." To be sure, it will take a little of Ms. Stavik's time to train her people to prepare more useful reports, but far less time and energy than she would otherwise waste in fuming about the reports and struggling to use them despite their inadequacies. As we have suggested elsewhere, the responsibility for setting up guidelines rests with supervisors, not with those who report to them.

Communication, then, is a two-way process. Successful communication requires a transmitter sending a clear signal and a receiver equipped to receive everything that is being transmitted. The human brain is an excellent receiver. With its power to reason, it not only can take in what is being transmitted but can also simultaneously analyze and evaluate it. The mind is not static; if it is well trained, it reaches out for messages and is ready to act as soon as it receives them. But this activity is not automatic. It may be subverted by emotional filters, by daydreaming, by external distractions. To these we all fall victim now and then. But well-trained readers or listeners will have reduced such lapses to a minimum and thus increased their effectiveness immeasurably.

335

ILLUSTRATIVE MATERIALS

1.

The following extract from Communicating at the Top, *by George de Mare,*[3] *for many years Director of Communications at Price Waterhouse & Company, focuses on the listening needs of top executives. Its ideas, however, should be equally valuable to anyone whose work involves listening to others.*

"The power of attention is the mark of the cultivated man," Lord Chesterfield wrote. In our modern world, it is something more. It is a matter of survival.

In the midst of the noise, the clangor, the myriad voices, to whom is the business leader or the man of affairs to listen and how is he to get others to listen also, when it is important that they do?

These problems involve something more than the technique of listening, a talent which has also unfortunately been almost completely lost amid the distractions and pressures of the day. Everyone knows that today it has become harder and harder to bring oneself to listen and even more difficult to induce others to do so. From the dull instructor through whose classes the young man must sit to the beloved friend whose talent for saying nothing has inured his acquaintances to a bright but fraudulent show of attention, everything conspires to train a man not to listen out of self-defense.

This training continues as he moves into the business world or the world of organizations, where he is often forced on his way up to attend elderly bores and many who possess the deadly combination of superior position, inferior brains, and the compulsion to display both. As he continues his rise, however, the noise grows louder and the demands on his time and attention grow more insistent, and it is an unfortunate fact of life that the worth of what he does hear as he goes up appears to decrease in proportion as his own abilities and skills develop, while the requirement to listen diminishes as his own position improves.

He now reaches the heights of the business leader, and as a reward he must sit through endless and often useless conferences, dull dinner speeches, and long-winded, time-consuming ceremonies. He must watch the moving lips of colleagues whose words and thoughts he knows by heart. He must anticipate the lumbering observation, the incoherent explanation, the meaningless ritual phrases which are poured out over him day after day. He must observe the thousand courtesies due those with inferior ability or failing powers who have a more than ordinary claim on him. It is little wonder, then, that not only is the ability to listen lost, but the ability not to listen becomes highly developed.

It is little wonder, but it is dangerous, and the magnitude of the danger is in direct proportion to the importance of the successful man's position and to his power to affect the lives and influence the thinking of others.

[3] New York: John Wiley & Sons, 1979, pp. 235–237. Reprinted by permission.

It is not just that he has grown to prefer the sound of his own voice to that of any other. It is not only that the deference of others has begun to lend an exaggerated importance to his thoughts and words. It is not even that he may overlook the fact that he himself is fast becoming one of those eminent bores he so decried on the way up, men who do all the talking and none of the listening. In all of us, perhaps, these tendencies may be observed to increase with age and with the diminution of ability. It is that this loss of ability to hear, this positive skill at missing most of what is said and ignoring the world's distractions, may well shut off the man of affairs from the most vital listening ability of all—the ability to observe, sense, and apprehend change, the ability to hear the whisper of the future.

The art of listening to others is a simple one and well known. It is also an elegant one well worth cultivating, not only for its importance and usefulness, but also for the increased depth it lends to your thinking and the graciousness it adds to all business and social occasions. The man who actually listens and pays attention to what others are saying generally stands out like a beacon of courtesy and fine manners in a sea of what appear to be compulsive talkers. In business affairs, the listener is often sought after for advice even when he may have no advice to give, because the habit of listening he has developed enables others in his presence to order and clarify their thoughts. The man of affairs can have no more engaging and fruitful characteristic nor one more likely to bring out for him the best others have to give.

PROBLEMS

1. The next time you hear a speech with a group of friends or fellow workers, ask each person to summarize the speaker's argument in 500 words. (Have the speech tape recorded, if possible.) Then compare the summaries.

   a. Are there any instances in which two reports are contradictory?
   b. Is there substantial agreement on the speaker's main point?
   c. Are there suggestions of preconceived antagonism towards the speaker's views? How are they revealed?
   d. Do you notice significant differences in the word choice used by the different reporters to record the same point? Do they suggest differing attitudes toward the speaker and the subject?
   e. Compare what seem to you the most accurate and least accurate accounts of the speech. Are there any clues to how the least accurate account got that way?

2. The next time you listen to a speech in which you have no vital interest, watch your fellow auditors. Record the symptoms of inattention that you see. Which individuals seem to be listening most attentively? What seem to be their common characteristics?

3. Select an appropriate photograph and try the parlor game discussed on p. 330. (You don't, of course, need a parlor to play the game. You can carry the photo **337**

around with you and ask a variety of people to interpret it.) Record the interpretations given, the more the better. Do the responses fall into any sort of pattern? Do they tend to vary considerably? Can you explain why?

4. Listen to a tape-recorded speech. Do not take notes. Then make an outline of its contents. Check the outline against the tape. How accurate was your outline? How well did you listen? What kept you from being more accurate?

5. The next time you hear a speech that you can tape, prepare yourself as we have suggested on pp. 328–329. As you listen, look for clues that indicate how the speech is organized. Take notes. Then outline the speech.

   a. Did the planning and the notes help you to make a more complete and accurate outline?
   b. Did it help to be able to see the person delivering the speech?

19

Speaking

M ost of what we have said about good writing is applicable to good speaking as well: considering the audience, using words efficiently, avoiding rubber stamps and jargon, adjusting the tone and style to the situation, avoiding the unnecessary passive, and reflecting meaning in sentence structure and organization.

Even more than a piece of writing, a speech reflects a personality. One should be extremely careful, therefore, to reflect one's *own* personality and to do it justice. On public occasions, the alert mind of many a speaker is obscured by his tired phrases or by the hail-fellow-well-met approach.

THE MOST IMPORTANT RULE:
BE YOURSELF

The best advice that one can offer a speaker is: Be yourself. No audience can be persuaded unless it believes a speaker is being honest and forthright, and only an excellent actor—which few of us are—can successfully maintain an assumed role for long. A speaker may sometimes get away with an assumed personality for half an hour or more, but eventually one small slip will occur: an awkward gesture, a misplaced word or phrase, or an insincere laugh. The 339 audience immediately recognizes the acting and questions the speaker's sincerity.

Being yourself, of course, requires knowing yourself. Any student of communication, oral or written, might well begin by saying with Sophocles' Oedipus:

> . . . I ask to be no other man
> Than that I am, and *will know who I am.*

Your attempt to discover who you are may take a significant portion of your life. We do not propose here to uncover a psychiatric couch and invite you to lie down. On the other hand, we do think that you might appropriately ask yourself questions like the following:

Is my outstanding characteristic my integrity, my feeling of dedication, my sense of humor, my informality, my enthusiasm, my seriousness?

Is my public smile a real one, or is it forced?

Do I tell stories well?

Are gestures natural to me?

If you tend to be a serious person, you will probably do better by impressing your audience with your earnestness and your sense of the importance of a problem than by trying to charm them with a pasted-on smile or a dragged-in story which obviously has nothing to do with your topic.

Any generalization about human behavior should, of course, be applied with care. Certainly some dedicated speakers put their audiences to sleep. The soporific effect, however, is generally produced by language, content, or boring delivery, rather than by seriousness of purpose. It is also true that people can learn to smile where a smile is appropriate and to tell stories that suit their own personality and their subject—and that they probably should attempt to do so. We are merely arguing that, for example, future Presidents should not attempt to use the delivery of a John Kennedy, a Franklin Roosevelt, or a Ronald Reagan. That may seem an all-too-obvious precept, but it is violated all too often.

The situation in which you find yourself will, of course, also help to determine your approach. Generally the smaller the group and the better you know the people in your audience, the more informal you can be. Few people would attempt to speak the same way at a sales dinner for ten customers as they would at a meeting of stockholders. Just as the setting for two such different functions should be different, so should the language. As we pointed out in Chapter 13, Judge Learned Hand's talk—because of the nature of the speaker, the subject, and the audience—was appropriately formal. Always the key is

the word *appropriate.*

SPEAKING

PLANNING THE SPEECH

Let's assume that you have been asked to give a talk on a subject on which you have done some research.[1] Obviously you must first have sufficient command of your subject to do a good job. If you do not, you have no business speaking. Sometimes a person invited to give a talk is well advised to refuse the invitation. One of our colleagues, a psychologist, was once asked to take part in a television program on mental-health problems during adolescence. He answered politely that he was not a specialist either in mental health or in adolescence, that he had no special interest in either (beyond, of course, the interest of the average educated person), and that he could not, therefore, appear on the program. The producer, however, brushed aside his objections and kept urging him to appear. Happily, the psychologist held out, and the producer eventually turned to someone who *was* qualified. Our colleague later commented wryly, "He didn't really care whether I knew anything about the subject. All he wanted was a body—preferably the body of a psychologist."

Our colleague might possibly have been so interested in aiding the producer or in supporting adult education that he would have undertaken whatever study was necessary to equip himself for the appearance. As a trained psychologist, he presumably would have had to do much less work to become knowledgeable about the area than an economist or a chemist. He was unable to spend the necessary time, however, and so he quite properly refused to speak.

Let us return to your situation: you have been asked to talk on a subject with which you are familiar. Even here, you should be cautious. Do you know enough to appear before the designated audience as an expert? Can you give them new insights, or will you bore them with material and ideas which to them are elementary and outdated?

A preliminary answer to these questions may not be difficult to make. Let's assume that you do have something useful and interesting to contribute. You should then carefully review the material you have on the assigned topic. Does it need to be brought up to date in certain areas? Are more statistics needed to support one or more of your points? Do you have what you need to refute objections which may occur to the audience and which may be brought up in discussion after the talk? Are there any gaps in the argument you will wish to put forward?

The best way to answer this last question is to make a preliminary sketch— a logical outline, perhaps, or a list of points to be made on each of the various aspects of the topic. When this step is completed, you will have all of the relevant information laid out so that you can determine easily whether or not it is complete.

---

[1] Because in Chapter 13, Tone and Style, we analyzed a speech by means of the Lasswell model, we will not repeat that demonstration here. To review how that model can serve as a device for thinking through a speech, the reader can turn back to that chapter. The present discussion will focus heavily on the last line in the Lasswell model—"With What Effect?"

There is another advantage to this procedure. It helps you to decide *what* you have to say before you begin to think about *how* to say it. As we have seen, the two steps should be kept separate. A good bit of the confusion in speaking as well as writing comes from trying to do the two things at the same time. Laying out the information first is as necessary for a speaker as it is for a suitmaker to lay out cloth. With everything before him, each can then cut, match, and arrange the material to meet the needs of the individual situation. One can imagine the fit of a suit which a tailor cut while unrolling a bolt of cloth. Yet many speakers (and writers) take a comparable first step. Some of them even try to sew the parts together at the same time.

With the material spread out, then, you are ready to prepare your talk. Here again many speakers go wrong. They assume that a logical outline of their material is also the best outline for their speech. In other words, they deliver the talk from the outline or sketch they worked up for their own use.

CASE STUDIES

Let us look at two examples to make this point clear. The Walters Marine Construction Company has been invited by an oil company to submit a bid on the construction of twenty-four seagoing tankers. The company would like to have the contract because it would enable it to expand into a new field. There are problems, however. In order to handle the job it would have to expand its dock facilities and deepen the channel which takes finished tankers from the shipyards out to the ocean. The estimator assigned to the job, Sarah Bolt, has been told to make an oral report to the Operating Committee in ten days. On the basis of her report, the committee will decide whether the company will submit a bid.

Sarah Bolt's first task is to collect and organize all the information that the Operating Committee will need to make its decision. Once she brings together her material, she will organize it, probably in some such way as this:

Cost of building tankers (broken down in some detail)	$ _____
Cost of extending dock facilities	$ _____
Cost of deepening channel	$ _____
Total cost	$ _____
Estimate of competitors' bids	$ _____
Difference	$ _____

This outline provides a sensible organization of the materials and reflects to some extent the way in which she gathered her data.

The Operating Committee, however, will want the last item first. Their problem is to determine whether costs for the docks and the channel can be held down enough to allow them to enter a competitive bid. They are willing to take the contract without any profit, or even at a small loss, in order to expand into the new field. The "Difference," then, is the crucial item for them. If it is in favor of their competitors, but very slightly so, they will know at once that they can probably get the contract by taking a certain loss. If the difference in favor of their competitors is large enough to give them pause, they will want to study the various costs to see where they can trim or take shortcuts. They may even ask for a breakdown of the figures and work over them for a few days. If the difference is overwhelmingly in favor of their competitors, they may decide against the project immediately and settle the issue in a few minutes, leaving Sarah Bolt with several pages of unreported figures.

If the Operating Committee decides to bid for the contract, Sarah must use the original outline (perhaps amended slightly as a result of the decisions of the Committee) to write up the proposal. Some figures, then, and many of the same facts may be used in three different patterns for three different audiences: first, for the estimator to get a picture of the situation; second, for the estimator to give her oral report so that the Operating Committee can decide whether to bid for the contract; and third, for the estimator to write up the proposal.

If Sarah were invited to lecture to a college class in engineering analysis and chose to use this particular example as the basis for her talk, she would probably fashion the figures into still another pattern. She would not need to report them in detail, as she had been prepared to do for the Operating Committee. She would, however, probably need to arrange an introduction so that the students, who were not familiar with the Walters Company and had had little practical experience, would understand the figures. And she would need both to explain how they were arrived at and to arrange them with a different emphasis from that used in the bid.

Here is one more example. An oil executive has just returned from a two-year tour of duty in the Middle East. During his first month at home, he is asked to give four talks: to a select gathering of officials in the home office of his company; to a convention of petroleum engineers; to the local Foreign Policy Association; and to the local Parent-Teacher Association. If he is to do a good job for each group, he will have to prepare and deliver four entirely different talks, even though he will be talking about "the same thing" in each: his experiences in the Middle East. His four audiences will arrive with different interests, different understandings, and different training. Should he also be asked to address a group which has a strong emotional attachment to Israel, he would have still another matter to consider in preparing a fifth talk.

MANUSCRIPT OR NOTES?

Now for the talk itself. How should you deliver it? If it is highly technical, you must take pains to be precise. If it is on a sensitive topic and you want to be very sure that you are not misunderstood, you may wish to write out the talk in advance and deliver it exactly as written. Actually, such precision is seldom necessary, though many insecure speakers like to insist that for them it *is*. Most people feel safer reading a speech. But they should not delude themselves. Only a person with long training and much experience can read a talk successfully. Most speech readers fail miserably and only manage to bore their audiences. Similarly, few speakers ever find themselves in a situation which really calls for memorizing a talk; and those who try to do so find that committing to memory a talk of more than four or five minutes is a tedious and time-consuming chore. Furthermore, few people other than trained actors can deliver a memorized talk without sounding mechanical.

If you feel that you must read a speech, your text should be prepared for easy delivery. That usually means avoiding long and involved sentences which depend heavily on punctuation for their clarity. It also means taking care not to be trapped into using phrases that are appropriate in a typed or printed text but not in a speech, either because of their reference to the medium ("As I indicated above . . .") or because of their formality.

Most good speakers use notes, which may be prepared in any of several different ways, depending upon what has proved useful in the past. Some, for example, write out their talks with key words or phrases underlined in red pencil and carry the typescript to the lectern. They plan to look only at the underlined phrases. Although an occasional speaker uses this system success-fully, it has serious dangers. First, it is not easy to keep one's place in such a manuscript. Second, there is a constant temptation to read instead of delivering the talk informally.

Most teachers of public speaking recommend that notes be typed on 3 × 5 or 4 × 6 cards. In that form, they can be carried in a pocket until needed and can be manipulated easily. Many speakers, however, prefer to have their notes on standard 8½ × 11 paper. They feel that the advantage of being able to see what comes next outweighs the possible advantages in handling and storing the smaller cards.

Whether you read or speak from notes, however, you should be sure that each page or card may be easily used. Since your material will be considerably farther from your eyes than the normal reading distance, the type should be dark and distinct. Manuscripts for reading should be double-spaced, or, if nec-essary, triple-spaced. Ordinary punctuation rules may be largely ignored in favor of a punctuation system which clearly indicates appropriate pauses and emphases. Conventional punctuation marks are often supplemented with sin-gle, double, and triple diagonal lines to group words for proper delivery, and with underlining (single and double) and capitalization of whole words or phrases to indicate appropriate degrees of emphasis. A sample page from a manuscript marked in this way is shown in Figure 19.1.

Your material should never be crammed into inadequate space or be al-lowed to pile up at the end of a page or card. Adequate margins will enable you to pick up each line easily with a normal sweep of the eye, and you will have room for jotting down the impromptu last-minute thoughts or local ref-erences that often improve a talk.

Manuscripts and notes should be placed on a lectern, if one is available, and then left alone, except when a page or notecard has to be turned over.

Neither manuscript nor notes should ever be held in your hand. They distract

in this city. // The mayor and councilmen have said, / not once but many

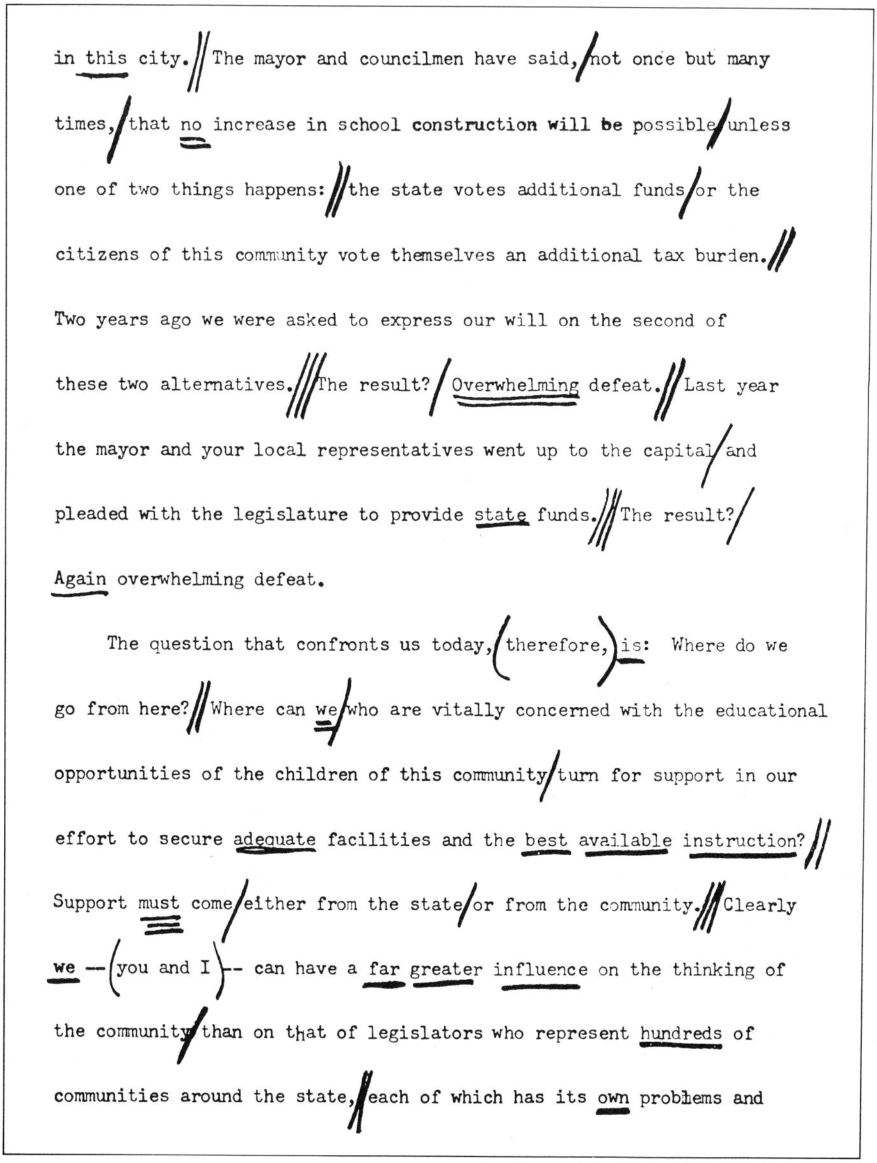

times, / that no increase in school construction will be possible / unless

one of two things happens: // the state votes additional funds / or the

citizens of this community vote themselves an additional tax burden. //

Two years ago we were asked to express our will on the second of

these two alternatives. /// The result? / Overwhelming defeat. // Last year

the mayor and your local representatives went up to the capital / and

pleaded with the legislature to provide state funds. // The result? /

Again overwhelming defeat.

The question that confronts us today, (therefore,) is: Where do we

go from here? // Where can we / who are vitally concerned with the educational

opportunities of the children of this community / turn for support in our

effort to secure adequate facilities and the best available instruction? //

Support must come / either from the state / or from the community. /// Clearly

we — (you and I) -- can have a far greater influence on the thinking of

the community / than on that of legislators who represent hundreds of

communities around the state, / each of which has its own problems and

Figure 19.1 A page of notes marked for speaking

the audience. If you are nervous, they will greatly magnify a slight hand tremor. They will also tempt you to fiddle with them; and while you speak, your audience will be fascinated as your hands bend, shuffle, tap, snap, roll, ruffle, drop, recover, and torture your notes. Meanwhile, your words will go un-heeded.

FACING THE AUDIENCE

When you use a lectern, you should be sure to stand several inches behind it. If it touches your body, you will have to look directly downward to see your manuscript or notes. As a result, your voice will be thrown into your throat, you will have difficulty keeping your place, and your audience will be distracted by the bobbing of your head.[2]

When you approach the lectern, you should already have examined the audience and picked out four or five individuals in different locations, most of them toward the back. If you talk directly to these people in turn, you will be heard by everyone. Even if the room is unusually wide, you need not rotate your head or body from side to side like a person watching a tennis match. An occasional slight turn in one direction or the other is all you need if you project your voice clearly to the back of the room (see Figure 19.2).

Figure 19.2 Two patterns for spotting people

Looking at particular individuals in the audience will also remind you that you are speaking to people, not to an unresponsive set of robots. As you notice and react to facial expressions—and perhaps even comment on them—your talk will become warmer and more personal and communication more effective.

TIMING

No speaker, however, should become so carried away as to lose track of time. If there is no easily visible clock in the room, you should remove your watch before beginning to talk and place it where you can easily see it. This precaution will prevent you from distracting your listeners by hauling out a pocket watch or pulling up your sleeve every few minutes.

Few things annoy an audience more than having a speaker run over the allotted time. Poor planning or deliberate disregard of arrangements not only

[2] Some speakers find it much easier to read a speech if it is typed on the top two-thirds of the paper only. This practice makes it easier for them to maintain eye contact with the audience.

is rude, but embarrasses the chair, who must call the infraction to the speaker's attention. Furthermore, it may force the audience to stay beyond the time anticipated and embarrass those in the front of the room who must leave for other appointments. If there are other speakers on the program, it may also eat up some of their time.[3]

There is no excuse, of course, for your exceeding the allotted time, for there is always opportunity to run through a prepared speech beforehand and work over the materials until they fit comfortably into the designated period. In addition, you can jot down in red at the top of every other page a figure (9:15, 9:22, 9:27, etc.) indicating when you should reach that page. Thus, if you reach the page marked 9:27 at 9:25, you will know that you can slow down a bit and make the most of opportunities for meaningful pauses. Or you may reinstate a point you reluctantly cut from the text. If you arrive at the same place at 9:31—four minutes late—you will have to speed up and perhaps drop an illustration. (If you don't know exactly when your speech will begin, you may, of course, record in the same way the number of minutes it should take you to get to every other page.) Using this procedure is even more important if you use note cards, for then it is much too easy to use up time with digressions or to get ahead of yourself by omitting essential material. Such a time schedule will constantly remind you of the obligation to finish on time.

POLISHING

Whether speaking from a manuscript or from notes, many speakers polish their delivery by tape-recording their talks. On occasion even the experienced speaker finds such trial runs useful. They give a good indication of the time the talk will take and familiarize the speaker with the material as no silent reading can. It will reveal not only tongue twisters and phrases that may look fine in print but do not sound quite right when read aloud but also errors in diction: the omission of syllables, the dropping of the g in words ending in *ing*, and the mispronunciation of vowels, as in *fur* for *for*, *ta* for *to*, *git* for *get*, and *lookit* for *look at*. A tape recording also provides a chance to check speed, emphasis, and the sound of one's voice.

---

[3] Except under extraordinary circumstances, no talk should be allowed to continue beyond its allotted time. If it does, the chair should intervene, first by passing a note to the speaker and then, if that does no good, by rising and insisting, politely but firmly, that time is up. On occasion, it may take a salvo of cannon to stop an inconsiderate speaker, but the chair owes it to the audience to do so. Here is how one of our colleagues recently handled the speakers on a panel. Taking his cue from the convention chair, he included in his letter about arrangements to each of the panelists the following paragraph: "From Mr. Allen's letter, I gather that my principal jobs are to introduce you and 'to insist ruthlessly and without exception that each speaker finish *on time.'* I promise to be 'ruthless' about time." He met with all the panelists briefly before they appeared and arranged to give a two-minute warning to those who wanted it. His demeanor, his good-humored frankness about his intentions, and his offer of help convinced the group that he was serious about time. They all kept within their allotted limits.

CONTROLLING NERVOUSNESS

Inexperienced speakers often think that seasoned speakers are never nervous. Seasoned speakers, however, disagree. Although experience does make for ease of delivery, very few speakers ever approach an assignment without qualms. Even veteran actors and actresses confess that they are nervous every time they go on stage. Some, indeed, are so frightened that they are sure they will not be able to go on. Once they walk on stage, however, they are all right. The same is true for most public speakers. Nervous while awaiting the job ahead, they perform admirably once they are doing it. And as every actor knows, some nervousness can be a good thing. Speakers or actors who are blasé about what they are doing may never quite get their act together and may wind up very unhappy about their performance. Nervousness, on the other hand, frequently "pumps one up"—provides the extra energy needed to project the voice and give appropriate emphasis, tone, and gesture. Hence, one should see nervousness not as something to be avoided, but rather as something to be controlled and turned to advantage.

There are ways of bringing nervousness under control. Since it often causes tension in the facial muscles, especially those controlling the eyes and tongue, one should consciously attempt to relax them. Many speakers make a practice of blinking their eyes and yawning as they wait to appear before an audience.

Having made your preparations, how should you proceed when you rise to speak? Once at the lectern, you should arrange your watch and notes, if they are not already in place. As we have suggested, you should stand several inches behind the lectern, so that you can see them easily. Finally—and perhaps this is the most important step of all—you should pause to look briefly at the audience. The pause informs them that you are about to begin. It gives them a chance to clear their throats, rearrange their legs, settle back in their seats, and do all the other little things that audiences seem to have to do when they are about to be addressed. Since it also suggests to them that their speaker is thoroughly in command of the situation, they automatically allow themselves to relax. If, on the other hand, you do not pause, they become tense: sensing that their speaker is ill at ease, they feel embarrassed. For you, this brief moment is invaluable; it provides you with an opportunity to settle your feet, square your shoulders, and raise your head. It also prevents you from rushing into the talk, an error which almost always results in stumbling over the first sentence, thus creating an unfavorable impression and markedly increasing your self-conscious nervousness. If you think that under the pressure of the moment you are likely to forget to pause, you should include a reminder at the head of your notes. Poise can be developed by conscious effort. The speaker who appears poised starts off with a great advantage.

HUMOR

Too many speakers try to prove that they are at ease by starting off with a
good story. "I'll show them I'm pretty comfortable up here," they think, "and

at the same time I'll loosen them up a little." So they begin, "My subject tonight reminds me of . . ." or "What your chairman just said reminds me of a joke I heard once from old Joe Smith. . . ." Too often, however, the joke is poorly told, has nothing to do with the topic at hand, and takes far too much time. Listeners are left wondering why it was told. They begin to suspect that the speaker probably doesn't have much to say, knows it, and is just making a lame attempt to win them over.

Thus, you should always keep in mind that humor is most effective when it arises naturally as a talk unfolds. Your audience will very easily tell the difference between wit that stems from your good-humored or satiric approach to a subject and wit that is pasted on. It is really a question of integrity. If you accept an invitation to speak on a serious subject about which you have special knowledge, you should not assume that the audience is most interested in being amused. We are not opposed to humor in a serious talk. Properly employed, it can be a very effective tool. Many speakers use it masterfully. But humor should not overshadow significant subject matter, should not be dragged in irrelevantly, and should not be used in lieu of content. It *should* be appropriate.

AUDIOVISUAL AIDS

Another effective tool is the audiovisual aid. Audio tape recorders seldom find their way to a speaker's platform, except perhaps to provide material for discussion. Aids that are truly audiovisual are used more often. The commonest are motion pictures, video tapes, and film strips. Even these, however, are used more often as substitutes for a speaker than as aids. After all, the most effective audiovisual aid is the speaker.

The aids most commonly used by speakers are purely visual: graphs, maps, charts, pictures, drawings, and printed messages. These may be projected on a screen; they may be drawn or lettered on a blackboard or on cards to be held up before the audience; they may be displayed on a flannel board or reproduced and distributed. They have one great advantage. They can clarify points for which words are inadequate. A single curve on a graph, for example, can demonstrate vividly what has happened to the cost of living over a period of years or describe fuel consumption in a particular engine under varying loads.

Manufacturers of projectors are becoming increasingly ingenious in helping speakers explain complex subjects. There is, for example, the "dynamic" slide (as opposed to the "static" slide) for use with certain kinds of projectors: it allows a speaker to build up or take apart a composite image, adding or subtracting sections as appropriate. The dynamic slide is a standard slide with transparent overlays hinged at the edges. Each overlay has a portion of a complete picture on it. Folding it over the face of the slide adds what is drawn on the overlay to what is already being projected on the screen. Colors can be used to emphasize or distinguish between different lines, curves, points, sections, or words.

Let us assume, for example, that the transportation manager of a company has been invited to discuss her major problems before a meeting of the board of directors. With a dynamic slide she can very easily demonstrate an important aspect of her problem. She may first project on the screen an outline map of the United States which shows the company's plants in blue and its chief customers' in red. After talking about them for a few moments, she may add an overlay showing available rail lines in black. Later she may add another overlay showing the navigable rivers in green, a third showing the airlines in orange, and a fourth showing the major truck routes by means of dotted purple lines. These overlays may be applied in any order, so that a particular mode of transportation can be examined separately or in relation to any or all of the others.

DANGERS OF VISUAL AIDS

In the use of visual aids, however, there are several problems. Too frequently they are used for their own sake, to demonstrate that the speaker is "up" on the newest gadget or the latest teaching technique. They should be used only as an aid to audience understanding of matters not easily explained in words, not as a prop for the speaker or to hide inadequacies in the speaker's material. If our traffic manager concludes, for example, that the best way to ship a particular product is by truck because trucking is fast, safe, and easily adaptable to the particular needs of the product, she should simply say so. Too often in such circumstances a speaker insults the intelligence of the audience by flashing on a screen:

> Trucking is . . .
>> FAST . . .
>> SAFE . . .
>> EASILY ADAPTABLE

and then reading the message to them.

Many a "speaker" actually does little more than present a series of charts and read them aloud. Nothing puts an audience to sleep more rapidly. And even if the words convey a message, the procedure gives members of an audience the impression that the speaker has been talking "down" to them.

PROPER USE OF VISUAL AIDS

In your talks, you should use visual aids smoothly. You should make sure that slides appear exactly when needed and in the proper sequence. The visual aid, after all, is presented for the sake of the talk, not the talk for the visual aid. If you need a pointer, it should be long enough to reach easily any item on the screen, chart, or board. (Some speakers prefer a flashlight to a pointer.

By fastening a stencil of an arrow over its lens, they produce an arrow-shaped beam of light with which they can point.) Insofar as possible you should face the audience, not the visual aid. Too often a speaker using a blackboard, for example, turns and talks to the board. As a result, the audience cannot hear what is being said. Finally, you should always keep charts, flannel boards, or blackboards covered until needed. Once used, they should be covered again, if possible. Exposed charts or figures distract your audience.

In determining how large charts or screen images should be, you should consider the size of the room. A diagram, picture, or sentence which spectators can barely see is often worse than no visual aid at all. Particularly at the beginning, when information is new, you should not put too much material on a single card or slide. As your approach and material become more familiar to the audience, you can increase the amount of information on each visual aid. Even so, each card or slide should concern a single idea or topic.

The principles of good speaking, then, are having one's material firmly in hand and tailoring it to the needs of the audience, matching one's delivery to one's personality, and calling on whatever mechanical aids are necessary to accomplish one's purpose. Speakers who are honest with themselves and with the audience will need no gimmicks. The integrity they project will insure that their views receive a fair hearing.

ILLUSTRATIVE MATERIALS

1.

A classic discussion of a common failing among speakers is John Davenport's "Slurvian Self-Taught,"[4] which is as relevant today as it was when it was written:

> Listening to a well-known Hollywood radio commentator some time back, I heard her say that she had just returned from a Yerpeen trip, and had had a lovely time nittly. I at once recognized her as an accomplished Slurvian linguist and, being a student of Slurvian, readily understood that she had just returned from a European trip, and while there (in Yerp) had had a lovely time in Italy.
>
> Slurvian is coming into common use in the United States, but I am, so far as I know, the only scholar to have made a start toward recording it. There is no official written Slurvian language, but it is possible, by means of phonetic spelling, for me to offer a brief course of instruction in it. In a short time, the student can learn enough to add immeasurably to his understanding and enjoyment of conversation wherever he travels in the country.

[4] Reprinted by permission of the author and Curtis Brown, Ltd. Originally published in *The New Yorker*, June 18, 1949. Copyright 1949 by John Davenport.

I first heard pure Slurvian fluently spoken by a co-worker of mine who told me that his closest friend was a man named Hard (Howard). Hard was once in an automobile accident, his car, unfortunately, cliding with another, causing Hard's wife Dorthy, who was with him, to claps. Dorthy didn't have much stamina but was a sweet woman—sweet as surp.

I soon discovered I had an ear for Slurvian, and since I began to recognize the language, I have encountered many Slurvians. At ballparks, they keep track of hits, runs, and airs. On farms, they plow furs. In florist shops, they buy flars. When hard up, they bar money from banks, and spend it for everything from fewl for the furnace to grum crackers for the children.

When Slurvians travel abroad, they go to visit farn (or forn) countries to see what the farners do that's different from the way we Murcans do things. While in farn countries, they refer to themselves as Murcan tersts, and usually say they will be mighty glad to get back to Murca. A Slurvian I once met on a train told me he had just returned from a visit to Mexico. He deplored the lack of automobiles down there, and said that the natives ride around on little burrs.

A linguistic authority of my acquaintance, much interested in my work in Slurvian, has suggested to me the possibility that the language may be related to, or a variation of, the one still spoken in England of which such a contraction as "Chumley," for "Cholmondeley," is a familiar example. However, I think the evidence insufficient for drawing such a conclusion. Surnames cannot be considered subject to the ordinary rules of pronunciation. In fact, the only one I have positively identified in Slurvian is Faggot, the name of the American admiral who won the Battle of Mobile Bay.

The name Faggot brings me to a discussion of what I designate as "pure" Slurvian. This includes those Slurvian words that, when spelled exactly as pronounced, also make good English words (such as "Faggot," "burr," and "claps"). The day that I can add to the lexicon such a word hitherto unrecorded, is a happy day for me. Here are some examples of pure Slurvian, alphabetically listed:

bean, *n.* A living creature, as in *human bean.*
cactus, *n. pl.* The people in a play or story.
course, *n.* A group of singers.
fiscal, *adj.* Pertaining to the body, as opposed to the spurt.
form, *n.* Gathering place of the ancient Romans.
gnome, *n.* Contraction for *no, Ma'am. Colloq.*
line, *n.* The king of beasts.
lore, *n.* The more desirable of the two berths in a Pullman section.
myrrh, *n.* A looking glass.
par, *n.* An attribute of strength, as in *the par and the glory.*
plight, *adj.* Courteous.
sears, *adj.* Grave, intent.
sport, *v.t.* To hold up, to bear the weight of.
wreckers, *n. pl.* Discs on which music is recorded for phonographs.

SPEAKING

Let me close with a final example, to make my meaning clear. Wherever you may be in the United States, if you hear the word "tare," the speaker probably is not referring to a Biblical weed growing in the wheat. More likely he is describing the sensation of extreme fear experienced by a movie fan watching Borse Karloff in a harr picture.

2.

Jargon, as we saw in Chapter 11, is present in much business writing. In speeches, the manager is likely to use an even larger percentage of jargon, trite phrasing, and standard metaphors than in letters. Each profession, we know, has its own jargon. So does each company. One special type we may call "informal speech jargon." It is found in most speeches in which business people attempt informality. It pretends to be direct and forceful; actually, like all jargon, it serves only to obscure a kernel of meaning by burying it in a mountain of words. Notice how little the speaker really has to say in the following talk:

The Composite Business Speech[5]

(This is not a parody. It is a loose compilation, based on a systematic count of the expressions and constructions most commonly used in current U.S. business speeches. Included are sixty principal clichés of reverse gobble-degook.)

COOPERATION—AN OPPORTUNITY AND A CHALLENGE
An Address

It is a pleasure and a privilege to be here with you today. These great annual meetings are always an inspiration to me, and doubly so today. After the glowing introduction by our toastmaster I must confess, however, that I'd like to turn the tables and tell a little story on Chuck. When I say it's about the nineteenth hole and a certain gentleman whose baritone was cracked, those of you who were at the Atlanta conference last year will know what I mean. But I won't tell it. Chuck Forbes is too good a friend of mine, and seriously, I know full well we all realize what a tower of strength his yeoman service has been to the association in these trying times.

Yes, gentlemen, trying times. So you'll pardon me if I cast aside the glib reverberation of glittering generalities and the soothing syrup of sugar-coated platitudes and put it to you the only way I can: straight English.

We're losing the battle:

From every corner the people are being weaned from the doctrines of the Founding Fathers. They are being detoured from the high-speed highway of progress by the utopian highwaymen.

Now, the man in the street is a pretty savvy fellow. Don't sell him short. Joe Doakes may be fooled for a while, but in the end he wants no part of the mumbo jumbo the global saboteurs are trying to sell him. After all, he is an American.

But he has to be told.

And we're not telling him!

Now let me say that I do not wish to turn the clock back. None of us do. All forward-looking businessmen see themselves as partners in a team in which the worker is a full-fledged member. I regard our employees as our greatest business asset, and I am sure, mindful as I am of the towering potentials of purposeful energy in this group of clear-sighted leaders, that, in the final analysis, it is the rock foundation of your policies too.

But the team can't put the ball across for a first down just by wishing it. The guards and the tackles can't do their job if the quarterback doesn't let them in on the play. And we, the quarterbacks, are muffing the ball.

How are we to go over for a touchdown? My friends, this is the question. I don't know the answers. I am just a plain-spoken businessman. I am not a soothsayer. I have no secret crystal ball. But I do know one thing: before we round the curve into the homestretch we have a job to do. It will not be easy. I offer no panaceas or nostrums. Instead, I would like to suggest that the real key to our problem lies in the application of the three E's.

What are the three E's?

ENTERPRISE! ENDEAVOR! EFFORT!

Each and every one of us must appoint himself a salesman—yes, a missionary, if you will—and get out and do some real grassroots selling. And when we hit the dirt, let's not forget the customers—the greatest asset any business has.

Now, much has been done already. But let's not fool ourselves: the surface, as our chairman has so wisely said, has hardly been scratched. The program is still in its infancy. So let me give it to you straight from the shoulder. The full implementation, gentlemen, depends on us.

So let's get on the beam! In cracker-barrel fashion, let's get down to earth. In good plain talk the man in the street can understand, let's remind Joe Doakes that the best helping hand he will ever find is the one at the end of his own shirt sleeve.

We have the know-how.

With sights set high, let's go over the top!

3.

One of the best known examples of persuasive speaking in our literature is Antony's speech to the people in Shakespeare's Julius Caesar. *The speech is delivered a few minutes after Caesar's enemies have assassinated him. The leader of the conspirators, Brutus, has brought the body to the Forum, has told the people that Caesar had to be killed because he planned to become a dictator. The cheering crowds want to carry Brutus home in triumph, but he asks them instead to stay behind and listen to what he assumes will be a standard funeral oration to be delivered by Caesar's long-time friend and protégé, Marc Antony. As Antony begins to speak, the mood of the audience is ugly, hostile. But gradually Antony wins them over, using every device in the orator's repertoire, and in the end he sends them off ready to tear the conspirators to bits.*

As you read, note the skill with which at every stage of the address Antony manipulates the emotions of his audience.[6]

ANTONY Friends, Romans, countrymen, lend me your ears:
  I come to bury Caesar, not to praise him:
  The evil that men do, lives after them,
  The good is oft interred with their bones,
  So let it be with Caesar. The noble Brutus,
  Hath told you Caesar was ambitious:
  If it were so, it was a grievous fault,
  And grievously hath Caesar answer'd it.
  Here, under leave of Brutus, and the rest
  (For Brutus is an honourable man,
  So are they all; all honourable men)
  Come I to speak in Caesar's funeral.
  He was my friend, faithful, and just to me;
  But Brutus says, he was ambitious,
  And Brutus is an honourable man.
  He hath brought many captives home to Rome,
  Whose ransoms, did the general coffers fill:
  Did this in Caesar seem ambitious?
  When that the poor have cried, Caesar hath wept:
  Ambition should be made of sterner stuff,
  Yet Brutus says, he was ambitious:
  And Brutus is an honourable man.
  You all did see, that on the Lupercal,
  I thrice presented him a kingly Crown,
  Which he did thrice refuse. Was this ambition?
  Yet Brutus says, he was ambitious:
  And sure he is an honourable man.
  I speak not to disprove what Brutus spoke,
  But here I am, to speak what I do know;
  You all did love him once, not without cause,
  What cause withholds you then, to mourn for him?
  O Judgement! thou art fled to brutish beasts,

---

[6] Anyone viewing a production of the play, the motion picture version, or the television film produced by the British Broadcasting Corporation will recognize that many persuasive devices— pauses, gestures, intonations, and the like—are not included in the play's text. Still the imaginative reader will have no difficulty in bringing the scene to life. The punctuation and capitalization are Elizabethan; they will suggest to the reader where the actor paused and what words he emphasized.

And men have lost their reason. Bear with me,
My heart is in the coffin there with Caesar,
And I must pause, till it come back to me.

1 PLEBEIAN Methinks there is much reason in his sayings.

2 PLEBEIAN If thou consider rightly of the matter, Caesar has had great
wrong.

3 PLEBEIAN Has he masters? I fear there will a worse come in his place.

4 PLEBEIAN Mark'd ye his words? He would not take the Crown,
Therefore 'tis certain, he was not ambitious.

1 PLEBEIAN If it be found so, some will dear abide it.

2 PLEBEIAN Poor soul, his eyes are red as fire with weeping.

3 PLEBEIAN There's not a nobler man in Rome than Antony.

4 PLEBEIAN Now mark him, he begins again to speak.

ANTONY But yesterday, the word of Caesar might
Have stood against the World: Now lies he there,
And none so poor to do him reverence.
O Masters! if I were dispos'd to stir
Your hearts and minds to mutiny and rage,
I should do Brutus wrong, and Cassius wrong:
Who (you all know) are honourable men.
I will not do them wrong: I rather choose
To wrong the dead, to wrong myself and you,
Than I will wrong such honourable men.
But here's a parchment, with the seal of Caesar,
I found it in his closet, 'tis his Will:
Let but the Commons hear this testament:
(Which pardon me) I do not mean to read,
And they would go and kiss dead Caesar's wounds,
And dip their napkins in his sacred blood;
Yea, beg a hair of him for memory,
And dying, mention it within their Wills,
Bequeathing it as a rich legacy
Unto their issue.

4 PLEBEIAN We'll hear the Will, read it Mark Antony.

ALL The Will, the Will; we will hear Caesar's Will.

ANTONY Have patience gentle friends, I must not read it.
It is not meet you know how Caesar lov'd you:
You are not wood, you are not stones, but men:
And being men, hearing the Will of Caesar,
It will inflame you, it will make you mad:
'Tis good you know not that you are his heirs,
For if you should, O what would come of it?

4 PLEBEIAN Read the Will, we'll hear it Antony:
You shall read us the Will, Caesar's Will.

ANTONY Will you be patient? Will you stay awhile?
I have o'ershot myself to tell you of it,

SPEAKING

I fear I wrong the honourable men,
Whose daggers have stabb'd Caesar: I do fear it.
4 PLEBEIAN They were traitors: honourable men?
ALL The Will, the Testament.
2 PLEBEIAN They were villains, murderers: the Will, read the Will.
ANTONY You will compel me then to read the Will:
Then make a ring about the corpse of Caesar,
And let me show you him that made the Will:
Shall I descend? And will you give me leave?
ALL Come down.
2 PLEBEIAN Descend.
3 PLEBEIAN You shall have leave.
4 PLEBEIAN A ring, stand round.
1 PLEBEIAN Stand from the hearse, stand from the body.
2 PLEBEIAN Room for Antony, most noble Antony.
ANTONY Nay press not so upon me, stand far off.
ALL Stand back: room, bear back.
ANTONY If you have tears, prepare to shed them now.
You all do know this mantle, I remember
The first time ever Caesar put it on,
'Twas on a summer's evening in his tent,
That day he overcame the Nervii.
Look, in this place ran Cassius' dagger through:
See what a rent the envious Casca made:
Through this, the well-beloved Brutus stabb'd,
And as he pluck'd his cursed steel away:
Mark how the blood of Caesar follow'd it,
As rushing out of doors, to be resolv'd
If Brutus so unkindly knock'd, or no:
For Brutus, as you know, was Caesar's Angel.
Judge, O you Gods, how dearly Caesar lov'd him:
This was the most unkindest cut of all.
For when the noble Caesar saw him stab,
Ingratitude, more strong than traitors' arms,
Quite vanquish'd him: then burst his mighty heart,
And in his mantle, muffling up his face,
Even at the base of Pompey's statue
(Which all the while ran blood) great Caesar fell.
O what a fall was there, my countrymen!
Then I, and you, and all of us fell down,
Whilst bloody Treason flourish'd over us.
O now you weep, and I perceive you feel
The dint of pity: These are gracious drops.
Kind souls, what weep you, when you but behold
Our Caesar's vesture wounded? Look you here,
Here is himself, marr'd as you see, with traitors.

357

1 PLEBEIAN O piteous spectacle!

2 PLEBEIAN O noble Caesar!

3 PLEBEIAN O woeful day!

4 PLEBEIAN O traitors, villains!

1 PLEBEIAN O most bloody sight!

2 PLEBEIAN We will be reveng'd: Revenge,
    About, seek, burn, fire, kill, slay,
    Let not a traitor live.

ANTONY Stay countrymen.

1 PLEBEIAN Peace there, hear the noble Antony.

2 PLEBEIAN We'll hear him, we'll follow him, we'll die with him.

ANTONY Good friends, sweet friends, let me not stir you up
    To such a sudden flood of mutiny:
    They that have done this deed, are honourable.
    What private griefs they have, alas I know not,
    That made them do it: they are wise, and honourable,
    And will no doubt with reasons answer you.
    I come not (friends) to steal away your hearts,
    I am no orator, as Brutus is;
    But (as you know me all) a plain blunt man
    That love my friend, and that they know full well,
    That gave me public leave to speak of him:
    For I have neither wit nor words, nor worth,
    Action, nor utterance, nor the power of speech,
    To stir men's blood. I only speak right on:
    I tell you that, which you yourselves do know,
    Show you sweet Caesar's wounds, poor poor dumb mouths,
    And bid them speak for me: but were I Brutus,
    And Brutus Antony, there were an Antony
    Would ruffle up your spirits, and put a tongue
    In every wound of Caesar, that should move
    The stones of Rome, to rise and mutiny.

ALL We'll mutiny.

1 PLEBEIAN We'll burn the house of Brutus.

3 PLEBEIAN Away then, come, seek the conspirators.

ANTONY Yet hear me countrymen, yet hear me speak.

ALL Peace ho, hear Antony, most noble Antony.

ANTONY Why friends, you go to do you know not what:
    Wherein hath Caesar thus deserv'd your loves?
    Alas you know not, I must tell you then:
    You have forgot the Will I told you of.

ALL Most true, the Will, let's stay and hear the Will.

ANTONY Here is the Will, and under Caesar's seal:
    To every Roman citizen he gives,
    To every several man, seventy-five drachmas.

2 PLEBEIAN Most noble Caesar, we'll revenge his death.

3 PLEBEIAN O royal Caesar.
ANTONY Hear me with patience.
ALL Peace ho.
ANTONY Moreover, he hath left you all his walks,
  His private arbours, and new-planted orchards,
  On this side Tiber, he hath left them you,
  And to your heirs for ever: common pleasures
  To walk abroad, and recreate yourselves.
  Here was a Caesar: when comes such another?
1 PLEBEIAN Never, never: come, away, away:
  We'll burn his body in the holy place,
  And with the brands fire the traitors' houses.
  Take up the body.
2 PLEBEIAN Go fetch fire.
3 PLEBEIAN Pluck down benches.
4 PLEBEIAN Pluck down forms, windows, anything.
                    Exeunt Plebeians with the body.

PROBLEM

Many people do not realize how little expression they use when they speak before a group. Try this experiment to see what you can do with your voice. From a novel or biography, choose a scene in which there is a good deal of excitement or action and familiarize yourself with an interesting passage of two or three pages. Then take the book and a tape recorder into a room that you can have to yourself and close the door.

Turn on the tape recorder and read the passage with as much expression as you can muster: "ham it up"; give it everything. Now listen to the tape.

a. Did you really put as much expression into the reading as you thought you did?

b. How close did you come to giving the passage its due?

c. Was there any variation in the intensity of your voice? In the pitch? In the volume? In the speed?

d. Leave the first reading on the tape. Read and record the passage again, trying to make your interpretation as meaningful and effective as possible. Compare the two readings for improvement.

20
Communicating in Group Discussion

Before calling a group together for a meeting of any kind, a supervisor should consider very carefully what is to be accomplished. Are they to be told something? Should they explore a problem? Should they reach a decision? Meetings for different purposes must be planned differently and must be conducted differently.

INFORMATION MEETINGS

Let us assume, for example, that a company's board of directors has decided to build a new plant. Just as the information on which their decision was based came up through the various levels of the company, so the decision itself must go down—and be translated into action as it goes. At each level the decision or a relevant aspect of the decision must be set out as carefully as possible so that there will be no misunderstanding. Too often trouble in carrying out plans comes from poor communication of policy.

Each person who calls a meeting to announce the decision to build a new plant should carefully prepare an announcement that will ensure that members of the group carry away precisely the appropriate type and amount of information. They should be given all the facts relevant to their own situation and their level in the company. And that information must be so presented that

360

they understand what is to be done and what it will mean to them. It must also allay unnecessary doubts about their own position and win the support of everyone on whom the project's success depends.

If each supervisor performs this assignment well, the decision to build a new plant will be transmitted to middle management in one way and to foremen in another. Whatever the level, a group leader will have to relay the decision, explain its significance for the group, provide whatever documentation is necessary, and allow sufficient time for questions. If the information is very important or very complex, the members of the group should leave with a document to which they may refer to refresh their memory or to clarify various aspects of the project.

We have gone into detail on what may seem a routine aspect of management communication because the apparent simplicity of a communication situation is so frequently deceptive. Management often fails to consider carefully the potential impact of its decisions on employees at various levels. It seems obvious that employees prefer to receive such information directly rather than from newspapers, a house organ, or the grapevine; but in too many companies the first news comes from such sources. A carefully planned meeting, on the other hand, ensures that these people get the information they need quickly and in detail, and it makes them feel that their roles are vital for implementing the decision. Furthermore, it ensures that no employee leaves an information meeting with any misconception which can become the basis of harmful rumors. Indeed, an information meeting is called partly to dispel such misconceptions and forestall the formation of such rumors.

Occasionally the person in charge of such a session leans too far in another direction and tries to avoid making it sound as though a decision is being relayed from above, when that is exactly what is happening. With all the current talk about teamwork, group dynamics, and togetherness, management sometimes seems to feel that all its decisions should somehow appear to be the spontaneous consensus of a "great big happy family." Such sleight of hand is really dishonest and seldom fools anyone. Management must make the decisions for which it is responsible. It should not try to appear "democratic" in situations in which it is not democratic or to make everyone in the company responsible for a decision which management alone has made.

EXPLORATION MEETINGS

An important decision by top management often calls for a second group meeting to explore the implications of the decision for a particular division or department of the company. If, for example, company policy on overtime is altered, the manager and department heads of each division will need to sit down and figure out what the change will mean for the division. Similarly, department heads will want to consider the matter with their assistants, some of whom may then need to study its ramifications with foremen under their jurisdiction. A similar need may occur if a division sends a proposal to top management—to purchase a license for a new product or to build a new plant, for example—and it comes back altered. The department heads will need to consider the nature of the changes and their effect on the original plans.

Before calling an exploratory meeting, the person responsible should see that all involved have had an opportunity to examine the decision to determine how it will affect them. A group discussion to which the members come poorly prepared is simply a pooling of ignorance. As someone has said, two half-wits do not make a wit.

Exploration meetings, in which no action is contemplated, are often very useful. Instead of asking immediately "How do we solve our problem?" they pose the very important prior questions: "What *is* our problem?," or "Do we have a problem?" Too often people attempt to solve a problem before they know what it really is. Getting together with the avowed purpose of exploring, rather than deciding, focuses their attention on the necessary first step of fruitful problem solving. Since they do not need to take immediate action, they are relieved of the dangerous temptation to take a position too early in the game which they will then feel committed to defend against all comers. Instead they may keep their thinking flexible until the appropriate time for reaching conclusions.

PROBLEM-SOLVING (OR DECISION) MEETINGS

In a third type of group discussion—probably the most widely used—the participants draw conclusions or make decisions. Faced with a problem, they must decide how to solve it. The resulting action may take many forms. It may be, for example, a recommendation to the president or board of directors. It may be a set of regulations for the subordinates of some or all of the group's members. It may be a series of instructions for some or all of the members themselves. It may be the postponement of a final decision until further evidence is obtained.

Although our analysis has distinguished three distinct types of group meetings (the information meeting, the exploration meeting, and the problem-solving meeting), in practice a meeting may be a combination of two, or even of all three, types. It may begin as an information meeting and conclude as an exploration meeting. Or the order may be reversed if a group which meets to explore discovers that it does not have all necessary information. Sometimes such meetings must be adjourned until more information can be provided. Or a group exploring a situation may discover it has a problem; then the meeting may become a decision meeting, where plans are made to solve the problem. A meeting may even start as an information meeting, shift to an exploration meeting, and then shift again to a decision meeting. At every point, however, the leader must know what kind of meeting is taking place at any particular moment in order to keep its purpose before the group and thus enable it to function efficiently.

MINUTES

Whatever the type of group session, the discussion leader should arrange for someone to take minutes. Often the task may be assigned to a younger person who should be present but because of inexperience will not have many comments to offer. If there is no such person in the group, the discussion leader may arrange for someone, probably a secretary, to attend the session specifically to take notes and write up minutes. The assignment should not be given to an active member, for no one can be expected to contribute effectively while attempting to record what is happening.

The minutes of a meeting are very important. They should not attempt to cover everything that is said. Usually they should simply record the major points discussed, the conclusions reached, and, most important, everything that the group as a whole or certain participants have agreed to do. Lengthy minutes take too long to prepare, require far too much checking, are likely to cause unnecessary resentment on the part of those who think they have been misquoted, and will not be read by most members of the group. Brief minutes which summarize the group's progress in exploring or solving its problem will provide all that the members need for their files. Before minutes are sent out, they should, of course, be checked for accuracy and completeness by the chairperson and by participants who have taken a prominent part in the discussion.

Prompt distribution is most important, especially because minutes serve to remind individuals of tasks that they have agreed to undertake. Minutes should be carefully organized, with materials clearly grouped for quick reference, and no significant item should be allowed to become lost in the middle or at the end of a paragraph. When the minutes must be longer than a page, it is useful to type participants' names in capital letters whenever they appear in the text. In some companies a secretary underlines in red the name of the person to whom a particular copy goes. The minutes below use still another mechanism for reminding participants of their responsibilities. The last paragraph is designed to assure that corrections are submitted promptly.

Minutes of the Meeting on
The Southeast Co. Project

Otco Headquarters
Rm. 1707, Eulalia Building
Chicago, Illinois

Wednesday, May 19, 1982

1:30 - 4:00 p.m.

Attending:

Otco	**Anderson-Jones**
B. D. Anson	B. F. Anderson
O. R. Friend	R. T. Anderson, group leader
P. L. Mandaya, group leader	E. C. Cohen
F. K. Salowski	A. J. Sanji

363

After a two-hour discussion of the division of responsibility for various aspects of the Southeast Co. Project, the group agreed that

1. *Otco's responsibility will be primarily planning and Anderson-Jones's primarily execution.*
2. *The two groups will communicate through their respective group leaders: P. L. Mandaya (Otco) and R. T. Anderson (A-J).*
3. *The next meeting will take place at*

Anderson-Jones Headquarters

Anderson-Jones Building

St. Louis, Missouri

July 22, 1982

1:30-4:00 p.m.

4. *In preparation for that meeting, the conferees indicated in the left-hand margin below will be responsible for providing each group leader with six copies of each of the following by Wednesday, July 8:*

Otco

a. preliminary plans

Anson   1) drawings

Salowski   2) specifications

Mandaya   b. dates for completion of plans by stages

Anderson-Jones

Sanji   a. analysis of labor costs in the project area

B. F. Anderson   b. project dates

      1) ground-breaking

      2) completion of plant

      3) turnover to Southeast Co.

Corrections to these minutes must arrive at Otco Headquarters before June 3, 1982, when the minutes will become the official record of the meeting.

Respectfully submitted,

O. R. Friend (Otco)

CASE STUDY: A WELL-RUN MEETING

At this point it may be useful to look in on a group discussion. The Southern Signal and Control Company manufactures railroad equipment. To be sure that it remains competitive, it has established a product-performance analysis group, which gathers and analyzes reports on equipment failures. Every three months—more often if the situation demands—the head of product-performance analysis discusses with the manager and staff of each operating department all reports on the failure of equipment manufactured by that department. The reports themselves are distributed to the department staff a week before the meeting, which is run by the manager, since he is responsible for the department. The head of product-performance analysis is present to supply additional information and to help in evaluating the reports.

The meeting begins as an information meeting. At the invitation of the manager, the head of product-performance analysis may summarize briefly the findings of her department. She may use charts or graphs to make her presentation more effective. If the problem on which she is reporting is not serious, her report will be simple. If she feels that the problem is significant, she will probably want to compare the results of the past quarter with those of the three previous quarters or of the same quarter of the year before. The manager will then see that everyone has an opportunity to speak, that everything is understood, and that the members of the group cooperate to elicit information rather than to place or avoid blame. The manager must also see that the group does not shift to problem-solving before it has all the required information.

The manager will then want to shift the focus of the meeting. The facts are all out in the open. Is there any problem? If there has been an unusually large number of failures, he will immediately be faced with a difficult decision. Should he invite the product-performance head to stay, or thank her for her help and suggest that they need not take up any more of her time? An alert group leader will have anticipated this situation and thought it through in advance. Will the product-performance head have anything to contribute to the solution of the problem in hand? Does she usually get along well with the group, or does she irritate them? Does she really try to help them solve their problems, or is she more interested in placing the blame for the failure of their products? Is she always even-tempered, or does she sometimes lose her patience? The manager who operates successful group meetings will not leave such important questions to be answered when he is distracted by other pressures. He will have thought them through before the meeting and reached a decision.

With or without the product-performance representative, the manager, functioning as discussion leader, is ready to lead his group into an exploration session. It may be very brief: the number of failures for the quarter may be so small as to indicate that there is no real problem. On the other hand, if the number has risen during the period, the group must consider whether it has a real problem or whether exceptional circumstances beyond its control have caused the rise. If the group concludes that there is a problem, it must then decide what to do. Here the success or failure of the department may depend on the manager's ability as a discussion leader. If the group makes wise decisions under his guidance, the meeting will be profitable. If he allows the group to dissipate its energies and abilities in wrangling over minor points, the meeting will be worse than useless.

As in most companies today, decisions at Southern Signal are not simply made by the manager and handed to subordinates for implementation. Some companies are still run by fiat, but they pay a high price. They deprive themselves both of the experience and ideas of subordinates and of the opportunity to train subordinates in the operations of the company so that they will be capable of assuming increased responsibility. The wise manager will consider very carefully, therefore, which matters he must act on personally, which he should delegate, and which he should submit for group deliberation. Having decided, he must let his subordinates know to what extent he wants them to assume responsibility in decision making.

STEPS IN PLANNING AND RUNNING A MEETING

Our analysis of the group discussion at the Southern Signal and Control Company demonstrates that the same steps that proved useful in planning and writing a communication are useful in planning and running a problem-solving meeting:

1. Determine the Problem

Depending on the situation, the chairperson can either define the problem or invite those attending to explore a particular situation in such a way as to isolate and define the problem themselves. Involving those attending the meeting is generally the more effective procedure.

2. Analyze the Problem

This step requires bringing together all relevant information and exploring different avenues for solving the problem. Again, as appropriate, the chairperson can either do the analysis or invite the members of the group to help do it. Inviting the people to participate is usually profitable.

3. Construct a Solution

At this stage the person in the chair will first guide the meeting toward a consensus, and then state that consensus as clearly as possible, both so that all participants will agree that it is in fact the consensus and so that the person taking the minutes will have a clear statement of the solution arrived at.

4. Check Against Problem

The chairperson should then invite the group to reconsider the proposed solution briefly to be sure that it is adequate to solve the problem discussed.[1]

---

[1] For a comparison of "satisficing" and "maximizing" models of decision-making in business, see Herbert A. Simon's "Theories of Decision-Making in Economics and Behavioral Science," *American Economic Review* 49 (June 1959), especially pp. 262–264, and his *Administrative Behavior,* Third Edition (New York: Free Press, 1976), pp. xxviii–xxxi and 240–244.

5. Confirm Solution

When the consensus or solution has been confirmed, the chairperson should state it again clearly and dismiss the meeting.

6. Recheck Against Purpose

When they read the minutes, all the participants can recheck against purpose. If they find what they believe to be an error, they should report it immediately to the chairperson. If they believe that the agreed-upon solution is inadequate, they should make known their reservations.

Information and exploration meetings, of course, will have fewer steps. In preparation for such a meeting, a responsible person or group will have gone through a problem-solving procedure like the one above and in the meeting itself may simply announce the results or may show how the solution was arrived at. Then, if members of the group see problems in putting into practice the newly announced decision or procedure, they may want to undertake the kinds of discussions suggested in steps 1 through 4.

Just as in planning and writing a letter or a report, one should not always expect, when planning and running a meeting, to move as neatly through the six steps as our description suggests. Sometimes the analysis of the problem (step 2) or an attempt to construct a solution (step 3) makes clear that the group should return to step 1 for a better definition of the problem. Sometimes during checking or rechecking (steps 4 or 6), the same necessity becomes clear. However, a chairperson who understands all six steps and the nature and purpose of each will lead a group discussion more effectively than one who does not.

GROUP DISCUSSION AND LEADERSHIP TRAINING

We know a small company in which inadequate communication interfered seriously with the company's operation. A new president and his executive vice-president agreed that the company would profit if its department heads were given more independence and were encouraged to take a greater interest in the overall operation of the company. Instead of being explicit about the change in their policy, however, they simply tried to give the department heads an opportunity to act on their own initiative. But the department heads, accustomed to tighter control, interpreted the apparent passivity of top management as lack of leadership. Group meetings ended in frustration for all concerned. The president felt that the department heads lacked initiative and the capacity for independent, creative thinking. The department heads complained that after a meeting with the president they could not understand what he wanted them to do. A management consultant who was called in sized up the situation and explained to the department heads what the president wanted.   367

When he had finished, one of them spoke up with considerable irritation: "Then why the devil didn't he say so?"

An important aspect of the good leader's job is training. Most executives know that in the day-to-day routine of running their company or department they can help subordinates learn what they need in order to grow, and so provide a continuous procession of capable managers for the company.

Supervisors have a double task, then, in running a problem-solving session: to lead the group in solving the problem and to help the individuals in the group and the group as a whole to grow. As leaders—or teachers, or coaches— they should liberate and develop the creative abilities of staff members so that they will become increasingly capable of individual responsibility and action and less dependent. On the other hand, supervisors who always tell subordinates exactly what to do merely develop poor reproductions of themselves. Furthermore, such rigid control frustrates and restricts subordinates and causes them to become narrow and inflexible, to do things as they have always been done, to distrust their own ideas and abilities, and to rely heavily on other people for instructions and support. A company full of such people has no vitality and soon ceases to be competitive.

Research has shown that group discussions are also useful in another way. Making changes through group decision instead of by issuing orders is a very effective method of reducing resistance to change. Employees accept much more readily those goals which are arrived at by group decision.

A supervisor who wants to help subordinates develop must, therefore, function as a discussion *leader* in group conferences and must maintain what psychologists call a "permissive" atmosphere. The members of the group should be encouraged to express their ideas. They should not feel that either the group leader or their colleagues sit in judgment or that they will be criticized or belittled. They must feel instead that their remarks will be treated with genuine respect and consideration.

THE ROLE OF THE DISCUSSION LEADER

The responsibility for planning any meeting rests, of course, with the discussion leader, who has important responsibilities not only before the meeting takes place, but also during and after it. Before calling any meeting, this person must determine what the meeting should accomplish, decide which individuals should attend, choose a date on which all of them can be present, and arrange for a suitable location.

As promptly as possible after that, the discussion leader should distribute a meeting notice and agenda: date, time, location; subject or subjects, each broken down, if possible, into subtopics; materials to be examined in preparation; materials to be brought to the meeting. The purpose of the notice is to enable each member to prepare for the meeting and come to it ready to contribute. Too often people are called to meetings without time to prepare and are therefore less helpful than they could be.

At each step, the discussion leader must decide how directive to be. Sometimes, in order to stimulate creative ideas, the group should try "brainstorming"—pouring out ideas without stopping to evaluate them. When the flow has degenerated to a trickle, the group can then go back to evaluate those suggestions that have some merit. At other times the discussion leader will want to keep the discussion firmly in hand—to put an end to useless wrangling, perhaps, or to keep the group from trying to avoid making a difficult decision. The leader should also make sure that all discussion focuses on the topic and head off promptly any pronounced tendency toward irrelevancy: "That's an interesting sidelight, Jim. Now about Ruth's comment that we dare not raise prices now, do you think that . . ." or, "Jim, that's something that we ought to talk over sometime. Why don't you see me when we're through here, and we'll discuss the advisability of scheduling a meeting just on that problem." One can, of course, be too ruthless in repressing *brief* remarks that give the participants a chance to relax momentarily: a quick joke, a pun, reference to a humorous situation. Discussions that rigidly adhere to the topic often become grim. A group functions better if it can relax now and then.

If, as often happens, a member of a group makes a remark which others do not understand, the discussion leader can clarify it quickly by asking, "Then you agree with Pat, John?" or "Are you suggesting a new approach, John?" Such remarks indicate to the previous speaker that what was said was not clear and prevent potentially embarrassing remarks by sharp-tongued participants.

A major responsibility of anyone running a meeting is watching for and heading off heated conflicts. If one participant replies angrily or disparagingly to another, the leader must point out quickly that the offender should desist: "Mary is entitled to her opinion, Fred," or "Getting angry isn't going to solve our problem, Fred," or even "Let's save the heat for next winter, Fred." If these efforts fail and the meeting degenerates into wrangling, the best course is to announce, "We're not getting anywhere. Let's recess long enough to give you people a chance to cool off."

Bullying, sarcasm, anger—all can disrupt a profitable discussion. The competent discussion leader should promptly rule them out of order. Only in an atmosphere in which each member is free to speak without fear of attack can the group accomplish a great deal. To be successful, however, the leader must constantly be alert to undercurrents in the discussion. In speaking as in writing, *how* one says something is as important as *what* one says.

CHARTING THE FLOW OF IDEAS

A device known as the sociogram, which charts the exchange of ideas among group members, has been used to determine to what extent a leader has been able to stimulate real group discussion. Figure 20.1, for example, is a sociogram for a brief meeting. Each arrow indicates the source and direction of a single comment. Notice that here each exchange of remarks was between the discussion leader and a member of the group. No discussion was directed across the table. Furthermore, only the discussion leader and two of the participants (*B* and *D*) said very much. *A* and *F* each had one exchange with the leader; *E* made one comment to him, which evidently warranted no reply; and 369

C said absolutely nothing. This, then, was not a group discussion, but rather a series of exchanges between the leader and a few of the participants.

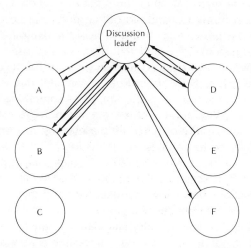

Figure 20.1. Sociogram of a leader-oriented meeting

Figure 20.2 is the chart of another meeting. It presents an entirely different picture. Here the discussion leader did relatively little talking, and every member of the group had something to say. *B* was drawn into the discussion twice by the group leader. *A* and *F* both did quite a bit of talking; and since they spoke only once to each other, it would seem that each assumed leadership during a different portion of the meeting.[2]

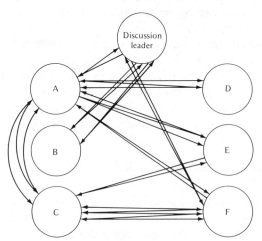

Figure 20.2. Sociogram of a productive discussion

[2] The discussion leader should not try to construct a sociogram while a meeting is going on. An observer (who is not sitting at the table) might make one, or if the meeting can be put on tape, the leader may construct one afterward. If members of the group are continually reminded that a sociogram is being made, they are not likely to contribute as freely as they normally would.

THE ROLE OF THE PARTICIPANT

To give this chapter focus, we have considered only the role of the discussion leader. But everything that we have said has obvious implications for the other members of the group. Just as the group leader should prepare for the meeting, so should the participants. They should read carefully and thoughtfully any material sent out in advance and be prepared to talk about it at an appropriate time in the discussion. They should think carefully about the meeting: who will be there, what its purpose is, what they hope to learn from it, how they can best contribute to it, and how each person will be likely to react. They should also gather whatever material they will need to function effectively in the meeting: reports, statistics, letters, and memos. A participant who expects to speak at any length or to make a particular point will also want to prepare a brief set of notes.

In the meeting, each individual should feel as responsible for its success as the group leader. Each should stick to the topic, avoid giving personal affront, listen carefully and courteously, contribute when appropriate, and keep all remarks as brief as possible. Each may also want to take brief notes to serve until the minutes are available.

As soon as possible after leaving the meeting, each participant should take a few moments to consider its implications and ask certain questions: "Did it resolve the matter under consideration? Did I promise to do something? If so, what do I have to do in order to carry out the assignment as soon as possible? Are decisions reached at the meeting going to affect me in ways that were not made explicit?" When the minutes are distributed, the participant should examine them carefully for errors and report promptly any which are significant. (Minor errors or omissions can usually wait until the next meeting.) Finally the minutes should be filed where they are readily accessible.

ILLUSTRATIVE MATERIALS

1.

A manager's style in dealing with subordinates depends on his or her self-image. Here is an analysis which distinguishes between "judgmental" and "judicious" managers.[3]

JUDGMENTAL MANAGER	JUDICIOUS MANAGER
The most efficient mode is to have one boss call the shots.	The most efficient mode is to make use cooperatively of the varied talents available.

[3] Reprinted by permission of the *Harvard Business Review*. Exhibit from "Creative Meetings Through Power Sharing," by George M. Prince (July-August 1972). Copyright © 1972 by the President and Fellows of Harvard College; all rights reserved.

I must protect my power to make decisions.	The best decision will emerge if I combine my power with that of the implementers.
I decide every course of action where I am authorized to decide.	I enlist my subordinates to devise courses of action, and contribute my thoughts as matters progress.
I must exercise all the autonomy my power permits.	I must use my power to help each subordinate develop his or her autonomy.
I use my power for my own growth.	I share my power so that my subordinates can grow as I grow.
I motivate people.	Accomplishment motivates people. I can provide opportunities for accomplishment.
I review, oversee, and control the efforts of my subordinates.	I use my experience, power, and skill to aid subordinates in accomplishing the task.
I take credit for the results of the groups I manage.	I explicitly recognize the accomplishments of subordinates.
To get results I must spot flaws and have them corrected.	To get results we must help each other overcome flaws.
When subordinates express themselves or act in ways unacceptable to me, I point out the flaws.	When subordinates express themselves or act in unacceptable ways, I assume they had reasons that made sense to them and explore the action from that point of view.
As mature people we are able to "take" put-downs and criticism without destructive consequences.	Even mature people are distressed to some degree by put-downs and criticism, and this makes cooperation difficult.
My role is to define the mission of my group.	My role in mission definition is to facilitate discovery by my subordinates and myself.
My role is to make judgments about the actions of my subordinates while they are carrying out our mission.	My role is to join my subordinates to make sure they succeed.

a. *What kind of leadership in a group discussion would you expect a judgmental manager to provide? A judicious manager?*

b. *From what you have read in this chapter and in the first three chapters of this book, would you expect judgmental or judicious managers to be more effective in running meetings of their subordinates? Why?*

2.

The following analysis breaks a discussion leader's task down into twelve functions, grouped according to purpose.[4]

The Two Major Types of Functions

Every group leader has two major functions. They are: (1) TASK functions and (2) GROUP RELATIONS functions.

The purpose of the TASK functions is to keep the group working on the task or project at hand, i.e., getting the group work done.

The purpose of the GROUP RELATIONS functions is to maintain constructive group relations among the members and to keep diverse individuals working together as a team. This means dealing with individual and group feelings and attitudes which may prevent the progress of the group towards its goals.

There are six TASK functions and six GROUP RELATIONS functions. They are defined below.

TASK FUNCTIONS

INITIATING: Proposing tasks or goals; defining a group problem; suggesting a procedure or ideas for solving a problem.

INFORMATION OR OPINION SEEKING: Requesting facts; seeking relevant information about group concern; asking for suggestions or ideas.

INFORMATION OR OPINION GIVING: Stating a belief; providing relevant information about group concerns; giving suggestions or ideas.

CLARIFYING: Elaborating, interpreting, or reflecting ideas and suggestions; clearing up confusion; indicating alternatives and issues before the group; giving examples.

SUMMARIZING: Pulling together related ideas; restating suggestions after the group has discussed them; offering a decision or conclusion for the group to accept or reject.

CONSENSUS TESTING: Sending up "trial balloons" to see if the group is nearing a conclusion; checking with the group to see how much agreement has been reached.

GROUP RELATIONS FUNCTIONS

ENCOURAGING: Being friendly, warm and responsive to others; accepting others and their contributions; regarding others by giving them an opportunity for recognition.

EXPRESSING GROUP FEELINGS: Sensing feeling, mood, relationships within the group; sharing one's own feelings with other members.

[4] Excerpted from Roundtable Films' Manager's Guidebook *Conference Leadership: The Critical Functions* (Beverly Hills, CA.; 1970).

HARMONIZING: Attempting to reconcile disagreements; reducing tension; getting people to explore their differences.

MODIFYING: When one's own idea or status is involved in a conflict, offering to modify one's own position; admitting error; disciplining oneself to maintain group cohesion.

GATE-KEEPING: Attempting to keep communication channels open; facilitating the participation of others; suggesting procedures for sharing opportunities to discuss group problems.

EVALUATING: Evaluating group functioning and production; expressing standards for group to achieve; measuring results; evaluating degree of group commitment.

a. *Which of these functions are appropriate for judgmental managers? For judicious managers?*
b. *Which of these functions are addressed in this chapter?*
c. *Are any of the functions inappropriate for a manager leading a discussion? Why?*

3.

Management specialists have developed a variety of strategems for promoting cooperation and minimizing conflict. Here is one such strategem that applies to group discussions.[5]

Managing Conflict

The most effective technique for managing conflict is to monitor the communication that takes place during group meetings. Managers who guide by encouraging positive talk and by discouraging negative statements and responses can help groups gain genuine skill in productive decision making.

What kind of communication strategies should be looked for and discouraged? A list might include:

Arm twisting: verbal force or coercion. "Admit I'm right, or you'll suffer the consequences." "If you disagree with me, you won't get promoted."

Status cop-out: rank or status-centered remarks. "Well, I'm the boss, and that's the way it will be." "It's my responsibility, so all I want you to do is concur with me."

Spanish inquisitioning: repeated questioning, but without dealing with the answers. "What do you mean?" "Why did you say that?" "What do you mean by that remark?"

The "later, you louse" look: just staring at someone with whom you disagree—a nonverbal "I'll get you later" response.

---

[5] Ethel C. Glenn and Elliott Pood, "Groups Can Make the Best Decisions If You Lead the Way," *Supervisory Management,* December 1978 (New York: American Management Association), pp. 4–6.

COMMUNICATING IN GROUP DISCUSSION

Stick-and-stoning: implied verbal abuse or name-calling. "What can you expect from a woman?" "You come up with the stupidest ideas." "I made myself perfectly clear the *first* time."

Butt-in-skying: never letting the other guy finish his thought. Constant interrupting.

Cheerleading: vigorous agreeing with everyone—the corporate yes-man. "Yeah, yeah, yeah—I like that idea." "Great, great, great!"

Physical dramatizing: semiconcealed headshaking, turning away from the group, shoulder-shrugging, downcasting eyes, but never verbalizing opposing ideas.

Intonating: the voice quality cuts, although the words may express agreement. Voice volume gets much too loud for the setting.

Cold-shouldering: excluding one particular group member; ignoring the opposition.

Tooth-pulling: making other group members act like dentists in order to pull out thoughts. "I didn't want to say it, but you made me."

This is a sample of some of the communication behaviors that discourage successful group decision making. Managers must help group members avoid these and other basically negative ways of speaking and responding with the body.

On the affirmative side, managers need to guide group interactions so that group members will:

—Be willing to accept and maintain opposing points of view.

—Clearly communicate their own ideas so that others can understand them.

—Freely and completely express disagreement verbally, without personal malice, not relying on someone in the group to pick up subtle gestures of disagreement.

—Listen completely and use feedback to check understanding of opposing ideas.

—Freely criticize the content of diverse ideas without criticizing those who express them.

—Be willing to accept criticism on an intellectual rather than on a personal basis.

—Be willing to take risks and to be vulnerable, with confidence in individual creative ability and the worth of contributions.

—Construct and convey logically structured arguments, with clearly evident reasoning processes. Brainstorming has its place, but not in a group that needs to move to a final decision.

—Leave disagreements in the conference room and not take them back.

a. *Is the recommended style judgmental or judicious?*
b. *How does the recommended style compare with the leadership style recommended in this chapter?*

PROBLEMS

1. Your group in a company training program or in a course in business communication has been asked to select a problem in the company or on the campus which you can use for a simulated group discussion or discussions, which will involve gathering information, exploring the problem, and solving the problem. Appoint a chairperson and a secretary, prepare yourselves for group discussion of what problem should be chosen. Have that discussion. Afterward have the secretary write up minutes.

2. Give each member of the group the minutes prepared for the above meeting. After they have had time to study them and take notes, have a new chairperson conduct a discussion of how useful they are. Tape-record the discussion. (NOTE: This exercise should be repeated after the discussions called for in Exercises 3 and 4.)

3. Select another chairperson and another secretary. Then prepare yourselves and have a group discussion of the problem chosen in Exercise 1. Once again, have minutes prepared.

4. From the tape recordings, have a member of your group prepare a sociogram for each of the above meetings and then conduct a group discussion in which the group tries to determine how its own discussions may be improved. Minutes should again be prepared by someone not actively participating.

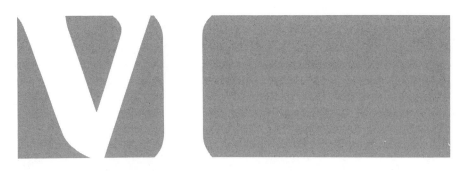

APPLYING
FOR A JOB

21

Communication and the Job Hunt

In no business negotiation is understanding the communication principles outlined in Chapter 2 more important than in seeking employment. To succeed in that search the applicant must consider again and again every element of the formula: who . . . says what . . . in which channel . . . to whom . . . with what effect? Though the way to a job may seem difficult and tortuous, individuals who keep these principles in mind and use to good effect the skills and techniques developed in this book should be out front in the competition for creative and satisfying employment.

WHO? THE PERSONAL INVENTORY

The desired end product of your job hunt is employment which promises opportunities for growth and satisfaction in an area where your talents can have full play. If the end you seek is merely a job—any job—not only are you unlikely to find satisfaction in what you do, but you are unlikely to find any employer willing to take you on. Only if you have decided what kind of employment *you* need is the search likely to be successful.

Before you enter the job market, before you begin thinking about job applications, résumés, or interviews, you must take a closer look at yourself than you have ever taken before. Ignoring for the moment any other considerations, you should set out to determine who you are, what your strengths and weaknesses are, what skills and interests you have, what you enjoy doing, and what you dislike.

Obviously, there is little use in conducting such an inventory unless you are prepared to be scrupulously honest with yourself, to consider very carefully how you would characterize yourself in relation to each quality or attitude assessed. Nor should you assume that any judgment you make is in itself "good" or "bad." Each of us is different. We have different skills and different interests. Each will function better in some situations than in others. Each has individual contributions to make. Your inventory will help you to determine where yours are likely to be most useful. It will also help you to decide what kind of job will be best for you. In the Illustrative Materials for this chapter, we have included a self-evaluation inventory. It is by no means all-inclusive, but filling it out will give you a good start toward knowing yourself better than you may right now.

After you have completed the inventory, you may wish to take one step more: reproduce all or a portion of the blank form and ask two or three people who know you well to use it in evaluating you. By comparing your evaluation with theirs, you will learn which qualities you project to others and which you do not—information useful to have as you move through the remaining phases of the job search. If, for example, you feel that you have confidence but others think you have little, you may wish to examine your behavior to determine what traits or habits have caused their misinterpretation. Or you may discover that in fact you are less confident than you thought you were.

IN WHICH CHANNEL?

If you have evaluated yourself, your talents, and your interests honestly and thoroughly, you will have a pretty good idea of what you can offer employers. To get a job, you will have to persuade them that you have qualities that they can use in their organization.

Most job seekers make contact with employers in one of several ways. They may use personal connections to secure an employment interview. They may set up an interview through a college placement bureau. They may telephone or call on a personnel officer or manager of a company in the area where they wish to work. They may answer a want ad. They may work through an employment agency. Or they may send out letters or résumés (about which we will soon say more) to a dozen or a hundred likely employers in the hope of securing an interview.

Where to Look

If you know of few obvious places to look for job information, you should

check out three major sources:

COMMUNICATION AND THE JOB HUNT

1. Your college placement office or career center. There you will find a wealth of information and people who will be happy to help you find what you want. They will have copies of the *College Placement Annual,* career opportunity booklets of all kinds, books on how to find a job, and guides to preparing résumés and cover letters. (If you are a graduate, your school's placement office will still be willing to help, and even if you have never been to college, any local institution will probably allow you to use its career center library.)

2. Your college and local public libraries. They will have copies of business and professional directories such as Standard & Poor's *Industrial Index* and *Corporation Records,* Dun and Bradstreet's *Million Dollar Directory* and *Middle-Market Directory,* and Moody's *Industrial Manual;* and the librarians can direct you to similar publications devoted to specific fields. These directories will usually provide not only names and addresses but also information such as size, names and titles of executives, sales volume, and number of employees. The library will also have copies of business publications: *Business Week, Forbes, Fortune, Changing Times,* and *The Wall Street Journal.* These journals will give you information about general business trends and where the best employment opportunities are likely to be. In addition, *The National Business Employment Weekly,* a tabloid, lists thousands of job openings in each issue.

3. The local Federal Job Information Center and local and state government offices. These will have up-to-date information on public service jobs.

If you wish to remain in the area in which you are now located, you can generate a file of company names by using the telephone yellow pages, lists available from the local chamber of commerce, and advertisements in the local newspaper. You should then try to find and record all the information you can about companies that seem particularly attractive, using the local business directories, employment offices, annual reports, and advertisements in national or trade periodicals. A thorough reading of the "Jobs Available" section of the local paper will give you some idea of the areas in which each company is hiring and the nature of its operations. If you wish to move, but to a specific location, you may use the same sources for the area in which you wish to settle.

Needless to say, the results you get from these researches will depend on the thoroughness with which you proceed. You will be going through a great deal of material. If you do not record your findings in a systematic way, details will very soon be swirling confusedly about in your head, and you will be unable to sort them out. You should put together a card file containing vital information about different businesses and industries where there may be opportunities for you. Eventually you should prepare a folder for each company in which you become seriously interested. As in any other endeavor, success favors the person who is organized and conscientious.

What Are Your Chances?

Even after all this work and in the best of times, however, the chance of any one contact's resulting in a job offer is very slim. Companies are always inundated by letters from job seekers. In times of economic instability the number of letters doubles, triples, quadruples. Most inevitably wind up in the wastebasket, a handful of applicants may be told that their letters will be put on file, and an occasional outstanding prospect may be invited for an interview.

Furthermore, the person who achieves an interview—whether by writing a letter, through a placement office or employment agency, or through some other contact—still has only a slim statistical chance of eventually receiving an offer. When employers set up interviews, they do intend to hire, but only, as a rule, when they run across an individual who can make significant contributions to their company. And only the applicant who is well prepared is likely to be able to demonstrate that he or she can do that.

SAYS WHAT? . . . TO WHOM?

The paths leading to an offer of employment may differ somewhat in detail, but for most individuals there are three basic steps to be taken: preparing a résumé (or, as one expert prefers, a qualifications brief);[1] writing a letter of inquiry or cover letter; and participating in one or more interviews.

The Résumé

The first step in your job hunt is preparing a résumé, the basic tool of job hunting. Its function is to indicate to an employer who you are and what you have to offer. That is not to say that you must be able to show that you have demonstrated every skill and every desirable quality under the sun. It does mean that the résumé should suggest that you have the potential to develop in such a way as to meet the employer's needs, both present and future.

Because every individual brings unique qualifications to the marketplace, there is no standard format or formula for a résumé. For some intelligent approaches, however, you may wish to examine the samples at the end of this chapter. And for more detailed information you may also wish to consult one or more of the useful guides which are also listed there. All of them have much to say on the subject. Here we can only discuss the general principles which should govern the preparation of the résumé.

Most important, as we have suggested, is to keep always in mind the person you are writing for—who your audience is. Ultimately that audience consists of all of the people in any company who may concern themselves with hiring

382   [1] Richard Lathrop, *Who's Hiring Who?* (Berkeley: Ten Speed Press, 1977).

an individual with your qualifications. Your résumé must give each of them the right impression of you. More immediately, it must impress the first person in any company who sees it: the personnel manager or other person who may be leafing rapidly through sixty or seventy résumés in the morning mail. If yours is just like all the rest in the pile, it will most certainly land in the wastebasket. If it is sloppy, poorly typed, or haphazardly arranged, it won't even rate a glance. Gimmicks are hardly likely to impress. What a hardened reviewer of résumés looks for is the rare example which brings forth the exclamation: "Now there's a person we could use! Let's set her up for an interview."

First Impressions

How can you increase your chance of being selected? To begin with, your résumé must be good to look at. It must suggest that you have taken care in its preparation: it must be neatly typed with no mechanical errors, no erasures, no corrections; it must contain certain obviously basic information; it must not be crowded on the page; and its format must be attractive and enable readers to pick up immediately those details which are of particular importance to them. Furthermore, it should contain only information that employers will want when they are first introduced to you through the résumé. They will not be interested at this point in your social security number, the names of your spouse and children, or, if you are or will soon be a college graduate, what high school you attended. They will, of course, want your name, address, and telephone number. Such information as your birthday, height, and weight need be included only if they seem relevant: a person who has been working for a number of years may feel it wise to include the first; one who is seeking a job requiring physical strength may wish to include the last two.

Career Objective

Most experts suggest that a person seeking a position of responsibility or one that will eventually lead to responsibility should begin with a statement of career or employment objective. This statement will let the reader know what the applicant's immediate and long-range goals are. Such statements are useful, however, only if they are clear and specific. "Management training program leading to executive responsibilities" is so vague as to convince any reader that the writer has failed to give much thought to career objectives. On the other hand "entry level position in management training for merchandising, with possibility of eventual advancement to managerial level" and "engineering position leading to opportunity to design heavy equipment for the petroleum industry" give the reader a good picture of what kind of opportunity the applicant is seeking.

383

What to Include

Once you have clearly stated your objective, you will spend the rest of the résumé convincing your reader that you are the person who should be hired. You must present a picture of yourself—your skills, your talents, your education and experience—which will cause a company to realize that you have what it needs, that you are the sort of person who will not only fit in with its organization, but also add strength to it.

The material for the résumé should come from your personal inventory. If that has been thoughtfully prepared, you will know what you have to offer, and you can fairly easily determine which elements of it will be likely to interest a prospective employer.[2] They are not difficult to spot if you keep asking: "Is this something the employer will wish to know at this point?" More difficult is determining how your qualifications should be presented: Which should you stress? How much should you say about each? In what order should they come? How should you phrase your statements?

There are no easy answers to these questions. Your answers will depend on what kind of job you are applying for and what your inventory says that you have to offer. It is safe to say, however, that nothing should go into this portion of the résumé unless it is clearly justified by its importance to the potential employer.

Always, too, you must put your best foot forward. You are neither required nor expected to include anything that might damage your chances of obtaining an interview. If you did not do as well as you could have in college, you need not offer your grade point average. At some later stage in the employment process, the matter will no doubt come up, at which time you can give your own analysis of why you did not do well. On the other hand, if you have an obvious physical defect, you may wish to include it: "When I was a child, I had poliomyelitis, as a result of which I have a slight limp. However, my normal activities are in no way affected." Such a statement will certainly do you no harm and may even increase your chances of being given serious consideration.

Most important, however, you should never tell a lie. Almost every fact on a résumé can, and probably will, be checked before you are hired. And any hint of deliberate dishonesty will cause you to be dropped immediately from consideration. Even if your deception is not discovered and you are hired, sooner or later it is likely to surface. A business organization can sometimes put up with incompetence, but never with dishonesty.

---

[2] Some people who are entering the job market for the first time may wish to explore opportunities in two or three different areas in which they have interests and talents. Those who do should certainly prepare a separate résumé for each area: for arts management and teaching or for industrial sales and public relations. Furthermore, any résumé should be flexible enough so that on occasion it may be revised to stress qualifications which are especially sought after by a particular company or group of companies in which the applicant may become interested.

Employment Record

The completed résumé, as we have suggested, should be a condensed summary stressing your qualifications for a particular kind of job. If you are a college student, it should not consist of more than one page, unless you have a very rich background indeed. It should certainly provide capsule descriptions of any jobs, paid or unpaid, that you have held, emphasizing those aspects which demonstrate qualities in which your employer will be interested:

Counter attendant for Miami Pancake House, London, Ontario. Letter of commendation for "diligence and friendliness in taking care of customers and initiative in devising a time-saving method for handling customer orders."

Life saving attendant at city pool. Medal from Centerville Police Department for aid administered to victim of heart attack.

Manager, Memorial Union Viking Room
   —improved customer service, which increased sales by 30 percent
   —introduced new billing procedure
   —initiated upgrading of facilities
   —trained, managed, and organized 26-student work force
   —coordinated all publicity for Viking Room activities
   —negotiated sales contracts for beverages and snacks
   —frequently acted as liaison between students, faculty, and administration

Even if you have had a relatively routine job, you can almost always make it work for you by emphasizing the qualities required to do it well. Even dishwashing, after all, requires promptness, diligence, and physical stamina.

Other Information

What other material goes into the résumé will depend on what you have to offer and what your potential employer is likely to be interested in. It may include education and academic honors, activity in campus or community organizations, special interests and hobbies, and personal information (birthdate, height and weight, health). You may also wish, if appropriate, to indicate how much of your college education you financed, what relevant vocational courses you have taken, the languages you speak and write fluently, travel abroad, and willingness to travel, to relocate, and to provide references on request. Much of what you present will be straightforward reporting, but you should keep in mind that it is always better to demonstrate a quality than to claim it. Thus any material that will *show* that you have a desired qualification should be used. If you look closely, you may find that you have more such material than you think.

385

The Cover Letter

Once you have completed your résumé, you will have to decide what to do with it. If you are a college student, you will want to have copies on file with your placement office. If you have contacts through parents, relatives, or friends, you may wish to send a copy to each with a carefully personalized letter: "Dear Mr. Saunders: Mr. John Peterson, for whom I worked last summer, has suggested that I write to you. . . ." Or, if nothing materializes through these sources, you may decide simply to send the résumé off to fifty or a hundred selected companies which may have an opening for someone with your qualifications.

If you choose this path, you will need to prepare a separately typed cover letter for each résumé, the contents varied in some instances to make the most of special circumstances: your familiarity with the area in which a company's research laboratory is located; your experience in working with government officials; or your knowledge of German if a company does a great deal of business abroad.

The letter should always be addressed to a specific individual by name, preferably the person responsible for filling the position you would like. (The name may be available in the company's annual report or other literature, in a business directory, or from the switchboard operator at the company's offices.) The letter should be brief, but it should do more than say: "I want a job. Here is my résumé."

Content of the Cover Letter

The letter should have a strong opening which does everything possible to suggest that you have something to offer to the particular company you are writing to. This should be a personal statement, perhaps a little provocative. It should certainly not sound like a canned or standard opening. One might start: "Dear Mr. Thornton: I have been told that there are no professional openings in the museum field this year, but I am determined to find one. Since I was a little girl, I have always believed that no other job would be right for me. As you will see from the enclosed résumé. . . ." Then this applicant could proceed to summarize briefly the training and other qualifications she would bring to the job. It may take a good deal of time to find exactly the right approach and the right wording for your opening, but the time will be well spent.

The remainder of the letter should focus on one or two major contributions you have to offer—leaving the rest of the résumé to speak for itself—and conclude with a request for an interview. Here it is most important to indicate clearly when you will be able to meet with the employer. "I will be in Milwaukee on vacation between April 6 and 18 and will be happy to come to Chicago at any time during that period for an interview." Employers will appreciate your being so specific, for you will be saving them time and extra correspondence.

Do not expect to hear from every company to which you write. You will be lucky if you hear from 20 percent, though you may do better if you are a senior in college and new to the job market. Don't let not hearing discourage you. To each company from which you have not heard after six weeks or so, write a brief note and send it, together with another copy of your résumé, to the same individual you wrote to originally. The note should say that on the chance that your original letter did not arrive, you are sending another résumé. And you will wish to add that you are still very much interested in working for the company. This strategy will not always work, but it has proved successful for many a job seeker whose first application has been lost in somebody's pile. It takes only a few minutes, a postage stamp, and a little luck.

The Interview

For most of us, the interview is the part of the job hunt we expect to enjoy least. We know that how well we handle ourselves may well determine the course of our life. Understandably we approach it with nervousness and perhaps some fear.

Certainly the interview is "nervous-making," as the British put it. But the person who understands the nature of such encounters and who is well prepared will look upon such nervousness positively. As we pointed out in Chapter 19 when discussing public speaking, the nervousness will get you "up" for the interview. If you are well prepared, it will largely disappear as soon as you and the interviewer begin your conversation.

Preparing for the Interview

How do you prepare for the employment interview? First of all, you have to come to a clear understanding of its real nature. Your initial interview with any company will be a screening interview—both for the company and for you. The man or woman sitting across from you will seldom be authorized to offer you a job but rather will be looking you over as a possible candidate, usually for a particular post or a particular training program. You, too, will be doing some screening. You will be asking yourself whether this is a company you want to work for, what the job involves, how good the training program is. Normally you hope that as a result of the interview you will be invited for further interviews, where screening on both sides can continue. On occasion, you may decide after the first interview that you do not wish to carry the process further with the company involved.

It is wise, too, to remember that the person whom you first see is not likely to be a "professional interviewer." If you are interviewed on campus, it may be an engineering or sales manager who has been asked to make a three-week interview swing through your area of the country. Or it may be a person who has served the company in several capacities, is near retirement, and is asked to take on more extensive interviewing responsibilities. If on the basis of a mail inquiry you are invited to visit the firm's general offices, you may first see a young person in the personnel office who will decide who else should see you. That may be a division manager or one of his assistants, neither particularly experienced in interviewing, and then the head of a specific department. Thus the person you are talking to seldom will have had special training in interviewing. "Mr. Jones" may be almost as new to the game as you are—and a bit nervous himself. And if you have done your homework, you may well have more to say about how the interview goes than he does. There is no need, therefore, to panic.

In any event, each company representative will expect you to have done your homework. Before you visit the company or see its representative on campus, you should review everything you have on it, and especially about the area—sales, public relations, manufacturing, engineering, overseas development, or whatever it may be—in which you would like to work.

If you do not have all the information that you think you will need, you will have to dig further in the sources we have mentioned. You may also be able to obtain information from individuals who know, or know about, the company. If you know in advance who will interview you, you should find out as much as you can about that person.

Once you have your information, you should consider how it relates to your own needs and desires. You will want to ask yourself such questions as what specific opportunities you are looking for, why you want to go with this particular company, what you have to offer that the company can use, and how interested you are in working for a company of its type and size and for how long. These and other questions are likely to be asked by the interviewer, and you must be able to answer them. Obviously, if you have anticipated and given serious thought to them, your answers have a better chance of being clear and articulate—and therefore, of impressing the interviewer. Conversely, you are not likely to find yourself thrown for a loss at any point in the interview.[3]

Making a Good Impression

Let's assume that you are being interviewed by Ms. Foxe, assistant manager of public relations for a major corporation. Your job is to convince her that you should be hired for her division. Your initial responsibility is to behave in such a way as to make a good first impression: be on time for the interview; wear appropriate "business" clothing; address her as Ms., Miss, or Mrs. Foxe (whichever is used by the person who introduces you to her); shake hands firmly, but not too firmly; remain standing until asked to sit down; sit naturally, but erect in your chair; give the impression of alert attention when she speaks; and answer her questions fully, but briefly. All of these actions are of great

[3] A list of fifty questions frequently asked in employment interviews will be found in the Illustrative Materials section of this chapter.

importance, for they establish her initial impression of you. And it has been demonstrated that a bad first impression seldom is changed in the course of an interview.

Interviews may be conducted in many different ways. They may be formal or casual, businesslike or conversational. Our Ms. Foxe—who will have seen your résumé—may begin asking questions immediately, or she may begin by talking about the weather, a recent television program, or something from the morning newspaper. When the questions do come, they may be general ("Tell me about your experience") or specific ("What kind of work did you do for the State Highway Department?"). You should be prepared to go along with the tone and format selected by the interviewer.

Certainly, however, you will not make much of an impression if you answer questions without being sure you understand them or if you confine yourself to excessively brief answers. Some questions will give you the opportunity to open up, to discuss experiences relevant to the job you want, and to suggest that you have what it takes to do that job. At certain points you may want to bring up a question of your own. ("May I ask you what type of . . .?") They may be about the nature of the job or the kinds of problems facing the staff you might wish to join. The answers you get may lead the conversation in a direction which will enable you to show—without laying it on too thick—that you have done your homework and that you have taken the time to think over what you have learned about the company and the job. You should also find opportunities to suggest—again without coming on too strong—that you have demonstrated qualities needed for the position you would like.

Throughout the interview you should be paying more attention to the interviewer's reactions than to your own. You should observe her closely so that you can react promptly to any hint of boredom, impatience, interest, or amusement. If you are talking a good deal and she seems bored, bring your remarks to a close. If she seems to have run out of questions, or if she is not giving you a chance to talk about qualities or abilities you can bring to the job, you should ask if you may talk about them. But always keep in mind that she is in charge of the interview. Don't try to take it over, no matter how much you may be tempted to do so.

On occasion you may find yourself being questioned in what seems a hostile manner, or Ms. Foxe may create a long pause while looking at the ceiling or staring at you. If these things occur, it may well be because she wants to test your reactions. Your best bet is to play it cool and avoid giving any evidence of anger or nervousness. She may ask what seems to be an unfair or irrelevant question. If so, you should take your time, and perhaps indicate that you do not understand how her question relates to the things you have been discussing. While she explains, you can be deciding how to respond. This sort of thing will not happen frequently, but you should be ready to handle it if it does come.

If you seem to be a likely candidate, the interviewer may well spend the latter portion of the interview selling the company: its training programs, benefits, and opportunities for advancement. And she may suggest the next steps

389

in the employment process: application forms, further interviews, perhaps specific tests to be taken. She will then ask if you have further questions, and the interview will be completed.

When you sense that the interview is about over, you should, if you still want the job, make clear that you are really interested and why you think you can contribute to her company. Be sure to thank her for the interview and offer to supply further information if the company should need it. Smile, shake hands firmly, and give an impression of confidence.

Now you have only two more tasks to perform to complete the interview process. First, you should jot down for your own information a brief summary of the interview, an analysis of your performance, and a list of things you learned from it. Such a report will prove useful if you review it, and others you have accumulated, as your prepare for your next interview. Second, you should write the interviewer a brief thank-you note—no rubber stamps, please!—in which you express your appreciation and indicate your present attitude toward the company she represents. You may also wish to mention some specific issue you discussed or supply information that you didn't have at hand during the interview. If you haven't heard from the company in two or three weeks, you may want to write or telephone about the status of your application.

WITH WHAT EFFECT?

Finding and securing the right job for yourself is often a lengthy and time-consuming operation. It requires energy, perseverance, sensitivity, tact, and above all a great deal of hard thinking about yourself and your future. It is *your* future that is at stake. You will want a job that will provide lasting satisfaction by giving you the kind of work you like and the opportunity to grow to fulfill yourself in the years ahead. Every minute of time and every bit of energy you put into your search should bring you closer to that goal. Beyond that, you should complete the process with a better understanding than you have ever had of who you are and what you may be able to do with your future.

Some useful books on the job hunt are:

College Placement Annual. Bethlehem, PA: College Placement Council. Revised annually.

Erdlen, John D., and Donald H. Sweet, *Job Hunting for the College Graduate.* Lexington, MA: D. C. Heath, 1979.

Figler, Howard, *The Complete Job Search Handbook.* New York: Holt, Rinehart and Winston, 1979.

Jackson, Tom, *Guerrilla Tactics in the Job Market.* New York: Bantam Books, 1977.

Lathrop, Richard, *Who's Hiring Who?* Berkeley: Ten Speed Press, 1977.

Medley, H. Anthony, *Sweaty Palms: The Neglected Art of Being Interviewed.* Belmont, CA: Lifetime Learning Publications, 1978.

Powell, C. Randall, *Career Planning and Placement Today*, Second Edition. Dubuque: Kendall/Hunt Publishing Company, 1978.

Singleton, John, and Robert Bao, *College to Career*. New York: McGraw-Hill, 1977.

Yeomans, William N., *Jobs*. New York: Paragon Books. Revised annually.

ILLUSTRATIVE MATERIALS

1.

Self-Evaluation Inventory

CHARACTER TRAITS

Rate yourself ($++$, $+$, ✓, $-$, $--$) on the following characteristics. Be *absolutely* honest in your evaluation.

Self-confidence	Ability to get along with people
Leadership	Willingness to take responsibility
Flexibility	Ability to communicate orally
Imagination	Ability to communicate in writing
Intelligence	
Initiative	
Energy	

1. What special skills do you have that might be useful on the job?
   _____

2. What do you most like to do with your free time?
   _____

3. What percentage of your free time do you spend with others? _____
   Alone? _____

4. Do you enjoy working under pressure? _____ Do you do your best work under pressure? _____

5. Are you good at following directions? _____ Do you like to explain things to others? _____

6. Do you take criticism well? _____

7. In what order would you rank your interest in working with people, with things, with figures, or with ideas? _____

8. Are you a patient person? _____

9. Do you become angry when things go wrong? _____

10. Are you a self-starter? _____

11. How good an organizer are you? _____

12. When you are with a group, do you tend to be the leader? _____
    An active member? _____ A passive member? _____

13. In what size community would you like to work? _____
    _____

14. Would you prefer to work indoors or outdoors? _____
    Would you prefer a nine-to-five job or flexible hours? _____

391

15. Would you like to work on salary, on commission, or on a combination of the two? _____

16. Would you be willing to travel 50 percent of the time? _____ 30 percent? _____ 10 percent? _____

17. Are you willing to work anywhere in the United States? _____ In the world? _____

18. Would you like to be responsible for the work of others? _____

19. What languages do you write well? _____ Speak well? _____

2.

Fifty Questions Asked by Employers During the Interview with College Seniors

1. What are your long range and short range goals and objectives, when and why did you establish these goals, and how are you preparing yourself to achieve them?

2. What specific goals, other than those related to your occupation, have you established for yourself for the next 10 years?

3. What do you see yourself doing five years from now?

4. What do you *really* want to do in life?

5. What are your long range career objectives?

6. How do you plan to achieve your career goals?

7. What are the most important rewards you expect in your business career?

8. What do you expect to be earning in five years?

9. Why did you choose the career for which you are preparing?

10. Which is more important to you, the money or the type of job?

11. What do you consider to be your greatest strengths and weaknesses?

12. How would you describe yourself?

13. How do you think a friend or professor who knows you well would describe you?

14. What motivates you to put forth your greatest effort?

15. How has your college experience prepared you for a business career?

16. Why should I hire you?

17. What qualifications do you have that make you think that you will be successful in business?

18. How do you determine or evaluate success?

19. What do you think it takes to be successful in a company like ours?

20. In what ways do you think you can make a contribution to our company?

21. What qualities should a successful manager possess?

22. Describe the relationship that should exist between a supervisor and those reporting to him or her.

23. What two or three accomplishments have given you the most satisfaction? Why?

24. What has been your most rewarding college experience?

25. If you were hiring a graduate for this position, what qualities would you look for?

26. Why did you select your college or university?

27. What led you to choose your field of major study?

28. What college subjects did you like best? Why?

29. What college subjects did you like least? Why?

30. If you could do so, how would you plan your academic study differently? Why?

31. What changes would you make in your college or university? Why?

32. Do you have plans for continued study? An advanced degree?

33. Do you think that your grades are a good indication of your academic achievement?

34. What have you learned from participation in extracurricular activities?

35. In what kind of work environment are you most comfortable?

36. How do you work under pressure?

37. In what part-time or summer jobs have you been most interested? Why?

38. How would you describe the ideal career for you?

39. Why did you decide to seek a position with this company?

40. What do you know about our company?

41. What two or three things are most important to you in a job?

42. Are you seeking employment in a company of a certain size? Why?

43. What criteria are you using to evaluate the company for which you hope to work?

44. Do you have a geographical preference? Why?

45. Will you relocate? Does relocation bother you?

46. Are you willing to travel?

47. Are you willing to spend at least six months as a trainee?

48. Why do you think you might like to live in the community in which our company is located?

49. What major problem have you encountered and how did you deal with it?

50. What have you learned from your mistakes?

Source: The Endicott Report, The Placement Center, Northwestern University, Evanston, Illinois, 1975.

3.

Negative Factors Which Most Often Lead To Rejection As Listed by 186 Companies (Factors listed by 10 or more companies)

(Number of companies listing factor in parentheses)

1. Poor scholastic record—Low grades without reasonable explanation—Low level of accomplishment (99).

2. Inadequate personality—Poor attitude—Lack of poise—Lack of self-confidence—Timid, hesitant approach—Too introverted (89).

3. Lack of goals/objectives—Poorly motivated—Does not know his interests—Indecision—Poor planning (80).

4. Lack of enthusiasm—Lack of drive—Not sufficiently aggressive—Little evidence of initiative (50).

5. Lack of interest in our type of business—Lack of interest in our company—Not interested in the type of job we have to offer (48).

6. Inability to express himself—Poor speech—Inability to sell himself (45).

7. Unrealistic salary demands—More interested in salary than in opportunity—Unrealistic expectations—Over-emphasis on management positions—Unwillingness to start at the bottom (39).

8. Poor personal appearance—Lack of neatness—Careless dress (35).

9. Lack of maturity—No evidence of leadership potential (35).

10. Lack of extracurricular activities—Inadequate reasons for not participating in activities—No accomplishment in activities (22).

11. Failure to get information about our company—Lack of preparation for the interview—Did not read the literature (22).

12. Objects to travel—Geographical preference—Unwilling to relocate (20).

13. Excessive interest in security and benefits—"What can you do for me?" (15).

14. Inadequate preparation for type of work—Inappropriate background (10).

Source: The Endicott Report, The Placement Center, Northwestern University, Evanston, Illinois, 1975.

4.

Three Sample Résumés

CHRISTINE L. CORYATE

Permanent Address: Address through June, 1980:
726 S. Monroe St.   723 E. John St.
Edina, MN 55436   Appleton, WI 54911
(612) 323-4672   (414) 739-3681 x 380

OBJECTIVE: A challenging career involving marketing and financial
                    analysis with exposure to a wide variety of opportunities
                    to utilize my analytical and communication skills.

QUALIFICATIONS: Double major in English and Economics...Sales experience..
                    business coursework in statistics, accounting and finance...
                    ambitious and hardworking...specialization in business
                    management and urban issues through college programs.

EDUCATION: Rigorous undergraduate studies at Lawrence University,
                    Appleton, Wisconsin. To receive B.A., June, 1981...
                    Cumulative GPA 3.4...Candidate for Mortar Board Scholar...
                    Vice President of House Council...organized campus
                    religious services...initiated Lawrence Social Issues
                    Group...Tutor in Economics and Writing...Field Hockey
                    and Track three years...Women's Chorus...Theatre
                    Production...held campus job throughout.

EXPERIENCE: Selected for Keller GSM: Women in Management Program,
                    Chicago, Summer, 1980...Interned at Marsh & McLennan
                    Inc. critiquing project proposals and working with
                    budgets...took night session Finance at Keller...
                    attended weekly management seminars for the Women
                    in Management group.

                    Participated in Urban Studies Program of Associated
                    Colleges of the Midwest, Chicago, Fall, 1979. Worked
                    as legal researcher for BPI law firm and as PACE
                    program volunteer at the Cook County Jail...took
                    seminars and classes concentrating on Chicago
                    Economics and Politics.

                    Worked for Larson Company of Saint Paul as a Sales
                    Representative, Summer, 1979. Attended a sales
                    training program and was placed in a field sales
                    position...Responsibilities included cold calling,
                    screening customers, giving demonstrations and
                    closing sales.

                    Employed by Perkins' Cake and Steak, Minneapolis,
                    Minnesota for two summers, 1977 and 1978...Began
                    as a waitress and was given additional responsibility
                    for training new employees.

PERSONAL: Born: May 7, 1959...Excellent Health...Willing to
                    travel.

INTERESTS: Competitive Sports, Music, Acting, Mathematics, Travel.

REFERENCES: Will be furnished upon request.

JAMES WILLARD SMITH

ADDRESS

326 Briarcliff Terrace   Born: May 27, 1956
Skokie, IL 60076   Languages: English, French,
Telephone 312-869-7302   Japanese

OBJECTIVE

    To use my varied experience in facilitating shipment of goods and
dealing with people in a management position, preferably in the transportation industry, either in the United States or abroad.

EDUCATION

Chicago Circle Campus   September, 1974 - March 1978 and
University of Illinois   September, 1981 - June 1982
Chicago, IL 60680   B.A. Degree in English

Waseda University, Tokyo, Japan (1976-1977). Studies in Far Eastern
history, Japanese, economics, and English Literature.

WORK HISTORY

December 10, 1979   Japan Air Lines Co., Ltd.
to August 18, 1981   O'Hare Int'l Airport, PO Box 66078
Title: Cargo Agent, II   Chicago, Illinois 60666

Responsible for aircargo handling, inventory, and documentation;
supervised unitization and transfer of same to shipside. Frequent
customer contact which emphasized maintenance of good relations with
an established clientele, through efficiency, confidence, and knowl-
edgeability. Participated in JAL certified training, including: a
general orientation seminar, "Cargo Tariff - Basic," "Cargo Handling I,"
and "Introduction to Restricted Articles." $1167.00/mo.

July 24, 1979   Palisades Merchandising, Inc.
to December 8, 1979   20 North State Street
Title: Shipping Co-ordinator   Chicago, Illinois 60606

Responsible for documentation, dispatch, and tracing of international
shipments of promotional materials. Salary upon termination: $800.00/mo.

April 1, 1978   Area Transport, Inc.
to July 21, 1979   300 South Dearborn Street
Title: Export Documentation   Chicago, Illinois 60606
        Clerk

Prepared documentation for containerized ocean freight shipments.
Salary upon termination: $600.00/mo. (approx.)

SPECIAL QUALIFICATIONS

Fluent in Japanese and French.
Willing to travel or to live in foreign country.

COMMUNICATION AND THE JOB HUNT

```
                        SANDRA M. CLAY

Present Address                          Permanent Address
937 East Alton Street                    530 Thomas Street
Appleton, WI 54911                       Columbus, OH 43228
(414) 739-3681                           (614) 243-9191

Objective:   To use my communication skills and knowledge of biology
             in a challenging job requiring initiative and dedication.

Education:   Lawrence University, Appleton, Wisconsin, 1977-1981
               - B.A. Degree expected, June 1981.
               - Major:  biology, emphasis on ecology, field biology.
               - Attended Associated Colleges of the Midwest Wilderness
                   Field Station, Ely, Minnesota, 1979.
               - Practice teaching:  Appleton West High School, 1980.

Work
Experience:  Consulting biologist - sales, Stratton Chemical Company,
                 Columbus, Ohio, Summer, 1980
               - Called on previous and prospective clients in fifteen
                   states around the nation.
               - Diagnosed and evaluated imbalances in privately owned
                   water bodies.  Increased sales of aquatic chemicals
                   and had positive feedback.

             Camp counselor, YMCA Camp Manito-wish, Boulder Junction,
                 Wisconsin, Summer 1979.

             Dental assistant and receptionist, 1978.
               - Learned receptionist and bookkeeping skills.

             Food Service worker, Lawrence University, 1979-1980.

             Receptionist, Lawrence Admissions Office, 1979-1981.
               - General office and computer work.

             Campus Tour Guide, 1978-1981.

Activities:  Lawrence University Community Council
               - Hall representative, 1979-1980.  Established hall forums
                   and door-to-door campaigns to keep communication
                   channels open.  Committee on Committees.
               - Vice President, 1980-1981.  Elected by all students and
                   faculty.  Responsible for $30,000 budget.  Reorganized
                   registration system.

             Alpha Chi Omega Fraternity, Foundations Chairman, 1980.
               - Initiated numerous service-oriented projects.
               - Organized reading program for blind student.
               - Raised $500 in quarters to buy braille typewriter for
                   Appleton Public Library.
               - Organized tutoring program for children at the Oneida
                   Indian Reservation.

Honors:      James F. Parker Memorial Scholarship.
             Phelps Prize for Scholarship and Service to the University.

             REFERENCES AVAILABLE ON REQUEST
```

5.

Two Letters of Application and Accompanying Résumés

723 East John Street
Milton, MA 02187
February 26, 1982

Dr. Edward M. Brucker
Vice-President for Research
Garrison Oil Company
1600 Industrial Park, West
Tulsa, OK 74108

Dear Dr. Brucker:

As you will see from the enclosed résumé, I will soon be completing my work for the B.A. degree in chemistry at Milton College.

For some time now, and especially since last summer when I was employed as a research technician for Patterson Oil Products, I have wanted to seek employment in the research division of an independent oil company. This decision has been reinforced by an honors project on "Problems of Extracting Oil from Shale in Two Montana Counties," which should be completed in April.

If you have openings in any of your research facilities, I will appreciate the opportunity to be interviewed. I will be at home in Des Plaines, Illinois, for spring vacation between March 22 and April 8, but if necessary I can fly out to Tulsa from here if I have a few days notice.

I look forward to hearing from you.

Sincerely,

Thomas W. Post

Thomas W. Post

THOMAS W. POST

Birthdate – 8/12/60

College Address	Home Address
723 E. John St.	321 Pelham Avenue
Milton, MA 02187	Des Plaines, IL 60016
(414) 731-7653	(312) 299-3216

Career Objective
A research or research-management position in the chemical industry or related fields; a position that allows creative thinking and full use of applicable skills.

Education
Milton College, Milton, Massachusetts. 1977-1981. Anticipated B.A. in June 1982, with a major in Chemistry. G.P.A. of 3.4 on a scale of 4.0. Dean's List Sophomore and Junior years. Independent study leading to an honors thesis to be completed in April. Subject: "Problems of Extracting Oil from Shale in Two Montana Counties." Also possess computer programming experience and outstanding writing skills. Have tutored students in chemistry, mathematics, and English.

Employment History
Summer, 1981
Research Technician with *Patterson Oil Products*, Des Plaines, IL. Received experience with applications of infrared (IR) and ultraviolet-visible (UV-VIS) spectroscopy. Largely concerned with the operation of a gas chromatograph/mass spectrometer (GC/MS) and its associated computer software. Was exposed to a variety of research topics through seminars.

Summer, 1980
Research Technician with *Central States Gypsum Co.*, Springfield, IL. Received experience with analytical chemistry techniques – gravimetric, titrimetric, thermometric, AA, and scanning electron microscopy (SEM).

1974-1979
Park District Swimming Pool positions, leading to Head Lifeguard position in 1978 and 1979. Required managerial and administrative skills, as well as an interplay with the public from a position of authority and high visibility.

Summer salaries provided approximately 30% of college costs.

Special Interest
Participation in competitive swimming since age 6. Recently voted MVP and Most Dedicated on Milton Varsity Swim Team. The demands of this sport have required considerable management of time and workload in order to satisfy educational, employment, and athletic commitments.

References
Furnished upon request.

6 Elam Terrace
Berkeley, CA 94721
May 1, 1982

Mr. Sheldon Zwicker
Zwicker Products Corporation
27 Coceran Boulevard
Minneapolis, MN 55436

Dear Mr. Zwicker:

Dr. Andre Pierrepont, one of my professors at the Graduate School of Industrial Relations here in Berkeley, has suggested that I write to you. He has told me that because of the rapid expansion of your business, you are planning to open offices in Paris, London, Brussels, and Rome and that you might be interested in training someone with my qualifications for service in Europe.

As you will see from the enclosed résumé, I am about to receive my M.B.A. degree from Berkeley. (At the last marking period I ranked fourth in my class.) I have had experience as a sales representative for a company which manufactures sophisticated pumps and for an insurance company. Having had two years schooling in France and having majored in French at college, I speak the language fluently. Numerous trips to Europe with my parents (my father is an importer) and my two years living in France have convinced me that I should seek a career in international commerce. I have always had many European friends and believe that I can contribute effectively to a company like yours which is planning to enter the European market.

If you do have a suitable opening for a person with my qualifications, I will appreciate the opportunity to have an interview. For the next two weeks I will be rushing to complete my studies. From May 15 to July 1, however, I will be at the above address (telephone: (415) 672-6191) and will be free to come to Minneapolis at any time.

Sincerely,

Sarah T. Porter

Sarah T. Porter

SARAH T. PORTER

6 Elam Terrace   Telephone: (415)829-2616
Berkeley, CA 94721

OBJECTIVE

To use my varied experience and advanced educational training in a position with
managerial responsibility. To be involved eventually in financial management
requiring innovative decision-making and close work with top management.

EDUCATION

September 1981 to June 1982: M.B.A., University of California, Berkeley. Courses
    included: Financial Management, Statistics (2 quarters), Analytical Methods,
    Managerial Accounting and Control, Management Information Systems, Economics (2
    quarters), Marketing, Organizational Behavior, Personnel Management, Business
    Law, Inventory Control, Government Contract Administration, and Procurement Law.
    Grade point average: 3.81.

September 1973 to June 1977: B.A., Pomona College, Claremont, California. Double
    major in French Literature and Theatre Arts (directing and stage management).

September 1970 to June 1973: High school diploma, Latin School of Chicago. Ad-
    vanced courses in French Literature and Biology.

October 1968 to July 1970: Middle School, Le Collège Cévenol, Le Chambon-sur-
    Lignon, France. All courses taught in French.

EMPLOYMENT HISTORY

April 1979 to August 1981: Amity-Southern Life Insurance Company, Huntsville,
    Alabama. Position: Licensed life insurance agent. Duties involved locating
    and advising clients; interviewing, negotiating, and pricing policy require-
    ments; servicing new and current clients; and counselling on estate planning.
    Earned certificate of completion in a course on advanced insurance practices
    and estate planning.

August 1978 to April 1979: Parker and Parker, Huntsville, Alabama. Position:
    Employment counsellor. Duties involved interviewing applicants for employment
    and arranging interviews with prospective employers.

July 1977 to June 1978: Tower Machine Company, Palo Alto, California. Position:
    Office manager/sales representative. Managed a branch sales office during
    expansion of both business and personnel. Developed and implemented adminis-
    trative and fiscal procedures. Responsible for all sales support and initi-
    ating inside sales, including follow-up, cost estimation, quotation, and
    contract or purchase order completion. Was in charge of all customer rela-
    tions. Coordinated various special projects and tasks including full
    responsibility for setting up and running a large sales seminar for current
    and prospective customers.

SPECIAL QUALIFICATIONS

Fluent in both writing and speaking French. Member, Board of Directors, Friends
    of the Warren Center for the Arts, Huntsville, Alabama. Serious interest in
    photography.

Willing to relocate for challenging opportunity. Available immediately.

SUBJECT INDEX

SUBJECT INDEX

feedback, 246
Felver, Richard I., 135–136
flowcharts, 136–137, 170–173, 183
Flower, Linda S., 155–157
Ford, Henry, 331–332

Galilei, Galileo, 285–286
Goddard, M. Lee, 327
good will, improving, 89–90
graphs
　use of, 173–176
　misleading, 176–178
group discussion, 360–375

habits
　changing, 14, 16
　need for good, 38–39
Hand, Learned, 241–243, 249
Hayes, John R., 155–157
heavy connectives, 192–193
　list, of, 196–197
Holt, Rinehart and Winston, 15–19
Home Mutual Insurance Company,
　290–291
hooks, 225–227
humor
　dangers of, 57
　in speeches, 348–349

　use of, 252–254
　in letters and reports, 14
　substitutes for, 252–254
information, supplying too much, 9,
　276–278, 299–302
informing, defined, 48–49
inquiry, letters of, 87–89
insurance policies, 10–11, 290–291
it is, 265–266

jargon
　accounting, 192
　financial, 215–216
　government, 11–13, 22–24
　in business talks, 353–354
　legal, 10–11, 282–285, 290–291
　technical, 192, 275–282
　see also language, rubber stamps

jobs
　hunting for, 379–401
　self-evaluation, 379–380, 391–392
　information about, 380–381,
　　390–391
　résumé, 382–385
　　samples, 395–397, 399, 401
　career objective, 383
　cover letter, 386–387
　　samples, 398, 400
　interview, 387–390
Jones, Gregory M., 22–24

Knight, Douglas, 255–256

language
　business, quaint, 19–21
　formal, 240–243, 245, 249–250
　government, 11–13, 22–24
　informal, 240, 244–245, 249–250
　insurance, 10–11, 290–291
　legal, 10–11, 241–243, 249,
　　254–255, 282–285, 290–291
　medical, 286–287
　pseudoformal, 245–252, 302–303
　redundancy of, 193–194
　technical, 274–282
　vulgate, 240–241, 249–250
Lasswell, Harold, communication
　　model, 28–29, 53–54, 81–82,
　　128–129, 242, 341, 379–390
leadership training, 367–368
legalese, 282–285; see also jargon,
　　language
letters and memos, business
　closings, 206–207
　cost of, 5
　cover, 386–387, 398, 400
　form, 90–93, 98–99
　headings for, 208–210
　openings
　　effective, 206–211
　　ineffective, 204, 208
　　marathon, 208
　requesting reference, 88–89
　routine, 31–32, 72, 87–89
　see also adjustment, appreciation,
　　collection, complaint,
　　congratulations, request, and
　　sales letters

404

INDEX OF
ILLUSTRATIVE MATERIALS
AND EXAMPLES

INDEX OF ILLUSTRATIVE MATERIALS AND EXAMPLES

INDEX OF ILLUSTRATIVE MATERIALS AND EXAMPLES

INDEX OF ILLUSTRATIVE MATERIALS AND EXAMPLES